William James's
"Springs of Delight"

Other titles in the series include

*Dewey's Empirical Theory of Knowledge and Reality*
John R. Shook

*Thinking in the Ruins: Wittgenstein and Santayana on Contingency*
Michael P. Hodges and John Lachs

*Pragmatic Bioethics*
Edited by Glenn McGee

*Transforming Experience: John Dewey's Cultural Instrumentalism*
Michael Eldridge

# WILLIAM JAMES'S "SPRINGS OF DELIGHT"

## The Return to Life

### Phil Oliver

VANDERBILT UNIVERSITY PRESS

Nashville

First Edition 2001

05 04 03 02 01    5 4 3 2 1

Library of Congress Cataloging-in-Publication Data

Oliver, Phil, 1957–
  William James's "Springs of delight" : the return to life / Phil
Oliver. — 1st ed.
    p. cm. — (The Vanderbilt library of American philosophy)
Includes bibliographical references and index.
  ISBN 0-8265-1366-2 (alk. paper)
  1. James, William, 1842–1910.  2.  Perception (Philosophy)
I. Title. II. Series.
  B945.J24 O55 2000
  191—dc21                                        00-010464

Published by Vanderbilt University Press
Printed in the United States of America

*For Sharon, Emma, and Katie—*

*my own springs of deepest delight*

To begin with, how *can* things so insecure as the successful experiences of this world afford a stable anchorage? A chain is no stronger than its weakest link, and life is after all a chain ...

*Varieties of Religious Experience*

The really vital question for us all is, What is this world going to be? What is life eventually to make of itself? The centre of gravity of philosophy must therefore alter its place. The earth of things, long thrown into shadow by the glories of the upper ether, must resume its rights.

*Pragmatism*

# Contents

# Preface and Acknowledgments

Ours is a planet sown in beings. Our generations overlap like shingles.... Once we get here, we spend forever on the globe, most of it tucked under. While we breathe, we open time like a path in the grass. We open time as a boat's stem slits the crest of the present.

—Annie Dillard, *For the Time Being*

Asked what my work on William James is about, I am always challenged to find a pithy reply. So wide was the range of James's concerns, so enduring is his broad relevance, and so habituated am I to finding a Jamesian slant on everything, that any terse statement feels irresponsibly shallow and misleading. But summaries *are* helpful, especially to prospective readers.

This book is, therefore, about the centrality for life of personal enthusiasms and habitual "delights" and their power to make our days meaningful, delightful, spiritual, and even transcendent. Such enthusiasms, or subjective ways of reacting to life and upon it, are natural for us. They are at the heart of a vision of life at once spiritual and deeply rooted in "the open air and possibilities of nature."[1] When our days become pale, tedious, or abstract, they sponsor our "return to life" in all its rich, robust, and personal concreteness. The natural provenance of such enthusiasms distinguishes them from the putatively supernatural incursions of convulsive "Enthusiasm" that Harold Bloom finds at the core of "the American Religion."[2] Jamesian transcendence is thus a variety of naturalism, though decidedly not that "present day materialism, which may better be called naturalism," which "leave[s] the destinies of the world at the mercy of its blinder parts and forces."[3] Jamesian naturalism, while not naive about those impersonal forces that largely shape material reality, assigns a destiny-shaping, evolutionary role to the emergent personal and cultural forces of intelligence and the human spirit as gifts of nature that may come one day to exert constructive influence on all our affairs. It finds nothing incongruous about nature and spirit in harness together. In fact, "the conception of spirit, as we mortals hitherto have framed it, is itself too gross to cover the exquisite tenuity of nature's facts."[4] We, in our teeming subjective particularity, are nature's most exquisite natural fact. We personalize nature:

> The only form of thing that we directly encounter, the only experience that we concretely have, is our own personal life. . . . And this systematic denial on science's part of personality as a condition of events, this rigorous belief that in its own essential and innermost nature our world is a strictly impersonal world, may, conceivably, as the whirligig of time goes round, prove to be the very defect that our descendants will be most surprised at in our own boasted science, the omission that to their eyes will most tend to make it look perspectiveless and short.[5]

Jamesian naturalism and the transcendence it favors have to do with the unique, partly incommunicable ways in which each of us may make vital connection with our respective personal, spiritual natures. It notices and celebrates our differences; but in the same glance it recognizes their anchorage in something we share, not just a common biology but especially a common capacity for embracing our own enthusiasms, just as we extend sympathetic respect for those of our compadres, ancestors, and descendants. In that light Jamesian transcendence is also about overcoming narrow egotism and expanding our sense of who we are, individually and as a species across time and space.

What objects of enthusiasm can imaginably promise so much? Any we can imagine, and then some—baseball, say, or the Beatles, beer, Great Britain, literature, science, science fiction, Monet, Mozart, Kentucky whiskey, Tennessee walking horses, walking, running, tilling the soil, raising kids, healing, praying, meditating, thinking, teaching, learning, and on and on. Whatever disparate items may show up on anyone's list (these are a few that crop up in my own family circle), their crucial essence is to point at, but not to replicate or make transparent to others' grasp, the depths of experience and personal significance they attempt to name. I can tell you that I love baseball, but I cannot begin to convey precisely why or how or the extent to which baseball is important for my peculiar ways of experiencing and living in the world. By the same token your account of the joys of macramé, soccer, or cat-dancing will leave me in the dark. But it is a darkness rimmed by the glow of a phenomenon we should all recognize and treasure.

This book, then, is a paradoxical rumination on possibilities of delight both *beyond* but still, somehow, to some unspecifiably partial extent, *expressible in* words. James, like the most thoughtful philosophers and poets, wavered between the earnest wish to affirm and extend our humanistic inheritance of understanding and sympathy through language ("philosophy is essentially talkative and explicit")[6] and an acute awareness of the intrinsic limitations of language that foreshadows the pragmatic elevation of deeds over creeds, actions over words, and engaged spontaneity over cool detachment. "The philosophy which is so important in each of us is not a technical matter; it is our more or less dumb sense of what life honestly and deeply means,"[7] a sense better enacted and enjoyed than enunciated. This creative tension was not resolved by James, who never stopped talking about the insufficiencies of talk:

> I am tiring myself and you, I know, by vainly seeking to describe by concepts and words what . . . exceeds either conceptualization or verbalization. As long as one continues *talking,* intellectualism remains in undisturbed possession of the field. The return to life can't come about by talking. It is an *act;* to make you return to life, I must set an example for your imitation, I must deafen you to talk, or to the importance of talk. . . . Or I must *point,* point to the mere *that* of life, and you by inner sympathy must fill out the *what* for yourselves.[8]

Having thus acknowledged the irony in pitching more words at rich phenomena that must elude them, I should explain the remainder of my title. James's richly imagistic phrase "springs of delight" equivocates judiciously between connotations of mechanism and organic nature, implying (as James does in general) the shared and natural sources of the varieties of human flourishing. Our transcendently delightful moments spring proximally from the body's marvelous biomechanism, and subjectivity modulates them with personal symbolism and the seeming spontaneity of pure and cleansing waters gushing from unplumbed depths. But then, curse our masochistically curious souls, we reflect and descend:

> A little cooling down of animal excitability and instinct, a little loss of animal toughness, a little irritable weakness and descent of the pain-threshold, will bring the worm at the core of all our usual springs of delight into full view, and turn us into melancholy metaphysicians.[9]

But usually, after suffering the "falling dead of the delight," we rebound: "the music can commence again;—and again and again—at intervals."[10] Our natural condition is to know both aspects of experience in turn, delighted "animal" spontaneity and angst-ridden cerebration. Our challenge is to reconcile them; our method, an uneasy mix of philosophy and untutored experience; our enemies, metaphysical malaise and that excessive intellectualism that discredits experience in advance. And our holy grail, the pearl of inestimable price, is no less than the promise and prospect of happiness, flourishing and fulfillment for ourselves and our kind.

Jamesian transcendence is not hostile to the verbal arts and, for some of us, is even inseparable from them. But it draws deeply from those subjective, personal realms of experience that in their fullness are truly beyond words, mysteriously and delightfully implicating "the fact that individuals vary from the human average in all sorts of directions . . ."[11] and dance to very different "music." Spontaneous deviation from the norm is not a total mystery, of course. The more we learn of our own evolutionary epic and the rich and growing complexity of life, the more we will have to say about the numinous nature that is our native habitat. But we can be confident and grateful that life will always exceed and overspill our words and, when they lure us into confusion or insubstantiality, will beckon our return.

The human spirit is intrinsically, inescapably personal but is also vitally related. If my book is occasionally more confessional than much contemporary philosophy, that is because my own vital relations have brought home to me the wisdom of "bond[ing] the personal narrative voice . . . to the human search for transcendence."[12] James says of Whitman that although he wrote autobiographically and in the first person, his practice was not from personal conceit but from the desire to speak expansively and vicariously for all.[13] Perhaps Whitman was ambitious, maybe presumptuous, but well motivated nonetheless. I intend my own voice in these pages to be illustratively personal, not exhibitionistic; but I know of no way to express the full meaning and importance of our subjective enthusiasms and commitments without speaking of my own. It may be customary to philosophize about such matters in abstraction and to hold subjectivity at arm's length from transcendence. My approach, however, is more like Thoreau's: "I should not talk so much about myself if there was anybody else whom I knew as well."[14] And Kierkegaard was right: Life is understood backwards but lived forwards—a homily best funded as the recognition that life is lived personally and concretely. There may be such a thing as a fallacy of misplaced concreteness, but not when it comes to understanding "the exuberant excess of [our] subjective propensities"[15] and the resulting spiritual dimensions of the subjective imagination.

Spirituality is the link of continuity between every human breath, every moment, and every epoch. It is what binds the personal, the social, and the philosophical. Life, as James says, is a chain: a flowing stream of succession to which we may contribute, not only through the spires of our genes but more overtly in our voluntary devotions and ideals. The living breath that measures our moments and days also marks the distance between an attentive present, coveted futures, and life's remote denouement. Respiration, inspiration, and aspiration are entwined aspects of the vision of life as a chain.

The year 1998 was full of remarkable, even surreal contrasts. It was an ignoble year: a sitting president of the United States found himself obliged to testify publicly about matters once thought too indelicate for words, especially those emanating from the mythically hallowed halls of the people's House and the Congress. He was required to defend his interest in the sublime artistry of our great national poet of democratic transcendence as other than just more proof of his own degeneracy. (Indeed, the president's accusers found his gift of *Leaves of Grass* provocative and possibly salacious.) But for me it was also a year of stunning, gratifying reverse: a new home-run king was crowned, and many of us who think the game sometimes "radiates a spiritual transcendence"[16] were seduced to end our unhappy estrangement. Baseball's spring is again, for those of us captivated by that old spell of our childhood, a recurrent source of delight.

Nineteen ninety-eight also brought a particularly personal day of transcendent delight; on a crisp February morning, my Vanderbilt faculty advisers—John Lachs, Michael Hodges, John Compton, John Post, and Paul Dokecki—approved an early version of this work and granted my admission to the club of credentialed scholars. Dr. Lachs's deft but unobtrusive direction allowed me finally to subdue the "Ph.D. Octopus" and discover the "personal and spiritual spontaneity" whose expression James considered higher education's greatest and most sadly neglected custodial responsibility.[17] In true Jamesian style, Dr. Lachs "barge[s] into the philosopher's lecture hall with the direct concerns of everyday life" to help his students "decide or discover what is important for them in their lives."[18] He personifies teaching's ideal.

I am indebted to so many inspirational friends, former colleagues, and teachers that I cannot thank them all here by name. I am very grateful to my family for their unstinting support, and particularly to my father, Dr. James C. Oliver, for all his exemplary ways (not only with words). I appreciate my in-laws, the Roths of Hohenwald, Tennessee, for their tireless help, and especially for their daughter. My wife, Dr. Sharon Roth, is a relentless motivator. Perhaps I could have done it without her, but I would not have. And thanks to our daughters Emma and Katie, I have also learned that "daily companionship with a questioning child is a reminder of what intelligence is for—not, ultimately, for dominion, but for communion."[19] This book is better for being the product of a writer whose stake in the future is as tangible as the flesh and blood and (I now understand) the spirit of precious others whose flourishing I cannot, *would* not distinguish from my own. American philosophers typically assert a preference for living realities over remote abstractions. My family has taught me what that means.

I thank everyone at Vanderbilt University Press for their equable professionalism in shepherding this book into print. I am proud to contribute to the important and growing Vanderbilt Library of American Philosophy.

xvi ℒ
PREFACE AND ACKNOWLEDGMENTS

Despite my reservations about the impact of computing in our time, I am happy to acknowledge the critical assistance of colleagues encountered in the cyberspace of various Internet forums.[20] Their mediated presence can be invaluable to those of us who have sometimes toiled, as I have, outside the conventional vineyards of academe.

And speaking of computers: in giddy anticipation of "Y2K," a surprising number of "survivalists" were taken more than half seriously, by as many normally sensible folk, in their apocalyptic predictions of a millennial crash when "the machine[s] stop"[21] counting years. But hope springs eternal for those who greet the future in the spirit of William James, with a stirring awareness of real risk, a promise of real gain, and the zestful expectancy that best suits an open, evolving, personal and pluralistic universe.[22]

Nashville, Tennessee
August 2000

# Introduction

## The Glimmer and Twinkle of
## Jamesian Transcendence

Philosophy lives in words, but truth and fact well up into our lives in ways that exceed verbal formulation. There is in the living act of perception always something that glimmers and twinkles and will not be caught, and for which reflection comes too late. No one knows this as well as the philosopher. He must fire his volley of new vocables out of his conceptual shotgun, for his profession condemns him to this industry; but he secretly knows the hollowness and irrelevancy.... In the religious sphere, in particular, belief that formulas are true can never wholly take the place of personal experience.

*Varieties of Religious Experience*

trans-end-dance: the ability to move beyond the end, otherwise called the dance of death.

Peter Ackroyd, *The Plato Papers: A Prophesy*

## "Circumscription of the Topic": Taking Experience Seriously

"Transcendence" is a rich but imprecise notion, calling up a wide range of overlapping associations. It may provoke thoughts of religion, spirituality, serenity, reverie, fantasy, enlightenment, ineffability, meditation, mysticism, metaphysics (in either the traditional or the New Age sense)[1] the meaning of life, the denial of death, art and aestheticism, psychopharmacology, neuropathology, parapsychology, or even epistemology, to skim only a portion of a list that scrolls on and on. But Andrew Delbanco, bemoaning the spiritual vacuity of an age so caught up in the borrowed prestige of brand identity, writes that "the idea of transcendence has detached itself from any current symbology" save that of mass market advertising ("the golden arches and the Nike swoosh").[2]

Transcendence may seem to be about God, or it may be sacredly secular and humanistic. Secular, humanistic, *and* sacred? Those who find "secular

I

humanism" intrinsically profane will not grasp, as James did, the possibility of this triple yoking. Dewey also affirmed this possibility, as do many liberals, Unitarian Universalists, and other "progressive" minorities in our time. Habit and convention, not empirical perspicacity, decree that public-spirited and earth-centered secularists must disavow a spiritual life. Transcendence may be cosmic or quotidian, reserved or refined, proselytizing or private. It may suggest supernaturalism, but it need not; indeed, one of my aims here is to strengthen the claims that, *for a Jamesian,* transcendence need not imply the supernatural and that strictly speaking, and in the spirit of James, it need not involve the transcendence *of nature.*

Transcendence may be strictly transient, momentary, and isolated, *an* experience discontinuous in each instance of its occurrence with the larger rhythms, patterns, and meanings of the lives it graces. Alternatively, it can compose the largest meaning in one's life, the pattern of a lifetime. Transcendence may be a fruition, an experience of conclusion—"consummatory," in John Dewey's language—or it may be less punctuated and more persistently enduring. Dewey himself wrote a great deal about consummatory transcendence, but the latter sort, transcendence of a more stolid and stoical kind, suggests the consistent pattern and meaning of Dewey's long life's work, perhaps more than does that of any other American philosopher. His gravestone paean to "the continuous human community in which we are a link" summarizes that pattern and meaning with simple but powerful eloquence.[3]

Transcendence might strike like a bolt from the blue or be more like the almost imperceptibly accretive sands on a beach. It may be an event in life, small or staggering. It may be a dispositional attitude toward life that raises one's sea level of happiness and the quality of experience in general, attuning the sensibilities to notice and appreciate a transcendent dimension of events that more somber natures miss. Or it may be the pessimist's prayer of salvation, his escape from an immanent existence he finds all too oppressively real.

Transcendence can be triggered, on the one hand, by a tiny incident, a random sensation, or an excavated memory; or, on the other hand, it can be produced by large and baffling public events. An example of the latter might be the apparently sudden collapse of the Soviet bloc in the concluding years of the last century, especially for those whose entire comprehension of human possibility had been conditioned from birth to accept its permanence. The resulting psychic dislocation and scramble for personal meaning must have occasioned much transcendence, East *and* West.[4]

Transcendence may be unexpected and surprising, or it may be the object of methodical cultivation. My delight in the game of baseball, for instance, or in a particular game, sometimes catches me by surprise but on other occasions has to be tracked down like a shot lined deep into the gap.

The "national pastime" is public, and frequently baffling, but—with a respectful bow to documentary artist Ken Burns[5]—it is a stretch to call it "large." It is only a game; but then, there are times when life is best *played* at, too (see the discussion of "flow" in chapter 5). And F. Scott Fitzgerald was just wrong when he called it "a boy's game, with no more possibilities in it than a boy could master, a game" without "novelty or danger, change or adventure." Closer to the mark is the observation that it "has been a touchstone to worlds elsewhere."[6] But for me the transcendent dimension of this game is not "elsewhere," it is (as in *Field of Dreams*) in my own back yard.

Transcendence may remind us of many a philosophical exercise in self-overcoming: the transcendental idealism of Kant, the ideal pessimism of Schopenhauer, the New England transcendentalism of Emerson and Thoreau, Nietzsche's misanthropic egoism, or Santayana's contemplative essentialism, to pick a random few. Jamesian transcendence actually has little to do with Kant's a priori deduction of categories of the understanding;[7] Schopenhauer, Nietzsche, and Santayana are all useful foils, illustratively antithetical to James in various ways. Emerson and Thoreau, as we will see, are closer to home in some respects, and we could cite countless literary allusions.[8] James's literary affinities, including Whitman and Emerson (suitably shorn of monistic, idealistic associations), reflect his commitment to taking personal, subjective experience seriously. The great critic Alfred Kazin graced us, shortly before his death, with sharp insight into James's passionate respect for each person's "own sense of the exceptionality of his existence" as part of "the axis of reality." His deepest commitment was to "the throb of our actual experience." His spiritual sensibility was not that of a true believer but of a "fellow soul."[9]

There is also the idea of transcendence as a weapon for combating extreme hardship and duress, or just boredom: we can transport ourselves imaginatively from the concrete situations in which we find ourselves, at least for a while, by taking thought of other times and places, by rehearsing poetry or listening (imaginatively if not aurally) to music, by meditating on eternity or its opposite, and by other ingenious mental strategies. This must be one of the single most valuable skills a person can acquire; certainly it always has been for the more resourceful innocents caught up in history's periodic eruptions of insane irrationalism. Accounts of mental stamina among concentration-camp and Gulag survivors are among our most inspiring narratives of human endurance.[10]

Transcendence may also take in the idea of personal accomplishment that exceeds expectation or overcomes special hardship: it is possible, many think, to transcend our genetic inheritance, the traumas of childhood, cultural deprivation, and so on. Poverty and ignorance are transcended much more often than we commonly appreciate. Astrophysicist Stephen Hawking transcended the horrible debility of Lou Gehrig's disease to write *A Brief History of Time*. And as a species we can speak of transcending the trend lines of natural and social history, becoming more cooperative, less belligerent, achieving some kind of progress in the transmission of an enlarged legacy to succeeding generations. This uplifting prospect of a cooperative, responsible, yet finite intelligence, *ours*, caring deeply enough about the millennial fortunes of remote posterity to identify strongly with them makes evolution, biological and cultural, the sine qua non of transcendence for some. The impact of the idea of evolution on humanity's self-image, to date *and* to come, cannot be overstated, nor can its influence on James and American philosophy in general.

The notion of evolution is a big part of what is meant by the "cultural transmission" of values, inviting us to imagine that the influence we succeed in spreading among contemporaries and immediate successors may ripple through the ages and make a difference for more distant descendants. The complementary reflection that we have been shaped by the past, that we are in fact evolving, is perhaps more unsettling, but James shares Dewey's enthusiasm for the speculation that, as Ray Boisvert puts it, "acts engaged in by individuals who are mere specks on the cosmic scale can have an 'infinite reach' . . . because the 'small effort which we can put forth is in turn connected with an infinity of events that support it.'"[11]

In itself, evolution cannot make us care about the long-term human prospect; that is a result of subjective factors like temperament. But it is an indispensable condition of our caring if we mean to relate it to purposive action such as parenting, itself a fertile ground of transcendence for some of us. Daniel Dennett makes this fundamentally humane point, surprising those who think his materialist biases are hostile to such an imaginative and even romantic view of human interconnectedness:

> One thing that does make us unique as a species is that for the last five or ten thousand years we have been the beneficiaries of conscious planning by our parents and their parents and the cultures in which we've resided. Today we are actively concerning ourselves with what the world is going to be like in the future. We have strong beliefs about this. They play a role in what Homo sapiens is going to be like a thousand years from now.[12]

Dennett's views in their totality, we will see, do not obviously make "elbow room" for this kind of "conscious planning" or, indeed, for a distinctive personal consciousness capable of transcending anything at all. But evidently his heart is in the right place; and I believe his head is, too, when he refuses to endorse a schism between nature and culture. All is in process, all is evolving, and this has the most profound implications for our place in a total scheme we see but darkly. Whether Dennett has entirely appreciated all the implications of the position he has taken is questionable.

James was an unusually fecund, imaginative, and suggestive philosopher. It would not be difficult to sustain a case for emphasizing each of these associations, in turn, as importantly related to his philosophy of transcendence. Yet it is also tempting to dispatch potential confusion at the start by arbitrarily decreeing this or that association irrelevant.

The better approach, I think, is simply to have my say about Jamesian transcendence as I have come to think about it and to assure readers that I intend no slight if in the process I neglect anyone's pet interests. The project of following James's resolve to take subjective experience seriously in the only way any of us can, from his or her own angle of vision, has the necessary effect of "circumscribing the topic" and neglecting areas others might prefer to pursue. A circumscription is really a partial transcription of one's own inner life. In particular, there are aspects of metaphysics, epistemology, and metaphilosophy that preoccupy contemporary neopragmatists such as Richard Rorty[13] but that I treat only lightly and in passing. Much more waits to be said on this topic, more than I can or want to say, and I hope others will say it. We must all tell our own stories. So here are some disclaimers:

My interest in Jamesian transcendence is not motivated by a futile quest for some standpoint outside both "reality as a whole" (whatever that might mean) and our statements about it. I am not attempting to draw a reliable map to all possible senses of "transcendence." I do mention several prominent vehicles and destinations in order to orient the reader who wonders what on earth transcendence might mean, but I have left others out. That is as much a reflection of my own subjectivity as a statement about important meanings.

Jamesian transcendence is in my view neither an epistemic nor an escapist impulse, both of which Rorty criticizes. True, James's radical empiricist commitment to personal experience does make him more hospitable to talk about transcendent entities and phenomena than traditional empiricists, but hospitable, we will see, within a naturalistic context and as a humane expression of his pluralism. He denies no important truths about the history and contingency of human convention and belief, or about human limits.

Transcendence is usually presumed by its possessors to emit self-certifying reverberations of "reality" or information about a world (natural or fantastic) beyond the theater of the mind. Hallucinations do, too, of course; but then they are sometimes found out: "Oh, I was hallucinating." Transcendent experiences do not usually get "found out" in this way by those who claim them. Transcendent attitudes or turns of mind are even less tractable than particular episodes, being the products of long experience and reflection. An exception would be in the "conversion" experience, sudden, unexpected, and revolutionary. But in every life of enduring commitment to ideals in which one has invested much of oneself, conversion—typically signaling antecedent dissatisfaction and unhappiness—becomes increasingly improbable.

Descartes's "clear and distinct perceptions" differed importantly from the "mental mark" of this sort of transcendence in at least one huge respect: Descartes meant to construct a foundationally coercive edifice of knowledge. Transcendent experiences may seem foundational to the individuals who report them, but their scope encompasses *at most* those individuals themselves, and even then are best understood not in terms of Cartesian certainty but more in the pluralistic sense of its absence. Others remain free to believe them hallucinatory, though the more charitable Jamesian response is usually a kind of agnosticism: not having had exactly *those* experiences, but noticing their evident power in the lives of those who report them, James urges upon us the epistemic equivalent of "hands off" wherever established facts trail what he calls "forced" and "momentous" circumstances of belief.

When someone identifies one of his own experiences as transcendent, he is making a much stronger statement about its vivacity and impressiveness *for him* than if he were simply to say that he had had a vision, an intuition, or a powerful feeling that might *for all he now knows* have been just a bit of synthetically or chemically induced mental weather signifying nothing. "I had a transcendent experience but . . . I might have just been hallucinating" or "my norepinephrine and serotonin levels were spiking" or "my medication was kicking in" would be very strange things to say in reflective response to one's own transcendent experience, even if accurate at an isolated level of neurophysiology. The personal quality of our specific experiences is rarely so isolated from our "real" world that we are prepared to dismiss them out of hand.

It makes even less sense to cash out a transcendent *attitude* or habitually high default level of happiness in terms of causal factors sharply removed from the form of a person's actual experience of life. Such a translation of personl experience into the generalized form of an explanation might not be literally false, yet it might be inappropriate, harmful to someone's ends, or incompatible with our happiness. Pragmatists and their foes argue incessantly about the relevance of such considerations, the former insisting that nothing could be more relevant. For a Jamesian, taking experience seriously involves the rejection of single-level description in favor of a multiplicity of self-reckoning.

This is an important point, but it is not easy to grasp or hang onto. We will revisit and challenge it. For now we can anticipate James's view by saying that in a way he thinks irrelevant the causes of our soaring and elevated moments. If we have such moments, their experiential quality must be such as to insure their own validation if anything does. They are "real as experienced," to an extent; that is, if we do not experience them as caused in this or that respect, do not know them as experiences of joyous insight or delight *caused by X*—where X might be neural network static, the brain's timing mechanisms, or protein microtubules[14]—then X is largely beside the point so far as transcendence is concerned. I say "largely" to suggest a limit, to the extent that certain epistemological and metaphysical issues are not allowed to take center stage or usher various candidate explanations from neurobiology, physics, or some other partial discipline into a starring role in place of subjective experience. For James the center stage of transcendence is always set by each of us in turn, however. Some transcenders, and some philosophers seeking to clarify the various modalities of transcendence, will undoubtedly prefer to keep issues and approaches on stage which will here be set aside, and that must be their prerogative if they mean honestly to tell the stories of their own enthusiasms.

But this is the story of Jamesian transcendence. Telling it accurately means emphasizing personal experience and identifying approaches he thought hostile to it. The reader can judge the adequacy and accuracy of the identification, but a few further comments to orient my approach may still be in order.

James derided the "bald-headed young Ph.D.'s" (ouch!) and their "desiccating and pedantifying" ways.[15] His evident objection was not to their baldness, their youth, nor even their Ph.D.'s but to their cocksure belief in the exclusive primacy of an approach to philosophy that begins and ends in questions about the establishment of "certain knowledge" and insists on technicality and jargon at the expense of clarity for all except a very few specialists. James always declared himself on the side of experience, *against* "philosophy," wherever the latter had been shrunk to fit the limited dimensions or stylistic exclusivity of a "school" or discipline. He scorned some epistemologists' implicit view of reality as something necessarily twinned and correlated to whatever questions we happen at the moment to be asking about what and how we can know, as though abstract knowing were the highest purpose of life rather than one among many.

Still, it must be admitted that James is best known for raising and answering questions of an intrinsically epistemic character, about the grounds of belief and the criteria for asserting knowledge. But its answers far exceed the bounds of epistemological propriety, not because James did not know better but because he intended to advance a radically different way of thinking from that current among the devotees of *erkentnisstheorie* in his own day as well as ours.

Philosophers, theologians, novelists, and others have written of transcendent experiences involving exalted self-surrender, when individual personality and identity are submerged or annexed by some mysterious larger force, power, or entity, and consciousness is pervaded by impersonal awareness, a sense of heightened reality, expanded perception, or unification with "the infinite." The object of so much psychic commotion has been designated "God" and countless cognate terms for divinity by some, but others have proposed different candidates for transcendent attachment. I will nominate a nonsupernaturalist candidate that I think James especially favored, while also remembering that he was temperamentally disposed to "favor" as many transcendent objects and ideals—metaphysical, natural, supernatural, or occult—as could be surmised to animate the inner life of even a single soul in the vastness of time and space.

So I must caution the reader always to bear in mind a distinction between James's own personal enthusiasms and his pluralistic hospitality to those of others. Tolerance or sympathy being itself one of his ideals, he often enthused over views—more pointedly, over *others'* enthusiasm for views—which in fact he detested personally.[16] He sympathized with almost everyone's spontaneous personal enthusiasms, their ways of meeting and "reacting on" life, without sharing them. And while he had his own clearly defined philosophical beliefs, he tried to refrain from using philosophy to discredit the experience of other persons. Many a commentator has failed to notice and apply this distinction and has run aground by miscasting James's broad sympathies as personal endorsements.

By whatever name or nature, the large and mysterious *something* in each separate instance of the varieties of transcendent religious, moral, or aesthetic experience is supposed to be a source of transformative energy. Such experiences may instigate in the transcender a crisis and a radical alteration of self-ascribed personal identity, or they may reinforce an identity already forged. They usually revolve around a compelling perception, intuited thought, or sudden shift of feeling that seems to the transcender to portend authentic discovery and may conflict with treasured prior commitments.[17] What is supposed to be "transcended" in such an experience is, in short, the subjectivity of the individual along with the "false consciousness" or conceptual errors that normally accrue to finite, limited beings like ourselves and that impede our achievement of happiness or personal fulfillment. "Fulfillment" presumably is relative: an epistemologist, unlike a graphic artist, musician, or truck driver, might be happiest and most fulfilled in studying the conditions or criteria of propositional knowledge. We all find fulfillment in terms closest to our own abiding interests and obsessions. But in each case, if discovery is claimed it is discovery of reality, some subset thereof, or some previously unnoticed aspect of one's relation to it.

The common denominator in all discussion of transcendence, from whatever angle, seems to be this: it somehow engenders happiness, personal fulfillment, or at least reconciliation to life in those who experience it, and it does so in part by radically altering the sense of self. In the extreme case, selfhood—not just one's previous personal identity but the very notion of identity as essentially personal—is abandoned, overcome, repudiated, declared an error or an illusion, or in some other way corrected by the liberating influence of whatever insight is supposed to be contained in the experience. Subjectivity, the condition and consequence of being a limited and error-prone self, might then seem an obstacle to transcendence. A too-intimate relation of attachment to one's own subjectivity, voluntary or not, might preclude the possibility of liberating insight and consequent happiness or personal fulfillment. So it might seem.

But the philosophy of William James affirms and celebrates subjectivity. Virtually every aspect of his thinking may be seen as an attempt to recognize and respect the integrity of individual experience as it is subjectively apprehended, no matter how odd it may seem from a more objective or intersubjective point of view. James also proposes, though, with his radical empiricism, that we acknowledge in our philosophizing a category of experience that is neither subjective nor objective but "pure" of such conceptual exclusions and discriminations. Pure experience is impersonal, apparently, in the fashion of transcendence as traditionally understood: impersonal because not concerned with the pretranscendent and limited self and not bound up in one's subjectivity. It might seem most likely, then, that if James has anything important to say about transcendence, it will come out of his philosophy of pure experience rather than from his affirming celebration of subjectivity per se.

My thesis, to the contrary, is that James is an advocate for a type of *personal* transcendence owing at least as much to subjectivity as to pure experience. The structure of this book mirrors this uncomplicated line of thinking: Chapters 1 and 2 lay the groundwork in establishing the importance and ubiquity of the concept of subjectivity in James's philosophy *because of its preeminence in experience*. Chapter 3 is the brief but crucial pivot point of the argument, considering and rejecting the suggestion that the impersonality of pure experience is strongly relevant to Jamesian transcendence. Chapters 4 and 5 reassert the primacy of subjectivity and personality in Jamesian transcendence and begins to explore a few of its implications.

I mean here to follow out some of the consequences of taking James seriously when he says, as in the epigraph above, that there is no substitute for personal experience. The "glimmer and twinkle" of transcendence is no exception. It is not enough to be "present," in some Zen-like fashion of transparent and selfless purity, to our most compellingly significant experiences; we must bring ourselves, our persons, our peculiarities and idiosyncrasies, our histories, and our anticipated futures—in a word, our subjectivity—with us, in our most transcendently stirring moments. Only thus, for James, may our lives accumulate concrete significance in their particularity. If this sounds more "existential" than pragmatic, perhaps that is because we have paid more attention to trendy existentialism than to the tradition of classical American philosophy. Alas.

"To the question about the meaning of life everybody answers with the story of his own life," said Hungarian novelist Gyorgy Konrad.[18] James heartily approves: this is how we should answer, and the existentialists were not the first to say so. But unlike many existentialists, pragmatists like James and Dewey also believe that the primacy of our personal stories need not preempt an inclusive social vision.

The *future* orientation of Jamesian transcendence, in particular, distinguishes it from alternatives and sits least comfortably alongside those more familiar eastern and quasi-eastern versions of transcendence that suppress subjectivity and will, renounce the self and its desires, and extol timeless passivity as the highest level of psychic ambition. Kitaro Nishida's Japanese Buddhist version of pure experience, for instance, takes James in a Zen direction that I think false to his own intentions, toward the fusion of self and universe dissolving into a timeless meditation on nothingness. For James, as we will see, self and universe are never really one; never mind *nothing!* He defends the experience of those who believe in this oneness, but he does not corroborate it. Nor does James concur in the sentiment that "there is nothing that is not a manifestation of God,"[19] though he sympathizes with the affirming sensibility uttering it.

"Pure experience," experience shorn of labels that may distort it or prejudice our perception—subjective and objective, material and ideal—is not more transcendently "real" than ordinary experience; it may just be a way of talking that James proposes that we adopt to remind ourselves not to let our overzealous conceptualizing intellects stand in the way of more immediate, less filtered relatedness to experiences of all kinds, to whatever extent that is possible at all. Our grasp of reality, or the sum of all actual plus all possible experience, grows as we come to appreciate the complexity of many points of view besides the one we happen to occupy. But of course we cannot remove the "filter" of our own subjectivity, though simply being aware of it is a big step forward in our respectful apprehension of so much experienced reality that lies beyond the borders of our own immediate consciousness.

My contention is that James's own preferred approach to subjectivity provides as well the groundwork of a naturalized, pluralistic approach to transcendence that reflects and advances the pragmatic tradition in novel and inspired ways. One example is how the identification with the vast human community of the future, an identification lauded by some current thinkers, may for James have been a suitable object of transcendent attachment, one fulfilling "religious" desiderata that is errantly thought by some James scholars to require supernatural backing. In addition, the discussion of Jamesian transcendence in chapter 5 touches on several related matters: the culture of computing and the unsettling, uncertain impact of new communications technologies in the so-called information age; the dangers of personal transcendence based upon subjectivity; the paradox of the future as a source of transcendence in the present; evolution and the idea of progress; destructive egoism vs. healthy subjectivity; the place of purposes and ends in human flourishing; the idea of "flow" or optimal experience; why Jamesian transcendence implies a fundamental continuity between the "inner" and "outer" realms of conscious human experience, and between the personal and the communal; and why pragmatists ought to be transcendently happy at least some of the time, and optimistic about the human prospect.

The importance of my thesis to James scholars, beyond whatever value there may be in showing that James has a philosophy of transcendence and that it more or less coheres with the rest of his thinking, is that it adds an increment of clarity to the always troublesome and problematic concept of pure experience. I should not presume to declare its importance to nonscholars, though I have tried to write with them in mind and, in fact, consider myself one of them. I do not share the disdain of so many specialists for "popular" scholarship. James certainly did not. It is good for specialists to communicate with one another so that they can gain the benefit of informed, thorough criticism, but it is not good for them to communicate *only* with one another, unless they really have nothing of wider interest to communicate. The greatest possible importance of my thesis to nonscholars, then, may be its implicit argument that philosophy can matter, that a philosopher dead for nearly a century can still speak to us in a voice that is fresh, lively, accessible, and relevant to our own life struggles.

That is also its greatest importance to me. I, too, find James "the most inclusive mind I can listen to, the most concrete and the least hampered by trifles."[20] I have been listening and responding to James for many years now, not always agreeing with him but almost always gaining from the experience.

## A Philosophy of Celebration

Robertson James once advised his brother to "stop your research for Truth (pragmatic or otherwise) and try and enjoy life."[21] William was probably touched by his sibling's concern. He often gave vent, himself, to a feeling that life and philosophy follow different tracks. But he must also have felt irritation at his younger brother's failure to grasp the motive forces in his life and philosophy that for him made philosophy, at least occasionally, a transcendently enjoyable activity.

He would have appreciated the satirical jab at those joyless and plodding scholars whose "research for truth" (the absolute truth, timeless and disconnected from any recognizably human circumstance or end) he also had no patience for. In fairness, James knew that some plodders and absolutists enjoy their work; but he would still have been mortified by the implication that he was one of them. Indeed, it is possible to think of the philosophy of William James as an extended meditation on the theme of enjoying life, a philosophy of celebration. James worked hard throughout his entire lifetime to create and hold a personal temperament capable of sustaining the celebratory, festive mood. It apparently did not come naturally to him, biochemically speaking. But another element of his native temper did predispose him to the social dimension of celebration: he was inveterately curious about the inner lives of everyone he met, regarding men and women as constellations of subjective fascination and potential insight. "When he met someone new," Linda Simon reports in her fine biography, "he probed persistently to discover all he could about them, to understand how their experiences made them who they were, to see where those experiences intersected with his own: all this, to learn more about himself"[22] and, we might add, to expand the field of his experience and its significant relations to others.

Only a redoubtable life celebrant and cosmic optimist would have responded, just weeks before his own looming extinction in the summer of 1910, to Henry Adams's dark musings about the Second Law of Thermodynamics, the "heat death of the universe" and so on, with this sort of blue-sky speculation:

> Though the ULTIMATE state of the universe may be its . . . extinction, there is nothing in physics to interfere with the hypothesis that the PENULTIMATE state might be . . . a happy and virtuous consciousness. . . . In short, the last expiring pulsation of the universe's life might be, "I am so happy and perfect that I can stand it no longer."[23]

The festive air of celebration in James is pervasive and insistent, but not unqualified. He rejects the more immoderate versions of "healthy-minded" optimism as callow and insensitive to the genuine, undeserved suffering of real individuals; yet even there[24] he finds merit, beneath the folly, for marshaling and directing constructive personal and social energies in the lives of enthusiastic postulants. But for himself, James proclaims a philosophical vision that refuses to ignore the world's unpleasant realities, even as it encourages the temperamental predisposition in some to focus on more pleasant possibilities. This is his meliorism.

James's lifelong refusal to "blink the evil out of sight" was firm, in an age that saw—at the very cusp of the Holocaust—a disquieting tendency by

Christian Scientists and other "New Thinkers" to deny the reality of evil.[25] Though he was in ways a representative man of his moralistic age, even the most casual acquaintance with his writings must leave an overall impression not of stern moralism but of a kind of joyous optimism, a life-affirming eagerness to fight humanity's battles and, on the personal scale, one's own in a spirit of confident insecurity. "Insecurity" here means the awareness of great stakes and real opportunities to seize or forfeit them.

This notion of the opportunity of insecurity bears on James's philosophy as much as on his personal temperament: in both, the celebrant is not separate from the naturalist or the pluralist, or from the pragmatist and radical empiricist, who (despite James's own disclaimers) in turn are bedfellows. "The difference between monism and pluralism is perhaps the most pregnant of all the differences in philosophy. *Prima facie* the world is a pluralism,"[26] fundamentally an open arena in which spirited combatants may enter real contests, score real victories, suffer real defeats, and fight for whatever real unity the world may bear. "My experiences and yours float and dangle, terminating, it is true, in a nucleus of common perception, but for the most part out of sight and irrelevant and unimaginable to one another."[27]

Less obvious on its face to some is James's claim that in addition to its dazzling, dizzying plurality the world is also pervasively, globally *natural*. This can indeed be a slippery term to use in describing James. He is hospitable to supernaturalism and does not prejudge anyone's experience, but his own personal tendencies of belief and expression are naturalistic in tone, even as they strain to meet the "spiritual" demands of his own and others' personal natures. John Edwin Smith sagely borrows Tennyson's lyric eloquence to express this commitment to safeguarding the reality of experience from reductive analysis: "the articulation and illumination of experience which is the goal of reflective thinking cannot contain less than that with which we started. If the splendor that falls on castle walls belongs to our direct experience, it must still be there at the end of analysis and not be transformed into wave lengths."[28] It is not that wavelengths cannot be natural and real, too; they can be. But James's pluralistic naturalism rejects the proposal that their reality can conceivably displace the concreteness of personal experience.

James was a resolute but un-Pollyannish yea-sayer and fighter, always insisting that life is a struggle but also a humane and "moral" one which, in contrast with "poor Nietzsche's antipathy" for weakness as such, should strenuously resist misanthropy and sublimate martial conflict.[29] We must acknowledge evil, pain, and loss; but we must acknowledge them not as intractable and permanent conditions rooted in the structure of reality from all eternity, but rather as the issue of present and inherited circumstance and the testimony of experience so far. These inevitable burdens invite resignation and pessimism in some natures; but they may also invite the deliberate cultivation of a different kind of reaction as well, calling forth our best efforts to construct a future that will be livable for the living. Cultivating this kind of reaction requires a special temperament, but perhaps a learnable one, to take real pleasure in contemplating a superior and perhaps distant future that will not be one's own to enjoy directly. It takes an even more enlightened temperament to move beyond contemplation and be willing to work for that future.

James's philosophy, I believe, aspires toward such a temperament and offers it as a model for what Dewey would later call "reconstruction" in philosophy and in life, both personal and social. It is a temperament that *confronts* disappointment and setback, instead of placing them in a scheme larger than life—larger, that is, than possible human understanding or acceptance—for purposes of resigned reconciliation. James would have us admit the existence of evil so that we need not admit its permanent necessity: "it might be an independent portion that had no rational or absolute right to live with the rest, and which we might conceivably hope to see got rid of at last."[30]

James is a philosopher of celebration not because everything occasions glee but because nothing in our future yet requires despair. We can act, and so we may hope. This forward-looking emphasis on the future and on what is possible, coupled with a rejection of any form of determinism that would require repudiation of all hope based upon possibility, is perhaps the most obvious sense in which James can be called a celebratory or life-affirming philosopher of happiness. This Jamesian emphasis is, with subjectivity, the mainspring of his philosophy of transcendence.

There is an uninvited guest at James's celebration: the charge that human freedom in the metaphysical sense is illusory and is, therefore, incapable of sustaining the celebratory mood toward possibility and the future. By his own insistence, the human spirit is hardly autonomous from the coarse urgencies of the body. For James, we all must learn

> how at the mercy of bodily happenings our spirit is . . . [A] cup of strong coffee at the proper moment will entirely overturn for the time a man's view of life. Our moods and resolutions are more determined by the condition of our circulation than by our logical grounds.[31]

As one who begins every day with strong coffee and thrives under its influence, I take particular interest in this passage. But I remain confident that my better early-morning moments *are* mine and not Starbucks.' Here again is implicit support for the suggestion that James is unconcerned about the causal antecedents of transcendence and is untroubled by the evidently corporeal origin of our states of mind. This is one leg of the naturalism I believe his philosophy of transcendence stands on. The relation between mental life and the brain's neurophysiological activity is in some fairly straightforward sense that of effect to cause, for James, but with a significant field of still-unanswered (and maybe unanswerable) questions about how that relation is actually effected and realized. There is still room for James to entertain, and to encourage others to entertain, various hypotheses of all sorts (including supernatural ones) concerning consciousness and regions of reality with which it may—through the brain's intercession—conduct an ongoing commerce.

Like a cup of strong coffee, many of the unexceptional events of daily life may yield exceptional moments. When I walk for an hour or more, I almost always experience at least a fleeting sense of heightened significance. There are natural chemical explanations of this, of course, having to do with the body's production of endorphins, the presence or absence of dopamine and other natural substances, and so forth. A naturalist admits and welcomes such explanations, and their contextual relevance to a physiological account of human functioning. But a walker does not want to hear about it, not while he is walking and not when he recalls the pleasures of walking. Is that because he prefers an ostrichlike posture or has a compelling "will to *make*-believe"? Bertrand Russell might say so, but James charitably presumes not; and as a walker I prefer simply to say that I take my walking experience seriously. Any insinuation that James prefers fantasy to reality ignores such ubiquitous statements as, "Woe to him whose beliefs play fast and loose with the order which realities follow in his experience: they will lead him nowhere or else make false connexions."[32] To be sure, there are deterministically or stoically pessimistic versions of transcendence that profess indifference to the metaphysical question of free will. Jamesian transcendence is not one of these. It must face the challenge of external causation.

But James not only believes in free will; he notices it in his own experience and accepts the like testimony of others. So long as he and we persist in representing mental life and subjectivity generally as more intimately identified with the self that acts, or the whole person, than with the brain either in isolation or in mysterious contact with 'nether-regions, then any account of how a person may sometimes act freely even though his acts are produced by brain events and "bodily happenings" must take seriously the subjective experience of free will. This is not finally negotiable. As a practical matter for James, free will is not a "problem" but a datum. But it is a challenging datum. James could respond to the challenge, in part, by distinguishing the mechanism responsible for mental events (the brain, its neurophysiological stimuli, and whatever other causes may be at work) from the experienced nature and content of those events. The latter is all interiority, personality and subjectivity. But does this provide adequate insulation? And should we want to insulate our minds in this way? Do not we court the bogey of dualism if we follow this line? Would it make more sense to re-think the prejudicial self-concept that treats the brain as somehow "exter-nal" to our persons and incapable of hosting or executing our spontaneity? But how do we do that?

I do not think James wants to insulate the mind, nor does he want to backslide into dualism. The brain is not external, though anyone who has ever spent more than a moment trying to hold the thought "I am a brain" will report that the identity issue here is not easy. If we could say all that we want to say about our inner lives and experiences by referring to *it*, instead of to minds and consciousness, James should not object. In fact, he thinks there are processes of consciousness and dimensions of experience that brain-talk may miss. Contemporary debates continue on this issue, as we will see. For some of us, though, it is just laughably obvious that extreme "eliminative" materialists are out of touch with the very realities betrayed by their own ac-tivity in the world. I once had occasion to point this out at a professional gathering of philosophers when the claim was presented, in all apparent se-riousness, that there are no persons but only organisms and their brains meeting a physical description matching our own. But brains do not attend philosophy conferences, persons do. And not uncommonly, many of *them* seem to have left their brains at home. One of the unfortunate "inveterate habits dear to professional philosophers" that James is eager to turn his back on[33] is an almost indiscriminate, juvenile posturing, so much in evidence at such gatherings, that is in defiance of common sense. "Common sense is *better* for one sphere of life, science for another, philosophic criticism for a third. . . ."[34] Why should not all philosophers know this?

James means to celebrate the self as both catalyst/instigator of future events *and* locus of intrinsically valuable experiences in the present. The second kind of celebration seems relatively untouched by the issues of free will and mind-body; the first may not be. In other words, a celebratory phi-losophy that aims simply to appreciate the varieties of human experience as they pass may sidestep certain metaphysical issues in a way not possible if it were oriented mainly to a future hanging in the balance of our freedom. James appears to be a celebrant of both types, so no full appraisal of his philosophy can postpone metaphysical contention indefinitely.

But there is a great deal more to the issues of happiness, subjectivity, and transcendence than any current or recent debate on traditional meta-physical problems (like free will and mind-body) reflects. This "more" be-gins where philosophy and conceptual discourse must end, somewhere in the neighborhood of every person's unique subjectivity as directly experi-enced. Presumably, we all know our own neighborhoods pretty well, in these terms, but others' neighborhoods only by analogy and sympathy and imagination. Much mystery must remain.

The claim that James is celebratory of the self as a locus of intrinsically valuable experiences means that he appreciates the marvelous diversity of ways in which human beings find the world interesting and important, ways that "make life worth living." This is the overt message of "On a Certain Blindness in Human Beings," James's essay that more than any other encapsulates the central themes presented here. And it is a crucial underlying motif in countless other James writings. The fact that one person's very reason for being leaves another cold and uninterested is at the heart of what he considers the enduring mystery of happiness and is part of the larger mystery of life.

## The Natural Mystery of Happiness

Happiness, thought James, is a vital and delightful mystery: something to wonder at, to cherish and promote. Often elusive, we must "conquer" it (in the manner of Bertrand Russell in his popular 1930 ode to joy, *The Conquest of Happiness*[35] or puzzle it out; but if it is not the kind of problematic mystery that requires final "solution," neither ought we to slip from active philosophical wonder and psychological inquiry into awed silence. Arriving at an impasse in his discussion of the knotty problems of how to relate mind and brain, consciousness and physiology, James asks:

> What shall we do? Many would find relief at this point in celebrating the mystery of the Unknowable and the "awe" which we should feel. . . . Others would rejoice [at a] "higher synthesis" in which inconsistencies cease from troubling and logic is at rest. It may be a constitutional infirmity, but I can take no comfort in such devices for making a luxury of intellectual defeat. They are but spiritual chloroform. Better live on the ragged edge, better gnaw the file forever![36]

And so James continued to gnaw for many years, at last hitting upon the radically empirical concept of pure experience: a profoundly suggestive approach to mind and body, and to much else besides, which unfortunately (though to the vocational benefit of succeeding generations of working scholars) he did not live long enough to expound in full.

James did not suppose, despite his refusal of spiritual chloroform, that happiness might be usefully quantifiable either precisely or in even the broadest terms. Claims that our respective predispositions to happiness are mostly, or half or forty percent, genetic, or the like, probably cannot be given a useful, consistently meaningful interpretation that will shed light on us all. How each of us exploits, squanders, neglects, or improves on the nongenetic side of his personal happiness quotient defies statistical analysis; but many "twins researchers" think they find the grounds in their data for minimizing the importance of environment and experience relative to heredity.[37] Siblings sharing similar or identical genetic endowments are yet uniquely themselves, though, unpredictably molded by their own biographies in ways subtle and ungeneralizable; and despite a current vogue for biological nature in the misconceived nature-nurture wars, the mirrored personal impact of variable experience still cannot be gainsaid.[38] Perhaps the ultimate vindication of this claim will come when we learn to clone ourselves and the imprint of unique experience at last becomes palpable. Scientists meanwhile will continue, correctly, to research the question; but here if anywhere is an appropriate invitation to philosophy.[39]

Popular and journalistic prejudice treats philosophy as an interim diversion and pastime on the way to real understanding: "The debate is still open as to whether the problem of consciousness—how felt experience is connected to the physical brain—is *purely philosophical, an illusory difficulty* that will be swept away by progress in neuroscience, or one that requires a revamping of all of science, starting with physics," began a recent article.[40] But if we are to achieve genuine progress in understanding consciousness, such prejudicial scientism—a species of intellectualism that discredits personal experience in deference to laboratory and armchair experts—is going to have to be "swept away" first. We are *all* experts in the matter of what our experience means to us. Nothing finally may be wrong with folk psychology that more folk *experience* cannot be trusted to fix, eventually. Unfortunately, patience for the long run is not an abundant commodity in the contemporary research environment. More in vogue is the expectation that scientists are about to pin down every last mechanical detail of conscious experience: "Neurobiologists . . . have located an area in the temporal lobe of the brain," we are told, "that produce[s] intense feelings of spiritual transcendence. . . ."[41] So much the worse for spirit, we are expected to conclude; but why not so much the better for the brain, if indeed it harbors a "religious hot-spot?" Like science, philosophy has a responsibility to correct errors in the representation of human experience. But it also has an obligation to balance correction with appreciation, to take experience seriously. Here is an attempted beginning.

An enduring paradox of our existence is that most of us are happiest when we are least troubled to understand why we are happy, when we resist the natural pull of our curiosity to reduce all phenomena to problems for research. Only when we are unhappy, or worse, do we profit from explicit attention to whatever hidden biochemical or emotional mechanism it may be that results in our states of conscious weal and woe. That is when we can least afford to ignore the causal springs of our workaday selves, when we possess the lowest tolerance for our own compromised spontaneity. The rest of the time, we probably do better not to look the gift horse of happiness too directly in the mouth. But are we most "spontaneously" ourselves when happy? Is mild depression normal and proper?

Severe clinical depression is one thing; the Prozac-popping refusal of so many in our time to confront the objective causes of personal discontent is another. But James is finally a Jeffersonian in the matter of happiness, on the side of those who proclaim its pursuit by any self-regarding means a basic human entitlement.

But why not study our happiness? Do we risk the evaporation of mystery? It must be an evanescent mystery, indeed, that vanishes under critical investigative scrutiny. But maybe there is a greater risk of overlooking a mystery beneath all serial causation. Multiply-subjective experience is unspeakably richer than the stunted imagination of the philanthropic trustee who, when asked for examples of intractable mystery worthy of his foundation's research dollars, mentioned the dietary regimen of a random Frenchman on an arbitrary day in the fourteenth century.[42] But far more puzzling than the mystery of what a medieval Gaul ate, or even the deep mystery of what it was like to be him, is how some of our contemporaries can be so intrigued by questions about his ingesta and the like but not about the peculiar, irretrievably personal quality not of his innards but of his inner mental and imaginative life. Can it be that, like the comic strip character in *Dilbert,* they believe "what's inside a person doesn't count because no one can see it?"[43] Of course, in courting mystery we ought also to note Darwin's rebuke: "ignorance more frequently begets confidence than does knowledge: it is those who know little, and not those who know much, who so positively assert that this or that problem will never be solved by science."[44] And James was no foe of facts, happy to gather and analyze them to solve what can be solved. But happiness is not just another problem on a list.

There is probably no simple statement clarifying what James thought mysterious about happiness. This book would be a very different project if there were. But I am convinced that the mystery of happiness, which for James is much more profound (and "deep") than any account of human behavior based solely upon physiological, neurological, psychological, computational, or cognitive science, is bound up with his general attitude toward the leading topics of this work: subjectivity and transcendence. In the present context, these are fundamentally about happiness, that is, about enjoying life and cultivating a deeper, richer, affirming and celebratory sense of what life means.

James continues and extends a quintessential American view of personhood, directly in the line of earlier celebrants of the frontier and the wild as symbolic of our national character, our perpetual quest for challenge and novelty. Thoreau and Emerson are in that line.

> Our village life would stagnate if it were not for the unexplored forests and meadows which surround it. We need the tonic of wildness. . . . At

the same time that we are earnest to explore and learn all things, we require that all things be mysterious and unexplorable, that land and sea be infinitely wild, unsurveyed and unfathomed by us, because unfathomable.[45]

Thoreau's tonic "wildness" is not just about weeds and rattlesnakes, but more the sense of a vital and open quality of experience that is ours if we have the fortitude and adventurousness of spirit to seize it. This is part of what "mystery" signifies for James as well, a quality invoked as much to inform his intellectual life as to counter what he considers its excesses. Mystery quickens our pulses, enchants our inner lives, and saves us from suffocating intellectual arrogance. We *need* it, Thoreau tells us; and James, ever sensitive to need, concurs. Whether this is true for us collectively, as a species, or just for some of us, as individuals, it represents a natural cap on our capacity for total knowledge.

Thoreau and James both imply that the mystery of life is palpable and perceptible for those who allow themselves the luxury of stillness in which to appreciate it. But teachers are not still. "What an awful trade that of professor is," James complained at term's end in 1892, "paid to talk, talk, talk! . . . It would be an awful universe if everything could be converted into words, words, words."[46] Richard Ford's character Frank Bascombe expanded on the same theme:

> Real mystery—the very reason to read (and certainly write) any book— was to them [his teaching colleagues] a thing to dismantle, distill and mine out into rubble they could tyrannize into sorry but more permanent explanations; monuments to themselves, in other words. In my view all teachers should be required to stop teaching at age thirty-two and not allowed to resume until they're sixty-five, so that they can live their lives, not teach them away—live lives full of ambiguity and transience and regret and wonder, be asked to explain nothing in public until very near the end when they can't do anything else. Explaining is where we all get into trouble. . . .[47]

Trouble, indeed. For one thing, our explanations tend to rely on unquestioned assumptions about the stability and permanence of our explanatory frameworks, the laws of nature, the scope of what can or cannot be explained, and even what it means to explain one thing in terms of something else.

James, we must always remember, holds out for real novelty as a pervasive top-to-bottom feature of the universe. This means being open to the possibility of evolutionary transformations at every level of existence, not only in biological organisms but in the universe at large, in the regularities of its diverse processes. James learned what he could from David Hume and, so, was not tempted to presuppose greater comprehension of "regular-ities" than we in fact possess. If such regularities might really be suscepti-ble of evolutionary transformation, we had best speak only loosely of the *laws* of nature. "We believe in all sorts of laws of nature which we cannot ourselves understand merely because men whom we admire and trust vouch for them."[48] Those who follow Hume in preferring to invoke the idea of constancies and habits, ever watchful for alteration, have James's implic-it sympathy. "New facts burst old rules. . . ."[49] He certainly agrees that the mania for exhaustive verbal explanations, and the vocations rewarding it, gets us into the trouble of assuming and asserting a great deal more than we know—more than we want to know, if we value not only our own spon-taneity but also that of a world with enough "movement and free-play"[50] in it to throw us a new pitch once in a while. Acceptance of a certain loose-ness in the laws of nature may be the price of indeterminism and a variety of free will someone like James would consider worth wanting.

On the other hand, we need also to notice an important difference dis-tinguishing James from other contemporary philosophers in the emphasis of his particular kind of "loose" talk about laws of nature. David Chalmers has said that "conscious experience itself is a fundamental property of the universe,"[51] coordinate with physical properties. Making theoretical con-nections between these two realms, which sounds a lot like the project of old-fashioned dualism, is the resulting challenge to philosophers and scien-tists. James rejects the dualism, of course. But he also rejects the displace-ment of experience that comes of representing it mainly as a property of the universe and not, derivatively, as a property of individuals. Conscious expe-rience is always, first and last, that of some individual. A naturalist will agree that individuals are natural constituents of the universe, but a natu-ralist who takes experience seriously in the fashion of James will be reluc-tant to speak of it with the impersonality of Chalmers's statement. Conscious experience is a property of the universe but, it is much more, too: the vital center of life, interest, significance, and personal meaning. It is the stuff of transcendence, for most of us not something that *as experi-ence* stands in need of theoretical connectedness.

But faith in the eventual casting of an explanatory net wide enough to snare even a frenetically evolving universe down to the last detail persists. Daniel Dennett thinks we can be confident that in time—a very long time, to be sure—evolution will spin out satisfactory explanations of "everything that happens" without demonstrable remainder, and that to lack this confidence is to conjure gratuitous, superstitious mystery.[52] E. O. Wilson has voiced a simi-lar faith in expectation of ultimate, total explanation, bemoaning what he sees as the philosopher's self-arrogated project of setting the limits of con-ceivable scientific probity and even of defensible human hopefulness. "Philosophy, contemplation of the unknown, is a shrinking dominion. We have the common goal of turning as much philosophy as possible into science."[53] But pluralistic humanists are not of Wilson's "we," spurning his peculiar form of "Ionian enchantment." In two thousand years we should all by now have become disenchanted with every variant of the attempt to demonstrate the reducibility to *something*—earth, air, fire, water, physics, information—of everything else. But the "astonishing hypothesis" that "'You,' your joys and your sorrows, your memories and your ambitions, your sense of personal identity and free will, are in fact no more than the behavior of a vast assembly of nerve cells and their associated molecules,"[54] astonishingly persists in various guises. People no longer trumpet "Social Darwinism" as they did a century ago, and "sociobiology" has nearly become a seventies curiosity; but "evolutionary psychology" preserves their shrunken spirit with unflattering depictions of human motivation as permanently, stupidly fettered by ancient, uneducable drives and instincts.[55]

Thomas Nagel—whose famous "bat" speculations[56] on the inaccessibility of first-order experience provided an irresistible hook for subsequent contention—is to Dennett one of the mysterian obscurantists whose "skyhooks" block the road of inquiry better traveled by "cranes"—the heavy (self-) lifters of growing human knowledge. Dennett is eager to reassure him that "we're making tremendous progress in getting information so we'll be able to say exactly what it's like to be a bat."[57] Subjective mystery is on the run, at least so long as no bats dispute our "information." But humans may not be compliantly batty enough for the research program. What must it be like to be Dennett? We are not likely to "get" that information anytime soon, not because Dennett's keeping it to himself but because it is no more than partially verbal (say the mysterians).

Dennett lumps John Searle with Nagel and indicts him for sponsoring "forlorn attempts to conceal the mind behind impenetrable mystery"[58] despite Searle's wish to place the mind on all fours with the rest of nature. But this statement from Searle seems perfectly complementary of Dennett's faith in the recession of mystery:

> As with the "mysteries" of life and consciousness, the way to master the mysteries of intentionality is to describe in as much detail as we can how the phenomena are caused by biological processes while being at the same time realised in biological systems. . . . I am not saying we should lose our sense of the mysteries of nature. . . . But I am saying that they are neither more nor less mysterious than other astounding features of the world, such as the existence of gravitational attraction, the process of photosynthesis, or the size of the Milky Way.[59]

Suppose Dennett, Wilson, and others are right, that one day science will "end" and consensus will gather around every big question concerning consciousness and life that anyone thinks to formulate. Is that all there is? Not for Searle. There are still "inner, qualitative, subjective states such as our pains and joys, memories and perceptions, thoughts and feelings, moods, regrets, and hungers,"[60] states obvious to all except, Searle suggests, Dennett and other "reductionists." But if Dennett does not repudiate the real existence of inner states, just their description as beyond explanatory reach *in principle,* he and Searle may be much closer than either of them will gladly admit.

Nor is that all there is for pragmatists like James, who remind us that explaining is often the last thing we want or need to do in order to understand and appreciate what our experience means. The road to transcendence passes more often through the nonbehaviorally, nondemonstably charted terrain of subjective experience than through the public domain of agreement about what needs explaining and what counts as an explanation.

Transcendence is an end or a contemplative resting place in the sense that it is intrinsically enjoyable when it transpires, but it can also be a beginning. The fresh perception of relations of all kinds that it offers, especially relations between individuals, communities, and generations past, present, and future, leads to action—though not in ways we can usually pinpoint, specify, and analyze. "Action" can mean appreciative enjoyment that alters the landscape of what we care about and what we care to explain. Transcendence can be fully engaged, in this way, in a normally active life. What we enjoy affects what we care about, take an active interest in, and *do.*

Beginning in the late twentieth century, we have come to care about the whole burgeoning culture of the computer, which has spawned a raft of exciting new work in the philosophy and psychology of mind. This new approach seeks for clues to the mystery of consciousness through the analogy of software and programs, in the chips and circuits and subroutines of the "thinking machines" in which we have invested so much energy and on which we have grown so dependent. I had none of this in mind when I began to think about James and happiness many years ago—not many of us did in the old Mesozoic typewriter era—but such issues deserve the most careful scrutiny. The nature of personal identity may have been an abstruse topic for professional philosophers then, but it is timely and relevant now.

James would not have lightly dismissed these new approaches, insofar as they remain diligently empirical in method. I think he would have been intrigued but finally put off by the "intellectualism" of an enterprise that proposes (according to some) to shed light on living realities through the contrivance of an abstract and disembodied conception of mentality: an old Cartesian mistake in fashionable dress. James would have maintained that there is a majesty and mystery to life that even the most circumspect computationalist is constrained by his method from realizing.

For a long time it was easy enough to see the obvious deficiencies of computational approaches: they abstracted consciousness from its world and tried to characterize its processes strictly in terms of the vacuum of self-referential programming languages, forgetting that human thinking so far as we know it at all is always embodied and situated in a world each of us represents from a unique first-person viewpoint.

Lately, however, a new sophistication is creeping into this field, and talk begins among cognitive/AI researchers of rejecting "the disembodied, atemporal intellectualist vision of mind" in favor of an explicitly biological and naturalistic account that will "put intelligence where it belongs: in the coupling of organisms and world that is at the root of daily, fluent action."[61] This is the sort of thing John Searle has been saying for a long time, that continental philosophers like Merleau-Ponty[62] and Heidegger seem to get most of the credit for originating, but that pragmatists like James and Dewey always knew.

Another contemporary cognitivist, Steven Pinker, conveys an excitement and passion not usually associated with computationalism:

> I believe that the discovery by cognitive science and artificial intelligence of the technical challenges overcome by our mundane mental activity is one of the great revelations of science, an awakening of the imagination comparable to learning that the universe is made up of billions of galaxies or that a drop of pond water teems with microscopic life.[63]

Here is a real hint of unabashed wonder at the workings of mind that seems to recognize its continuity with a nature more marvelous in complexity and scale and sheer evocativeness than any supernaturalism ever dreamed of. Yet, Pinker says in an autobiographical aside, he has ignored nature's "solemn imperative to spread my genes. By Darwinian standards I am a horrible mistake. But I am happy to be that way, and if my genes don't like it, they can go jump in the lake."[64]

But wait, now: if our personal happiness sometimes requires us to deviate from nature's genetic and other default programming, our minds—we, really—either are computers of such unimaginably stupendous sophistication as to be able to rewrite the program spontaneously as we go, or else they (we) are not really computers in any remotely familiar sense at all. That is, minds and persons do computations, but they do something else, too: they pursue happiness.

This may be just an empirical question the answer to which will change how we (or, more likely, our remote descendants) think about computers and brains and (if there remains any felt need for these terms) minds and persons. For now, the field is crowded with intuitions but not with many conclusive answers. And, for now, the upshot of computational research seems to be that if the brain is a computer, it is tremendously less algorithmic ("mindless and purposeless") than any yet conceived. My own intuition, and James's, is that no science now conceivable will get to the bottom of happiness because none can ever do more than point at the phenomenon of variable subjectivity from the outside. The experiential content of subjectivity, the stuff of happiness and personal transcendence, must still be grasped from the inside or missed.

Wishing to deflate Star Trek–style extrapolations of hopefulness for a progressively more humane, enlightened, and technologically sophisticated future, science journalist John Horgan says that there is "only one scientific fantasy that seems to have any likelihood of being fulfilled": our creation of "machines that can transcend our physical, social, and cognitive limits and carry on the quest for knowledge without us."[65] It is doubtful that James would embrace this speculation, if taken to imply the possibility of nonbiological "life forms" in whose experience we may now vest a vicarious proxy. The coidentification of ourselves with future generations that is at the heart of Jamesian transcendence depends on the solid perception of *human* continuity across time, and at this date most of us remain unabashed biological chauvinists, even if we *have* overcome racism and *specie*sism. But it is an empirical question, and an intriguing one, whether our attitude on this will change. Perhaps there is a "Mr. Data" in our future.[66] Or perhaps Searle is right: "Increased computational power in a machine gives us no reason whatever to suppose that the machine is duplicating the specific neurobiological powers of the brain to create consciousness."[67] Horgan has lately taken up this banner himself, seemingly backing away from his earlier speculations about transcendently smart machines:

> I suspect that the more intelligent or aware or enlightened we become—whether through drugs or meditation or genetic engineering or artificial intelligence—the more we will be astonished, awestruck, dumbfounded by consciousness, and life, and the whole universe, regardless of the power of our scientific explanations.[68]

We need not posit science's end, it seems, to acknowledge its limits. No one, no method, no research program can capture all that marvelous variety of first-person experience and reframe it inside a new, all-encompassing perspective. We do not even know what it would mean to be able to do that, although some suppose that God does it and others that a sufficiently complex supercomputer might do it someday. To the extent that these *are* empirical claims or predictions, Jamesian radical empiricists will be content to wait-and-see; but because they take experience seriously, they must also be skeptical of an approach that on its face seems liable to exclude vastly more experience than it can capture. We already know what that is like; it seems to be our natural condition. If the analogy of brains to hardware and minds to software is even approximately accurate, the new science is sure to replicate that feature of our existence. But the residue of life-enriching mystery may be transformed into stultifying confusion, if we come to think of experience as just another program variable and not the living content of reality.

The mystery of consciousness will disappear, Searle suggests, when our mapping of the "biology of consciousness" approaches the depth of our general biological understanding. "We will understand consciousness when we understand in biological detail how the brain does it."[69] But is that achievement even imaginable? And how deep is our general biological understanding, really? As Searle never tires of pointing out, "We don't have a clear idea of how anything in the brain could cause conscious states."[70] But the crucial point is that even if we did, we would be no closer to an intimate understanding of the relation between those states and the felt, lived experience of being in each instance the singular person who knows them.

In a revealing discussion Searle suggests that our problem of consciousness is going the way of a previous generation's problem of vitalism: we now know better, he implies, than to invoke a mysterious "life force" whose function is better executed by a detailed account of the "mechanism" involved in standard, current biological explanations. Maybe so. But the "élan vital" responded to an area of wonder that seems outside the scope of most accredited research programs in biology. Being out of vogue in a scientistic age is not the same as being intellectually vacuous or obsolete.

It seems that Searle hasn't grasped the mystery that impresses James any more than Dennett. He is surely right, a Jamesian is bound to think, when he says that "biological brains have a remarkable biological capacity to produce experiences [that] only exist when they are felt by some human or animal agent,"[71] but the mantralike, incantatory iteration of "biological" may mislead: calling consciousness biological not only does not demystify it; it does not even really point the way to eventual demystification. We do not possess a "depth of understanding [of] the biology of life" that can even begin to model an exhaustive science of consciousness. A biological approach to consciousness may remove many cobwebs of gratuitous mystification, but the probability that it will answer all our questions is thin. That is good news to a Jamesian.

The Jamesian point Searle may not fully appreciate, even while spelling out its intuitive foundation in first-person subjective ontology, is that mystery is built into our experience of reality. Our biological brains create first-person experiences, each of us is a "first-person," and none of us is omniscient. Searle grasps each of these "obvious" facts well enough in isolation from the others but seems inadequately impressed (from a Jamesian point of view) by the profundity of their merger. We will not "understand consciousness when we understand in biological detail how the brain does it"[72] because such understanding must describe brains in general. In the end full understanding of consciousness cannot *possess* anyone's conscious experience in particular, never mind everyone's.

This is a point either too subtle or too obvious, apparently, to persuade the unpersuaded. It is commonly conceded that scientific usefulness depends upon generality. The fact that subjectivity is the form of our experience is general enough, but experience itself is inescapably, irreducibly, delightfully specific. Every person, indeed every moment of every person's conscious experience, is necessarily opaque to every other to a degree sometimes trivial but oftentimes not. Thanks to language and the extension of sympathy based on presumptive and evident similarities, not all is mystery. But plenty is.

This can seem trivial, or it can seem profound beyond words. Perhaps it is finally temperament, as James says, that inclines each of us to be either struck or unmoved by the force of mystery. Likewise, temperament makes some of us naturalists, others supernaturalists; some scientistic, others mystical. And some few, like James, manage to mix these and other elements in an original, personal compound that causes consternation in minds less practiced in the "negative capability" of holding contraries in solution. It is a rare bird that can in the same breath praise those who "throw the doors of their minds . . . wide open to the supernatural" *and* caution them not "to relax their vigilance as to evidence."[73]

So James is happy to be a "mysterian," a steadfast proponent of the idea that life is enhanced and dignified by the perception of permanent mystery at its core, flattened and misrepresented by excessive positivism, *naive* verificationism, and unimaginative naturalism. But he is also a kind of positivist and verificationist, and he is a naturalist, despite some current scholars' claims to the contrary. One, for instance, rejects interpretations of James's theory of consciousness "involving a consistent and farseeing naturalism"[74] while another asserts that where "Dewey's philosophy is naturalistic all the way down," James's is "spooky all the way up."[75]

Can James consistently honor both impulses? Can a mysterian be a naturalist and not a spook-monger? I believe the answer is yes, but only—as I will attempt in the next section to explain—with more circumspection than has been customary in recent debates.

## The Temper of a Pluralistic Naturalist

In this section I want to reinforce by way of further introduction the crucial distinction we have already noted between James's own beliefs and enthusiasms and his arms-length advocacy of others' perspectives. James's naturalism, evolutionism, and faith in the future cannot be understood in isolation from his pluralistic esteem for diversity, his classic Millian liberalism from the conviction that every perspective offers a partial but indispensable window on reality. Jamesian transcendence cannot be truly understood apart from his remarkably candid personal effusiveness and natural exuberance of temper.

What kind of a naturalist was James? This is not an easy question. James was a naturalist not simply in the manner of a Muir or a Peterson, or even of Thoreau, though he *was* a hiker and a believer in the restorative possibilities of the outdoors. But ordinarily James's naturalism should be understood in two senses: (1) as *biological* naturalism, the view that all observable life phenomena admit of explanation at some level, whatever such explanation may be worth in the terms of biological science—and we have noted that it is not always worth so much for James; (2) as *global* naturalism, the view that everything experienced and experienceable is real and in precisely that sense is a part of nature. Being natural and real is not the same as being entirely objectifiable, predictable, or lawlike. But it is honorific, in the sense of something to be respected and taken seriously, whether one experiences it oneself, directly, or as something reported in the experience of others. Where hallucination is suspected our respect may be less, but since we do not have foolproof diagnostic or epistemic tools for distinguishing real experiences from false ones in every case, James solicits our tolerant forebearance.

James had strong personal tendencies toward both senses of naturalism and strong sympathetic tendencies away from them. A radical empiricist's last word, forever penultimate and not conclusive, must always be to wait and see. But some of James's earliest words on the subject remained instructive throughout his philosophic life: "I'm swamped in an empirical philosophy. I feel that we are Nature through and through . . . and yet, notwithstanding, we are *en rapport* with reason . . . all is nature *and* all is reason too."[76] Because James's ubiquitous Nature shares equal billing with "reason"—"spirit" might for once be the more usefully descriptive term, here—it is not hard to find examples of his scornful rejection of unsophisticated naturalism. "The purely naturalistic look at life, however enthusiastically it may begin, is sure to end in sadness. . . ."[77]

But James is not a *pure* (or "mere") naturalist, or a "popular science evolutionist" in contrast to someone like Henry Adams (recall James's response to Adams, above). "To ascribe religious value to *mere* happy-go-lucky contentment with one's brief chance at natural good is but the very consecration of forgetfulness and superficiality." James's naturalism is saved from arid "purity" by this attitude, which begins to tell us something important of his philosophy of transcendence:

> The lustre of the present hour is always borrowed from the background of possibilities it goes with . . . [L]et faith and hope be the atmosphere which man breathes in;—and his days pass by with zest.[78]

"Zest" is one of James's favorite words, charged with the vibrancy of experience not as a metaphysical category but the felt movement of life as literal *inspiration*, something to draw in and express through all the pores of one's being.

Is this "spooky"? James's 1904 essay "Does 'Consciousness' Exist?" concludes with the bold assertion that "the stream of thinking (which I recognize emphatically as a phenomenon) is only a careless name for what, when scrutinized, reveals itself to consist chiefly of the stream of my breathing."[79] The bodily anchorage of thinking, for James, prevents him from wholly embracing a supernatural account of the phenomenon of transcendence as he encounters it in his own experience. But notice that he is careful to speak of "*my* breathing." Let others scrutinize the phenomena of their own inner lives and draw their own life-quickening conclusions. "Hands off," again.

"Not God, but more life," said James, is the most natural human impulse[80] and the ultimate source of religious variety. And, as he informed a correspondent in 1901, his own sense of life was most quickened by what he could not help regarding as the *progressive* epic of evolution. "I believe myself to be (probably) permanently incapable of believing the Christian scheme of vicarious salvation, and wedded to a more continuously evolutionary mode of thought."[81]

James considered philosophies "religious" if they reflect and support a personal style of confronting life and enable their possessors to act, hope, and dream instead of withdrawing in resignation and despair. Such philosophies may be supernatural, but they may just as well not be. So may the talk of subliminality and "a wider self through which saving experiences come," in the conclusion of *Varieties*, in *A Pluralistic Universe* and elsewhere. The surface spookiness of such talk is much alighted when we recall that for James the "self" is substantially, naturally constituted by relations, including not only those already established and recognized but significantly by other relations both anticipated and unforeseen. "Every bit of us at every moment is part and parcel of a wider self, it quivers along various radii like the wind-rose on a compass, and the actual in it is continuously one with possibles not yet in our present sight."[82]

But was James's own personal religious philosophy supernatural? We must resist any quick or easy answers here, lest we simplify and distort an issue that was complex for James, and ought to be for us, too. He sometimes does, indeed, write forcefully as an advocate and practitioner of supernatural speculation; but beneath all the varieties of our religious experiencing, he also suggests, we can still detect a common natural impulse in each of us to live meaningful, coherent lives *by our own lights*. This is the impulse that wants to honor our respective, personal, subjective commitments but without in the process affronting the conditions of communal sympathy and civility. In view of this emphasis, the supernatural "over-beliefs" James sometimes professes or flirts with may be seen as idio-syncratically personal curiosities, peripheral to his central insight into the natural ground of all kinds of religious speculation, including the supernat-ural. Again, supernaturalism for James is not strictly opposed to what I have called his global naturalism. This is no concession but a nod to the sophis-tication of James's peculiar form of naturalism. The simplistic dilemma be-tween naturalism and supernaturalism is, for him, simply false. His affirmation of naturalism is subtle and diffuse because it aims, prima facie, to take everyone's experience seriously; and this means recognizing the po-tential integrity even of those experiences of others that for us ring fantastic and strain our own credulity.

What is this "nature," for James, that undergirds experience in its end-less and unpredictable variety? Is it something essential and fixed? Can we even pose such a question without insinuating an unwarranted and unprag-matic essentialism? Is there a *nature* at all, or do we experience *natures*, which we gather together under an abstract concept or metaphor that we then hypostatize and exalt as Nature?

These are the right kinds of nominalistic questions for a Jamesian to ask. We should not essentialize nature in any sense that implies arrest or fi-nality, these being intrinsically counter-evolutionary states. James, like all pragmatists in the vanguard of philosophic Darwinism, was no turgid clas-sicist on questions of being and becoming. The evolutionary, antiessential-ist cast of his thought is unmistakable. His interest is not in specifying timeless conditions for the possibility of experience and understanding in general, but in discovering the actual content and meaning of our experi-ence in and of (global) nature, in particular. Indeed, for James we are con-scious bits of nature ourselves. "Common men feel the question 'What is Nature like?' to be as meritorious as the Kantian question 'How is Nature possible?' So philosophy, in order not to lose human respect, must take some notice of the actual constitution of reality."[83] And this means taking notice of the experience of actual persons, as they report it, and "taking no-tice" means taking *seriously*.

But does James's global naturalism so inflate the conception of nature as to render it pragmatically inefficacious? No. The category of nature, to be truly helpful as well as accurate, must accommodate the full range of human sensibility and experience. For a Jamesian there is simply no other handle on "reality" than this. And whatever "efficacy" means, exactly, prag-matists do not value it above helpfulness and accuracy, and probably should not distinguish those criteria sharply in any case.

James's personal religion as well as his philosophy, we can fairly surmise, included evolutionary thinking as an important element of belief in human solidarity. As made plain in an earlier quotation, James rejects "vicarious sal-vation." But clearly he also regards evolution as a natural-historical process whereby "saving experiences" are generated for those with the breadth of sympathetic imagination to identify vicariously as links in the chain of genetic and other influence. The totality of this experience, with all those other links who are our brothers and sisters (and mothers, fathers, sons and daughters) *is* human reality. A bestselling book[84] argues that, for genetic reasons mostly, the decisive influences in children's lives are provided not by parents but by peers. James would not be impressed, preferring the healthy tension of the open Emersonian question "Who shall set a limit to the influence of a human being?" in combination with the sagacious injunction to let children "be themselves, and enjoy life in their own way."[85] A link is no mere placeholder; it is a support, a lead, a connection, and sometimes (for better or worse) an influence. Sometimes the best influence is benign neglect, but sometimes not. "Nothing is more alarming than the impoverishment of our children's capacity to imagine the future,"[86] except the evident disinterest of too many parents in awakening that capacity.

Another 'ism crowds the stage of James's philosophy: *humanism*, most succinctly the view that human "experience as a whole is self-containing":

> I myself read humanism theistically and pluralistically. If there be a God, he is no absolute all-experiencer, but simply the experiencer of widest actual conscious span . . . [This is] essentially *a social* philosophy, a philosophy of "co," in which conjunctions do the work . . . refusing to entertain the hypothesis of trans-empirical reality at all.[87]

Facile scholars sometimes portray James as a hyperindividualist and an asocial, if not antisocial, philosopher. They do not understand the depth of his commitment to the communion of human ends: a commitment not unlike that of Emerson and Whitman, which dares speak the name of God in the most worldly of temples. For James, we may all aspire to be experiencers of widely conscious span. That does not mean that we can each be God ourselves, in the derisively antihumanistic sense, but that we can throw off the narrow egoism of a constricted self-conception and choose a wider identity.

The role of temperament in philosophy is one of James's better-known preoccupations, with his distinction between tough- and tender-mindedness and his insistence on the rightness of seeking a well-tailored fit between individual traits of character and personal assent to propositions. Roughly, this is the view that our prejudices precede all argument and that we tend, as if instinctively, to find reasons for believing what we have already accepted.

Two personal experiences of James's deserve special mention as illustrative of his temper and its formative influence on his philosophy. The first, discussed in chapter 1, is the "Walpurgisnacht" he spent atop Mt. Marcy in the Adirondacks. He described its physiological and emotional manifestations in a letter to his wife testifying eloquently to his preference for risk and challenge in life, and to his sense that such preferences are importantly related to our corporeal nature. The second is James's personal account of the great San Francisco earthquake, an account that must be at least curious and possibly illuminating to anyone who has ever been visited with an earthquake experience of his own. My own small quake experience was in Palm Springs, California, on May 7, 1995, a relatively insignificant shimmy on the Richter scale (5.0) but enough to awaken me from a deep sleep at 4 A.M. with an immediate, inexplicable awareness of exactly what was happening. I confess that the dominant feeling for me, then, was fear.

James's firsthand account of the events of April 18, 1906 is, by contrast, not one born of fear at all:

> [L]ying awake at about half past five . . . I felt the bed begin to waggle. . . . Sitting up involuntarily and taking a kneeling position, I was thrown down on my face. The room was shaken like a rat by a terrier . . . [My] emotion consisted wholly of glee . . . at the vividness which such an abstract idea or verbal term as "earthquake" could put on when translated into sensible reality and verified concretely. . . . I felt no trace whatever of fear; it was pure delight . . .

James described his total quake experience as "mind-enlarging," reporting in the quake's aftermath a sense of cheerful solidarity among the survivors, "a kind of uplift in the sense of a 'common lot' that took away the sense of loneliness that (I imagine) gives the sharpest edge to the more usual kind of misfortune. . . ."[88]

It is no coincidence, I think, that one of the first things James wrote after the quake was an essay called "The Energies of Men." Like Emerson and Thoreau before him, he was alert to the very *human* significance of natural events. An earthquake, even a puny one, is a release of vast amounts of energy. We are conservators and expenders of energy, too, but much of our effort is dissipated. "The human individual lives usually far within his limits . . . [H]e energizes below his maximum, and he behaves below his optimum,"[89] habitually. But here is our greatest seed of hope: our bad habits were made to be broken. Like Emerson, James is a champion of self-reliance and the spirit of reform. Perhaps more than Emerson, he is also a champion of hope as the collective human urge so admirably displayed by those San Franciscans whose "hearty frame of mind" and eagerness to make a fresh beginning amidst natural devastation he found so uplifting.[90]

"All attempts to explain our phenomenally given thoughts as products of deeper-lying entities . . . are metaphysical."[91] James was never shy about doing metaphysics himself, even in the psychological writings when he announced a deliberate methodological intention to write from the standpoint of a new science in the early stages of collecting its data. Far from treating it as a bogey, he insists that "metaphysics means nothing but an unusually obstinate effort to think clearly."[92] But his most developed metaphysical stance—a blend of pluralism, radical empiricism, and naturalism—does not speculate *coercively* about deeper-lying entities. Instead he invites all of us to follow the arc of our own subjectivity in accounting for the particular constitution of our inner life.

Nonetheless, it is a mistake to think that James's naturalism and semi-conventional empiricism in *Principles of Psychology* was halfhearted or a sham, disingenuously masking a barely concealed "spookiness." It would be more accurate to say that the younger James wrestled with his own conventionalism and the prejudices of his scientific training—we should not forget that he held an M.D. and that he worked in the field as a practicing scientist with Louis Agassiz's Brazil expedition—and sought to balance it by cultivating an appreciation of "spookiness" in the experience of others that was not wholly native to his own spontaneous expression and temper. His peculiar brand of naturalism is more strongly akin to that of an Emerson than to the scientism and positivism of most self-avowed naturalists in our time. James was no Concord Transcendentalist, but he had that Emersonian purity of heart that instinctively exults in the experience of mystery and is prepared to admit that while we are intimately of nature, not foreign to it but related by "consanguinity," we are also "as much strangers in nature as we are aliens from God. We do not understand the notes of birds . . ."[93] But as we will see at the end of chapter 4, some know more of "birdsong," and the occasional impulse to render life's music without words, than others.

Yet a Jamesian naturalist revels also in the experience of discovery, not as mystery's rival but as its natural complement. The reconciliation of science and religion lies, if anywhere, in mutual respect for variable personal experience combined with fidelity to its shared natural conditions. A Jamesian is committed to both and can echo biologist Richard Dawkins's claim that "the feeling of awed wonder that science can give us is one of the highest experiences of which the human psyche is capable . . . a deep aesthetic passion to rank with the finest that music and poetry can deliver."[94] But Jamesians repudiate any reflexive scientistic hostility towards supernaturalism. It too, they allow, may fire passions natural and real. Emerson wrote in *Nature:*

> The best-read naturalist . . . will see that there remains much to learn of his relation to the world, and that it is not to be learned by any addition or subtraction or other comparison of known quantities, but is arrived at by untaught sallies of the spirit. . . .[95]

This Emersonian regard for nature as realized in spontaneous, personal, endlessly idiosyncratic human form distinguishes Jamesian naturalism from the misanthropic visions of many a naturalist. The poet Robinson Jeffers spoke of our "wild swan of a world" and evidently meant by that, among other things, a world fundamentally indifferent to human needs and demands. But nature and culture are not antipodal for James. Some elemental part of us is indeed irretrievably wild ("game-flavored as a hawk's wing"), but the domesticated, partly civil human animal is of nature, too. Poetry is of nature. Jeffers wrote: "I hate my verses, every line, every word."[96] James also lapsed into moments when such sentiments escaped his breast. But like Jeffers, he always took up his pen again.

## ". . . more day to dawn"

It was an inspired scriptwriter who once had Captain Picard of the starship *Enterprise* give a book by James (*A Pluralistic Universe?*) to young Ensign Crusher.[97] James's pluralistic naturalism is just the sort of freewheeling, ready-for-anything openness to novelty and variety that a deep-space explorer will want to travel with. James quotes Renan: "*In utrumque paratus*, then. Be ready for anything—that perhaps is wisdom."[98] James is that kind of philosopher because he wanted to be that kind of man: an explorer, adventurer, and happy traveler. He would be right at home on a starship, provided frequent shore leave visits to Keene Valley in the Adirondacks, to Chocorua, New Hampshire, and anywhere else in the traversable universe as fine. Here is a fine statement of the heroic temper that James so hungered to possess and to press upon our imaginations:

> The great affair, the love affair with life, is to live as variously as possible, to groom one's curiosity like a high-spirited thoroughbred, climb aboard, and gallop over the thick, sun-struck hills every day. Where there is no risk, the emotional terrain is flat and unyielding. . . .[99]

In as many places as intrepidity can carry us, James urges cheerfully firm resistance to the obstacles before our understanding and happiness. He opposes any diluted, accommodated, shadow version of happiness as inadequate to the spirit of a dreaming and aspiring species. Then, at the end of the day, we may still have recourse to whatever fatalistic or Stoic elements in our philosophic arsenal that may give some kind of succor for those best efforts that have landed short. But the end of the day is but a temporary terminus, a stage in an ongoing cycle. The future always beckons with the hope—no guarantees—of more fruitful engagement in life, of richer relatedness, refreshed perception, desired possibilities actualized, delightful new possibilities envisioned.

It is that Jamesian vision of "saving possibilities" in a future we can begin to enjoy in the present that integrates the leading themes here: subjectivity, mystery, naturalism, evolution, religion, personal flourishing, and social solidarity. All are ingredient in my notion of *personal* transcendence based on present identification with future possibilities and interfused with the delightful potencies of the preverbal sensorium. My aim is to depict these themes as points on that continuum of human experience at once stubbornly personal, constructively social, and *globally* natural; to emphasize some nonegoistic possibilities inherent in the fact of human subjectivity; and to highlight not deficiencies of human capacity due to our intrinsically localized points of view but opportunities in the way of a kind of transcendence that in the manner of James celebrates our condition and spiritedly welcomes its challenges.

I hope to signal in this book the relevance of American philosophy to issues emerging from the incipient culture of the computer, which may be *the* ubiquitous mark of our age. Jamesian transcendence can shed needed light on ways in which cyberculture threatens to compromise the texture of experience for the unwary and to misdirect our understanding of what it means to be alive and conscious. One way to reclaim that understanding is through a return to the measured elegance of the best imaginative literature, possibly our oldest and most reliably product-tested virtual reality technology. Great fiction and poetry can transport us, as nothing else can, into an approximation of the subjective sensibilities of other souls. James flags the incapacity of language to contain the robust subjectivity of ordinary experience; the best poets admit and accept that limitation and still create verbal illumination of interior worlds beyond their words. By that criterion, James was a marvelous poet. Richard Poirier has noted that James's pragmatism *works* "by effecting a change . . . carried out entirely within language." But he also recognizes that James's largest sympathies, like those of the surpassingly prolix Emerson, remain poetically anchored in a region beyond words but well within the province of life.[100]

Jamesians should greet the new century with eager anticipation, not worry. "There is more day to dawn," concluded Thoreau in *Walden*. "The sun is but a morning star."[101] James's favorite rhetorical question sounds the perfect echo: "What has concluded, that we might conclude in regard to it?"[102] This is a philosophy of exertion and hope, of transcendent subjectivity, of celebrated delights, and of life endlessly reclaimed.

# I

# Taking Subjectivity Seriously

Bring the past for judgment into the thousand-eyed present, and live ever in a
new day.

Emerson, *Self-Reliance*

Nature and human life are as various as our several constitutions. Who shall
say what prospect life offers to another? Could a greater miracle take place
than for us to look through each others' eyes for an instant?

Thoreau, *Walden*

## Perceptual Multiplicity and James's "Vision"

It is almost cliché to begin a discussion of William James with the porten-
tous mention of his own remark that "a man's vision is the great fact about
him" and then to offer a boiled-down statement of a position or proposition
that is supposed to capture the essence of his philosophical project. This
approach may be harmless or even useful, for expository purposes, but it
also affords the danger of violating the spirit of James's thought, even while
one is in the very attempt to grasp it.

James's philosophy mirrors the man: inclusive and multifaceted as he
was expansive and eclectic, and unwilling to stifle any voice or to constrict
the domain of attested human experience. So, let the reader beware. If
there is *a* center, it is in motion. I think I am within hailing distance of it
most of the time here, but markedly different approaches are, too. Truth is
not always well served by strident competition.

"Hands off: neither the whole of truth, nor the whole of good, is revealed to any single observer, although each observer gains a partial superiority of insight from the peculiar position in which he stands."[1] Failure to
respect a multiplicity of interpretive insights would be an instance of the
deplorable but *natural* "blindness" by which we so frequently misconstrue
one another. James did advance a striking vision; but one great fact about
him, and the most arresting thing about *it*, is that his vision (like Emerson's

"thousand-eyed present") defies every conceivable attempt to reduce it to a single point of view, including his own. It is "self-reliant" only to a point.

That is the paradox and the genius of James's pluralistic naturalism, in this an amplified and refined echo of Emersonian individualism: he had distinctively original views that he articulated with passion and clarity, but his vision also included an intrinsic impulse to transcend itself. He believed what he believed, saw what he saw from his own uniquely angled perspective, as we all must. But he knew as well that others believed and saw differently, often from motives as compelling and reasons as good as his own. He was convinced of the rightness of personal predilection in philosophy and in life, and he committed to defending the varieties of belief, action, and sensibility that it reflects and engenders.

I begin this discussion, then, by reiterating my disavowal of exclusive insight into William James, except in the sense applying to every observer by virtue of his or her "peculiar position." Instead, I propose to shed what light I can by looking for the importance of a few points of emphasis that have impressed me in my reflections on James. One of these is perceptual experience and multiplicity.

*Perceptual experience* is a notoriously open-ended term of philosophical art, or can be; and multiplicity is for James a natural fact requiring and validating such open-endedness and latitude in alternative definition. It would be foolish, he thinks, to suppose that a single definition might picture all the realities of perception any more than a single photographic portrait can capture every possible nuance of facial expression.

But provisionally let us understand perceptual experience to mean an awareness that usually involves one or more of the senses in a relation of immediacy to objects or events constituting some part of a percipient's environment. This is not exactly the same as *sensation,* but the terms bear enough similarity that it is not always important to distinguish them in a given context. Both terms normally signify a state of awareness caused, provoked, or otherwise brought to someone's attention by that person's engagement in the environing world.

This provisional definition does not exclude much, and in fact permits us to include very interior, subjective, cerebral types of experience as "perceptual." But even the most tenuously sensual experiences typically presuppose the possibility of immediate experience that is engaged in the world and not immersed in isolated consciousness, like a brain in a vat or Descartes in his study. Empiricists and radical empiricists make much of this possibility; rationalists do not.

Our provisional definition brooks no special concern about the general reliability of the bulk of ordinary human experience and understanding. It does not entertain skeptical doubts about the placement of persons in a natural setting wherein they may establish real, unmediated relations that are exactly what they are experienced *as*. Such experiences may be falsely interpreted and reported, but they cannot be falsely undergone.

The "great fact" about James may finally elude formulaic precision, and his vision may ultimately resist capture, but my starting point is the belief that much insight is to be gained from an analysis that investigates this theme. The strategy here is simply to follow James's own program of taking perceptual multiplicity to heart and exploring its conditions and implications.

I hope, with this strategy, to convey the significance of multiplicity in James's philosophy as (among other things) a crucial link to reality, a necessary condition for understanding our commerce with reality as more than personal, subjective awareness that is seriously vulnerable to skeptical doubt; a spur to action; an antidote to melancholy; a vehicle of "transcendence," possibly even a transcendent object capable in its own right of sustaining exceptional experiences or experiential patterns that stand out from dull or merely habitual routine; an objective relation between different parts or aspects of "pure experience"; a corrective for "intellectualism" or unwarranted confidence in the probity of human intellection, and a corresponding neglect of the life of the senses; and a cure for the aforementioned "blindness": the obtuse nonrecognition of, and insensitivity to, other persons' inner lives.

Blindness of this sort has no total cure, but James thought that awakening our sensitivity to perceptual multiplicity would more than palliate, and might even provoke partial remission. But it must be an inner self-awakening, beyond even the most extended or intended reach of words, which will hasten our heralded "return to life." James was always uncomfortably aware of the irony (if not the untenability) of his own vocational role as provocateur:

> vainly seeking to describe by concepts and words what I say at the same time exceeds either conceptualization or verbalization. As long as one continues *talking*, intellectualism remains in undisturbed possession of the field. The return to life can't come about by talking. . . . I must deafen you to talk, or to the importance of talk. . . . Or I must *point*, point to the mere *that* of life, and you by inner sympathy must fill out the *what* for yourselves.[2]

Perceptual multiplicity is the fact in back of James's ubiquitous talk about the "varieties" of experience, a fact we dare not neglect if we want to understand him.

"The deeper features of reality are found only in perceptual experience."[3] James points to the ephemeral, fleeting quality of immediate perceptual experience as the insuperable barrier to complete human understanding of the real. We cannot compass all experience, and it is only an "intellectualist" error to suppose that any avenue of experience can be bypassed on the way to full understanding. We can in some way hope to "extract" a conceptual translation of it, but concepts are not "deep," and discourse about experience is not experience in the primary sense (that is, it is not immediate or perceptual, though it may still be "perceptive"). Some sympathetic modern readers of James, particularly impressed by this last point, think he anticipated certain late trends imported from the European continent (especially France) and meant not only to deny that the world beyond our words sanctions those ideas and conversations that "agree" with it, but to detach language from the world.

Richard Rorty's neopragmatism seems to hold something like this view. Its least circumspect defenders typically reside in university departments of literature; philosophers who defend it usually describe their orientation as defiantly literary and historical rather than philosophical, reserving that term for the opprobrious censure of unreconstructed realists, antirelativists, and other reactionaries who do not concede the wisdom of a radically historicist and deconstructivist approach to intellectual life.

James appreciated and sometimes espoused versions of historicism and relativism—*relationalism* is a better term for his view—but was no deconstructionist. He was a marvelous writer of accessibly literary philosophy, but he was at last a philosophical intellectual and not just a kibitzing conversationalist. Like Dewey and the other "classical American philosophers," he regarded all intellectual disciplines warily but with a real conviction of purpose. He believed that philosophers have an important function in our cultural life that is more than just talking, though talk they must if they are to execute the role assigned them with any competence.

The deconstructive pragmatists follow James in thinking that what we call the world or reality is for us an abstraction from the totality of our experience. But they depart from him (and Dewey) abruptly and irrevocably when they fail to distinguish depths from shallows in that totality, and to preserve for philosophers an explicit responsibility to acknowledge and ply the distinction. Fortunately, says Edward Reed, "others have picked up the notion from James and Dewey that one can believe in real, thick experience and still be a philosopher."[4] Despite being troubled by its occasional and maddening descent into trivia, James was unashamed to admit that he "believ[ed] in philosophy myself devoutly."[5]

James's emphasis on perceptual immediacy as the touchstone of something "deep" in our experience, whether trenchant and profound or merely misguided, is one of his most characteristic and recurrent motifs. It may be possible to be a "pragmatist" while renouncing the Jamesian depths, but it surely is not possible to do so and still be a Jamesian.

But in the Jamesian spirit of inclusion, I will not here attempt to establish membership requirements for some closed "Friends of William James" society. I simply note the fact that James was painfully aware of difficulties in coming to terms with perceptual experience philosophically, some of them also Rorty's reasons for renouncing philosophy's traditional problems and purposes; but still he stuck with them. James's unremitting commitment to the presence of real depths in experience, which philosophy easily misses and discourse did not invent, is not easily skirted or dismissed by those who would represent themselves credibly as his lineal intellectual descendants.

I dislike deconstructive pragmatism (by which I mostly have in mind Rorty's creative and deliberate misreading of James and Dewey, evidently aimed at eliding their distinctive differences from the continental tradition of Heidegger, Derrida, and others). I think James would dislike it too, for failing to take seriously the subjective experience of depth beyond words. It would be mean-spirited to deny the deconstructionists their insights. Rorty's genius for "antiphilosophical" narrative and synthesis has raised the profile of American philosophy generally. But his sweeping attempts to transform the Pragmatists into irrealists of a specific sort are misleading.

The attractiveness of dispensing with the notion of perceptual depths is undeniable: what can we really say about an experience that begins to lose clarity and vividness precisely when we speak of it? How, indeed, can we be sure that our talk about experience does not fundamentally alter our recollection of it, or even that any experience is "immediate" and "perceptual" at all? In other words, do we have grounds for asserting a phenomenal distinction between deep and shallow experience?

James clearly thinks we do, with his admonition to "take reality bodily and integrally up into philosophy in exactly the perceptual shape in which it comes."[6] This is an intriguing, paradoxical challenge; for he has told us that the conceptual order of discourse is intrinsically incapable of replicating the full-blooded reality of immediate perceptual experience. The perceptual "shape" of it is lost in the translation to language. But this again raises questions about the status of philosophical activity. Does James mean that philosophy can and must "take reality up" by deliberately and explicitly refusing to make philosophical claims about reality? Or does he mean that, by directing us away from concepts, philosophy may succeed in turning us toward reality?

Something of this sort is suggested in his defense of Bergson: "In using concepts of his own to discredit the theoretic claims of concepts generally, Bergson . . . show[s] us to what quarter we must *practically turn* if we wish to gain that completer insight into reality which he denies that they can give."[7] This comes in the context of James's denial of any overt contradiction in such a procedure, inasmuch as concepts here are performing a practical (and not a purely theoretic) function.

Presumably, there *would* be a contradiction involved in using concepts to demonstrate the inferiority of concepts, but James denies the need (indeed, the possibility) of such a demonstration. The strength of his denial is bound not to impress anyone who associates "insight" with communicability; but perhaps this association belongs to the sphere of the purely theoretic understanding, not to that of what James calls "our aesthetic and practical nature."[8]

In any case, we are faced with a confusion about the nature of the activity that would urge a "practical turn" away from itself. Does it undermine the cogency of radical empiricism or merely rankle the epistemologist's demand for unambiguous evaluative criteria?[9] But one can almost hear James chuckling at the form of this confusion and waving it impatiently away. It is rooted in the philosopher's stubborn vocational refusal to lay aside his "conceptual shotgun" even for a moment and enjoy the renewal of fresh perception and a new day.

"The day is good . . . in which we have the most perceptions," for "there is something in all of us that ought not to consent to borrowing traditions and living at second hand."[10] This is a part of James's gloss on Emersonian transcendentalism, delivered in a remarkable oration in Concord, Massachusetts, on the occasion of the 1903 centenary celebration of Emerson's birth. The pregnant notion of "something in all of us," whatever else Emerson or James thought of it in detail, refers to the permanent availability of fresh perceptions and a native human ability to receive them.

Every perception is a unique opportunity, potentially, to recast one's estimation of things. Emerson's "thousand-eyed present" is a perpetual invitation to slough off our hardened and restrictive old conceptual skins and swim for awhile in the bracing medium of novelty. We do not have to assimilate every experience as though we were building a tower to heaven that might collapse in the presence of a new idea. That is the famous "*foolish consistency*" of "little minds . . . philosophers and divines," which may be the single most familiar but least understood Emersonian aphorism of all.

In this sense James is a transcendentalist: like Emerson, he touts the primacy of the present moment as an originative, creative source of revelation and a force for real innovation in shaping one's destiny. But unlike Emerson, James is no metaphysical idealist; Emersonian transcendentalism is ultimately a species of monism, which aims to account for the lucidity of perceptual experience in terms of higher powers and intuitive faculties. I think there are, in fact, Jamesian ways of understanding "higher powers"— about which James is eager for others to speculate and which he himself can embrace—but these are not Emerson's transcendently ideal ways. Emerson asserts that we "cannot be happy and strong until [we] live with nature in the present, *above time*,"[11] where James insists on observing pantemporal continuities in our experience as fundamental to the experience of transcendence. And, James takes care to distance himself from what he characterizes as Emerson's and the "transcendental cult's" belief in the "immanent divinity in things, the essentially spiritual structure of the universe."[12] But James is not quite fair to Emerson when he refers to the "worship of mere abstract laws," since Emerson attested as powerful an interest as James's in the pragmatic fruitfulness of those "abstractions" to enrich the day-to-day lives of those who profess them.

Transcendence for James is not so much about transcending time as such as about breaking down exclusive identifications with any one temporal modality. Thus James speaks of the value of hope and the transcendent experience of joy, which is both momentary and present *and* prospectively futuristic; while Emerson says that "in the hour of vision, there is nothing that can be called gratitude, nor properly joy," just a contented feeling that "all things go well."[13] For James, some things go well, but others await our best efforts at meliorism.

But Emerson, too, betrays frequent and intense interest in temporality. He applauds "the fact . . . that the soul *becomes*," and in a very Jamesian spirit he observes that "power resides in the moment of transition from a past to a new state, in the shooting of the gulf, in the darting of an aim."[14]

James's "transcendence" is an experience that heightens a person's awareness and feelings of importance, significance, or value, and which (to an external observer) seems incongruous with, and disproportionate to, the circumstances which occasion it. Curiously (if not paradoxically), the most "transcendent" experiences for James are precisely those involving the greatest degree of immersion in what is immanent and at hand in so-called ordinary experience. Emerson himself reported such a moment of transcendence in this well-known passage from his essay "Nature": "Crossing a bare common, in snow puddles, at twilight, under a clouded sky, without having in my thoughts any occurrence of special good fortune, I have enjoyed a perfect exhilaration."[15]

Citing this and other like episodes, James asks, "in what other *kind* of value can the preciousness of any hour, made precious by any standard, consist, if not in feelings of excited significance like these, engendered . . . by what the hour contains?"[16]

He is adamant and explicit in localizing transcendence in the familiar matter of everyday life. Remarking on the sensorial numbness and insensibility that befalls all of us as we become slaves to our routines, James contends that the world is chock full of "essential divinity" and "eternal meaning," if only we would allow ourselves to notice; and he is quite clear in rejecting any requirement of otherworldliness.

One man's "inanities" provide the occasion of another's transcendence, "of all the excitements, joys, and meanings that ever were, or ever shall be."[17] This is Emersonian to the core but without any hint of an underlying theoretic rationale, an "Oversoul," or anything else to confer significance on present perception except the fervor of someone's actual experience. Indeed, James declares himself quite cogently on this most "existential" of questions when he says that "the solid meaning of life is always the same eternal thing, the marriage, namely, of some unhabitual ideal, however special, with some fidelity, courage, and endurance; with some man's or woman's pains."[18] An "ideal" may or may not be eschatologically otherworldly, for someone, but if it is to play any part at all in making a human life meaningful it must enter into the daily round of living; and this, for James, involves the immediacy (not only the symbolism) of perceptual experience.

"There can be no very black melancholy for him who has his senses still and lives in the midst of Nature," declared Thoreau.[19] The echo of this sentiment is easy to catch in James, whose own struggle with depression was a primary impetus for his thought. It is significant that James's definition of free will emphasizes the capacity to direct and hold one's attention voluntarily and not submit to thoughts and feelings that would sap the will and spirit. If the stuff of transcendence constantly surrounds us, and awaits only our attentive gaze to become active, then it is not surprising that James would implore us to pay attention. The link between free will and emotional stability is familiar to students of James's life and thought, but the importance of perceptual experience in forging this link has not received the emphasis it deserves.

I have mentioned the personal form of transcendence in James, the extraordinary dimension of so-called ordinary experience that promises to transform the routine into the exceptional. This is the form of experience affording the possibility of personal happiness and joy, the "something in all of us" which, by its extreme variability and ultimate ipseity, seems indifferent or even hostile toward the conceptual harness of philosophical expression.

But might there be forms of transcendence that can validate (or even require) philosophic industry and ambition? Perhaps, if the evasion of philosophy results in severe distortions and diminishments of our personal and collective experience. That seems to be a looming threat in the current atmosphere. James's disdain for the profession of philosophy (more precisely, for the professionalization of philosophy) is well known, and he often spoke of his purpose as that of defending experience *against* philosophy. Richer, then, is the irony of James's views of perceptual experience and personal transcendence not only finding a home in philosophy but keeping philosophers professionally occupied in manning the barricades to repel the enemies of experience.

Philosophers have important work to do just now, at the present moment of multidisciplinary speculation about what our experience can possibly mean in the light of so much unassimilated, unintegrated research from various branches of science involved in "consciousness studies." And our culture, always eager to jump on the latest quick-fix, magic bullet bandwagon, is presently inundated by mood-enhancing pharmacological solutions to all our emotional problems. Philosophers agreeing with James that our experience is too important to be left in the hands of specialists, and the drug manufacturers, had better get busy.

## The Philosophy and Biology of Joy and Melancholy

> Happiness is probably a matter of temperament, and for anything I know it may be glandular. But it is not something that can be demanded from life, and if you are not happy you had better stop worrying about it and see what treasures you can pluck from your own brand of unhappiness.
>
> Robertson Davies, *Table Talk*

> We all want to be happy, and we're all going to die....You might say those are the only two unchallengeably true facts that apply to every human being on this planet.
>
> William Boyd, *Stars and Bars*

For James, happiness *is* very largely a matter of temperament; most everything is. And it is certainly "glandular," subject to the body's influence, its chemical dips and surges and its responsiveness to the world's endless parade of stimuli. That is why James detected a "worm at the core of our usual springs of delight" and why happiness can seem so problematic when we force ourselves to face these simple facts of biology squarely.

James could not disagree more, though, with the idea that our relative susceptibility to happiness is just a given, and that—happy or not—our peace depends upon accepting this with stoic dispassion. Temperament may be a given for most of us, but it is not a fixed given for James. We have every right to demand happiness of life, to press our personal needs upon the universe, and to do what we must to quell the perverse demons in our breasts who intend only our agitation and hopelessness.

But apparently we also tend, most of us, to revert to our respective happiness and misery "setpoints" no matter what disasters or serendipities life may visit upon us. We might wonder, then, whether our biologically based temperaments are more permanently intransigent and less amenable to our needs and demands than James wanted to believe.

We all want to be happy, and we are all going to die. These "unchallengeable" facts of life may both be called biological necessities, yet so much of happiness within a mortal frame comes for some only through the consolations and imaginative liberations of philosophy. Certainly that was so in James's own case. Consider, first, the uncompromising moralism and "manliness" of this statement:

> The attitude of unhappiness is not only painful, it is mean and ugly. What can be more base and unworthy than the pining, puling, mumping mood,

no matter by what outward ills it may have been engendered? What is more injurious to others? What less helpful as a way out of the difficulty? It but fastens and perpetuates the trouble that occasioned it and increases the total evil of the situation. At all costs, then, we ought to reduce the sway of that mood; we ought to scout it in ourselves and others and never show it tolerance.[20]

This does not sound like the attitude of someone temperamentally disposed by nature to tolerate or extend sympathy or compassion toward public sadness in himself or others, and it is clearly not in support of the fixed-temper theory. James arrived at his hard and heroic bootstrapping view of happiness only by passing through and besting the worst assaults of his own nature's "pining, puling, mumping" tendencies: he conquered happiness. When he says that life feels like a fight, this is no small part of his meaning.

James was an emotional man who did not avoid confrontations with the melancholy side of his nature. Not uncommonly for a thoughtful and sensitive person of his time, he recognized tendencies in himself toward what then was called "neurasthenia" (what we are more likely to diagnose as depression). An early diary entry is frequently cited to show that his attempt to reconcile this rogue element of his personality was pivotally important in the subsequent development of his thought:

> Today I about touched bottom, and perceive plainly that I must face the choice with open eyes: shall I frankly throw the moral business overboard, as one unsuited to my innate aptitudes, or shall I follow it, and it alone, making everything else merely stuff for it?[21]

The "moral business" is the possibility of self-determination through the application of will. At this time (1870; he was 28) James genuinely doubted this possibility, in the absence of a firm conviction of the will's metaphysical autonomy. James's apparent capacity to be laid low by the perceived want of appropriate philosophical arguments, to the extent that this was an actual and objective cause of his discontent, is surprising in retrospect. In later life he almost always conveyed the impression of a man whose interest in ratiocination was dictated by professional considerations but whose personal temper was gloriously untouched by any putative gap between, on the one hand, what he could not help believing and, on the other, "proof" (or conclusive philosophical reasoning).

Indeed, it is almost a tenet of James's mature thought that proof is not appropriately sought in those large questions (like that of free will and determinism, in his own case) which serve as fundamental orienting markers of life itself. He approvingly insisted that "the whole man is at work when we form our philosophical opinions,"[22] not just the self-styled dispassion of some insouciant philosophizing faculty. What is lacking is not an argument, then, but a passional decision and commitment to a belief neither proved nor refuted but whose ultimate vindication could well hang in the balance between risk and caution, action and hesitation. This anticipates "Will to Believe" (1897), but the thinking that guided James's notoriously misunderstood position in that essay can already be detected in the much earlier "crisis" texts.

The youthful James credits the French philosopher Renouvier with providing a persuasive argument for free will, but he insists that his favorable response is (in the spirit of the issue) a free act. He does not bend to the argument (as to a "coercive demonstration"); he chooses to accept it because it satisfies his "moral demand" for a hospitable (if not comfortable) universe in which the will is not superfluous:

> I see no reason why his definition of Free Will—"the sustaining of a thought *because I choose to* when I might have other thoughts"—need be the definition of an illusion. . . . My first act of free will shall be to believe in free will. . . . I will go a step further with my will, not only act with it, but believe as well; believe in my individual reality and creative power. . . . I will posit life (the real, the good) in the self governing *resistance* of the ego to the world.[23]

The "resistance" in which James lodges so much confidence as the ground of his life-affirming "posit" is not itself a posit, or hypothesis; it functions instead as a perceptual datum that the free will theory (in contrast with determinism) is supposed to render coherent. The basic experience of agency that he says is implicit in all conscious activity includes the feeling of "resistances which [the ego] overcomes or succumbs to."[24] The *feeling* of resistance is a datum, but the resolution to believe in resistance as something more than mere feeling, as evidence of our capacity to engage the world in deliberate interaction, and willfully to initiate events that depend upon our exertions, is a hypothesis.

James displays an early, instinctual anchorage in the felt experience of living, and this lighted the way out of suicidal despair. He did not feel himself in any way cut off from the world but, rather, was at a loss for an appropriate response to the feeling of pressure and the summons to personal responsibility and vital engagement it posed. The fear that he might not possess a strength commensurate with the world's undeniable push and pull was finally overmatched by a greater fear: that his hesitancy would render him entirely impotent, ineffectual, and truly cut off from active participation in life. This was the nightmare vision of an all too imaginable version of himself, thinly veiled, which he related years later in *Varieties of Religious Experience:*

Suddenly there fell upon me without any warning, just as if it came out of the darkness, a horrible fear of my own existence. Simultaneously there arose in my mind the image of an epileptic patient whom I had seen in the asylum . . . moving nothing but his black eyes and looking absolutely non-human. This image and my fear entered into a species of combination with each other. *That shape am I*, I felt, potentially. . . . It was like a revelation; and although the immediate feelings passed away, the experience has made me sympathetic with the morbid feelings of others ever since.[25]

This experience must indeed have been revelatory for James. I believe it convinced him that the human situation is fundamentally precarious, that the line between robust sanity and pitiful invalidism is thin, and that the only way to conquer these feelings of helpless vulnerability is by taking life strivingly, aggressively, with combative high spirits and alert senses, and a gambler's sense of risk.

The melancholy side of James, and his "moral" resistance to it (which is not to be sharply distinguished from his decision to "posit life in the self-governing resistance of the ego" to the world's felt demands), has much to do with the substance and tenor of his philosophy. His nightmare vision of physical invalidism became the model for a kind of philosophical invalidism which, in one form or another, was his constant polemical bête noire. "Intellectualism" and "rationalism" were not merely names for philosophical alternatives he found uncongenial, but theoretical embodiments of isolation and disconnectedness, of exile from the world.

James was the most good humored of intellectual adversaries, always prepared to brook any philosophical dispute with personal charm and friendliness. All the more striking, then, is his scathing attack on "Bertie Russell trying to excogitate what true knowledge means, in the absence of any concrete universe surrounding the knower and the known. Ass!"[26] Nothing appalled James like the casual willingness of some philosophers to dismiss or do without a concrete, surrounding universe of real events and real resistances. This is philosophizing that diminishes and eviscerates, and in so doing it repels the "entire man" who "will take nothing as an equivalent for life but the fullness of living itself." He may retain visiting rights with philosophy, but

he will never carry the philosophic yoke upon his shoulders, and when tired of the gray monotony of her problems and insipid spaciousness of her results, will always escape gleefully into the teeming and dramatic richness of the concrete world.[27]

James was not a mystic, though he was perfectly hospitable to the notion that mystical experience may be as real (and as revealing of the real) as any experience could be. He downplayed the suggestion that his hostility toward rationalistic philosophical systems may have been motivated by mystical strains in his own makeup, contending instead that "it is the ordinary sense of life that every working moment brings, that makes me contemptuous of rationalistic attempts to substitute thin logical formulas for it."[28]

The ordinary sense of life, if not mystical, is nonetheless something we experience as large, elusive, and literally unspeakable. "There is something in life, as one feels its presence, that seems to defy all the possible resources of phraseology."[29] Our words are frozen and discrete; they do not follow the subtle shadings, overlaps, continuities, and constant movements of subjective experience. Would James then dispute the attitude which contends that when we transform our inchoate thoughts and affections into words we participate in a creativity of the spirit, "a divinely-inspired art [that] grounds us in the sacred"?[30] Not at all, so long as we recall that our words do not spring into existence ex nihilo any more than we did; nor do they create the world that *was* before the words and that *is* beneath them still.

James admits that successful communication depends upon careful attention to meanings, deliberately discriminated and qualified, and that "meaningful" personal experience requires our deliberate direction and selection of what we will attend to. Discrimination and selection are verbal activities.

But there is "something else," besides. There are "living moments" whose

> meaning seems to well up from out of their very centre, in a way impossible verbally to describe. . . . Something forever exceeds, escapes from statement, withdraws from definition, must be glimpsed and felt, not told. No one knows this like your genuine professor of philosophy. For what glimmers and twinkles like a bird's wing in the sunshine it is his business to snatch and fix. And every time he fires his volley of new vocables out of his philosophic shot-gun, whatever surface-flush of success he may feel, he secretly kens at the same time the finer hollowness and irrelevancy.[31]

Here again is the marvelous imagery of wildness that fed James's soul and gnawed at what he could not help but see as the pretensions of his professional, professorial identity. In the immediate perceptual experience of life, but *not in words*, "intellect, feeling and will, all our consciousness and all our subconsciousness together melt in a kind of chemical fusion."[32] For James the gulf is insuperable between living and theorizing. Even our most penetrating attempts to haul a chunk of experience into the domain of discourse are doomed to inadequacy. "Ever not quite" conveys his sense of the ultimate futility and hubris of any philosophy that imagines that it can faithfully "snatch and fix" the essential meaning and worth of what Dewey and others would call primary experience in verbal form.[33] "Philosophy must pass from words . . . to life itself."[34]

Experience itself does not suffer the philosopher's inadequacy and is no poorer for it, since it needs no "lateral support"; its meaning is self-sustaining, self-contained, and (as experience) self-evident. Granting James this point, and granting the impertinence of philosophy when it would say what cannot be said, how are we to approach an understanding of the heightened kind of experience so secure within its own borders that it requires no further elaboration in philosophical terms?

In other words, how do we identify or even notice a kind of experience so elusively "fused" that it must evade our discursive grasp? Perhaps the best suggestion on this point, R. B. Perry's, is simply to pay attention:

> There are occasional moments when experience is most fully tasted— in the exhilaration of a fresh morning, in moments of suffering, or in times of triumphant effort, when the tang is strong, when every nuance or overtone is present. James would arrest us at such moments, and say, "There, *that* is it. Reality is like *that*."[35]

The idea of human transcendence usually is taken to mean a kind of surmounting of the normal range of experience. It is supposed to involve a detachment and removal from the everyday patterns of life, which by implicit contrast with the reported significance of transcendent experience are judged to be mundane and dispiriting. Perhaps because we are inured to some such picture of the difference between customary and exceptional states of mind, we tend to identify the exceptional states with peculiarly mystical, religious, or otherworldly forms of experience.

We do not expect to be enchanted or enthralled by the familiar furniture of our lives, and so we do not attend to our ordinary affairs with the same pitch of alert anticipation that true believers muster in their ritual devotions. We submit to self-administered doses of what James called "moral anaesthesia" and spend too many of our waking hours bored or unimpressed by the world at our feet. Ennui becomes familiar, the normal way the world is. But then, one day, unnamed dissatisfaction penetrates the threshold of consciousness. This is when some seek escape, or envy those who seem to find it, in schemes of belief and value that leave the world behind, as though knowing in advance that our so-called ordinary experience must be prosaic, tedious, and dull, or else it would not be "ordinary." Thus do we conflate different senses of the word: *ordinary* can just mean whatever tends to happen in the normal course of our days, or it can mean unexceptional, uninteresting, dull. Is it so hard to believe that every day can bring exceptional, interesting, enlivening moments? Must we surrender our experience to the narrowness of a restricted definition, an "ordinary" word?

Many of the traits we associate with transcendent experience of the supernal variety are also characteristic of what James portrays as transcendent. Such experience is exceptional: it stands out as superior to the routine or habitual, and it heightens a person's awareness and feelings of importance, significance, or value. It is an intensely interior affair, seemingly incongruous with, and disproportionate to, any visible conditions and circumstances that may occasion or accompany it.

Unlike many traditional accounts of transcendent experience, James's version regards its perceived worth as instantaneous and local ("made precious by what the hour contains") instead of promissory (based upon the promise of another plane of being, separate and wholly apart from the commonplace, to which the experience supposedly beckons). Rather than distancing its subject from the world, it brings some part of the world into sharper focus for him and infuses it with a value that formerly it did not seem to possess.

Jamesian transcendence literally embodies possibilities of excitement, joy, meaning, and happiness, which in the light of his pluralism and naturalism are the most highly personal, therefore variable, forms of human aspiration. The literal embodiment of happiness is its carnal anchorage in physiology and all the processes of the human organism impinging upon consciousness. Its variability means that what is transcendent for me may be uninteresting, distasteful, or even flatly incomprehensible to you. But because the human physiological constitution is not variable, something else *must* be if we want to understand transcendence in its particularity. Subjectivity fits the description.

There is no single object that all our respective transcendent moments must intend or imply, nor is there assumed to be one true interpretation of them. They are not necessarily to be thought of as glimpses behind a veil or special revelations of a reality concealed by phenomena—though of course that is how some interpret their exceptional experiences, and James does not presume to correct them. But James does point to an experience of transcendence that is more like a shock of recognition, a fresh perception of something that has been regarded before but without interest. Transcendence is an awakening of vitality. It announces the simple message that one is alive and surrounded by a world of presentations that may elicit an enduring fascination and foster a sense of connection with objects and events falling outside the narrow bounds of our habitual self-absorption.

Emerson's aforementioned experience of "exhilaration," unbidden, unexpected, and inexplicable on its face, prompted James to observe that the seeds of transcendence are entirely dependent for their fruition upon a host's receptivity, "on the capacity of the soul to be grasped, to have its life-currents absorbed by what is given."[36] This is the capacity to be surprised by our experience, to encounter the world with a minimum of prejudicial expectation and to allow the novelty of an event or of a moment to confer its own significance. This is what it means to be receptive to nature (as opposed to artifice, not necessarily to the supernatural): to retain an attitude and a posture of expectancy that yet does not anticipate the specific content of all possible experience. James thought such openness to the new had been substantially subverted in his own day by an overrefined parlor aestheticism:

> Life is always worth living, if one have such responsive sensibilities. But we of the highly educated classes (so called) have most of us got far, far away from Nature. We are trained to seek the choice, the rare, the exquisite exclusively, and to overlook the common. We are stuffed with abstract conceptions, and glib with verbalities and verbosities; and in the culture of these higher functions the peculiar sources of joy connected with our simpler functions often dry up, and we grow stone-blind and insensible to life's more elementary and general goods and joys.[37]

In our day, paradoxically, an age seemingly overrun by new kinds of experience, new ways of experiencing ourselves and the world, the numbing of sensibility has gone further than James could have dreamed. The parlor is not the only enemy of novelty and spontaneity in experience. The Victorians did not have cable or the Internet.

> The remedy under such conditions is to descend to a more profound and primitive level. . . . The savages and children of nature, to whom we deem ourselves so much superior, certainly are alive where we are often dead. . . .[38]

This passage indicates James's own preference for, and just possibly (let us admit) his idealization of, a rustic and "primitive" corrective for the numbness and aridity of so-called civilized life. It is impossible, when noting the almost childlike spirit of playful delight permeating his discourse, to believe that he truly covets "the happiness of both thinking of nothing and doing nothing."[39] He sings the praises of perception as such, divorced from all mentation; but the suspicion is unavoidable that James's own most characteristic form of transcendence is the singing itself. In other words, the pulse-quickening activity that most effectively fueled his own sense of transcendence may have been that of writing and talking about nature, the senses, and nonverbal experience. This is speculation, of course, but invited by James's own liberality in sanctioning a rich and varied conception of transcendence. James wants to make special claims for immediate perceptual experience as an unparalleled repository of transcendental possibility, but he does not rule out any source or deny any testimony:

> Wherever a process of life communicates an eagerness to him who lives it, there the life becomes genuinely significant. Sometimes the eagerness is more knit up with the motor activities, sometimes with the perceptions, sometimes with the imagination, sometimes with reflective thought. But wherever it is found, there is the zest, the tingle, the excitement of reality; and there *is* "importance" in the only real and positive sense in which importance ever anywhere can be.[40]

There is a marvelous moment in the film *Manhattan* (United Artists, 1979) when Woody Allen's character, Isaac Davis, wonders why life is worth living. He compiles a list including, among other "things that make it worthwhile," Willie Mays,[41] the second movement of the Jupiter symphony, and Cezanne's "incredible apples and pears."

The compilation of such a list, far from trivializing transcendence, instead presses the Jamesian point that we do not discover the importance of things without first discovering which things actually are important to *us*. Listing the things that make (my) life worth living is a way of professing the belief that it is, and so of "helping create the fact." This reverses the order of procedure that would have us conform our affinities to an objectively prescribed and conventionally esteemed canon of excellence. The arbiters of taste in music agree that the Jupiter symphony is a classic, but that is not what makes it an occasion of transcendence *for* Woody (Isaac); and if I fail to resonate to its strains, that means neither that I am deficient nor that Woody's "eagerness" is misplaced. It simply illustrates the profoundly personal quality of transcendence, which springs (James suggests in "Is Life Worth Living?") from "the deepest thing in our nature," a "dumb region of the heart," which yet is "our deepest organ of communication with the nature of things."[42]

Call that quality subjectivity. But we should resist the usual connotations of that label, those that imply an element of caprice or arbitrariness in our respective determinations of value. The incommunicable thrill I feel at an impossible game-saving shoestring catch, the rush of elation on hearing a particular piece of music (it might be Mozart, or it might be John Fogerty singing, "Put me in, Coach!" depending on the mood of the moment), the surge of sheer, undirected satisfaction in the middle of a long walk in the woods: these moments feel neither arbitrary nor voluntary, but their qualities are as stable and recognizable to me as anything can be. Yet, they *are* purely subjective in the sense that they are my moments, having about them a felt aspect that I would not know how to objectify for your perusal. They are not debased for being subjective in this sense. On the contrary, subjectivity and transcendence are mutually ennobled by the condition of their relation to personality. That makes them living realities.

If we recall James's position that "the deeper features of reality are found only in perceptual experience," it is not clear what he means to say about the metaphysical status of feelings aroused by experiences not straightforwardly perceptual. If my feelings of zest are provoked by formal logic or mathematics, and the "excitement of reality" is most pronounced in me when I am engaged in such activities, then James must either explain how they are ultimately perceptual in nature or he must deny that those feelings have metaphysical import (while admitting that they have the same degree of *personal* importance for me as your more sensually oriented feelings of transcendence have for you).

But a possible third alternative might be to deny that any feelings as such, however engendered, have metaphysical significance. We might encounter reality perceptually but be wrong to conclude that we had done so on the basis of feelings attributable to particular perceptual experiences. I believe that the third alternative would be unacceptable to James because it insinuates an artificial barrier between experience and feeling, denying immediacy.

This leaves the dilemma of either analyzing seemingly nonperceptual experiences as perceptual, after all, or distinguishing metaphysically different levels of feeling. Yet, it would be typically Jamesian to deny the destructive character of this dilemma, and in fact he likely would address any particular challenge of the sort posed here with some combination of alternatives. Perhaps a perceptual, not strictly intellectual, element functions in the capacity to enjoy logical and mathematical operations, even if the enjoyment gathers unspecifically in some unlocalized region of experienced mentation. But some feelings are simply experienced as more remote from familiar patterns of perception than others.

James would be pleased and unsurprised to learn that researchers have verified the palpable personal benefits of a happy disposition. Natalie Angier reports:

> Science has applied far more zeal to the anatomy of melancholy than to the understanding of unfettered joy. Researchers have analyzed the stress response in exquisite detail. They know that perpetual surges of adrenaline, noradrenaline and cortisol sear the body like a drizzle of acid and that chronic stress, along with its loyal comrades hostility, anger and depression, can sicken and even kill us. They suspect, however, that sensations like optimism, curiosity and rapture—the giddy, goofy desire to throw the arms wide and serenade the sweetness of spring—not only make life worth living but also make life last longer. . . . Why happiness is healthy, though, and what the body is doing when it exults in itself, science has only the most suggestive of clues.[43]

The body chemicals known as endorphins (commonly credited with producing the so-called runner's high) actually suppress the perception of pain
but apparently play no more positive role in producing pleasure and joy in
their own right.

The Jamesian implication here is that joy *is* a positive and independent
phenomenon and not merely the privation of pain. In other words, it is "its
own decidedly active state of possession, the ripe and gorgeous feeling that
we are among the blessed celebrants of life" enjoying "a delicious, as opposed to a vicious, spiral of emotions."[44] Further research will certainly
shed more light on this mystery (as, for instance, the hormone oxytocin,
"the possible mediator of feelings of satisfaction and harmony," becomes
better understood). Meanwhile, philosophers ought to find something felic-
itous to say about joy and happiness, and we all ought to allow ourselves
permission to have some. But ours apparently is now a "culture of com-
plaint" in which personal happiness is déclassé. The leader of an organiza-
tion committed to "bring[ing] happiness out of the closet" observes that we
are oversupplied with "12-step programs that support your wounds, but
there's nothing to support you if you went to Sonic this afternoon and had a
great lemonade or had a great golf shot and you want to talk about it."[45]

James supported others' small personal ecstasies, and despite his oft-
expressed contempt for the hyperanalytical tendency (acutely developed in
some philosophical tempers) which seeks for explanation where instinctive
enjoyment is the more human response, he talked felicitously about happiness and joy. Consider, for instance, the act of enjoying supper. Of course
there is great health and survival value for humans to enjoy what they eat
(even if we could plausibly imagine that a real alternative might actually involve fasting and starvation); but

> not one man in a billion, when taking his dinner, ever thinks of utility.
> He eats because the food tastes good and makes him want more. If you
> ask him why he should want to eat more of what tastes like that, in-
> stead of revering you as a philosopher he will probably laugh at you for
> a fool. . . . It takes, in short, what Berkeley calls a mind debauched by
> learning to carry the process of making the natural seem strange, so far
> as to ask for the *why* of an instinctive human act.[46]

At the risk of debauchery, then, let us continue the discussion of joy as a
human phenomenon. It may in some sense be instinctive for us, but our sophistication and our habitual ways of confronting the complexity of modern
life seem to have dulled our sensibility to simple joy.

The philosophy of joy, therefore, must aim for more than elucidation: it
must lead the charge for a recovery of innocence and immediacy, conditions
that seem to be indispensable for a meaningful human life. Seen in this light,

the consideration of joy is part of the wider project that James identifies as the philosopher's vocation, namely, to assign all "mental objects" to their proper positions, and in their many relations, relative to all the others.

This is a metaphysical project, but the most compelling motive we have for undertaking it is ethical: we need to understand how to take the inner lives of others (and, not least, of ourselves) to foster a climate of respect and tolerance for ways of pursuing happiness that are not penetrable by the disinterested onlooker's external gaze, and constantly to renew ourselves through the varieties of novelty in experience that our "ancestral blindness" would neglect.

James is fond of citing the famous passage from Emerson describing the "perfect exhilaration" that can sometimes sweep over a person whose sensibilities are attuned to novelty, not just of an outward kind but also, and for a deeply reflective temperament *especially,* when literally nothing unusual is going on in the surrounding environment. All of us have an inner life, but fewer of us actively attend to it as to a garden, and far fewer still possess that Emersonian refinement that comes to regard externalities as forming a backdrop for the truly important processes of life which transpire internally.

James wholly applauds Emersonian refinement, but he does not treat it as a higher or more evolved form of life than that of the so-called common person. The total push of his contribution to this discussion is toward a more inclusive understanding of how subjectivity transforms every process of living, for its most earnest practitioners, from barren meaninglessness to vibrant ideality. Again, this transformation occurs quite locally and outside the direct comprehension of those who do not share in it. Addressing an audience of collegians, James is at pains to discourage the notion that the only ideals genuinely worth living for are their own:

> Sodden routine is incompatible with ideality, although what is sodden routine for one person may be ideal novelty for another. This shows that there is nothing absolutely ideal: ideals are relative to the lives that entertain them. To keep out of the gutter is for us here no part of consciousness at all, yet for many of our brethren it is the most legitimately engrossing of ideals.[47]

If that is incomprehensible to us, we need to think some more about the role of subjectivity in drawing the many maps of personal happiness and idealism.

## Subjectivity and Reality

"The *fons et origo* of all reality is subjective, is ourselves."[48] James did not mean that the source and origin of reality is to be found in a supraindividual act or faculty of Kantian constitution, or that thought literally creates everything.

Yet, it is not obvious what he did mean, and we will not even come close to the "center of his vision" unless we can be fairly sure of his intent in making such a startling declaration.

The context of this statement in *Principles of Psychology*, a discussion of the familiar Kantian/Humean denial that existence is an additional property distinguishing real objects from objects of thought *simpliciter*, indicates that James is rejecting the proposal that we seek the principle of reality in conceptual analysis alone (while ignoring the genesis and relational status of our concepts). But if the phenomenon of subjectivity is to provide an answer to the question of reality, we need to know what we are asking.

In part, the question seems to wonder how we should understand the role of subjectivity in the light of objectivity, insofar as we think it useful to distinguish between ideas, beliefs, attitudes, and forms of activity that directly reflect and essentially depend upon a specific person's own situation, values, goals, and projects, and those that do not.[49] James was committed to the guiding presupposition of empirical scientific investigation, which holds that much can be gained by treating our experience as fodder for objectifying research. He believed in the existence of important facts about the world and ourselves that we should attempt to discover; and he believed that this enterprise of discovery, to the extent that it succeeds, yields objective knowledge, or genuine understanding and insight that is independent of what any particular person may happen to believe and that should be acknowledged as having the authority to compel rational assent. The celebrated "will to believe" does not apply to beliefs that are strongly sanctioned by reliable, authoritative consensus, only to those for which no consensus exists and that require us to act in an evidentiary vacuum.

*Principles of Psychology* was James's attempt to summarize the state of objective knowledge (and ignorance!) in one corner of human experience, the fledgling science of psychology, as it stood in his day. Subsequent revisions of that stage of our rudimentary understanding do not undermine the governing principle that there *are* objective facts for the discipline of psychology to unearth. Misunderstanding of James's attempts to convey the fluidity of human experience and belief (nature grows, humanity becomes, truth happens) has led some to an impression of him as a total subjectivist. No impression could be more false. Whatever it means for truth to happen to an idea, when it *does* happen it happens objectively. But because ideas are personal as well as social, it happens subjectively, too. Nothing in this is either contradictory or pernicious.

James anticipates Nelson Goodman's *Ways of Worldmaking*[50] (or Goodman echoes James) in insisting that virtually any constellation of ideas and descriptions that is even minimally coherent (and therefore separable from alternatives simply to the extent of being recognizable and discussable) contains a reliable, and perfectly objective, determination of its own truth conditions. The world of Sherlock Holmes, no less than that of Albert Einstein, is an enveloping reality. It is objectively true that Holmes lived on Baker Street and false that he was abstemious. Truths about Holmes do not depend on anyone's subjective fancy (except, of course, Conan Doyle's) because they are embedded in a network of relations—constituted in this instance by a collection of sentences in books—whose authority is backed by broad consensus based on funded experience. The experience in Holmes's world as so embedded is the product of a fictive imagination, but the experience of being compelled, moved, and motivated by fiction is as real as anything in our world. That is something to bear in mind as we grapple with the significance of *virtual* experience in a natural world.

James's commitment to applying the notions of subjectivity and objectivity where applicable, coupled with a liberal resolve to take seriously the life of the mind and a respect for the varieties of immediacy in experience, sets the problem with which James wrestles in his treatment of subjectivity and reality. He refuses to discount any "sub-world" in anyone's experience. Besides the sensible world of physical objects, the scientific world of microphenomena, and the world of abstract mathematics, he recognizes the worlds of illusion, mysticism, religion, opinion, and even madness. We ignore most of these worlds most of the time, but "the complete philosopher is he who seeks not only to assign to every given object of his thought its right place in one or another of these subworlds, but he also seeks to determine the relation of each subworld to the others in the total world that *is*.[51]

This is no idle or aesthetic exercise, but a concession that no single world comprehends all of reality. "Each world *whilst it is attended to* is real after its own fashion."[52] James's interest in the varieties of subjectivity (as manifested in our worldly multiplicity) is thus in furtherance of an objectivist agenda: to limn the boundaries of the real in its marvelous diversity. Still, reality is in fundamental, inescapable ways a subjective phenomenon. "The trail of the human serpent is everywhere," and James delights in mocking every philosophical attempt to evade this most realistic condition of life.

Thomas Nagel—whose own examination of the thorny issues that complicate our thinking about the distinction between subjectivity and objectivity touches provocatively on many central Jamesian themes—sees both attitudes as indispensable; but he allows that "the view *sub specie aeternitatis*" may be "a very poor view of human life." If so, "we should start and end in the middle of things"[53] and give up any pretense that ultimate objectivity may carry us beyond our subjective anchorage in medias res.

This threatens even a limited objectivist agenda (that of James's "complete philosopher"). Even if we jettison the quest for ultimate, unqualified objectivity, the subworld kind of objectivity may be either out of reach or else simply irrelevant. If there is a problem about how we put together our conceptions of subjectivity, objectivity, and reality, it has to do with these subworlds, their mutual relations, and whether it is possible to assign every mental object to its "right place" without distorting its significance for the human subject whose object it is. James will endorse no advance toward objectivity that compromises the personal dimensions of life, no philosophical theory "whose principle is so incommensurate with our most intimate powers as to deny them all relevancy."[54] He thinks some versions of materialism are guilty of such a diminution of human powers; his own early psychological account of emotion may seem materialistic in this objectionable respect. His later radical empiricism was in part an attempt to address that concern with its stipulation of a "stuff or material . . . of which everything is composed," which is no "material" at all in the problematic *old* sense but the momentarily pure stuff of immediate experience.[55]

"Reality means simply relation to our emotional and active life . . . whatever exalts and stimulates our interest is real."[56] James overstates his own position, not wishing to claim that we are "interested" in everything real to the same extent. But his general point is that our "perception of reality" is more than a simple and passive registering of whatever happens to fall before our attentive gaze. Rather, we perceive and acknowledge the full-bodied reality of objects selectively.

Our principle of selection is the recognition of *importance,* which compels our *interest.* Interest and importance are experienced subjectively: what interests me may be a matter of indifference to you. But a great deal of what interests me has to do with the kind of being I am; and this means that we will share many interests (as fellow humans or countrymen or co-parishioners or democrats). Interest and importance, then, are not exclusively subjective. This may be small consolation to the objectivist who wishes to keep subjectivity out of discussions of reality altogether and who thinks that in snagging it we must necessarily overcome our subjective selves—an impossible and undesirable proposal for James.

Subjectivity is the importance-conferring aspect of our being, the condition and permanent possibility of "meaningfulness" (not as a feature of language but much more broadly, as what is usually called the deep philosophical question of whether life has meaning, purpose, and significance). Human subjectivity is problematical because we also possess notions of objectivity that seem (on some accounts) to threaten the respectability of subjective life. As Nagel says, from a sufficiently detached and "objective" point of view, nothing seems to matter (have meaning, purpose, significance). Yet, most of us would find it psychologically impossible simply to abandon the objective side of our nature, even if we wanted to; and there are powerful and obvious reasons why we should not want to, given our commitment as a civilization to science and technology and our moral commitment to personal responsibility and social justice.

"Living realities" are those things to which we are drawn with what James calls a "stinging" perception of personal need. What fails to sting in the appropriate fashion is, for us, uninteresting and unimportant (and relatively deficient in the reality we are prepared to accord it). Our sense of reality thus hinges on our capacity to be excited and engaged by some "sub-world" or other.

This capacity is most acute in childhood, when virtually all is novel and vital and curiosity is aroused at every turn. The question of subjectivity is nothing less than the question of how we may lay firm hold of the childlike capacity for excitement in the presence of our environing worlds and carry it with us into our maturity, where it faces the challenge of survival in the shadow of our "adult" capacity (and yearning) for more objective, less fevered ways of ordering our experience. The child in us is delightedly astonished and intrigued by the seemingly endless procession of new experiences, new relationships, new revelations of what might be possible in the vast openness of time and space. No wonder young children are so receptive to stories. If "reading is the art of welcoming other minds into one's own, of making room for new ideas, foreign landscapes, unknown creatures, exotic dreams,"[57] of using words to transport oneself beyond them, then children are born artists. How wonderfully wise and nurturing, those "Native Americans [who] tell stories to children instead of hitting them"[58] to impart life's lessons.

As adults, we develop an ever more urgent demand for stability and predictability in our experience. What we formerly reveled in, the shock of the new, we now find unsettling. We actively resist exposure to novelty, preferring to rest on predictably familiar laurels. Ironically, however, the ordered systems of objective reality to which we refer all unassimilated experiences, so that they will cease to perturb our restful disinterest in the surfaces we meet, have the unwanted consequence of dulling our capacity for enjoyment. Enjoyment recedes as our subjective sensibilities give way to objective indifference.

But James concurs with Robert Louis Stevenson: "to miss the joy is to miss all."[59] This observation occurs in the 1899 essay "On a Certain Blindness in Human Beings," which is to me the most affecting and eloquent Jamesian statement of the crucial importance of subjectivity in making human life meaningful. It is also one of the essays that most impresses upon us James's hard-won temperamental optimism about life, an optimism that is not itself blind but that begins to find its own enlightenment in the diagnosis of a kind of congenital mental blindness for which we must all learn to compensate.

# II

# Blindness and Optimism

Each, from his peculiar angle of observation, takes in a certain sphere of fact and trouble, which each must deal with in a unique manner.... Each attitude being a syllable in human nature's total message, it takes the whole of us to spell the meaning out completely.

*The Varieties of Religious Experience*

## A Certain Blindness

The 1899 essay "On a Certain Blindness in Human Beings" contains, both by letter and implication, the core of James's devotion to the subjective life and its seminal importance in making human life meaningful. It is important for the interpreter of James not only because of its clarity and compactness of statement, but also because it dates from the time of his philosophical maturity (appearing in print nearly a decade after the publication of *Principles of Psychology*) yet is addressed to an audience (teachers) whose interest is pedagogical and broadly psychological. It is reasonable to suppose that psychological concerns were not far from his consideration when he penned this essay, at least to the extent of checking any philosophical excesses that the *Principles* might have disallowed.

That point may be a bit obscure, but I raise it in anticipation of a background objection that some of James's psychological positions do not easily square with their more overtly philosophical counterparts, especially where the latter emphasize the inward significance of personal experience, interests, and enthusiasms (the theory and the account of emotion is a prime example of this). In "On a Certain Blindness," if anywhere, we can expect to find James wearing both the philosopher's and the psychologist's hats, almost simultaneously.

James begins the essay with an observation that echoes *Principles* in linking our determinations of "the worth of things" with our feelings (as distinct from intellectual judgments). Interest and importance, recall, guide our perception of reality; and, our perception of worth being closely allied with our sense of reality, *feelings* are necessary if anything is to seize our interest: "If we were radically feelingless, and if ideas were the only things our mind could entertain, we should lose all our likes and dislikes at a stroke, and be unable to point to any one situation or experience in life more valuable or significant than any other."[1]

This is a crucial first step in the development of James's position on subjectivity: he rules out the possibility that preferences of value might in the first instance be objectively founded, for they would not exist at all to a thoroughly objectivist sensibility (whatever that might be like). Notice that he is not saying that preferences cannot be defended or ranked in an objectivist manner, in something like a rational reconstruction of value; he is saying, emphatically, that they do not first recommend themselves to our intelligence and then pass over into active expression as our actual values. This order is precisely reversed from what he thinks is the actual and necessary direction of our lives as thinking *and* feeling creatures.

A feeling, thinking organism is one whose normal commerce with the world begins from a profoundly egocentric orientation. A pure *res cogitans* would not be a particular person at all, but a particular person is inescapably caught up in a variety of relations having to do with much more than pure intellection. It may be that our normal egocentrism reinforces and rewards a tendency to be preoccupied with our own feelings, to the exclusion of the feelings of others, and that our long, unsteady ascent toward civilization and civility has been purchased only at the price of some part of our instinctive self-regard (which is not at all the same as self consciousness). If so, James thinks, it is a price well paid. The alternative is surrender to the "blindness with which we all are afflicted in regard to the feelings of creatures and people different from ourselves."[2] We are naturally inclined to take up an external vantage when we think about others, and really we have no other way of relating ourselves to them: my inwardness, unless we believe in a kind of spiritual migration usually found only in imaginative works of science fiction, is not available to you; nor is yours to me. We can of course exchange information about ourselves (our Selves), but nothing you say will ever convey a real and living sense of what it is like to be you (or vice versa). Even the most intimate of couples must confess a barrier to complete mutual understanding. We may speak of true love as the merger of disparate identities into one, and perhaps this kind of love is best defined as the willingness and desire to accomplish some such merger. But in the end this is not an option for beings like ourselves. We are limited to one consciousness, one self-apprehending Self, per person.

Still, there are alternatives. We can either allow our blindness to insulate us from our fellows and set us in opposition to them, or we can attempt to grasp the inwardness of others, not at first hand but through an extension of empathy that accords others a full measure of recognition as similar to ourselves, not in the specific quality of their inwardness but rather in the simple fact of it. If I concede your humanity, I must also concede that you have an internal life as rich and complicated, and as inaccessible to others, as my own. If "others are too much absorbed in their own vital secrets to take an interest in ours,"[3] it is, nevertheless, not too much to ask that they acknowledge our absorption as possessing the same urgency for us as theirs does for them; and in our mutual acknowledgment lies the beginning of mutual tolerance and respect.

James is by no means original in calling attention to the extraordinary difficulty of establishing and sustaining a genuine marriage of minds and to our inveterate habit of missing the inner springs of others' words and deeds; but he places a distinctively humane stamp upon these observations by finding human "blindness" not simply deplorable but also emblematic of the deepest spring of our shared humanity, our subjectivity. And for James subjectivity is to be celebrated, as the ground of purpose in our lives; and reflection on the moral implications of subjectivity leads to a principle of caution whereby we refrain from denigrating and dismissing any process of life whose subjective sources we cannot comprehend. James's account of subjectivity has profound implications not only for metaphysics and episte-mology, but for ethics and political life as well.

James illustrates his point about subjectivity with numerous examples, the most fanciful of which likens our predicament to that of a canine regard-ing his master engaged in reading. The poor pooch is constitutionally inca-pable of making sense of such an outwardly placid activity. Yet, we may credit the dog with far more tolerance (we usually call it loyalty) than humans cus-tomarily show toward the strange and unfamiliar in their own experience. Another example, closer by analogy to our own case, is that of illiterate primi-tives who misconstrue reading as a kind of medicinal eye bath. Here is an in-stance of the misapplication of intelligence in order to demystify something not understood by substituting a plausible but false interpretation of it.

One of the moral imperatives issuing from James's account of subjec-tivity is that we ought to renounce the impulse always to translate others' experience into the categories by which we understand our own. Respect for the varieties of subjectivity embraces a greater capacity for benign igno-rance than we routinely exhibit: a capacity for neither understanding nor feeling compelled to understand the inner significance of the lives of oth-ers, and for not leaping to judgments that condemn their opacity.

As James was unable at first to see more than a charred and ugly land-scape in the Carolina mountaineers' forest clearing (which "was to them a symbol redolent with moral memories . . . duty, struggle, and success"[4]), so the mountaineers were ill-equipped by the predominant patterns of their own lives to understand "my strange indoor academic ways of life at Cambridge." We might hope to narrow the chasm between such radically different systems of meaningfulness through earnest and open discussion, but in the end we must be prepared to invoke a rapprochement by which each party concedes the other's right of ultimate inscrutability. "Eagerness" is the sign and warrant of importance in life, and no rules restrict its sources:

> Wherever a process of life communicates an eagerness to him who lives it, there the life becomes genuinely significant. Sometimes the eagerness is more knit up with the motor activities, sometimes with the perceptions, sometimes with the imagination, sometimes with reflective thought. But, wherever it is found, there is the zest, the tingle, the excitement of reality; and there *is* "importance" in the only real and positive sense in which importance ever anywhere can be.[5]

James cites a charming fable recounted by Stevenson, of the monk whose instantaneous rapture at hearing a songbird in the woods consumes half a century. The practical bent of our lives makes it difficult for us to appreciate the profound moral of this myth, namely that the quest for a "bird" whose song uniquely resonates for each of us (and the exquisitely rare discovery of one) is nearly the whole point of living.

Such is the message James hears in the poetry of Wordsworth and Whitman (whose respective "birds" seem to have been immersion in, and celebration of, the subworlds of physical nature and human intercourse: Whitman "felt the human crowd as rapturously as Wordsworth felt the mountains . . . as an overpoweringly significant presence, simply to absorb one's mind in which should be business sufficient and worthy to fill the days of a serious man"[6]). James agrees with Stevenson that poets may be the most realistic realists: they do not exclude from reality the "phantasmagoric" inner worlds for which human beings actually consent to live.

It is possible, of course, to regard Wordsworth's mountains or Whitman's crowds from an external point of view that strips away the subjective, emotional elements of their discourse. But what would remain would be less real, even if more objective; and for James this would be equivalent to saying that the objective mountains and masses of men and women are less interesting (ergo, less important) to those poets whose subjective excitement bathed the mountains and persons in charged significance. In this respect we are all poets and should all wish to be better ones. But we are poets chained to our own muses, minimally sympathetic at best to those of our peers. Charles Lamb wrote to Wordsworth of being happy "without your mountains," and that his own "attachments are all local."[7] Exactly: our attachments and enthusiasms are "local"; they belong to places and environments (in both the geographical and imaginative senses) where we are at home. But our sympathies may roam, they may be tutored to cosmopolitanism.

James frequently reminds us of the role that personal temperament plays in inclining us toward this or that philosophical position, and this is especially so where the positions at stake are tied to our fundamental determinations of value and meaningfulness. Whitman presented himself as a kind of everyman, and his poetry exalted the common run of experience that lies open to all. But it is an exceptionally expansive and open temperament capable of being moved to joyous celebration by the ordinary spectacle of a saunter down the street, a ferryboat ride, or a blade of grass. Whitman's contemporary Carlyle, reputedly one of the intellectual giants of his day, was nevertheless reported to be incapable of taking in the majesty of the night sky without recoiling in disgust. Schopenhauer, so brilliant a metaphysical thinker, found only tedium in the recurrent cycles of passing time. "What is life on the largest scale, he asks, but the same dog barking, the same fly buzzing, forevermore?"[8]

James's response is from the opposite side of the temperamental divide separating the yea-sayers and celebrators from the pessimists. "Yet of the kind of fibre of which such inanities consist is the material woven of all the excitements, joys, and meanings that ever were, or ever shall be, in this world."[9] But, he points out, the capacity for joy is not equally distributed. It may not be a real, spontaneous, unassisted possibility for many. For them, assistance in various forms (including pharmacological intervention) is a godsend.

It is unfair that a natural capacity for happiness is not evenly distributed. But for probably many more than will ever admit it to themselves, the compensatory discovery of personal meaning in medias res—in the satisfaction of our simplest bodily and emotional needs, in that flip side of our practical nature not closed off to aesthetic appreciation of everyday occurrences, and in the recognition of natural, historical continuities that connect each with all—is a live option.

And so, a kind of optimism becomes optional, too.

## Optimism

An optimist is a guy who has never had much experience.

Don Marquis, *Archy and Mehitabel*

Optimism: the doctrine or belief that everything is beautiful, including what is ugly.

Ambrose Bierce, *The Devil's Dictionary*

When Voltaire's Pangloss articulated his Leibnizian conviction that "all is for the best in the best of possible worlds," he was engaged in a form of metaphysical apologetics which, James would agree, gives optimism a bad name (calling Leibniz's theodicy "superficiality incarnate" and his sense of reality "feeble").[10] If to be an optimist is to believe that we live in the best of all possible worlds already, and if (with James) we find this belief unpalatable, myopic, and dispiriting, then we may be tempted to court pessimism as the only intellectually respectable alternative. Or we might conclude that the "optimists," though attitudinally confused, are descriptively right to declare that nothing could be better. Unlike them, however, we would find this declaration cause for the most profound sadness and, perhaps, despair. It would damn our faith in the human imperative, felt and acted upon by so many, to *make* things gradually but progressively better in a world so acutely in need of improvement. "Nothing could be better," for those wedded to that imperative and to the melioristic pluralism that is its source, would mean that we can do nothing though everything is to be done. "The world . . . may be saved, *on condition that its parts shall do their best*. But shipwreck in detail, or even on the whole, is among the open possibilities."[11] Safe steering is not guaranteed; passengers, skipper, and crew are only human.

So unless we are confident in a just and beneficent Master Plan for the universe, executed by cosmic "hands" other than ours and that leaves nothing to be done *by us*—nothing, that is, not already orchestrated and planned from the start and in that sense not really *our* doing—we will be nonplussed by the optimists' proclamation of a readymade, perfect world. Besides, we want—our nature may even *require*—some constructive work to do. How strange a worldview, which denies the need (in this, of all worlds) to employ able and willing hands in ameliorating the conditions of life and growth, and in altering the "normal" course of events.

But James lived and worked among some of the most adamant and undaunted metaphysical absolutists in the history of Western philosophy, in their heyday. While he would therefore agree that their worldview was "strange," it was, a century ago, anything but odd or unfamiliar to him or anyone else to whom philosophy mattered. They were the mainstream traditionalists, not he. And James befriended most of them, even sponsoring the fledgling career of possibly his most intractable opponent, Josiah Royce, who had utter confidence in a "Plan" of rational, absolute, universal salvation.[12]

Those of us who relish the fight and fire of James's polemics are glad for the resistance that ignited his philosophical passion: concepts and philosophical fashions whose vogue is mostly long past and which can seem to exude a certain quaint mustiness that fails to match James's fire: monism, absolute or transcendental idealism, monolithic "block universe" cosmologies, and so on. Yet, we see the absolute temper and disposition still, in contemporary garb. It might even be argued that some of the neo-pragmatists and so-called postmodernists who would lay claim to James's intellectual legacy are, in some ways, representatives of the very patterns of rigidity and a priorism that James derided. However, it is not my purpose here to engage such neopragmatists in a new round of polemics. Let us permit James's views an independent hearing; we can draw comparative conclusions later. We should nevertheless be aware that nothing intrinsic to the name *pragmatism* (whether prefixed by *neo, pseudo,* or whatever) confers immunity to the scourge of dogmatism.

James was a philosopher who lived and participated in the philosophical disputes of his historical moment and who did not cavil about taking his own sharp stands. But it would be a mistake to think of James as a philosopher only in opposition, defined by what he resisted. He was *for* a great deal: affirming a constructive and ongoing role for humanity in the shaping and unfolding of reality, in absorbing disappointment and gamely continuing the "fight," as he liked to call it, and in trumpeting our successes, large and small. Above all, his keynote *celebrates* the fight and the spirit of sober-yet-cheerful work (as we may prefer to call it, with a less martial turn of mind), as we push back against the stubborn sources of our discontent.

These reflections surely underscore the Jamesian refusal, the *radical empiricist's* refusal, to allow that either the optimists or the pessimists, as conventionally and historically defined, can be right. If "the optimist proclaims that we live in the best of all possible worlds, and the pessimist fears this is true,"[13] James will insist on another way around or through the poles of this dilemma. It cannot be true that total perfection reigns in the actual world of our experiencing. We can only believe so by shutting our eyes to the obviously real ills and injustices by which humans are regularly visited—by disallowing, in short, the evidence of our experience. Those rare individuals who are personally charmed to lead lives free from affliction must know—or, minimally, must have heard or read of—others who are not; or else they are living ostrich lives and are more to be pitied than envied.

What is more, unqualified optimism that denies real suffering and deficiency in the world insults our real capacities; it disables our remedial impulses. Can our humanitarian and compassionate responses be so misguided, our felt regrets so misplaced? James certainly had no tolerance for dilettantism and the effusion of idle regret, disconnected from responsive action. But what of the active regret that fuels reform? Are the heroic deeds of good men and women, the noble benefactors of humanity (not merely the acclaimed, the Schweitzers and Mother Teresas, but the unsung and underappreciated community volunteers, the "Habitat for Humanity" workers, et al.) superfluous? Or (what comes to the same thing for anyone possessed of the kind of philosophical temperament James exemplifies) necessarily ineffectual?

It needs saying, here, that of course the Leibnizian optimist has his "theodicy" and his rational response and denies that anything—absolutely anything—is "superfluous," or gratuitous, or unnecessary. All is Rational Necessity. For Hegel "the Real is the Rational, the Rational is the Real."[14] What a startling, potentially stultifying attitude, for anyone who purports to live and act in the world of our collective experience!

Is our humane compassion entirely provoked by events foreordained and beyond our influence? Is it thereby made gratuitous except as an aesthetic phenomenon? From the God's-eye-perspective envisioned by rationalists, of course, necessity cannot be gratuitous. But this is just to notice the rationalist prejudice against an unfolding, unforeordained experience. As for an aesthetic-subjectivist rationale, that is the least persuasive theodicy of all, unless one has already accepted the sensibility of the aesthete and moral subjectivist.

We may speculate that such emotional and personal responses build our character or enhance our inner lives and make us better people than we might have been in a world not summoning such qualities. We might further aver that a world in which some of us get to be "better people" is a better *world* than one in which others of us get to suffer (and die) less. We might; the others probably would not concur. *They* might be expected to quibble with our definition or application of "better."

Crossing the divide between rationalists and empiricists has never been easy, nor should we anticipate a resolution here. But we of a decidedly empiricist bent have never grasped how everything can be anything, metaphysically speaking; how "all [can be] Rational Necessity." It seems intuitive to us that ours is a multiplex world of disparate objects hanging together loosely at best and sometimes only because we connect them conceptually (and voluntarily, not in deference to antecedent metaphysical necessity). We forge connections, or relations, where they do not already obtain in the nature of things, because doing so seems to serve purposes that we have framed. Their unity is purposive and emergent, not primordial.

The main point to emphasize here is that an empiricist, and especially a *radical* empiricist like James, is bound to find unqualified optimism objectionable on the grounds that it renders our most admirable traits and putative powers (compassionate regret for the way some things are, resolute determination to make things better a little at a time, sympathetic feeling for others' pain) apparently superfluous and ineffectual *from his or her own point of view*. Of course that is not the point of view of the rationalist, who may feel compassion, may in fact *feel* the same total range of feelings as the empiricist. But the rationalist's official, theoretical stance requires detachment of such feelings—from the formal description and the metaphysics that rationalism ascribes to the world and, most tellingly, from personal activity in the world.

This last point about the rationalist-absolutist's complicity in sundering experience, philosophy, and action one from another brings us to James's critique of what he calls "subjectivism," especially as mounted in the early essay *Dilemma of Determinism* (1884). It is important not to confuse this term with "subjectivity," which James normally lauds, in its particularity and person-specificity, as the principal source and indispensable condition of value and enjoyment in our lives (and, we have noted, the *"fons et origo* of reality").

Subjectivism for James is the view that the actuality of events is less important than what and how we think or feel about them. It places private sensibility above public conduct in the chain of being (and *doing*) and declares, or at least implies, that the real consequences of real actions matter less than the way in which we internalize and conceptualize them. "But then the moral judgments seem the main thing, and the outward facts mere perishing instruments for their production."[15] Practically, subjectivism is "either a nerveless sentimentality or a sensualism without bounds [that] fosters the fatalistic mood of mind. It makes those who are already too inert more passive still; it renders wholly reckless those whose energy is already in excess."[16] "It makes the goose-flesh the murder excites in me a sufficient reason for the perpetration of the crime. It transforms life from a tragic reality into an insincere melodramatic exhibition."[17]

In James's estimation, subjectivism trivializes and deracinates life and withdraws the bite and sting of reality in favor of more purely aesthetic interests. His repudiation of the subjectivist point of view is unvarnished, unreserved, and probably unfair; but it is also refreshing in its directness. And we who read James at the opening of the twenty-first century are likely to catch a hint, in these polemics, of how James would react to our contemporaries the "deconstructionists": he very likely would find them unacceptably subjectivist in their turn away from immediacies and living realities in deference to theory.

James would preserve optimism's good name by restoring what he considers its original and commonsensical signification, namely, the hope and belief that our exertions may make a constructive difference; but he would also temper this faith in our powers by a sober recognition of limits beyond which human powers may be unable to carry us. He wishes, as we have noted, to avert any brand of pessimism which fears that all is as it must be, and any brand of optimism which asserts that nothing could be better. "Meliorism" is one of the names James gives this sane but elusive middle position:

> [T]here are unhappy men who think the salvation of the world impossible. Theirs is the doctrine known as pessimism.
>
> Optimism in turn would be the doctrine that thinks the world's salvation inevitable.
>
> Midway between the two there stands what may be called the doctrine of meliorism, tho it has hitherto figured less as a doctrine than as an attitude in human affairs.[18]

James would be content for meliorism to remain an attitude and not become a doctrine, if only the attitude were sufficiently widespread and not so prevalently swamped by the more entrenched doctrines of optimism and pessimism. Of course, the same can be said of pragmatism. Indeed, the points of similarity between pragmatism and meliorism are so many and so prominent that we could almost interchange the terms in most contexts alluding to the attitude toward life that James most characteristically extols. Pragmatism, to invoke the old Lockean theory of value, is about our resolve to own the future by mixing our labor with it. And in the language of theology, it is about "salvation":

> Meliorism treats salvation as neither inevitable nor impossible. It treats it as a possibility, which becomes more and more of a probability the more numerous the actual conditions of salvation become. . . . Some conditions of the world's salvation are actually extant, and she can not possibly close her eyes to this fact: and should the residual conditions come, salvation would become an accomplished reality. . . . You may interpret the word "salvation" in any way you like. . . .[19]

That last is an interesting and generous—possibly overgenerous—allowance, in his fashion; but James does seem to mean something definite by "salvation." If rationalist absolutists mean by it some kind of eternal preexisting unity underlying all phenomena—a kind of guarantee of ultimate universal perfection and disallowance of history as a real unfolding of events whose outcome awaits contributions unforeseen and unforeseeable—James rejects this entirely. Instead, he points to "saving possibilities" *in*, and emergent from but certainly not guaranteed in *advance* of, the experiences of individuals. There is *potentially* a "rational unity of all things," he thinks, in their actual empirical unification; but whether such will ever be achieved and enjoyed by finite individuals is an open question, and it is James's willingness to be intrigued and motivated by the question of unity in full acknowledgment of the world's extreme past and present disunity that accounts for the forward-looking and progressive orientation of his philosophy.

Meliorism is an optimism shorn of the "necessity" so cherished by rationalist metaphysicians and an acknowledgment of the pessimists' observation that tragedy and senseless suffering are not infrequently found in the normal run of human experience. "The problem still remains," argues Henry Samuel Levinson, commenting on George Santayana, James's student, colleague, and occasional antagonist, "how to display suffering's meanness and then transcend it by celebrating 'passing joys and victories in the world.'"[20] This, in my view, is also a marvelously succinct statement of what *James*, in part, is up to.

"Doing nothing," or nothing either overtly premeditative or pointedly purposive, is importantly ingredient to some occasions of transcendence. James celebrates such transcendent moments (for instance, Emerson's exultant perambulations) and the subjectivity which is our human condition, as well as a "condition" or prerequisite of such transcendence.

"I fully believe in the legitimacy of taking moral holidays," Jame wrote, meaning those marvelous respites from care and concern and struggle, typically coincident with the aggressively pursued leisure we call "vacation" (and the English call "holiday"). A moral holiday, then, is a vacating, an emptying, a withdrawal from the daily grind and the daily hand wringing, when we tell ourselves that it is truly morally acceptable just to relax, not only our bodies but especially our consciences, with regard to the world's (and our own) panoply of worrisome and regrettable facts; to accept ourselves and the world for awhile, despite our flaws and its corruptions and depredations; and so, to renew ourselves for return to the fray.

"Moral" may seem misapplied in description of a deliberate period of neglect toward issues of the greatest moral gravity, but James denies any contradiction here. Our world is the scene of every kind of event, from joyous and ennobling to perverse and profane. In such a world, moral holidays are not merely tonic; they are probably essential to our sanity and, viewed in evolutionary terms, to our survival.

Most of us find at least a week or two out of the year for this kind of renewal, but we allow ourselves to believe that time for renewal year-round is unthinkable. Apparently, we prefer to collapse into our vacations than to take them more nearly as needed, tonically and often. In a still-timely 1873 essay James contrasted our busy-ness with the artful approach to life practiced elsewhere, inviting us to consider "the shopkeeper in Germany, who for five or six months of the year spends a good part of every Sunday in the open air, sitting with his family for hours under green trees over coffee or beer and Pumpernickel, and who breaks into *Achs* and *Wunderschons* all the week as he recalls it." His "contentment in the fine weather, and the leaves, and the air, and himself as a part of it all" is a springboard of renewal that propels him cheerfully back to work, back, as we say, to "reality." But he knows that his recreation is *at least* as real as his work (which would suffer as surely as he would without his springboard). Perhaps the shopkeeper knows something that we do not or that we have forgotten.

James may be a melioristic optimist, but an optimist he surely is. Yet, he remains wary, even of optimism that he credits with avoiding the snares of self-inflicted metaphysical necessity. Among his ideological bêtes noires in the camp of the self-proclaimed optimists are some whom he calls "healthy minded" (including the self-anointed "mind cure" practitioners and others whose vogue in the late nineteenth and early twentieth centuries in some ways anticipated the so-called New Age movement and "spiritual healers" of our own time). We shall see, however, that James's opposition to "healthy mindedness" and the "mind curists" was by no means entire or unequivocal. In fact, he typically defends the unorthodoxy of beliefs and practices that prescind from the genuinely motivated subjectivity of individuals, not because they are unorthodox—although given James's penchant for collecting eccentric characters,[21] it sometimes seems that way—but because they reflect a genuine piece of experience laid hold of and tenaciously held onto, against all merely theoretical objections. James always presents himself as the friend of experience and of those who seek to possess and honor their own experience and as the foe of abstract and exalted sacred cows—especially philosophy's sacred cows. And so we will have to be very cautious about how we characterize the nature and intent of James's opposition to "healthy-minded optimism."

> Some men and women, indeed, there are who can live on smiles and the word "yes" forever. But for others (indeed for most ), this is too tepid and relaxed a moral climate. Passive happiness is slack and insipid, and soon grows mawkish and intolerable. Some austerity and wintry negativity, some roughness, danger, stringency, and effort, some "no! No!" must be mixed in to produce the sense of an existence with character and texture and power.[22]

This is why James had such ambivalent reactions, and some revulsion, toward the Chautauqua movement of "spiritual uplift," which achieved its zenith during his lifetime. He despised its insipidity, its mediocrity, and its overall atmosphere of preening priggishness. He was put off by the walls of psychological sanctimony it erected to keep any risk or danger at bay. The author of "The Moral Equivalent of War" was not inspired by this model of life as never ending adult education in a scoured, antiseptic, and safe environment that to someone of his temperament was assuredly toxic to the spirit.

"Healthy mindedness" in essence is the belief that we ought not concede the independent and real existence of negativity in any form, lest we in some way incur the handicap of negative thinking and thereby predispose ourselves to failure. Agreeing substantially with what he calls the "ascetic" attitude toward extreme optimism,[23] James insists on our clear-eyed admission that the world sometimes disappoints, wounds, or destroys the lives it harbors. He means not simply that lives are, in fact, damaged and destroyed as a matter of course and, as it were, as a "normal" feature of human reality. This is a self-evident and even banal observation (to recall Hannah Arendt's insightful limning of the ubiquity and plain-faced commonness of evil). Nor does he intend to argue that bad things happen for reasons beyond our ken, but that they happen for no "reason" at all, in any ultimately rational sense.

It is sophistry or worse to contrive explanations for a dimension of experience none of us can fathom. What was the *reason* for the holocaust? There may be many historical or psychological explanations for why a madman in the 1930s was driven to found a political movement based on his obsessive belief in the superiority and triumphal destiny of "Aryans" and the inferiority of Jews and for why a proud and culturally sophisticated people were in thrall to his insanity. But the assemblage of such causal hypotheses will never constitute a rationale for the unredeemable human loss—of life and dignity and integrity and basic *humanity*—which those horrific events entailed. The *Why?* that spotlights ineradicable mystery is not dissolved by that kind of answer because the empathic human heart participating in fellow suffering is not assuaged by heartless, mechanical explanations. We are rightly stunned and unsettled by the sabotage and destruction of a planeload of innocent travelers, the deliberate detonation of deadly explosives in a place of public celebration, or the slaughter of children. And this says nothing about the sorrowful emptiness we feel for the victims of so-called physical evil, when the earth opens and swallows whole communities, or about the other natural events sundering human life.

We tend to think of examples from our own time when we compile such litanies of misery, and while our century has exceeded imagination in both degree and extent of tragedy and pain, it also bears reminding ourselves that we did not invent suffering. James similarly felt the helplessness of rage without a suitable object in his own age, which we tend to over-romanticize as innocent. It is that universal sense of helplessness, and the urgent need to find some way of resisting and turning back the forces of destruction, or at least of identifying them, that leads us to an attribution of evil as malevolent deed rather than as random misfortune. This is undoubtedly a species of mythic superstition and primitive supernaturalism. Malevolent deeds were, of course, tragically in evidence in the century we shared with James, their actions anything but random. But it is likely that the greater part of human misfortune, day by day, has no metaphysically special or supernatural referent that we can name. Human acts of cruelty are, sadly, of our nature. And life-destroying catastrophes flow from physical (geologic, meteorologic, seismic) nature.

But whatever face we place on experiences and events that are deeply and mortifyingly injurious to our hopes and our flourishing, there seems to be a fundamental human need to strive in our own behalf against the collective "forces of darkness" (to borrow yet another coinage of the mythic imagination)—hence, the indispensable usefulness of the concept of evil. "I cannot bring myself, as so many seem able to do, to blink the evil out of sight, and gloss it over," James wrote to his brother as a young man in 1870. "It's as real as the good, and if it is denied, good must be denied too. It must be hated and resisted while there's breath in our bodies."[24] And sixteen years later: "There is no full consolation. Evil is evil and pain is pain."[25] Here as with so many aspects of the Jamesian soul and psyche, James's student, colleague, and biographer R. B. Perry nicely conveys a sense of the man:

> He was too sensitive to ignore evil, too moral to tolerate it, and too ardent to accept it as inevitable. Optimism was as impossible for him as pessimism. No philosophy could possibly suit him that did not candidly recognize the dubious fortunes of mankind, and encourage him as a moral individual to buckle on his armor and go forth to battle.[26]

And yet, as we have seen, he believed wholeheartedly in "moral holidays." Holidays are celebratory times, and James never forgets the celebratory elements of experience, most especially the moments of "transcendence." They are the saving elements that "make life worth living." Ordinary experience is positively studded with opportunities for such moments, if we will but train our attention to notice. Transcendence for James is our entree into, not an escape from, the deepest realities of corporeal existence and "mundane" experience. It is not the ascension to a peak far removed from ordinary life, but attentive immersion in fields of experience and worlds of meaning we typically swim through in forgetful oblivion.

The idea of evil strikes many as an embarrassingly outmoded concept, retaining the musty reek of previous generations' crippling repressions, obsessions, and superstitions. Yet, we cannot shake it because it conveys, as no other idea can, an ineradicable part of our experience. If we are no longer comfortable to designate evil a substantive, a noun, we are yet hard put to deny that it persists in adjectival form as a plain fact of life.[27]

Every day brings news of more evil acts, assaults, debasements. Our task is not to ignore such news, although Thoreau was surely right when he said that once we have gained acquaintance with a "principle" we begin to dull our humane sensitivity by paying detailed attention to repeated instances of it. Rather, our challenge is to devise intelligent, civilized responses to the daily round of disaster that balances our natural sympathies with our limited individual powers and connects us to the ongoing human project of amelioration, which also allows us our moral "holidays." No small challenge!

Perhaps it is really circumstance, accident, chance, or brute fact that we mean to curse, or should, when we attribute malevolent agency to "the world" and shake our fists at "evil," or when we decry misfortune that we cannot pin directly and unambiguously upon someone, or when no amount of causal explanation even begins to alleviate the sense of utter devastation and absurdity and pointlessness and cosmic wrong that washes over us in the wake of some humanly executed cruelty. This must be why some of us who entertain no serious thought of Satanic supernaturalism are nonetheless unwilling to put aside the concept of evil. And besides all else, it is deeply unsatisfying, psychologically, to condemn such events with anything less than the harshest language in our verbal arsenal.

Indeed, it is difficult not to see declarations of unqualified optimism (as in the Panglossian "all is for the best")—even when they are grounded in some supposed prudential principle such as the healthy-minded conviction that "negative thinking" invites failure, while more affirmative attitudes and feelings summon success—as evidence of a deficient feeling for reality. This judgment needs to be qualified, however, before we attribute it to James; for he seems unwilling to condemn those whose worldly ignorance secures their personal bliss. Such persons do exist, and good for them (so long as they are not philosophers!). But most of us cannot, and should not, ignore most harsh realities. The deliberate cultivation of some forms of healthy-mindedness appears a vain attempt to do precisely this:

> The method of averting one's attention from evil, and living simply in the light of good is splendid as long as it will work. It will work with many persons; it will work far more generally than most of us are ready to suppose; and within the sphere of its successful operation there is nothing to be said against it as a religious solution. But it breaks down impotently as soon as melancholy comes; and even though one be quite free from melancholy one's self, there is no doubt that healthy-mindedness is inadequate as a philosophical doctrine, because the evil facts which it refuses positively to account for are a genuine portion of reality; and they may after all be the best key to life's significance, and possibly the only openers of our eyes to the deepest levels of truth.[28]

Notice that James does not repudiate what we may call aversion as a religious attitude *for those whom it well serves;* he simply denies that it serves philosophers and others whose professional vocation is not merely to feel personally at home in the world but to tell the truth about it as well. This distinction will surprise those who expect James to disavow any interest in truth apart from personal satisfactions; but it is perfectly consistent for him to characterize the adequacy of a belief in terms of the purposes and interests that it subserves, and to observe that many religious beliefs have nothing to do with any abstract conception of "the truth" as an intellectual proposition. Philosophical beliefs about religion, however, are required to be truthful in a way that personal religious attitudes are not: they must take account not only of one's own experience but of as much personal experience as there is, has been, or will be. It is an enterprise of almost unspeakable chutzpah to think it possible even in principle to compass all of experience in any fashion. At best, it functions as a "limit concept" or a regulatory ideal fated never to be realized concretely, but for the radical empiricist this imposed requirement of experiential inclusiveness is the difference between dogmatism and open inquiry.

By distinguishing the (real) truth about evil and religion from "healthy-minded" beliefs about them, we may seem to be departing from a suitably Jamesian circumspection about the limits of truth, as distinguished from strongly motivated personal belief. T. L. S. Sprigge evidently thinks so when he says that if we distinguish the internal goal of thought, namely, *truth*, from external goals like emotional value and satisfaction, then it seems that James blurs this distinction or defies it by urging the abandonment of the internal goal altogether.[29] A Jamesian must reply that this internal/external distinction is arbitrary and practically irrelevant. If emotional satisfaction is not integral to the goals of those whose search for truth—in pragmatic terms itself indistinguishable from satisfaction—creates the importance of goal seeking in the first place, we have lost the thread of our own identity.

"My own view," Sprigge says, "is almost the opposite of James's. For it seems to me that it is quite satisfactory to go for beliefs which work well in practice for the purposes of daily life, without much bothering about their real truth, but much less desirable to do so in matters of great religious and moral moment."[30] He adds, "'True' is the main success word applicable to thought," and thought, or thinking (viewed in Darwinian terms, as James views it), is essentially a survival mechanism. Apparently, then, James *ought to* praise true thought (defined in conventional correspondence terms, for its survival value), but he does not, instead denigrating it as a vapid conception of truth. If this is what Sprigge means, he has missed the boat in two big respects: for one thing, James does praise true thought. But, for another, he praises thinking that has demonstrated its own survival value and earned a presumptive claim to some part of truth; and always, he reserves the right to revise the appraisal in the light of further experience.

If we view thinking as playing an essential evolutionary role in our development and progress as a species and as individuals as well, and also regard the metastasized concept of "thought" as something of a philosophical fifth wheel—as James does—then it seems much more natural to follow James in loosening the old definitional constraint that shrinks truth to correspondence with preexisting states of affairs (that is, those that preexist judgments and ascriptions of truth). Thought is good; thinking is successful when it conduces to our flourishing, enhances our growth, and so aids and abets our survival. We pay our debt to such thinking by calling it true, for its role in procuring the fulfillments and satisfactions we so appreciate. James's is an importantly different emphasis and a sharp departure from the old static view of truth: it says, in effect, that truths correspond to realities, to be sure, but no less than realities correspond to truths. This may sound maddeningly paradoxical if not trite, but it serves to remind us that when we formulate beliefs and ascribe truths *from out of our experience* and with an eye to future satisfactions, *we* alter the "fit" between the world (conceived statically) and our dynamic contributions to its evolution. When our formulas (beliefs, sentences, propositions, or whatever media express the principles and expectations we are prepared to *act on*) "work," the world must be reconceived so as to reflect this additional fact *about* the world. And our contribution is another fact about the world as well.

James's main point about truth, I think, can be seen as a rejection of a certain coupling of propositions. He thinks it very peculiar, unacceptably so, to hold both that (1) X has contributed materially to our, or to someone's, survival, growth, or flourishing, at least more so than any yet-imagined alternative to X; *and* (2) X is false. I know, and James knows, that some people find this coupling perfectly natural and intuitively sound. Suffice here to say that he does not. He may be mistaken in this but not obviously or absurdly mistaken, as alleged by some who insist on a more "realistic" understanding of truth-as-correspondence. These are two very different intuitions of what truth is, and what it is *for*. Is it primarily an instrument of future evolution and present "satisfaction" as ingredient thereto? Or is truth simply a transcription of the way things are (a phrase meant somehow to anticipate and include the unforeseen issue of evolutionary history, or meant as eternal Truths that are temporarily—or should we say *temporally*—unavailable to our finite consciousness)?

It is crucial to remember that James means to ascribe truth adjectivally, not to beliefs and sentences in the abstract but to actual thinking and real life. Some may say they equate living with copying or transcribing an august and impersonal reality, but not many live as though they really believe it. Correspondence theorists must negotiate life a day at a time, too, not once for all time. This is not simply a flip remark, for James or for pragmatic empiricists generally, but an observation recognizing the vitality and real movement of our world, so far as our experience reveals. If our philosophizing is to reflect this observation, and this recognition, then it must not rest in a static account of things, or of how we may *know* them.

In the final analysis, we need to recall that James's central question, first and last, was never How do we demonstrate that we possess justified true beliefs? Instead, he was drawn to personal and existential concerns, and philosophized about truth in order to address *them*: What shall I do? On what grounds can I believe what is not scientifically proved, or disproved? How shall I go about constructing my character and my self, so that I shall be up to the daily challenges of living? What is the significance of my own experience and that of others? How can I make my beliefs, actions, and hopes consistent and complementary? And so on.

If James's theory of truth is not fully satisfactory as a theory of truth generated from, and supportive of, rigid assumptions about what is internal to Truth itself, that is because it is not meant to be. It is intended to be much more: a clarification of what beliefs are, an appeal for openness and tolerance,[31] and a call for relevance in our philosophizing about truth, belief, and action (and an insistence that these three issues are also *one*). This attempt has been successful and will have been so even when the last journal article has been printed in refutation of the Pragmatic Theory of Truth.

By now it must be very clear that James is a philosopher of subjectivity: he sees his main task as that of exploring its implications for the quality of human, and humane, life. And he believes that living a good life means taking everyone's experience seriously. Here a contrast may be instructive. F. C. S. Schiller, a contemporary and ally of James's in the philosophical wars of their day, was also a philosopher of subjectivity; but in important ways Schiller was more "subjective," less a realist about nature and our experience in and of it, indeed, *as* its progeny. He may be more deserving of the lineal recognition that Richard Rorty sometimes hastily confers upon James.

Schiller called himself a "personal idealist," in deliberate contrast to absolute or transcendental idealists like Green and Bradley. James, on the other hand, bristled at the charge that his radical empiricism was in any important metaphysical sense "idealistic." Like James, Schiller defended and celebrated subjectivity; but it is highly misleading to lump him and James with Rorty, indiscriminately, as antirealists.

Of course, James held that human volition, with purposive intelligence its most useful tool, contributes mightily to the perpetual determination of a reality that is metaphysically underdetermined from the start: there are always more *real* possibilities at any moment than the actual facts (minus the undetermined and unexecuted choices of individuals) can account for. Schiller and Rorty, and the "objective" pragmatists, agree on this. But James is distinctive in his conjoint emphasis on intractabilities as no less real than the world's plasticity. It sounds paradoxical, but James is a realist in part because he is so attuned to the different ways in which personal views and enthusiasms shape very "subjective" descriptions of the world, which are useful, accurate, and—in pragmatic terms—*true*. Here he distinguishes his own brand of realism from what he saw as Santayana's peculiar irrealism:

> I am a natural realist. The world per se may be likened to a cast of beans on a table. By themselves they spell nothing. An onlooker may group them as he likes. He may simply count them all and map them. He may select groups and name these capriciously, or name them to suit certain extrinsic purposes of his. Whatever he does, so long as he

takes account of them, his account is neither false nor irrelevant. If neither, why not call it true? It fits the beans-minus-him, and expresses the total fact, of beans-plus-him. Truth in this total sense is partially ambiguous, then. If he simply counts or maps, he obeys a subjective interest as much as if he traces figures. Let that stand for pure "intellectual" treatment of the beans, while grouping them variously stands for non-intellectual interests. All that Schiller and I contend for is that there is no "truth" without some interest, and that non-intellectual interests play a part as well as intellectual ones. Whereupon we are accused of denying the beans, or denying being in anyway constrained by them! It's too silly![32]

James here enlists Schiller in the cause of pragmatic "natural realism." But charity toward an ally in the philosophical wars seems to have unhinged his judgment in this instance. Schiller was no natural realist.

Peirce claimed that Schiller occupied a position in philosophy intermediate between himself and James, but the more accurate mapping places James between Schiller and Peirce. Realism, expressed as a general attitude toward life, is something like believing that what there is does not depend on what anyone thinks there is. The pragmatic difference between making and creating reality, or between making and discovering it, impresses James and Peirce in a way that it does not impress Schiller. In addition, there is an important motivational difference between Jamesian realism and more orthodox varieties: many realists want philosophy to exalt an ordered world, and this they hope to find in a world independent of mind. But James believes that the real world is various and disordered, not because our minds are such—though they surely are—but because that experience he is sworn to take seriously reveals variety beyond ordering by any one perspective or system and because he affirms the general reliability and even purity of immediate experience.

# III

## Pure Experience

What is the aboriginal Self, on which a universal reliance may be grounded?
What is the nature and power of that science-baffling star ... which shoots a
ray of beauty even into trivial and impure actions, if the least mark of independence appear?

Emerson, *Self-Reliance*

### The Purity of Pure Experience

Here, again, is where we have been, where we are, and where we are going.
James celebrates personality and subjectivity as preeminent life phenomena
to be taken seriously—not distorted, diminished, or denied by intellectualist faithlessness to experience. Yet, subjectivity is limiting, a source of error
and blindness in our relations to the world and especially to other persons.
It might seem that a too-intimate relation of attachment to one's own subjectivity, voluntary or not, might preclude the possibility of transcendence.

James also proposes, with his radical empiricism, that we acknowledge
in our philosophizing a category of experience neither subjective nor objective but "pure" of such conceptual exclusions and discriminations. What is
the element of purity in immediate experience? Is it, for James, a fount of
transcendence? Maybe "pure experience" is impersonal in a way that fulfills
the apparent prerequisite of impersonality in transcendence: unconcerned
with the pretranscendent and limited self and not bound up in one's personal subjectivity.

The suggestion sounds plausible enough, but I think it is wrong. My
thesis, to the contrary, is that James is an advocate for a type of *personal*
transcendence owing at least as much to subjectivity as to pure experience.
In the two preceding chapters I tried to lay the groundwork in establishing
the importance and ubiquity of the concept of subjectivity in James's philosophy *because of its preeminence in experience*. In this chapter I will consider and reject the suggestion that pure experience is impersonal in a way
that makes it strongly relevant to Jamesian transcendence, setting the stage
in the last two chapters for the reassertion of the primacy of subjectivity

and personality in Jamesian transcendence, and some tentative explorations of why this matters.

James, like Emerson, was a rugged individualist who regarded institutions and authorities of all kinds as derivative, compared to the men and women whose spontaneous activities are the real creative force at work in the world. Despite sharp differences, noted in the previous chapter, the two agree that independence and originality of perception is a natural human entitlement that beatifies all it touches.

That is why the "aboriginal" reality for James is not a Self at all, strictly speaking, but concrete immediacy as the anterior possibility of personality and selfhood. It is not an Emersonian oversoul, an Absolute Ego, or God, though he hopes its effects may be universally salutary for all who learn to rely upon it. It is aboriginal for language and thought, as well as action; so words may fail to corral it. We possess it as an *attitude,* a receptivity to freshness and novelty in our experience. It "baffles" science because it is subjectively interior and not perfectly general, an attitude felt but not seen except through its fruits. It is, as Emerson says, "spontaneity."

We noted in the introduction that some Far Eastern adaptations of James go much farther east than he ever did, when they allow personal selfhood to melt into a cosmic unity that does not distinguish me from you from the universe. James's position on what was called the problem of the one and the many was pragmatic to the core: how we choose to characterize the relations between things, and between things and ourselves, depends on our purposes and the contexts in which we are discussing them. But in the end, and with apologies to Robert Pirsig, among others, James is too much the Emersonian individual and pluralist to sympathize deeply with a view whose last word on the subject is that all is one.[1]

That is why I said in the introduction that it is not enough, for James, to be "present" in some Zen-like fashion of transparent and selfless purity at our most compellingly significant experiences; we must bring ourselves, our persons, our peculiarities and idiosyncrasies, our histories, and our anticipated futures—in a word, our subjectivity—*with* us to our most transcendently stirring moments. Only thus, for James, may our lives accumulate concrete significance in their particularity. The purity of pure experience is not that of renunciation in the eastern sense, of personal desires and attachments. James was quite at home with the idea that we *are* the particular bundles of wants, preferences, valuations, and (especially) experiences, and actions that uniquely individuate each of us. As they change and grow, or stagnate, so do we. The people, places, and things to which we sustain voluntary attachments are the most important constituents of our respective identities. To renounce them, or detach from them, would be to die.

What then, we will wonder, is so pure about pure experience? The answer, in a word, is *immediacy.* It retains the combined senses of presence, concentrated attentiveness, and (to whatever extent is humanly possible) presuppositionlessness, an indispensable element of experiences that are unbiased and open to novelty. Pure experience is *momentarily* forgetful of past and future, and so in that sense transcendent of time. But past and future in the particularity of our attachment to them, through the particular window of appreciation we all bring to our own experience of the world, are conditions of continuity: we bring that attachment with us (or it brings us) to the bar of experience; we have our marvelously forgetful, briefly untethered moments of vision, insight, and delight, and then we fumble again for the reassuring tug of the rope of memory and anticipation that carries us forward into a future that may be transformed by the afterglow of what went before. True enough, for James "you can reach a state of consciousness called 'clear consciousness' in which the mind is perfectly lucid, without being caught up in discursive thoughts."[2] We can reach such a state, but James does not advise futile efforts to stay there. Life presses forward.

Unlike the rose under Emerson's window, whose aura of timelessness and perfection depends upon its own utter lack of self-regarding consciousness combined with our aesthetic and anthropomorphizing, projective regard for its form, we must strive to win and retain our limited perfections. We are not "perfect in every moment of [our] existence." But then neither, really, is the rose: ask a gardener.

According to Eugene Taylor and Robert Woznick, editors of a useful volume on the reception given James's earliest public presentation of his idea of "pure experience,"[3] James's view "that knowing is an affair of relations within our own experience was solipsistic in its implication that certain knowledge of existence beyond the self is impossible." But this is a misreading, based first of all on a failure to grasp the historical meaning of pragmatism and American philosophy more generally. James does not entertain genuinely skeptical doubts about the possibility of knowledge. Nor do the editors appreciate the extent to which James denies that self-knowledge is basic and prior to all other understanding, all other significant experiencing. James calls the self "incidental" to pure experience. Following the editors' line of thinking applied to this statement, we would conclude that even knowledge of the self, let alone knowledge beyond the self, is dubious for James.

But knowledge in the pragmatic sense is not strictly a matter of *observing* the relations we have encountered within our own experience to date; it also involves the ways in which we act upon those relations *and* relations intended but not yet observed. And in any case, the "relations within our own experience" include relations to other persons and minds, to social facts and purposes beyond oneself, and to the future. In short, "knowing" in the Jamesian sense cannot possibly collapse into solipsism.

The idea of solipsism is parasitic on a range of philosophical and metaphysical assumptions that James is eager to suppress, those that give us the

categories of subject and object (among many others) and propel our confusion about what it means to know, how we know, and so on. James's philosophy of pure experience is an attempt to show how we can suppress
those troublesome assumptions and remain true to our multiple, endlessly
various experiences of subjectivity.

But James's idea that we can give up the interdependent concepts of
subjectivity and objectivity in philosophy has misled many to think he was
in some way repudiating the phenomenon of subjectivity in life. Not so.
James always means to take personal experience, and therefore subjectivity,
seriously. Even in the midst of experiential immediacy, there is a person
whose experience of immediacy it is, whose previous experience of life has
created the receptivity to whatever immediacies and delights that person is
capable of receiving, whose experience of the future may be subtly or profoundly altered by present immediacies.

## Pure Experience and Transcendence

Pure experience is James's name for immediacy that has not yet been dis-
tilled into categories or placed in a system of theoretical relations, but simply has been *had* by someone. Transcendence may assume the form of
delighted absorption in what is "given" in experience, whether taken amidst
ordinary, familiar patterns of living or in the exceptional states of awareness
associated with mysticism, and whether it stresses the continuities or the
"breaks" in life. It may seem natural to suppose, then, that transcendence is
just pure experience in which an immediate perception of value is the
salient feature.

James's position concerning "value" is mostly implicit and must be
drawn out; but there is no question about his commitment to the full reality of value as a primal human phenomenon that pervades and flavors our
experience. The very term *experience* is itself sometimes used by James as
an index of value, when contrasted with untested theory or alleged rational
necessity as an a priori condition of experience. Simply stated, James is predisposed to exalt experience as such.

He may be said to beg the question against rationalism, since he does
not have an argument for his "postulate" that "things of an unexperienceable nature . . . form no part of the material for philosophic debate."[4] But
this is a saw that will cut both ways; rather than reverse the charge by accusing rationalists of failing to grapple with radical empiricism's starting
point, let us honestly acknowledge the temperamental schism at the heart
of all philosophizing. Rationalists are temperamentally and constitutionally
incapable of conceding James's postulate, no less than radical empiricists
are incapable of giving it up. The fundamental value of experience per se is,
in this sense, nonnegotiable and incommensurable. Beyond the elementary,

axiomatic dispute between rationalists and empiricists over the intrinsic value of experience, the determination of value differs between empiricists of various stripes. Some would refer all questions of value to a fixed standard of utility, a consensus of thoughtful opinion, or some other desideratum that is externally and retrospectively related to any particular experience. Others would declare value an amorphous, unassayable product of social custom or individual idiosyncrasy. But to be radically empiricist is at least to entertain the possibility that value is embedded in, not projected upon, experience.

James not only entertains this possibility; he affirms it and recurs to his own experience for confirmation (as he invites others to the bar of their own respective biographies). In other words, he rejects any account of value that reduces it to mere emotive or subjective expression as inadequate to the felt experience of life at first hand, where value is first met. Pure experience is metaphysically prior to the instrumental categories of objectivity and subjectivity; and value itself is sometimes "pure," immediate, restricted to a moment, and momentarily regarded without thought of extensive relation. The ascription of value that comes later, when time has passed and consequences have been registered, is not so pure. We ascribe value when we attempt to place an object or an activity in hierarchical relations with other objects or activities; placing is a matter of categorizing, and categorizing is a form of mediation.

Moreover, the ascription of value can seem more problematic than other kinds of categorization; it seems by its nature more variable than other features of experience, more directly tied to the peculiarities that distinguish you from me than (say) our respective visual experiences. We may be tempted, then, to think that our visual experiences are more real than our experiences of value, or indeed to deny that there are any *experiences* of value at all, as something apart from our ascriptions of value. From here it is a small step to the complete relativizing of value: we conclude that value is subjective, that is, dependent upon the quirky, nonrational or irrational ascriptions of value ("value judgments") for which human beings are so notorious. But pure experience subverts this reduction by admitting that value is relative to experience but also by denying that the immediate experience of value is subjective. The whole subject-object division comes later; strictly speaking, there are no "subjects" in the radical empiricist equation.

James's most straightforward statement of his position on value is made in the context of a discussion of what he calls "the hybrid or ambiguous group of our affectional experiences, of our emotions and appreciative perceptions."[5] They are hybrid in the sense that they sometimes seem to belong to both our inner feelings and external realities, and they are ambiguous to the degree that we cannot (and need not) be any more specific than this about their proper referents. Such appreciations "form an ambiguous sphere of being, belonging with emotion on the one hand, and having objective 'value' on the other, yet seeming not quite inner nor quite outer."[6] Does the fireplace emit a pleasurable warmth, or do I derive my pleasurable warm feeling from the heat of the fire (a heat which, thus shorn of adjectival qualifiers, is valueless)? Is the sunrise magnificent, the wind violent, the song sad? Or, do such attributions anthropomorphically misplace the locus of value outside of pure subjectivity? If we are content to be narrowly pragmatic but not metaphysical, we will answer that it makes no practical difference how we answer these questions: the important thing is that we know how to warm ourselves at hearth side, that we remember to button our overcoats in a gale, that we are free to appreciate the experience of sunrise, that we enjoy (or despise) the song, and most importantly, that we not inflict our respective determinations of value upon those who do not share them. If you would rather sleep until noon, I must not insist on dragging you into the dawn.

A radical empiricist is not content with this response, although his respect for the variability of experience combines with his value-to-experience relativizing to produce the same admonition that we not be imperious in trumpeting our own predilections. The difference is that he understands this admonition as something more than social courtesy, more even than a requirement of civilized life. Tolerance of others, for a radical empiricist, is the generalized recognition of real value as an immediate perception of experience. True enough, practical life generally does not impel us to be decisive in resolving the ambiguity of our value statements; but from this it cannot be concluded that the underlying value that they express is of a different metaphysical order than is commonly supposed to attend our less ambiguous utterances. James wishes to credit ambiguity with as much reality as our actual experience of it may happen to convey, and it is for this reason that he rejects the narrowly pragmatic treatment of emotions and "appreciative perceptions":

> [pure experience is] a primitive stage of perception in which discriminations afterwards needful have not yet been made. A piece of experience of a determinate sort is there, but there at first as a "pure" fact. . . . Something like this is true of every experience, however complex, at the moment of its actual presence. . . . With the affectional experiences . . . the relatively "pure" condition lasts. In practical life no urgent need has yet arisen for deciding whether to treat them as rigorously mental or as rigorously physical facts. So they remain equivocal. . . .[7]

"Equivocal," but hardly dispensable. Value literally quickens the pulse and arrests the attention. It enters into the web of physical events and announces itself most palpably where we are least able or inclined to feign indifference, within the ambit of our own corporeality:

It is those very appreciative attributes of things, their dangerousness, beauty, rarity, utility, etc., that primarily appeal to our attention. In our commerce with nature these attributes are what give emphasis to objects; and for an object to be emphatic, whatever spiritual fact it may mean, means also that it produces immediate bodily effects upon us, alterations of tone and tension, of heart-beat and breathing, of vascular and visceral action.[8]

The same eruption of value infusing the world with interest, James says, also delivers this insistent, localized bid for our acknowledgment. "The 'interesting' aspects of things are thus not wholly inert physically. . . . [This] is enough to save them from being classed as absolutely non-objective."[9]

Indeed, the palpability and dynamism of our acute interest is more than enough, really, since interest directs not just our awareness of things but also our future relations with them. Value, whether in the form of "appreciation" or passionate aversion, becomes objectified through our acts and thoughts. In other words, my "inner feeling" of exultation at the spectacle of sunrise might appropriately be called *merely* subjective if I never felt the impulse to repeat it or in any other way to bear witness to it, if it never came again to mind. But to the degree of my exultation, *sunrise* acquires a concrete status for me as one of the realities constituting my world. My thought of sunrise comprehends both physical (mainly visual) and affectional aspects univocally; and it requires a special exertion of abstract analysis for me to possess the thought as an elemental compound rather than as the unitary presentation that I naturally take it to be. This is why James thinks that value governs our thought processes:

> It is by the interest and importance that experiences have for us, by the emotions they excite, and the purposes they subserve, by their affective values, in short, that their consecution in our several conscious streams, as "thoughts" of ours, is mainly ruled. Desire introduces them; interest holds them; fitness fixes their order and connection.[10]

James punningly concludes that value is indigenous (but not restricted) to our "streams" of thought: "the ambiguous or amphibious status which we find our epithets of value occupying is the most natural thing in the world."[11] That we can become aware of a world (that is, a relatively stable and coherent medium in which experience may be refined and personalized) at all is only because value is equally at home on the dry land of external reference and in the fluid channels of internal feeling:

> If one were to make an evolutionary construction of how a lot of originally chaotic pure experiences became gradually differentiated into an

orderly inner and outer world . . . [t]his would be the "evolution" of the psychical from the bosom of the physical, in which the esthetic, moral and otherwise emotional experiences would represent a halfway stage.[12]

On the one hand, James means not that value is a stage that must be passed through and left behind, on the way to what we misleadingly hypostatize as "consciousness," but rather that the constantly shifting awareness discriminating between self and "thing" is literally unthinkable in the absence of value. Its presence, on the other hand, is the spotlight by which we make our way across the landscape of our perceptions. Most of the time we are not aware of it in any explicit way, but it assuredly is there; and when we *are* aware of it, the exceptional type of experience I have been calling "transcendence" becomes a possibility.

What kind of awareness of value is it that must accompany transcendence, if transcendence is a form of immediacy? How explicit might it be? Is it a form of "understanding" in any cognitive sense of the word? The temptation is to say no, but then we come across passages like this:

Ought we to listen forever to verbal pictures of what we have already in concrete form in our own breasts? They never take us off the superficial plane. We knew the facts already—less spread out and separated, to be sure—but we knew them still.[13]

James means facts like our experience of striving self-awareness at the locus of conscious impulse, activity, resistance, and accomplishment. Fidelity to such facts is crucial if we are to enjoy a sustaining relation to the original sources of delight in our lives.

## Self-consciousness

It seems like the me that is really me and was bein' held back by the I that I am is comin' out all over my face.

Goober Pyle (*The Andy Griffith Show*)[14]

Naturalist and writer Annie Dillard writes, "It is ironic that the one thing that all religions recognize as separating us from our creator—our very self-consciousness—is also the one thing that divides us from our fellow creatures. It was a bitter birthday present from evolution, cutting us off at both ends."[15] Well, that is one way to look at it.

Then there is James's way, emphasizing subjectivity (rather than self-consciousness and separation) and the transcendent feelings of exalted awareness to which it sometimes gives rise. This is more a point of emphasis than a signpost of real dispute or opposition, but the emphasis is importantly different nonetheless. It is the difference between viewing the self, on the one hand (as implied in Dillard's observation) as abandoned and alienated; and, on the other hand, as vitally related to an endlessly engaging, often fascinating environing field of "pure experience," in which each of us is privileged to possess sole (and *soul*) occupancy of the point of view from which we apprehend the spectacle and launch our own participation in it. The "soul" may or may not be an immortal entity, for James, but the living mortal soul is the self-aware locus of intersecting planes of pure experience.

James rejects alienation—the "puling and mumping mood" of helpless despair—and exalts pure experience as both an enjoying and a doing, at once passive and active. He finds in our "normal" or everyday consciousness of self not only a sense of potentially terrifying contingency but also the opportunity and invitation to regard our lives as so many occasions of excited expectancy and unmatched perception.

Dillard's perspective confronts the melancholic sense of tragic diremption from a lost or imagined preternatural wholeness that *can* accompany our solitary self-regard, when we give ourselves over to such ruminations (as in Plato's famous mythic parable of the divided self and the origin of gender). James denies none of this, but he also sees in it another aspect. The flip side of separation is uniqueness and opportunity to cultivate one's own subjective states as the character-forming, personality-marking, identity-conferring traits that do make us different from each other, to be sure, but different in a way wholly compatible with healthy and vitalizing connections of all kinds. Uniqueness need not mean disconnection and alienation. If we conclude with James that our human condition is more than just an occasion for wistful ontological regret, that it presents genuine opportunities for self-possession and personal growth, we will celebrate such traits as the subjective building blocks out of which we create essential elements of our very selves.

But before we can appreciate James's celebratory approach, and in fairness to the quite legitimate point of Dillard's reflections on self-consciousness, we need also to realize that he came to *his* perspective only after wrestling with other impulses; and he retained his "healthy-minded" perspective only by continuing to grapple with them almost constantly. "Healthy mindedness" itself made a complicated, not unqualified appeal to him. He fought to achieve a form of it in his own makeup and fought ever after to maintain with it an accommodation he could accept and defend.

We must consider also a further point in Dillard's favor: a good case can be made that our day-to-day or normal experience furnishes an ample objective basis for evaluating self-consciousness more like Dillard does, in the passage cited, than like James does—for instance, how easily and often human beings miscommunicate. If we only knew just how often our words and deeds have been misconstrued by others, even or especially by those to whom we are closest and from whom we expect the greatest understanding and sympathy, we might very well be tempted to emphasize the discontinuities and rifts in our collective experience, rather than the possibilities of connection . Each of us lives surrounded by a social chasm, as a castle is surrounded by a moat. Dillard is surely right about that. Not to make this case—or if James does not—is a testimony of hope for improved relations as much as a report of already-existing frictionless intercourse and freely flowing relations. James's commitment to the radical dimension of his empiricism, with its insistence on noticing the conjunctive relations in experience no less than the disjunctive, may sometimes seem to incline him to an excessive appreciation of continuities. Perhaps he does overcompensate for what he perceives as traditional empiricism's neglect of such relations.[16]

But let us not digress. James does not much philosophize about the self in tragic isolation or (in the modern argot) the self as "dysfunctional," because philosophy was for him the life jacket he used to break *away from* isolation and dysfunction. He was more concerned to philosophize about connection and health, because this was the personal condition which he felt compelled to strive for and to emulate; it was the condition whose absence he felt as an intolerable oppression. James was anything but sunnily, blissfully ignorant of the "sick soul," the impaired self, the troubled consciousness. Parodists of American philosophy who lampoon it as the intellectual equivalent of "can do" boosterism, and so forth, do him the greatest disservice on this score.

The parodists notwithstanding,[17] James was no stranger to melancholy. He never actually succeeded in throwing it off altogether, not even after making his bold resolution in 1870 to reject depression and despair in favor of "my individual reality and creative power."[18] Depression, though held at bay throughout most of his adult lifetime, was evidently a hovering presence from which James never felt entirely free.

But his philosophical enterprise very substantially subdued the depressive tendencies in his personal constitution by finding and clutching hard the silver lining behind Dillard's cloud. In brief, our condition of being "cut off" from both supernatural divinity, if such there be, and our fellow mortals—although James prefers not to invoke such imagery—is also the precondition of our uniqueness and our individuality. Our uniqueness and individuality, in turn, spawn the peculiarity of perspective we call subjectivity. And because subjectivity is the inescapable form of our perception, we are able to have and enjoy an experience of transcendence uniquely our own, rooted in our respective interests, enthusiasms, and orientations to the totality of our own experiential histories. In other words, our personal biographies supply the elements of our unique and personal forms of transcendence. Let us not brood in bitterness about having been cut off from the cosmos or from humanity, James would say to Dillard, unless we also acknowledge and celebrate the privileged opportunities for experience that this very circumstance has engendered in us.

What is more, we are not insuperably "cut off" in either direction. Indeed, some among us continue to resonate to the idea of divinity; some have undergone experiences that seem to testify (to *their* satisfaction, at least) to the workings of divinity in the universe and in their lives. In addition, through the practiced extension of sympathy and empathetic understanding, and through persistent efforts to communicate and to share our experiences, we can sometimes, to some extent, begin to bridge the gulf separating us. The "varieties of religious experience" can connect those who feel the need for that kind of connection to a larger, more-than-human universe.

This is really what *Varieties* is mainly about and what James intends to demonstrate. By illustrating the liveliness of religious hypotheses, practices, and experiences *for some individuals,* James means to reveal such connections (my term; *relations* more typically is James's) as latent in the experience of those individuals. He does not, however, mean to generalize the validity of the connections beyond the experience of those whose connections they are purported to be. In other words, we are no more or less cut off from God and our fellow humans than our experience reveals us to be, and our experience is not monolithic, univocal, or collectively authoritative. Mine is mine; yours is yours. Yet, I am bound by ties of sympathy and simple civility to guard and respect the integrity of your experience, as you are mine. In the specific case of religious experience, there is no presumption here of a shared quality of experience, common motives, common etiology or eschatology (or any other "ology") to elicit or account for our mutual sympathy. The only "grounding" required is supplied by our common humanity and all that it implies. James is not mining the common ore, the universal essence of religious experience, but rather the rich particularity and multiplicity of it.

To repeat: the varieties of religious experience connect the religiously inclined to the universe in a more meaningful way than is possible for them in the absence of such experiences. And sensitivity to the varieties and shades of human subjectivity, coupled with commitment to liberal and communitarian virtues, connects us one to another, despite our differences or because of them or because our differences are attributable to the fact of our common humanity. And this is another way in which the phenomenon of subjectivity may be said to form an objective backdrop for religion and, more generally, for life. It contains the seeds of a robust pluralism whose fruits are tolerance, natural humility, and perhaps even a kind of intellectual curiosity.

To summarize: in discussing so-called normal self-consciousness, or the attitude we habitually take in our day-to-day reckoning of how our individual selves relate to others and to any transcendent entity or force about whose existence we may wish to speculate, I have suggested that there are two different attitudinal tacks that present themselves. One is exemplified by Annie Dillard's remarks about self-consciousness as a source of disconnection, separation, isolation, and existential loneliness,[19] the other by James's view of self-consciousness as betokening our subjectivity and the possibilities of personal liberation that it affords. But at the same time I have tried to do justice to Dillard's remarks by noting that James himself was initially drawn to the more brooding, less effusive view. His positive evaluation of normal self-consciousness was hard won, not instinctive or reflexive.

The upshot of the discussion concerning subjectivity thus far is that, for James, subjectivity connects us to our own experience and to the practically unbounded total sphere of possible experience, in a unique way; and the way in which we are thus each connected is due in no small measure to contributions we singly make to the direction and texture of our own experiencing. We select and direct the nature and degree of our connection to the total field of experience that we are to enjoy by deploying our attention, or by allowing it to be deployed, by choosing to entertain some thoughts and not others, by aligning our wills with some acts and courses of action and not others, or, perhaps, by aligning ourselves with someone else's choices and active intentions. The *we* is really *I* in every separable instance, of course: "I choose," "I select." We do not always consciously experience ourselves in the act of selecting, attending, choosing, willing, or even doing, as we move somnambulistically through time-worn routines or submerge our identities in some larger collectivity of which we imagine ourselves mere inoperative appendages. Yet, personal responsibility is, *ex hypothesi*, nontransferable and ineliminatable. The hypothesis here, of course, is free will, the starting point and touchstone of James's philosophy. Put another way, James's emphasis on subjectivity is a banner-raising of individualism, a call to each and all to become aware of the ways in which we can regain active direction of where and to what extent we are linked to wider fields of experience, aware of how we may appropriate an authentic relation to "pure experience" in our own lives, and aware of the importance of recognizing the inspiriting significance of such relations in the very different lives of others.

Scholars tend to sidetrack themselves by focusing on questions like What is it? and What kind of stuff, if not material or ideal? when dealing with the proposal to think in terms of pure experience rather than the old metaphysical categories of matter and spirit. James's last word on the subject was that so far as he was concerned, and so far as his concept of pure experience is meant to extend, "there is no *general* stuff of which experience at large is made."[20] The better question, from a Jamesian perspective, is *What is it experienced as?*

One answer to that question is that pure experience is experienced as possibility and opportunity, as endless points of possible relatedness between oneself and other experiencers, prospective experiences, future achievements, and so forth. In a word, pure experience is experienced as *connection*. But for James we must always insist on this caveat: No single rope of connection, no antecedent guarantee of ultimate and harmonious unification binds all the experiences that have transpired or will ever transpire in constituting our universe. Nevertheless, "the unity of the world is on the whole undergoing increase."[21]

It has been helpfully suggested[22] that pure experience be liberated from its misleadingly "idealistic overtones," which, admittedly, may be impossible to do entirely. But it would surely take us some distance in that direction if students of James, and especially those eager to enlist him on the side of "neutral monism" in the old mind-body debate, could be persuaded to substitute the phrase "neutral *pluralism*" instead, in characterizing his view. James thinks that our confusion in this, as in most metaphysical debates, comes about when we insist on pigeonholing our thought and fail to state clearly what our perplexity means, concretely. If calling a fact "mental" or "physical" does not help to minimize perplexity and, indeed, if such categories become murkier the more we invoke them, then the solution may be to find different categories or, instead, to do away with categories and turn flexibly and attentively to how individuals actually encounter themselves and others in the world and to what they mean to accomplish. Just as the solution of puzzles like whether a man circling a tree circles also the squirrel residing there depends largely on one's meaning and purpose, so it is for the more interesting cases of metaphysical perplexity.

We will come much closer to an accurate report of James's intentions, even if it sounds to some less bold, in saying that a correct and open regard for the varieties of experience requires our neutrality with respect not to the *source* of experience but to the numberless *sources*. James, then, would have done us all a service if he had spoken not of pure experience but rather of pure *experiences*.

It was suggested earlier that James may have had an excessive tendency to correct what he perceived as traditional empiricism's historical neglect of "conjunctive relations." Perhaps his nominal unification of experiences in the concept of pure experience, as a singular designation, is symptomatic of this tendency. Or perhaps the misleading name was selected casually and inadvertently. There is ample precedent for this in James: at various times he regretted most of his coined names and phrases that captured the popular mind, not least including *pragmatism* and "will to believe." Whatever the explanation, James was in what surely must have felt to him like a pinched and somewhat awkward halfway position, where he was vulnerable to criticism from all sides. He stood midway between the empiricists who called forth his natural and spontaneous allegiance but who gave short shrift, in his view, to a very large class of experienced relations, and the rationalists who recognized these relations but only in a way that vastly exaggerated their scope and majesty relative to the totality of experienced relations. And the rationalists in their turn neglected the relations of disconnection, disjunction, mere "with-ness," and what might be called, in partial echo of David Hume, *contingent conjunction.*

James tried to appreciate rationalism's strengths, but he did not truly stand "midway" between these extremes. He was much more partial to empiricism, warts and all. For James, even rationalism's insights were skewed: granting the truth of conjunction, still "rationalism tends to treat [conjunctive relations] as being true in some supernal way."[23] James's way, instead, is to concede the reality of every kind of experienced relation just as experienced; but none is "supernal," none the *really* real by comparison to all the rest.

Yet, there is a kind of philosophical priority granted to conjunction after all, by radical empiricism, in what James calls the relation of continuous transition. To speak more plainly, he is talking here about the experience of *change.* "[T]o be a radical empiricist means to hold fast to this conjunctive relation of all others," or else to court the "metaphysical fictions" that come of freezing and atomizing our experience into bits that then seem to require an elaborate, extraneous, *gratuitous* theoretical accounting. The experience of change is so very basic to our grasp of reality because it *is* the fundamental reality of growth and evolution and history, above all the personal history of our most intimate acquaintance, "self." In the first instance we know ourselves as "processes of change in time,"[24] and while we can come to know others as similar "processes" we arrive at such understanding of them only through thought and analogy, not (as in our own case) by direct acquaintance. This is no skeptical questioning of whether we can "know other minds," no dalliance with solipsism—James never doubts that we directly experience other persons and the reality of society—but it is a sharp insistence on recognizing the order of our experience. He is not saying that we have to infer the existence of other persons but that we have to bridge a discontinuity in the quality of our experience of them. The discontinuity is never jarring enough to cause us to wonder whether there *are* other persons—of course there are!—but it is a disruptive obstacle in the way of our appreciating their angles of vision, their points of view, the way the world *feels* to them. It is the underlying cause of "a certain blindness in human beings" that James does not want us ever to forget.[25]

Before we proceed with this discussion of "pure experience," we might do well to anticipate an objection. Some will charge that James has the cart before the horse here, particularly if the aim is to shed light on the phenomenon of self-consciousness. Does it make sense to begin talking about experience from the outset if we mean to understand that species of experience called self-consciousness? Should we not be working *from* the more fundamental datum, the self, *toward* the self's experience, which after all is a derivative and secondary phenomenon? Or is it?

It is not, for James. That is part of the reason for calling the experience in question "pure," primordial, spontaneous, or original rather than reflective, considered, elaborative, or such. "[T]he Self as a system of memories, purposes, strivings, fulfillments, or disappointments, is incidental to this most intimate of all relations" between continuous states of mind. *Incidental!* Our experience is pure until it has been filtered through the verbal and conceptual constructions and abstractions of talk. James invites us to recur to an experience antedating all "Self"-attribution, to bypass what is truly derivative and secondary. In his judgment, most of what we think we know about the Self is actually contrived and artificial, the invention of an ingenious species comparable to the intricate old astronomical epicycles "explaining" the movements of the planets. They were complex, elaborate, clever, useful, and literally false. James thinks falsehood is bound to result when our focus is on redressing deficiencies in previous theory rather than holding fast to the raw data of experience itself. No, he says, do not begin with the Self; it is incidental to deeper features of reality that are ours to know. But before we can know, we have to *look*. "The deeper features of reality are found only in perceptual experience."[26]

Of course, "raw data" is about as controversial a notion in philosophy as there is, to say nothing of "deeper features of reality!" James knows that. But it is doubtful that anything that anyone has said, during the century since he philosophized, about the "myth of the given" or the ubiquity of "discourse," and the like, would dislodge him from a belief anchored in the intimate and ongoing personal experience of change at first hand. His challenge to the reader, even to critics and skeptics, is to take experience at "face value . . . just as we feel it."[27] Turn away for awhile from *talk*, from writing and conceptualizing and theorizing, and see if you do not notice something beneath all that in the field of your own introspective awareness. Then, if you honestly find nothing there, go on and talk if you must.

Some (like James) must talk, because talking is their vocation and their habit, or because they can only imagine that everything found in their fields of introspection got there via talk. Or, more simply, they just like to talk. If only all professional talkers and teachers were so motivated! Talk of all kinds will always be with us, and we are the richer for its variety. "The world is wide enough to harbor various ways of thinking,"[28] and talking and writing are what acquaint us with them. But are they extrinsic to reality, for James? No. He does not deny that there is something fundamentally constitutive of our humanity in the meaningful utterance and interpretation of signs. If "the first man" was the first of a pair of aboriginal creatures to deploy or to comprehend "a mouthy little sound . . . as 'meaning' something they beheld in common," as Walker Percy put it,[29] James would simply add that he or she brought to that first meaningful episode a primordial and prelinguistic capacity for mute exhilaration and delight in the qualitative immediacies of sensation. As that capacity becomes ever more entwined in our civilized, evolving, verbalizing condition, it becomes ever more humanizing and civilizing for us to acknowledge, appreciate, and cultivate its contribution to our humanity. But we should also admit the truth of Whitman's statement that "words are spiritual—nothing is more spiritual than words. —Whence are they? Along how many thousands and tens of thousands of years have they come?"[30] They, too, are links in the chain of life.

In the end, James is concerned not so much to battle the talkers as to offer an alternative to the snares and seductions of intellectualism, or the habit of forgetting and losing ourselves in talk that misses what is real. "Over-subtle intellects" want a conceptual understanding of self and the world not as a supplement and aid to primary perception but as a substitute for it; but we should not fool ourselves into thinking that Royce, Bradley, et al., are the only oversubtle intellects in James's purview. His point is that we are all oversubtle intellects until we learn to attend our own experience with minimal preconception.

How *do* we break down our preconceptions about the world's real elements, and overcome doubts about our own perceptual and cognitive abilities to encounter them directly? How do we disabuse our intellects of overweening subtlety? James's answer is that first we must resist the temptation to find an intellectual—or an *intellectualist*—solution.[31] Rather than thinking our way around skepticism, he proposes that we just allow experience to run its course and that we not impose artificial roadblocks in the form of stipulated theoretical expectations to which our experience must then conform, or else be disavowed.

And to a considerable extent, James thinks this crucial first step in overcoming intellectualism was taken by the classical British empiricists. It oversimplifies the case only a little to say that the correct equation for understanding James and his radical empiricism is: Hume + radicalism = radical empiricism ("radicalism" in this context meaning a closer scrutiny of all kinds of relations, and greater fealty to those—conjunctive relations in particular—which in James's view Hume neglected). James means to continue and to enrich the empiricist tradition, not to supplant and certainly not to discredit it. In the previous discussion we noted James's rejection of Hume's belief that everything we perceive is "loose" and disjointed. But James saw himself as a good and faithful empiricist, cleaving to the spirit *and* the letter of empiricist principles by reporting his experiential awareness of conjunctive relations "between" percepts—relations that are themselves perceived. Insofar as the percepts and the relations—the "perch-ings" and "flights" of experience—merit full equality of recognition, they really are "between" only in a relative and perspectival sense: we might just as accurately reverse the terms and say that the Humean percepts are ex-perienced between the conjunctions. But however we *say* it, James pre-dicts, if we allow all the relations in our experience their full due we will begin to notice a seamlessness beneath the garment of our everyday per-ception that belies any great preference or priority for either the "between" states or the terms they mediate.

Philosophers, psychologists, and others concerned with identifying and analyzing the processes of thought have a precise use for the contrived act of introspection and for other mental operations. And the requirements of daily living impose a practical value on discriminating those parts of experi-ence that are relatively stable and substantive from those having a more evanescent and fleeting quality. Those same requirements may trick us into discrediting the full reality or worth of the latter, especially if we have not cultivated a sensitivity to transient and unexpected moments of aesthetic or spiritual deliverance. But most of us, much of the time, are well positioned to notice and appreciate the flow of what James recognizes as *streams* of thought and experience, for practical as well as for aesthetic ends.[32] If we ignore this flow, from ingrained habit or theoretical preconception, we miss a great deal. Again, James echoes Stevenson: To miss the joy is to miss all. Most of us are good at catching those forms of joy that are surrounded by ritual and the stamp of our culture's habitual approval; but so many of life's potential golden moments are small, unmarked, and uncelebrated.

James aims to do full justice to the conjunctions as well as the disjunc-tions in experience and thereby finally to fulfill the letter of the Humean program: to out-*Hume* Hume, as it were. The classical empiricists were clearly on the right track, James thinks, when they insisted on tracing the contents of consciousness to experiential "originals" in sensation and in seeking to account for whatever else occupies our minds in terms of (in principle) experienceable mental operations (like Hume's "reflection"). They were right, though Hume for one was intemperately, gratuitously provocative with his famous call for the incineration of flabby metaphysics and to reject speculative theoretical constructs in place of solid experience; and this hard-nosed commitment to experience formed a watershed in the history of human understanding.

But the classical empiricists erred, James thinks, in not grasping the wholly speculative and shakily theoretical implications of their constricted, exclusive criteria of what was to count as original in experience. If we an-nounce that a person is a bundle of sensations, is bound only by habit, is "constant conjunction," or some such, we are burdened with an incoherent and deeply unsatisfying picture screaming for completion. In the absence of a more satisfying picture drawn perceptively and persuasively from experience, speculative metaphysicians *will* complete it, each in their own imaginative ways. We have introduced a mystery into our philosophy—in itself not a bad thing—but we have simultaneously subverted our ability to solve it by excluding from consideration all perception that does not fall under the narrowly defined category of "sensation." And if we claim that the world is a concatenation of such sensations, having nothing to do with one another, we have exceeded the bounds of experience; thus, to what original in sensation or reflection can we assign general statements about the world? But more importantly, says James, such statements ignore vast realms of experience containing the information we need to solve our mystery of discontinuity between the self and its experiences, and between self and world. The mystery in question is that which is generated by mistaken and incomplete thinking. James does not claim that experience necessarily or generally holds a solution to ultimate mystery, which remains the province of religion for some, philosophy for others. In truth, probably the great majority of persons do not experience ultimate mystery as problematic; we can argue that they *should*, that it is a fool's paradise into which no wonder and mystery creep. But James begrudges no one any happiness honestly come by and does not denounce the blissful ignoramus as such, unless his bliss is purchased at the unacceptable social cost of untended obligations, or the like.

But if James does not find in experience a uniform response to the mystery of existence, or even a uniform experience of mystery, neither does he debar us from addressing, in our own experience and in our own way, any mystery that we, singly, may find compelling. The point: the experience of mystery, and how we choose to confront or to evade it, is personal and not universal. This point, more than any other, carries the practical significance of James's radical reconstruction of classical empiricism.

Again, Hume and the classical British empiricists were fundamentally correct about the sources of experience in contrast with their idealist brethren. But in James's estimation they did not appreciate the breadth and scope of their own insights.

We have said that the purity of pure experience is corrupted mainly by "talk," for James. So long as we put off the discursive reconstruction of past experience—with the unavoidable selection and revision this entails—and attend to the felt immediacy of experiences as they transpire, we cannot mistake them. They are real *as experienced*. James simply rejects the tendency of thought—so prevalent in philosophy especially since the advent of positivism—to represent language and conceptual thinking as pervasive, ubiquitous, inescapable, and determinative of the entire contents of consciousness. He admits that the discursive intellect possesses a powerful inertial force that *may* overrun pure experience, but it need not.

The danger of taking this position, of course, is that we risk painting ourselves into a corner of ineffability from which we may never emerge, if "emerging" means saying something incisive and truthfully descriptive about pure experience beyond the bare claim that it must be possible to have direct experience of relations which preexist all subsequent talk about them.

We must take care not to misrepresent or overstate the linkages between thought, conception, language, and speech, when we talk about "talk." The linkages are tight enough, for James, if still much looser than those later to be enshrined by the "linguistic turn" of positivists who, in the name of ontological parsimony, were so quick to dismiss whatever did not lend itself to precise, perspicuous, verifiable verbal dissection. Their preference for language and linguistic analysis had largely to do with an aversion to woolly metaphysics that spawned vague and unverifiable claims. Yet, the positivist impulse, ironically, seems to spring from the same mania for order and tidiness and *economy* in their total worldview as motivated the absolute idealists: neither could tolerate a universe, whether of things or theories, with parts just strung alongside one another and not demonstrably integral to a closed and ordered system. James, by contrast, is typically at ease with a world of chaotic profligacy and loosely external relations. Unlike the absolutists, however, the positivists had no use for the nonindependently, non-*extra*-systemically verifiable. Hence their turn to the dissection and analysis of language. There, they thought, is a public arena in which it is impossible to obfuscate or conceal meaning behind allegedly impenetrable personal experience.

James would not take this turn because he recognized the seductions of language, the ways in which it lures us into a zone of complacency about the depths of experience and feeling—the "mysteries" if you will—which are deep and mysterious precisely because they are *not* public in the way of language. Language is the bearer of public memory, the keeper of our collective history, and the domain of shared understanding; but because it can be such, it is also a cause of forgetfulness, where subjective, personal, and private understanding is at issue. It beckons us into the public world; only by an effort of self-possession do we voluntarily turn away from that safe world, safe because not solely our own, not wholly our individual responsibility. The subjective and private self is just that. Successful living means negotiating the passage between public and private realms, repeatedly, without losing our way.

The relations in experience, as we first encounter them, roughly correspond to grammatical connectors (*and, with*). We may wonder if we speak this way because these connections first occur in pure experience, or whether speech covertly places them there. James seems confident that the experience of conjunction is at least coeval with conjunctive speech. He seems not to have taken seriously the proposal that we regard the former as parasitic or derivative.

Now, despite his emphasis on the potential pitfalls of *conceptual* activity in distorting our picture of *perceptual* reality, James does not claim that pure experience is absolutely pure or unadulterated by thinking and speaking. As "the immediate flux of life," it is brushed by the same influences that dominate our everyday consciousness; but James is talking about a stage of consciousness that is *relatively* primitive and uncomplicated, that recurs perpetually, and that we can tune into or not. No one in a normal, noninfantile, or nonpathological state of awareness—ever has "an experience pure in the literal sense of a *that* which is not yet any definite *what*,"[33] but our experiences may still be pure in the intended sense if they embody some unspecified (but presumably substantial) degree of "unverbalized sensation." It is unclear whether or to what extent it might be possible to quantify the threshold amount of unverbalized sensation prerequisite to an experience's being pure; but we can take James's point, surely, without the need for that kind of measuring instrument.

Perhaps we do not need a procedure for quantifying purity precisely, but it would be useful to have at least an informal criterion of how we can correctly judge an experience to embody sensation as such. Perhaps it is enough that we withhold or suspend categorical judgments about an experience ("mental," "physical," "subjective," "objective") to preserve an element of purity, of "plain, unqualified actuality." But if so, must we, in fact, suspend judgment, or is it enough to adopt a merely methodological doubt, after the example of Descartes (despite any inclination we may have to think that our experience actually belongs to one or another category which, for philosophical reasons extraneous to the experience itself, we decline to name)?

It would be convenient for James to take the methodological approach: he could just say then that "pure experience" is a *stance* toward our experience that we may assume at will, which may or may not have a foundation in real perception but which is nonetheless a useful tool for clarifying our ideas about the philosophically rich phenomena of continuity and immediacy and the relations sustaining them.

Convenient, yes; but not consistent with James's real motives and purposes in philosophizing. We said before that James does not take a "linguistic turn," and that is exactly what this proposal to take "pure experience" as a methodological stance and not, necessarily, as a perceptual reality, amounts to. It is an attempt to achieve philosophical results by shrinking the universe to proportions commensurate with the conceptual tools that seem manageable to us: an alluring move, but, if James is right about pure experience, a move in the wrong direction. *Your universe is too small*, he effectively tells the positivists. If he did not believe it to be a perceptual reality, he would not discuss it as such. Pure experience is not for him just a useful fiction; it is a living reality.

The above phrase "stage of consciousness" as a description of pure experience may mislead; but the confusion is constructive and illuminating, I think, because it illustrates why James wants to talk about pure experience as a living reality and not just a *façon de parler*. Most frequently James speaks of pure experience as a stage not of consciousness but of *perception*, a perception of relations. Colloquially, however, we find it most natural to revert to the former locution. That is because colloquially, or in an everyday sense, it will seem to us that pure experience is "experienced *as*" a state of mind, if at all. But saying that misses James's point in invoking pure experience, namely that there are qualities of perception and ranges of experienceable relations that antedate their assignment to mind. "The peculiarity of our experiences, that they not only are, but are known, which their 'conscious' quality is invoked to explain, is better explained by their relations— these relations themselves being experiences—to one another." Hence we *should* speak of pure experience as a stage of perception, so as not to trick ourselves with the question-begging connotations of "consciousness."

James, not unlike Schiller and Bradley (and perhaps all the absolute idealists) in this, was a panexperientialist, holding some version of the claim that all is experience, that no part of human reality is wholly outside the realm of actual or possible experiencing. He knew that one obstacle to widespread acceptance of radical empiricism is that it sounds idealistic. In fact, Schiller was not a radical empiricist at all, even if he and James seem to have assumed that he was. Rather, Schiller was a "personal idealist" (as distinguished from absolute and transcendental idealism). This must have much to do with the widespread tendency of commentators to hear eastern resonances in the notion of pure experience.

But James resisted the insinuation that radical empiricism and the "doctrine" of pure experience were idealistic. We noted differences with Schiller that make it plain that radical empiricism was for James implied by, and supportive of, fundamentally *realistic* intuitions. James was a realist, albeit a different kind of realist: one who takes subjectivity and individualism as the most basic and profound realities of all. This is why there was such an affinity between James and Schiller in the first place, despite their distinct differences over realism. And his differences with Bradley make it equally plain that James had no wish to be allied with phenomenalism or the view that physical realities are reducible to sensations; but Bradley's first impression of pure experience was that it was precisely that.[34]

James did not intend to suggest that physical realities—that realities *simpliciter*—reduce to anything at all. They are what they are, no more and no less. An experience of physical reality, experienced *as such*, is an experience of physical reality and not "really" an experience of something else our naive senses and untutored common sense have failed to apprehend. But by the same token, an experience of *ideal* reality (if anyone reports such an experience) is what it is, too; and so also for experiences of pink elephants and liberal Republicans. We find, however, that pink-elephant reports tend not to sustain stable continuities with other experiences as well as the gray. Those of us with limited firsthand elephant experience do not, therefore, usually base our elephant expectations on those reports. It would be irrational of us to do so.

The point here is just that for James, the arena of pure experience is not the place to adjudicate existence claims, nor is it a foundational place where anyone, particularly any rationalist philosopher, should wish to lay the cornerstone for a system of certain knowledge. But it is the place where immediate experiences of mostly unverbalized sensations are possible. Some of these get reported in a way connecting fruitfully to other experience, some not. In neither case do more complex objects, or nonexperiential objects, get "reduced" to sensations.

James is no phenomenalist, but because of the confusion surrounding this he has often been the target of misdirected arguments against phenomenalism based on the fact that different perceivers perceive the same objects differently. But this kind of argument cuts no ice with radical empiricism which, being largely a recognition of the fact of human subjectivity and an affirmation of the reality of subjective experience, accepts and even predicts perceptual relativity. More than that, as the next section will consider, it embraces the endless varieties of ways in which human beings perceive, honor, and pursue the conditions of their own personal fulfillment.

# IV

## Pursuing Happiness

Happiness is a mystery, like religion, and should never be rationalised.

G. K. Chesterton

### Religion and the Pursuit of Happiness

Happiness may in fact be a mystery and a gift, but for James it is also a pursuit. That is where religion comes in. James defines religion as "the feelings, acts, and experiences of individuals in their solitude, so far as they apprehend themselves to stand in relation to whatever they may consider the divine."[1] He claims to reject the notion that defining religion so broadly automatically includes any fanatical fascination, systematic obsession, or prolonged piety that anyone may happen to profess for anything at all; presumably, then, he would apply strictest scrutiny to the late Flip Wilson's "Church of What's Happenin' Now," Annie Savoy's "Church of Baseball," or Garrison Keillor's "Sacred Shrine of the Republican Revelation,"[2] for instance, before accepting their own self-descriptions as religious.

But on its face his own preferred definition seems little different, practically, from a declaration that religion has *no* definition, if a definition is supposed to stipulate rigid "necessary and sufficient conditions" for membership in an exclusive and privileged class. His rather vague formulation ("whatever they may consider the divine") is unlikely to regulate the turnstile of admission into the ranks of what counts as "religion." Maybe this is not a bad thing. James did not think that it was, and there is no good reason—certainly none implied by his own philosophical goals and commitments—why *he* should wish to erect stringent entrance requirements at religion's gate. James philosophizes about religion in his customary role as a zealous guardian of personal experience, no matter whose, and is most of all concerned (in *Varieties*) to get down an accurate and insightful record of how real men and women have actually experienced the pull and power of those alternately self-abasing and exalted feelings of connection with something "more," something larger and greater than themselves, commonly called religious. He is not interested in producing either a revisionist or a prescriptive account of what we do or ought to mean by *religion*. He does mean to present as honest and revealing a portrait of what individuals in fact experience while in the throes of what they themselves describe as religious experiences, to the extent that such is in another's power to tell.

Religionists (churched religionists especially) are most prone to debate this issue of inclusion, some from motives worthily self-interested[3] but some not. The spiritually paranoid among them may be afraid that they will compromise their own presumptive salvation if they welcome "imposters," ideological lightweights, or (worst of all) freethinking skeptics into the faith. Their tickets to paradise have been punched, think the True Believers, and they want no *poseurs* coming along for the ride, sullying their credentials or possibly even disrupting the journey.

But James is a social meliorist, as we have seen: his focus is on our collective salvation. This is not to say that he was at all indifferent to questions of personal salvation. First and last he was an intensely individualistic philosopher, with a compelling interest in saving himself from the personal demons (chiefly depression and tendencies to what he called "morbid" reflections on the precipice-like contingency of human flourishing) which haunted him. But his philosophizing was always undertaken in a constructive spirit of communal progress. The lessons he learned, the progress he achieved, he meant to share. Nothing so permanently mobile and fallible as a personal creed can punch one's ticket, as it were, for all eternity. James's view is that we all might be saved, or we might not be, but whichever it is to be, we are all in the same open boat so far as that *possibility* (not *impossibility*, not *inevitability*) goes. Our destiny has yet to be decided as a historical matter, but it is *ours*, not exclusively mine, hers, or yours. We are bidden to join our private and individual efforts to the collective endeavor, so that we might *all* enjoy personal salvation. When a meliorist works for salvation, he works for an achievement that all might reap, corporately, but that each might enjoy singly, as well as socially. He aims to balance public good with private fulfillment, assuming that one without the other is unacceptable (even if imaginable).

We should say a word more here about the term *salvation*, which may mislead with its freighted implications of supernatural or eternal life. James is certainly aware that many or even most religious persons in our Western religious traditions are deeply wedded to belief in the persistence of their own personalities or "souls" in incorporeal form. He is himself not hostile to such a belief and sometimes seems to entertain the possibility as what he would call a "live option," a candidate for his own belief.

Yet, the record seems fairly clear that he remained neutral, publicly, about the extent or the supernatural status of his own personal faith. James's frank responses to a questionnaire on religion in 1904 provide real insight: *Do you believe in personal immortality?* "Never keenly; but more strongly as I grow older." *Do you pray?* "I cannot possibly pray—I feel foolish and artificial." *What do you mean by 'spirituality'?* "Susceptibility to ideals, but with a certain freedom to indulge in imagination about them. A certain amount of 'other worldly' fancy. Otherwise you have mere morality, or 'taste.'" *What do you mean by a 'religious experience'?* "Any moment of life that brings the reality of spiritual things more 'home' to one."[4] I know that many will read in these responses a Jamesian tilt toward supernaturalism, but I am more inclined to view them as a nod of sympathetic recognition and moral support, an instance of neutral distancing and what Perry has called his belief in (others') believing. In any case, his use of the term *salvation* in the present context is neutral with respect to any supernatural implications. It means something like "deliverance from evil," where 'evil' is not taken *necessarily* to imply a malevolent supernatural agency at work in the world, and where it is hoped and supposed that natural human powers are equal to the task of resisting it successfully, not always but often, at least in the long run.

There is a substantial body of precedent supporting liberal inclusivity in the designation of the religious. For instance, many socialist intellectuals earlier in this century—atheists not excluded—considered themselves intensely religious. "Whatever a man will labour for earnestly and in some measure unselfishly is religion,"[5] said writer and mystic D. H. Lawrence. Others have been known to exhibit an astonishing quasi-religious enthusiasm for what nonenthusiasts stubbornly persist in calling mere games, diversions, recreations, or pastimes. We have already alluded to *Field of Dreams* and its "Church of Baseball" and its many high-minded penitents who have waxed spiritual and poetic about the national pastime. Does "time begin on opening day"? For some of us, that is when it *stops* in the salutary sense of transcendence. Satchel Paige said that maybe he would "pitch forever," and in the sense of a naturalized concept of eternity (see below) maybe he did. James's student, the pragmatist Morris Cohen, once published an essay entitled *Baseball as a National Religion* in which he reported actually bringing the idea to James's attention.[6] James did not, apparently, warm to the idea. But he would have implicitly understood Paul Simon's plaintive rhetorical lyric "Where have you gone, Joe DiMaggio?" We humans have a powerful need for inspirational icons we can revere and yet still, somehow, "relate" to.[7] Beyond the simple "team concept" and its instrumental focus on victory, baseball actively rewards such dwelling in the past and encourages the eager anticipation of future occasions of dwelling there again, at the park and in the imagination. Those creatively spliced video reels in which a swatting Ruth melds with an Aaron, Mantle, Maris, Mays, or McGwire demonstrate at some level how this mere game can encourage its devotees to slip the bonds of time, in transient green reveries. The late Renaissance scholar and baseball commissioner Bart Giamatti wrote with unscholastic passion of the *inner* fields of play where we mortals may visit paradise.[8]

James's esteem for the human condition of subjectivity, with his appreciation of the varieties of life it sponsors, leads directly to the thoroughgoing and enthusiastic indulgence (for which he was notorious) of anything whatever that imbues individual lives with "significance." It also goes far toward an explanation of why he was so tolerant, and even *fond*, of eccentrics and their quirky, crotchety obsessions.

Theologians have divided along these lines as well, the liberals being as fond of Paul Tillich's definition of religion as an attestation of "ultimate concern"[9] as conservatives are appalled. Chesterton, again, speaks against liberal inclusiveness when he says that "a man can no more possess a private religion than he can possess a private sun and moon."[10] But we *do* possess "private" suns and moons: one person's "moon like a flower in heaven's high bower" is another's "moon over Miami" and yet another's "harvest moon." The pagan's sun as object of veneration is very different from the dreaded source of toxic radiation against which we armor ourselves in slathering layers of protective unguent.

Yet, the analogy also reminds us that our respective "private" objects and the several worlds ("*sub*-worlds,"[11] James called them) which they populate do nevertheless supervene on a stable and shared constellation of public objects. The same sun does warm the pagan and the beach bum, after all, no matter how differently they may represent and interiorize this still-solid fact. Our subjectivity requires a backdrop of objective reference for clarity and contrast. And so does our private religious experience require some minimal stipulated agreement about what religion is. In just that minimal sense, James's broadly expansive definition is a success in its own terms. It supplies an answer, in every case, to the question Why do you call that *religious?*—because it relates the religious fruitfully to their own experience in a way which, for them, is suggestive of what they consider the divine; and it provides meaning or significance in their lives that will place them in more satisfactory relations to their experience in the future—or something of the sort.

One other important point here: There is a deeper sense in which James's definition supplies an objective backdrop and positive sanction for countless "private" religions; it implies an explanation of the very phenomenon in question. And if we find what he says plausible and persuasive, we will likely find ourselves unable to imagine the case being otherwise, unable to conceive a world in which private religions do not proliferate. In other words, James's broad definition of religion points to, and (loosely) follows from, his understanding and appreciation of subjectivity; and if we accept what he says about subjectivity, we will come to think of *it*—the fact of subjectivity as perhaps the most important constitutive element in a human being's make-up—*as* something like the objective backdrop that religious peculiarity and difference requires.

James's liberal and inclusive definition was crafted so as to broaden the scope and interest of his remarks in the school lectures that became *The Varieties of Religious Experience;* but James also has extrapedagogical reasons for "circumscribing the topic" in this way. He cites a contemporary's proposal to define religion as any "habitual and regulated admiration,"[12] and although he rejects it as unhelpfully indiscriminate he still agrees that "any persistent enjoyment may *produce*" religious feelings.[13] We have seen that the liberality of James's definition of religion is virtuously inclusive, consistent with his melioristic approach to salvation, and implied by his general position on subjectivity. Some of the great literary and theological figures of modernity have been participants in this debate about inclusiveness; so James's position is in good—or at least, all will admit, in prominent—company. His definition may be more inclusive than even he intended, but it is hard to imagine James agonizing about the risk of that sort of liberal excess.

But on his own terms James ought to be less sanguine about this concern, if it could be shown that his approach misrepresents or ignores the actual experience of large numbers of religious persons and practices. It might be contended by some devout persons, in this regard, that a focus such as James's on religion as a source of personal happiness, satisfaction of desire, or need misses the point of genuine religious devotion. In calling attention to the fact that various kinds of enjoyment can lead to religious feelings that may then find expression in some ritualized practice, discipline, or devotion, James is pointing to the central importance of personal happiness in religious experience, but is he in danger of *reducing* religion to the pursuit of happiness? Most religious persons would insist that a great deal more than happiness or personal satisfaction, whether their own or that of humanity generally, is involved in religious practice and discipline.

C. S. Lewis is a familiar example of a religious person, in his case an important religious leader and opinion maker, who claims to demote the pursuit of happiness below other religious values. He is in fact doubtful that happiness and, more generally, the satisfaction of desires, are religious values at all. Consider his repudiation of religious "consolation" in the face of personal grief : "Talk to me about the truth of religion and I'll listen gladly. Talk to me about the duty of religion and I'll listen submissively. But don't come talking to me about the consolations of religion or I shall suspect that you don't understand."[14]

Lewis notwithstanding, most of the figures James examines in *Varieties* certainly seem to exhibit a thirst for religious "consolation." Indeed, the outward manifestations of their religious passion become largely unintelligible, *from the outside,*[15] without our supposition that such ardent faith is motivated by a definite interest in something more than religious truth or duty. It appears to be the case that there is also present, in fervent religious practice, an unmistakable element of *need, want, or desire*. Call it what you will, it is a powerfully animating force in the lives of those whose religious experience takes center stage in *Varieties*. This is not to deny that some individuals feel an impulsion of duty or a devotion to the truth, even truth in the abstract, which to them is the very heart, the *point*, of religious belief. This may have been the case with C. S. Lewis.[16] It may have been so with Immanuel Kant and with others whose mental temperaments fit them for the remoteness of ideal abstraction. But the ideal commitments of most religious persons are not quarantined from the vitality of daily and sensory perception.

For those whose religious convictions flow from feelings of rectitude and the impulse to imbibe universal principles capable of sustaining or "verifying" those feelings, there is an overriding dual imperative: (1) Discern your duty, and (2) do it. And to these, perhaps, should be added: (3) State it truthfully and parsimoniously. And further: (4) Disregard and denigrate all merely personal inclination and desire. Such individuals perceive no great difference between the purpose of religion and that of ethics. Both, they hold, are born of a felt compulsion to align oneself completely with the universe's own rules of order; and this means suppressing and rerouting our spontaneous desires, which are presumed to come from a different place. The ethical and religious imperatives, so understood, rest upon a settled hierarchy of universal obligation that God decrees. To be religious, to be morally correct, is to be an obedient instrument of God's will. Moral and religious obligation are founded in God and adjudicated by a correct interpretation of religion. Kant, of course, sought an independent philosophical corroboration of religious truth, but he seems never to have abandoned the religious precepts of his earliest years. James, to the contrary, holds that moral obligation is rooted in our human relations.

Lewis seems to find the quest for personal consolation and reward almost embarrassingly self-regarding, spiritually debased, or otherwise somehow inferior to correctly attuned religious practice. This is diametrically opposite James's attitude. In "The Moral Philosopher and the Moral Life," he articulates a view of the relation between personal desire and ultimate worth, which pervades his entire philosophy. "[E]very de facto claim creates in so far forth an obligation,"[17] he declares in startling defiance of conventional ethical assumptions. But let us take a step back in order to understand James's defiance.

Many conventionally religious persons have difficulty with the suggestion that someone might be spiritual *and* agnostic or atheistic and are hostile to something they have heard demonized as "secular humanism." Many humanists, on the other hand, have difficulty understanding how their commitment to the "religion of humanity" strikes mainstream believers as undermining morality and decency. The question of the existence of a god, though fascinating, is to them subordinate to questions about what we owe our fellow humans, what hopes, dreams, fears, and sorrows they might harbor, and how to ameliorate their woes. On the one hand, humanists never suppose that such concerns might actually hinge on the real status of an omnipotent, transcendent, otherworldly being. On the other hand, it has never occurred to many traditional religious persons to think otherwise.

"If God does not exist everything is permitted." That Dostoyevskian, Nietzschean, Sartrean knell of nihilism so intuitively obvious to fundamentalists baffles a *Jamesian* humanist: "existentialism is *a* humanism." James would never accept a voluntarism so radical as Sartre's, for instance, which starts by assuming that we are "nothing" until we act and thereby choose a wholly contingent personal identity. For James a shared, largely biological human nature accommodates our endlessly various particular *natures*.[18] Our choices and acts do not create our respective natures ex nihilo but only actuate or frustrate them.

Dostoyevski should be required reading for all humanists, not to dissuade them of their humanism but simply to educate them about the polar opposition of a perspective so different from that to which they are accustomed. Traditional believers would do well to study (among many other essential documents in the corpus of what might be called the library of humanistic spirituality) John Dewey's *A Common Faith*, Bertrand Russell's "A Free Man's Worship," and James's "The Moral Philosopher and the Moral Life." James's purpose in that essay is to raise and answer the question of where moral obligation and duty come from, or what makes a claim on our conduct and belief legitimate and compelling? Whence its warrant, validity, and appeal?

The old view that most of us absorb osmotically in our youth—represented, typically, as the "voice of conscience"—says that the validity of ethical claims and moral statements ("You ought to do X," "Y is wrong") "rains down upon the claim . . . from some sublime dimension of being."[19] The correlative implication is that in times or in regions of moral drought, when validity does not rain down, "everything is permitted"; or at least *nothing is settled and nothing is prohibited*. This is one way of viewing the explosion in our time of moral relativism: as the natural consequence of a widespread but mostly unacknowledged presupposition to the effect that morality and ethics *must* fail to resolve issues wherever there is lack of consensus about the sublime origins and status of validity. Now, except perhaps in small monastic communities organized around a common faith, and alternatively in monolithic religious institutions whose members uniformly cede moral authority to the institution, there never has been this kind of consensus among most human beings at any given time about any given issue of moral import. Sublimity is not commonly recognized or referred to the same object(s). We handicap our efforts to achieve ethical results from the start when we stipulate a requirement that validity take this form.

Against the requirement of sublimity, James proposes something very different: "Take any demand, however slight, which any creature, however weak, may make. Ought it not, for its own sole sake, to be satisfied? If not, prove why not."[20] But is this not an invitation to moral anarchy, a leveling of all demands and an obliteration of all distinctions? No, it does not level the demands. It levels the playing field on which the demands are to compete for social sanction. It invites distinction, discrimination, thought, evaluation. James is proposing the moral equivalent of the legal presumption of innocence; call it the moral presumption of entitlement. Just as the legal presumption does not prevent deliberative bodies from finding guilt and assessing responsibility, so does the moral presumption stand ready for correction.

In the best of worlds every demand would be reasonable, none would be injurious or hurtful to others, all would be satisfiable. No two desires or demands would ever conflict. It is intuitive to James that such a world would be the best. Perhaps Lewis, Kant, or others committed to a duty-based view of human good would not share this intuition. But in this hypothetical world, there would be no reason to begrudge any desire or demand that anyone might make for any reason, and certainly no basis upon which anyone would be right to set about frustrating the achievement of another's satisfaction. How could one prove the illegitimacy of what someone else seeks? "The only possible kind of proof you could adduce," James continues, "would be the exhibition of another creature who should make a demand that ran the other way." It is, alas, a fantasy world in which demands fail to run up against one another in incompatible ways.

Even those who have already taken the same steps as James toward throwing off the old inveterate habits of thinking, and who no longer expect to demonstrate a sublime source of ethical validity, still frequently wish somehow to speak for, or with the imprimatur of, the universe: "The universe is such that one ought to do X." James resists this tendency to personify the universe so as to smuggle the old sublimity in through the back door. We would not want to do this unless we believe in a universal or divine consciousness that actually exists.

> If there be such a consciousness, then its demands carry the most of obligation simply because they are the greatest in amount. But it is even then not *abstractly* right that we should respect them. It is only *concretely* right . . . life answering to life. A claim thus livingly acknowledged is acknowledged with a solidity and fulness which no thought of an "ideal" backing can render more complete. . . .[21]

This is a repudiation of Platonic and transcendental idealism, but more impressively it is a turn toward a naturalism that discerns its own concreteness in the living expression of the inner lives of embodied and yearning souls, and discerns in "actually living minds" allof the "ground" that a moral life needs. "Wherever such minds exist, with judgments of good and ill, and demands upon one another, there is an ethical world in its essential features."[22]

James's parable of "the rock" conveys our situation, as he sees it, and invites us to draw the appropriate implications for the status of "desire" in our world. Far from the base and defiling instigator of duty forsworn, as we have been discussing it, desire is the natural source of purposes, values, and significance. It commands our presumptive respect, in the absence of proof of its unworthiness:

> Were all other things, gods and men and starry heavens, blotted out from this universe, and were there left but one rock with two loving souls upon it, that rock would have as thoroughly moral a constitution as any possible world which the eternities and immensities could harbor. It would be a tragic constitution, because the rock's inhabitants would die. But while they lived, there would be real good things and real bad things in the universe; there would be obligations, claims, and expectations . . . [T]here would, in short, be a moral life, whose active energy would have no limit but the intensity of [their] interest in each other. . . .[23]

The "rock" is no science fiction fantasy, it is our home: the natural cradle of our aspirations and the repository of our hopes and efforts. It is an inherently "ethical" community constituted by the plurality of needs, claims, and desires that our condition requires us to sort and order. Desire, and what we make of it, makes our world.

> We, on this terrestrial globe, so far as the visible facts go, are just like the inhabitants of such a rock. Whether a God exist [or not] we form at any rate an ethical republic. . . . And the first reflection which this leads to is that ethics have as genuine and real a foothold in a universe where the highest consciousness is human, as in a universe where there is a God as well. "The religion of humanity" affords a basis for ethics as well as theism does. Whether the purely human system can gratify the philosopher's demand as well as the other is a different question. . . .[24]

Let individuals take their consolations and their happiness wherever and however they find them, James says, but the philosopher as philosopher occupies a standpoint outside religion. His discipline requires more circumspection; it does not recognize "divine revelation" as a legitimate, authoritative, overruling source of ultimate knowledge. The philosopher is vocationally committed, whatever his personal predilections (including any religious beliefs he may entertain or hold), to give reasoned reflection, rooted in a dispassionate survey of our collective and individual experience: this is the philosopher's *provisional* final word, until tomorrow.

Yet, this attitude and this distinction place James in an odd spot as a philosopher committed to defending "experience *against* philosophy": "if we are true philosophers we must throw our spontaneous ideals, even the dearest, impartially in with that total mass of ideals which are fairly to be judged."[25] And:

> The problem I have set myself is a hard one: *first,* to defend (against all the prejudices of my "class") "experience" against "philosophy" as being the real backbone of the world's religious life—I mean prayer, guidance, and all that sort of thing immediately and privately felt, as against high and noble general views of our destiny and the world's meaning; and *second,* to make the hearer or reader believe, what I myself invincibly do believe, that, although all the special manifestations of religion may have been absurd (I mean its creeds and theories), yet the life of it as a whole is mankind's most important function. A task well-nigh impossible, I fear, and in which I shall fail; but to attempt it is *my* religious act.[26]

James's "religious act" is, in essence, his formulation and dogged advocacy of a naturalistic creed that can permit itself to take seriously the experience of the private imagination and lonely heart in its struggle for release from isolation and despair and its striving for the vindication of hopefulness.

## Exceptional Mental States

> He has short hair and a long brown beard. He is wearing a three-piece suit. One imagines him slumped over his desk, giggling helplessly. Pushed to one side is an apparatus out of a junior-high science experiment: a beaker containing some ammonium nitrate, a few inches of tubing, a cloth bag. Under one hand is a piece of paper, on which he has written, "That sounds like nonsense but it is pure onsense!" He giggles a little more. The writing trails away. He holds his forehead in both hands. He is stoned. He is William James, the American psychologist and philosopher. And for the first time he feels that he is understanding religious mysticism.
>
> Dmitri Tymoczko, "The Nitrous Oxide Philosopher,"
> *Atlantic Monthly,* May 1996

James's abiding fascination with religious mysticism is just one instance, but was possibly the most elusively compelling for him personally, of his more comprehensive interest in "fringe" experiences of all kinds. He was a great patron of marginal men, a defender of extraordinary and sometimes quite literally unbelievable experiences that gripped his imagination, not because he had undergone them himself but, perhaps, especially because he had not. They intrigued him and offered the richest imaginable territory in which to explore his intuitive sense that there is a great deal more to reality than crosses the threshold of our mundane consciousness. He hoped to "verify" at least some of those remarkable experiences, either for himself or for others. Of course, there are limits to our ability to verify another's experience, but at the least James wanted to push back the barriers—in the form of a priorism, narrow scientism, and mainstream conventionalism—which would prevent individuals from owning their own original experiences directly and without the prejudice of artificial stipulations about what is empirically possible.

Professional philosophers, alas, verify few enough realities of any kind, at first hand. James was always thrilled for the opportunity to engage the world outside his study directly, without the filter of others' interpretations or the natural drag of inertial blindness—hence his oddly elated response (mentioned in the Introduction) to being shaken from his bed in 1906 by the great San Francisco earthquake. He claimed to have felt "no fear, only admiration for the way a wooden house could prove its elasticity, and glee over the vividness of the manner in which such an 'abstract idea' as 'earthquake' could verify itself into sensible reality."[27] Excitement in response to external events, large or small, is itself an "exceptional mental state" in its own right besides being provocative of such states, for some temperaments. In James's view, it taps in to "dynamogenic" reserves of energy, and we all possess access to such reserves. As I read James on this, he intends no mystical or supernatural claim but an assertion of natural capacities within our normal constitution but beyond our normal consciousness.

So it was that he attended seances, defended alternative medical "healers" against his own medical profession,[28] and generally lent sympathy and support to embattled claimants of the offbeat and unusual. In some ways his attitude is the purest application of J. S. Mill's classic liberalism as expressed most famously in *On Liberty*: if we would learn the truth and discard error we must not merely allow, we must *cultivate* minority points of view.

What makes a fringe experience different from the ordinary and everyday run of events, what makes it "exceptional," is both its comparative rarity and an element of surprise. Undergone by relatively few individuals, and by them only infrequently, the experience seems to the experiencer in each instance to deliver an unexpected twist of insight or perspective. It invariably changes how such experiencers think about themselves and the world, in profound and subtle ways. It may precipitate an extreme transformation of belief, a "conversion" of one kind or another, and it usually has for the experiencer a "meaning" not evident to third parties who must necessarily regard it remotely, even if sympathetically. "You really had to be there" is probably the fringe experient's best, though least enlightening, rejoinder to skeptics. This is a sphere of experience in which subjectivity is truly in the saddle.

The changes wrought in a fringe experience may be relatively ephemeral or lasting. In James's case we can speculate that the changes of outlook he himself experienced while under the influence of psychoactive substances, as reported above, were relatively impermanent: the intoxication passed; he donned again his philosopher's hat and set about trying to make sense of it after the fact. Those who are most profoundly and permanently altered by fringe experiences tend to accept them at face value and do not seek explanation in other terms. But James's experiences with mind-altering chemicals is also indicative of the philosopher's vocational immunity to fringe phenomena. It is one thing to accept experiences at face value, another to make retrospective sense of them in terms of a larger explanatory framework. The fact that James wanted to do both is remarkable and rare. Radical empiricism is just this attempt to do full justice to all our experiences while not abandoning critical acuity and the will to formulate truths about the world.

It is small wonder that so many philosophers and psychologists have had so hard a time grasping the scope and import of radical empiricism, and that James so frequently experienced frustration in the attempt to serve both of his chosen masters, experience and critical reflection. But it is significant that in his frustration he never wavered in his commitment to the first part of the program (doing justice to every experience); more often he grumbled about the second, the critical aspect of the philosopher's task. But as Wittgenstein's example would later show, we *can* stop doing philosophy whenever we choose. James would rather have chosen to let philosophy go than to falsify experience "as it comes." But his own work stoppages, when he would announce his conviction "that the desire to formulate truths is a virulent disease,"[29] were never more than holidays.

If James was immune to the fringe, he was enough impressed by what he clearly regarded as the profundity of his experiences with intoxicating substances to philosophize about them. He was not a "drinker" or habitual substance abuser; his drug use was "experimental" and infrequent. The painfully close experience of an alcoholic sibling must have disabused James of any temptation to engage in recreational mind bending. But his experiments did reinforce his strong sense of the varieties of possible experience, consciousness, and reality that elude our normal apprehension. He was an outsider to the spiritual longings characterizing most religious and mystical consciousness, but he was hardly a disinterested outsider. He came as close to sharing those feelings, those cravings for "more" than empirical consciousness has been thought capable of delivering, as he possibly could without actually possessing them.

He *was* an outsider to the experiences that most fascinated him and drew his philosophic attention, for the most part. By all accounts James did not himself undergo a fringe religious experience of the sort that is most often associated with religious mysticism. But he did have, and report, exceptional experiences, for instance, what he called his "Walpurgis Nacht" experience during a hiking vacation on Mt. Marcy in the summer of 1898. "I now understand what a poet is," he wrote to Mrs. James, in a flush of quasi-mystic excitement and "spiritual alertness" in which "it seemed as if the Gods of all the nature-mythologies were holding an indescribable meeting in my breast with the moral Gods of the inner life."[30]

What is a poet? Like many readers James had probably once thought of the poet as someone simply having a facility and a love for aesthetically pleasing arrangements of words, for the combination of aural and semantic properties of language artfully deployed. It is enough, this view holds, for a poet just to enjoy creating these effects without grasping their provenance in a complicated theoretical way: poets, after all, like to rhyme, either literally or figuratively, through the elegant use of figures and resonances. James the naturalist and democrat would have appreciated Poet Laureate Robert Pinsky's remarks that "poetry calls upon both intellectual and bodily skills," that "the medium of poetry is a human body: the column of air inside the chest, shaped into signifying sounds in the larynx and the mouth," and that the chief skill of poetic interpretation is one's own embodied awareness.[31] But after his sleepless night in the Adirondacks, James was perhaps in a position to view himself and his thought in a more seriously poetic way. The philosopher-as-poet is witness to an inner pageant involving personal impulse and impersonal nature, sometimes in conflict, often in turmoil, prospecting for meaning and for an unnamed "more," struggling in delight and frustration for words.

The mystic and romantic poets certainly seem to have lived their poems, or tried to, before penning them. But one who writes his experience is necessarily separated from it: in the act of putting it down he recreates the experience imperfectly and creates afresh the possibility of a *new* experience, the aesthetic experience of poetic appreciation or the cognitive experience of shared, communicated meaning. And so poets attempt to render, or anticipate, their experience symbolically, allegorically, with only the resources of this strange, wonderful, but limited linguistic medium to paint and point with; likewise does the philosopher attempt to render it, with words and concepts and metaphors and even the occasional graphic image. Poets and some philosophers are convinced that there is something deep but inchoate in the experience awaiting significant encounter, something potentially revelatory, pulse quickening, immediate, normally concealed, and rapidly remediated in words and associations if not entirely lost and forgotten.

Keats said that poetry ought to evoke a feeling of familiarity in the reader "as a wording of his own highest thoughts."[32] Wallace Stevens agrees that this is how most of us do in fact read poetry, those of us who read it at all: we listen for familiar "echoes." But there is also an experience of strangeness in poetry that can seem not exactly unfamiliar but also exceptional and sublime. Many of Stevens's poems, for instance, couched in familiar settings and dealing with everyday moments, can evoke this feeling. His "Sunday Morning" concerns skipping church, sipping coffee, and eating oranges in the sunshine while regarding the "freedom of a cockatoo." It has been called "the greatest spiritual poem in American literature."[33]

But what is the spiritual quality of an arrangement of words and sounds in ordered cadence? Can words, even in exquisite poetic combination, catalyze an experience of sharp immediacy, if not of full-blown transcendence? The answer must reside not in the words or the poetry considered in isolation, but only in relation to a particular person's peculiar sensibility, and in specific circumstances. In my own case I must report that while I love to read and have enjoyed particular occasions of reading and hearing immensely, I have never found the written word to be a catalyst of immediacy so much as a faint reminder of past experiences and a harbinger of future possibilities. I seem to recall a time in remote preadolescence when it was possible to so lose myself in a text that the experience was entirely luminous, self-containing, and in some ways self-transcending; but while I can still luxuriate in the experience of reading, reflecting, and verbally ordering my own thoughts, that particular form of youthful self-forgetfulness now seems much harder to come by.

I would not presume to generalize from my experience in this respect, except to suppose that children as a rule probably are much closer to their own sources of personal transcendence. That is what makes "mindful parenting" both a challenge and a deeply gratifying delight: children are naturally receptive to occasions of spontaneous and unforced learning, playing and doing (those distinctions themselves being artifacts of adult convention) that exploit their own native curiosities and predilections. I believe that children are naturally predisposed as well to the idea of personal relatedness in many directions and, so, are intuitively equipped to comprehend the idea of life as a chain, to internalize it and to construct all their outer relations in its light. In short, children are natural-born poets.

A poet may also, by the way, be someone who gets so stirred up about some inner commotion that he behaves unwisely in his outward conduct, in a rebound and an excess of high spirits. James evidently did this, hiking far beyond sensible limits the day after his Walpurgisnacht. But no one ever claimed that fringe experiences and exceptional mental states were "sensible"!

A few words in passing, now, about all the specific "exceptional states" James studied but that we will pass over lightly here. James is popularly associated, among those who are at least passingly familiar with his interest in fringe phenomena, with religious mysticism and chemically induced alterations of consciousness. But the subject titles of his 1896 Lowell Lectures[34] reveal a wide eclecticism of interest in fringes of all kinds, the only obviously common denominator being the suspicion and unease that most of them tend to elicit from most of us: dreams and hypnotism, automatism, hysteria, multiple personality, demoniacal possession, witchcraft, degeneration, and genius. Much of this material later made its way into the Gifford Lectures, which were to become *The Varieties of Religious Experience*. Discussions of the subliminal and the subconscious anticipated and reflected the incipient cult of Freud and presaged the more speculative elements of James's conclusion in *Varieties*. These and other ideas in the Lowell Lectures fed many of James's popular essays such as "The Energies of Men." James thought that we fail to exploit our reserves of mental and "moral" energy because so much of our life goes on at a level that is unexceptional in the extreme; but exceptionality is not hostile to the everyday, just unfamiliar to it.

Exceptional mental states, mystic consciousness, alternative states of awareness, psychic phenomena, the subconscious, religious experience, mental healing, mind cure: all of these, for James, demonstrate that everyday consciousness is but one possibility and far from the most interesting. James's treatment of exceptional mental states is consistent with his views on subjectivity and transcendence, and he means to corroborate those views in turn. Similarly, his point in emphasizing religious experience is not that it is religious but that it is *experience*, genuine, heartfelt, intense, undismissable, and, likewise, for psychic experience or alternative consciousness generally. When experience is marginal, understanding is weakest; that is where our attention and study stands to gain the most.

The suggestion I want to entertain here is that exceptional mental states may be *candidates* for transcendence, as James understands this phenomenon, but they may also provide *analogies* of transcendence for those who have not experienced such states. But let us be quick to remind ourselves that James rules out the old-fashioned, pre-Kantian, precritical variety of naive transcendence as knowledge beyond, behind, or above experience—rules it out, that is, as a subject of fruitful philosophical investigation (but not as a respectable personal conviction for anyone who happens to find such beliefs vitalizing or hopeful). And James rules it out for himself, insofar as the radically empirical hypothesis he favors is incompatible with the notion that we can speak sensibly and knowingly of that which transcends all possible human experience:[35] "the only things that shall be debatable among philosophers shall be things definable in terms drawn from experience. (Things of an unexperienceable nature may exist *ad libitum*, but they form no part of the material for philosophic debate.)"[36]

This "postulate" of radical empiricism is a working hypothesis, or better, a proposal based on past futility: all previous attempts to illuminate the "unexperienceable" have foundered, for reasons not hard to fathom. Calling the restriction or prohibition against debating the unexperienceable a postulate does not of itself eliminate the possibility that there *are* unexperienceable things (for us) in our universe, as James acknowledges in his bracketed caveat. Nor does it render otiose the speculation that some philosopher has said, or will, say something true about it (though we could never know or show this). But of course an unexperienceable *object* is, for purposes of understanding, communication, and discourse, a philosophic oxymoron. An object is supposed to complement and fulfill the perceptual or intentional act envisioning it; but the unexperienceable is, by definition, excluded from the field of what can possibly enter into our perceptual range.

Yet, James frequently attests a personal belief—perhaps more a personal hope and wish—that the universe contains wider spheres of consciousness than we ordinarily apprehend. This sense of something "more" that is tantalizingly near the threshold of our awareness but still not quite tangible, which exceptional mental states may possibly approach, leads him to temper the predominantly celebratory spirit of his appreciation for the multilayered varieties of experience with an expression of regret for the tragic dimension of a life whose soaring moments are all too often yoked to toxic degradation:

> it is part of the deeper mystery and tragedy of life that whiffs and gleams of something that we immediately recognize as excellent should be vouchsafed to so many of us only in the fleeting earlier phases of what in its totality is so degrading a poisoning.[37]

The catalytic poison in this instance is alcohol, but James's gleaming, fleeting "excellences" may arrive through many and various portals of experience. What is the strange, wonderful, darting mysterium we recognize but cannot hold? No very precise answer is possible for James, of course, or there would be more than a "whiff" to inspire us. Evidently, though, he intends not intoxication, as such, but whatever it is about this state that leads one to affirm and embrace the world even while admitting its deficiencies.

There is a serious danger, however, in radical empiricism's willingness to accept the personal testimony of individuals as the best and final arbiter of what their own experience means, of critical surrender to superstition and delusion. The late Paul Feyerabend's intellectual anarchy may have been a good motivator of valuable reflections in the philosophy of science; but whatever the worth of "anything goes" as a slogan and working principle in tightly contained spheres of inquiry, as a general rule of life it is disastrous. James was not unacquainted with human eccentricity, and we have noted that he had a real affection for "cranks" and characters of all kinds (which is partially but not wholly accounted for by the present discussion of his philosophical interest in fringe consciousness). But what would he make of *our* cranks, our alien abductees and "recovered memory" twelve-steppers? We can be sure that he would feel a healthy portion of spontaneous sympathy for many of them, but we can be equally certain that he would stop short of conceding to them the last and total word in accounting for their own peculiar psychobiographies. Unfortunately, many of our contemporaries are less immune to silliness committed in the name of professional rectitude.[38] We must wonder: if organic origins do not matter in our evaluation of an experience, what is the check on misreporting personal experience?

We have noted the biographical fact about James that he did not personally, habitually undergo experiences of the sort he classifies under the rubric of "exceptional mental states." There was his Mt. Marcy Walpurgisnacht experience and perhaps some others like it, but our understanding of what exactly he experienced on such occasions is necessarily scant; and there were his experiments with drugs. There may be a tendency among some inquirers to suppose an important distinction between spontaneous and artificially induced experiences, in this regard. But "artificial" is a difficult and problematic adjective for a radical empiricist. It may not matter, for James, what precipitates an exceptional mental state. There may be no "check"; we may have to err on the side of excess.

Generally, James insists that organic explanations of mystic vision, indeed of subjectivity in any form, are largely beside the point. Again, for instance,

> the sway of alcohol over mankind is unquestionably due to its power to stimulate the mystical faculties of human nature, usually crushed to earth by the cold facts and dry criticisms of the sober hour. Sobriety diminishes, discriminates, and says no; drunkenness expands, unites, and says yes. It is in fact the great exciter of the *Yes* function. . . . Not through mere perversity do men run after it.[39]

Some might call alcohol and other intoxicants "artificial," but James is not pointing to the genesis of an episode of imaginative flight but, rather, emphasizing the resultant expansiveness, the sense of cosmic unity and affirmation, and the general feeling of existential reconciliation. *These* are not artificial, no matter the instigating agency. They are vehicles of transcendence. But subjectivity and transcendence are not unqualified goods; they are rimmed by relations of consequence that must figure prominently in our final evaluations.

James did not want to *sanctify* psychic phenomena, mystical experiences, religious feelings, or alternative forms of consciousness with the imprimatur of science; he wanted to enrich science and philosophy with the recognition that all of these marginal experiences are real and worthy of systematic study. They do not need sanctifying, if we trust experience, because they are as sanctified, as legitimized, as they need to be. But they are challenges to our understanding. James did not understand the dismissive attitude. Even a marginal experience, if pervasive enough, can portend depths of insightful awareness unavailable to ordinary consciousness.

We need, however, to qualify these remarks about James's broad hospitality to the margins of religious or spiritual experience. Millions in our late twentieth century society who were previously disaffected from mainstream religion have sought to recover some semblance of institutional devotion, thus producing an explosion of interest in experimental "spirituality." The New Thought movement, that "deliberately optimistic scheme of life" James helped to propel,[40] has flourished and spawned offshoots that are sometimes difficult to distinguish from the more recent enthusiasms and excesses of the "New Age." James would mostly be delighted, I think, at so much fervor fomenting around so many "untaught sallies of the spirit" (in Emerson's happy phrase). The new spirituality poses questions and engenders practices not conventionally or exclusively of either the flesh or the devil, practices evidently a great deal more satisfying to those who resonate to them than the old-time religion.

However, this spirituality also propounds attitudes and assumptions a Jamesian is bound to reject. A relatively moderate, representative example of this is the popular contemporary writer Ken Wilber, whose views seem to span several of these new spiritual camps. Here is a dust jacket sample of his thought:

> The desires of the flesh, the ideas of the mind, and the luminosities of the soul all are perfect expressions of the Radiant Spirit that alone inhabits the Universe, and sublime gestures of that great perfection that alone outshines the world. There is only One Taste in the entire Kosmos, and that taste is Divine, whether it appears in the flesh, the mind, or the soul. . . . From One Taste all things issue, to One Taste all things return. . . .[41]

This insistent assertion of "Kosmic" unity, not as an ideal but as a present reality—all appearances notwithstanding—is about as un-Jamesian as one can imagine. Perhaps a case can be made for its congruence with Emersonian idealism, but it is also a standard tenet of many of the avatars of New Thought who like to invoke Emerson and James together as their co-inspirational patrons. The Unity School of Christianity, for example, affirms in its standard liturgy "only one presence and one power in all the universe, God the good, omnipotent." And the motivational/self-help industry is glutted with advocates of the related idea that we can "manifest" reality simply by holding our heartfelt desires steadily in mind, or in "Divine Mind." This is the essential message of Wayne Dyer and Deepak Chopra, for instance, in books outlining how we can "get what we really, really, really want." And The Celestine Prophecy,[42] a "spiritual mystery," generously heralds "a new era of increased awareness and spirituality."

On the one hand, I am sure James would not mind lending a little moral support, but, on the other, despite superficial resemblances to familiar Jamesian themes—the idea of tapping latent spiritual energies and connecting with "your own personal energy" to "make a difference" in the world, for instance[43]—this is decidedly not James's own worldview. A pluralistic universe contains many tastes, sensibilities, and sources. It contains no set destiny or return destination. All is not divine, nor do all souls show signs of being on a journey of expanding consciousness and growing spirituality. We do not inhabit a universe without limits, nor can we always "manifest" and enjoy our hearts' desires and get what we want. James, and the Rolling Stones, knew better.

A less moderate example of the neospiritual "taste" of our time is suggested by the best-selling books of James van Praagh. Not only is he open to the possibility, as James evidently was, that "mediums" can put us in touch with the dear departed; van Praagh claims he is one himself, with a "hotline" to the spirit world. Many of our contemporaries seem to believe him. Maybe he (like Jane Roberts's "channel" Seth?) has James's number. According to van Praagh, "Being spiritually disciplined does not mean that we have to live a serious life. Why get bogged down in temporary earthly conditions?"[44] This may not sound like a serious question, but the sober pragmatic response is that we are planted on terra firma whether we like it or not, and only a responsible seriousness—not bleak solemnity—about our situation can de-bog us. The attitude of indifference toward "local" concerns does not make for healthy communities or a full spiritual life. Real engagement in the affairs of neighborhood, city, nation, world, and planet is indispensable.

James's interest in the margins was partly motivated in the first instance by his "personal search for a workable solution to his own emotional and physical difficulties,"[45] but this can be overstated. Certainly the marginal experiences reported in Varieties were as alien to James's own personal experience as could be, yet his personal sympathy for those who reported such experiences could not have been stronger. It makes a great deal more sense to take James's commitment to experience at large, as well as his overall sense of cosmic mystery, as endlessly particularized and personalized, as the straightforward explanation of his interest in the margins they appear to be. "Not only that anything should be, but that this very thing should be, is mysterious!"[46]

## Absorption

"Contentment" is work so engrossing that you do not know that you are working. . . . It is always the paradox of contentment—of happiness or joy—that to remain at its pitch it must include no consciousness of itself; you are only content when you have no notion of contentment.

Donald Hall, *Life Work*

. . . once attention is shifted from the future and we begin to enjoy activities at the time we do them and for what they are, we have transcended the mentality that views life as a process of mediation toward distant ends.

John Lachs, *Intermediate Man*

We have considered the definition of "transcendence" as "joyous and forgetful absorption in what is present to perception, without regard to spatiotemporal conditions." Of course there are also experiences of absorption that are neither joyous nor forgetful, which seem in fact to wallow immersed in acute consciousness of time, place, and circumstance: painful and unpleasant experiences in which our undivided awareness is suffused with negative emotions or undesired sensations. A chronic toothache may be impossible to transcend. So may be a rancorous quarrel, a violently traumatic incident, an ugly confrontation. Typically, we endure and outlast these upsets to our equipoise, but just as typically they exact a price and leave a scar. Happily, this is not the species of absorption concerning us here.

We are occupied instead with *absorption as transcendence*, "the form of experience which affords the possibility of personal happiness and joy," that "something in all of us" which, by its extreme variability, and ultimate ipseity, seems indifferent or even hostile to the conceptual harness of philosophic expression." It is tied to our more exceptional experiences, and for James this links it inextricably with the subjective, the personal, and the ineffable. We *can* talk about it, but we need to be aware that our talk cannot capture or contain the experience in its vitality and total importance for life, cannot preserve the way it *feels*, and that, the way it feels, is its very core and substance. A transcendent experience minus the subjective is no more than a pale and partial rendition of something originally vibrant and compelling. The experience of transcendence is primary, immediate, dynamic; the discursive reconstruction of the experience is derivative, detached, arrested. This must be ridiculously obvious to the person in the street. Who but a philosopher or other professional talker and writer would entertain for a moment the notion that *talk about* happiness can even remotely approximate the intrinsic value of happiness itself or begin to approach it experientially?

This resistance to "talk" or "speech" is the anti-intellectualist wariness of conceptual distortion and insufficiency we have already encountered in James. The intended contrast is not with speechlessness as such but with the experiential immediacy that talk tends to obscure. Radical empiricists need not commit vows of voluntary silence, then, but if they do not they are stuck with the problem of how to reveal and articulate an immediacy that most talk covers over. If they are smart they will not commence to solve the problem with sweeping denunciations of all talk, which after all is the only way we know of sharing and learning from one another's experience. They may agree with the sentiment that "under all speech that is good for anything there lies a silence that is better,"[47] but they should also register the irony that the author of that statement wrote a great many volumes of distinctly *un*silent books.

And then there is the early Wittgensteinian kind of silence, which nobly abstains (for awhile) from the vice of hypocrisy. In the preface to his then-final word in philosophy, the *Tractatus*, Wittgenstein wrote: "What can be said at all can be said clearly, and what we cannot talk about we must pass over in silence."[48] And then, defying tradition, expectation, and precedent, he *was* philosophically silent for many years, until with the *Philosophical Investigations* he regained his voice (or assumed a new one). Philosopher of science Karl Popper had the exactly right rejoinder (or "conjecture"): "But it is only here," in the regions of our deepest perplexity, "that speaking becomes worthwhile."[49] That was a response that the mature Wittgenstein evidently took to heart. In this he acted at last as James did always: proceeding with caution, *but proceeding*.

While *transcendence* is often interchangeable in meaning with *happiness*, they are not the same. All transcendence contains elements of happiness and joy, but the reverse is not always so: there are occasions of immanent happiness just as there are of sorrow and pain. There is, for instance, the joy of gustatory delight in a pint of good stout—to select a personal example not everyone will relate to but which comes immediately to my mind. Perhaps most of the simple sensory pleasures fall into this category, as events giving instant, immanent happiness, more-or-less precisely located (to the extent that this is ever true of *any* sensation), and then passed by. But if I linger over my stout, if I become aesthetically transfixed by its savor, if in the process I forget my (present) self in an upwelling recollection of the past, and so on, in some such fashion what begins as simple, immanent enjoyment may then ascend to another level of appreciation altogether. It may even attain a level of what we might wish to call transcendence, not unlike Proust's evocation of childhood in the unassuming experience of tasting a madeleine cake in *Remembrance of Things Past*. I do not mean, necessarily, anything quite as vaulting as what we just saw James calling an intoxicated awakening of the "mystical faculties." I rarely consume enough stout at a sitting to do that in any case, though perhaps it was different—although he said it was not—for Walker Percy and his bourbon:

> The joy of Bourbon drinking is not the pharmacological effect of $C_2H_5OH$ on the cortex but rather the instant of the whiskey being knocked back and the little explosion of Kentucky U.S.A. sunshine in the cavity of the nasopharynx and the hot bosky bite of Tennessee summertime—aesthetic considerations to which the effect of the alcohol is, if not dispensable, at least secondary.[50]

Again, James finds no contest between the experience of transcendence, per se, and *talk*—philosophical or otherwise. One is a primary and living reality, the other a derivative and parasitic reverberation. But our concession that the simple and immanent enjoyment of some sensory stimulus (such as a favorite libation or a tea cake) may escalate into full-blown transcendence should give pause. Consider: there are some individuals whose paradigm of personal happiness is found in talk, of one kind or another. They include the readers, writers, and dramatists among us. Some are philosophers. James himself is a perfect example. May they not find transcendence in the scratching of a pen, the tap of a keyboard, the resonance of a lecture hall?

We need, then, to distinguish the content and intention of talk from the experience of it. When our focus is on that, on the experience of communicating, verbalizing, manipulating symbols as not only a purposive activity but as a thing worth doing for its own sake and for the sheer joy of doing it, we have come full circle from intellectualism back to life.

Joy, enjoyment, happiness, and contentment are all names for a quality of experience that is most propitiously realized, it seems, unconsciously. If we transfer our attention deliberately, with the express purpose of cultivating the present and reaping momentary happiness, we may compromise what Donald Hall calls the paradox of contentment and lose that fragile flower of unforced delight. Maybe it is possible to be too intent, too methodical, too deliberate in our quest for transcendence; maybe a "quest for transcendence" is doomed to self-destruction from the start, but, then, so must what Russell called the "conquest of happiness." This is unacceptable, for James at least. He insists on thinking of the universe as hospitable to our "innermost" demands, the most urgent of which is happiness.

Hall is right to stress the forgetfulness, the unconsciousness of transcendent happiness. But he surely overstates the case. We can be happy and know that we are, and still have the experience of time and space and circumstance seeming to "drop away," in a manner of speaking. But he expresses an important point, in calling attention to the absorptive quality of our greatest contentment.

Our definition of transcendence ("joyous and forgetful absorption in what is present to perception, without regard to spatio-temporal conditions") stipulates an insouciance or lack of regard for time and place, and this is the kind of unconsciousness that may be a condition of transcendence. But "without regard to" may be confusing or misleading: we *are* spatio-temporal beings. Our lives would not last long if we actually and frequently acted without such regard; we have no choice. Nearly everything we do reflects the mostly tacit and unconscious *but essential* regard we must have for our situation and circumstances in general, if we are to stay (as the psychologists and law courts say) "in touch with reality." The practical demands of life decree a severe check on all our more imaginative impulses: the uncontested reality, the only reality that "practicality" requires us to acknowledge, is the public and impersonal sphere of unexceptional everydayness.

This is a miserly point of view, this "practicality." In any balanced and rounded view of life it is indispensable; but if we allow it to be our only window on the world, or the only point of view we privilege as real and important, it represents a most desultory and impoverished mentality. It then ignores (or worse, castigates) the available riches of a varied and immediate inner life, with levels upon levels of awareness surpassing the everyday.

The varieties of inner experience exceed formulation. This is one reason why James and the other pragmatists (and Santayana) are so insistent that we recognize, appreciate, and *enact* the possibilities of existence. If there were no such alternative plateaus of consciousness within the range of our perception, the legal convenience of reducing our touch of reality to this single point would be a metaphysical terminus as well. It would exhaust the field and simplify life immeasurably, and unconscionably, if we agree with James that "the world of our present consciousness is only one out of many worlds of consciousness that exist."[51]

When James speaks of the "many worlds of consciousness," he does not just mean those exotic and intriguing netherworlds of the supernatural about which he and others speculated so cryptically, and which they supposed to intrude into our consciousness in extraordinary and mysterious ways: via the unconscious, in dreams and visions, or through the agency of ingested substances such as made James seem to speak, almost Pentecostally, in alien "tongues." Or so he thought, when he was under the influence of nitrous oxide; later it seemed to him, as it seems to his sober readers, so much gibberish. His "Hegelisms"—"nonsense and on-sense"—read like pure (if clever) parody, however profound they may have seemed on first entering James's pickled consciousness.

James also has in mind those more "normal" altered states of awareness that can accompany relatively simple activities but which, for a time, take us out of ourselves and permit a re-visioning and renewal. Walking can have this transformative effect. It certainly did for Alfred Kazin: "I need to walk in these streets as I need to pray and to dance; somehow it is only when I walk alone that I feel the possibility of doing either."[52] There are physiological reasons why this should be so, and James is interested in them. In his view, however, that is a separate issue that in no way undermines the potentially transcendent character of such experiences, no matter how they come about. However we get there, when we are in a transcendent state of mind we have entered a different "world of consciousness." As noted in our previous discussion of Jamesian subworlds, there may be as many such realms of conscious experience as there are occasions for individuals to take an active interest in anything they can thematically uphold and elaborate for their own or others' attentive gaze.

We discussed the jejune "practicality" that has no use for any but the most common and conventional ways of taking things. But here we must introduce a crucial pragmatic proposal for the revision of what is ordinarily understood as "practical." That sense of practicality dismissive of the exceptional, the rare, and especially the privately transcendent, is not James's. Instead, he recognizes the practicality of anything that produces real and desired effects in anyone, whether anyone else experiences the same effects or not, whether anyone else even grasps them as realities or not. James concludes *Varieties* with the insistence that "that which produces effects within another reality must be termed a reality itself, so . . . we [have] no philosophic excuse for calling the unseen or mystical world unreal." And, "God is real since he produces real effects."[53]

Does "God" produce the effects? Or does the God *hypothesis?* This distinction, and this way of posing the question, may strike the religious experient as *extra*-experiential, an outsider's question. As a matter of plain fact, the God hypothesis produces "real effects" in countless individuals only because they have taken it beyond the hypothetical stage in the conduct of their own lives. For the rest of us it remains at most (pending "verification") a hypothesis. The first point here is just that whether we call the invigorating agency "God" or something else will and should depend upon who *we* are (and on the role "God" plays in the disposition of our lives). A second point, also important, is that James would stand by his claim that "God" produces real effects and, so, must be real, even if the evident fact of widespread religious devotion among humans of all times and places were very different, if there were only one lonely soul to report a vital firsthand relation to the divine. Why should the impulses of a single individual be sacrosanct? Because for James, as for Emerson, experience is always some *one's*, and if it is real for them it is presumptively to be respected by us. We are social beings, and pragmatism is a social philosophy; but we are also all still "single individuals" at the bar of experience that constitutes for us the only world we can claim truly to know. "Other world! there is no other world," James significantly reports Emerson saying, "than this one, namely, in which our several biographies are founded."[54]

Of course the hypothesis of "another reality" may seem question begging from the start, but James's point—consistent with radical empiricism's allegiance to the integrity of individual subjectivity—is that if we are to respect the experience of those who attest active, personal commerce with the unseen, we must accept the reality of their reports. *Within the ambit of their own experience*, the unseen produces real effects in them and is, therefore, real.

The "unseen" produces the effects?! *Delusions* of the unseen, reasonably counters the skeptic. Here the radical empiricist has a large bullet to bite: yes, he admits, perhaps the mystic is deluded. But his own experience, as he knows and shares it, is authoritative *for him*. Something real has produced these salutary effects. Calling it delusory simply displaces the question of what that reality may be. If the skeptic wishes, it is a "real delusion"; but if so, and if the effects are really salutary—if they "make life worth living"—then perhaps we all should wish to be so deluded.

But this is too easy. It is the *Brave New World* mentality that harbors tyranny under the cover of tolerance and is unable or unwilling to recognize deluded happiness as a perversion of human good. The drug-induced bliss and passivity of Huxley's vision is the reductio ad absurdum of the claim that "if it feels good it *is* good." Pragmatism and radical empiricism are committed neither to this attitude nor to the acceptance of any delusion that happens to "work" for someone. It is possible to take the hedonist's experience seriously without being tempted to honor or emulate it.

James the psychologist knows the difference between psychotic delusion and genuine experience. It is just that James the philosopher knows of no way to capture and convey the living reality of transcendence from an external vantage. Attempts to do so always end in the annihilation of the subjectivity at its core, and thereby sacrifice the transcendent character of the experience. But unlike some philosophers who also speak of verifying realities, he does not conclude that their elusive quality renders them unreal. If the cost of respecting and preserving genuine experience is to leave an unknown quantity of delusion uncorrected, he will gladly pay it. And as a practical matter we have little choice but to pay. Beyond the extreme instances of delusion, we have no sure way of identifying or even characterizing many of the lesser falsehoods to which we are all likely susceptible.

How many successful ventures are launched under banners of questionable confidence and driven by doubtful assumptions? A little delusion, sometimes, may be our greatest asset in producing the "real effects" we need to achieve desired ends. That is one of the large lessons James conveys under the banner of "will to believe."

This liberality in tracing trails from "real effects" to real causes, and discerning realities at the trailhead, is related to one reason why James ultimately rejects, and rejects sharply, transcendental idealism. His contention is that if this or that description of the world fails to manifest practical differences in particular ways, in our individual experience, it is a verbal sham. It must produce real effects to be real. But some "transcendental metaphysicians" are "refined supernaturalists":[55] they describe a reality not recognizably different from that of naturalism and science, in its effects as we encounter them; yet they suppose that because their descriptions allege an invisible genitive mechanism beneath and behind all our particular experience, they have articulated a lively alternative account of things. By contrast, the religious supernaturalism of the philosophically uncorrupted "common" folk at least expects the religious hypothesis to make a difference in definite and noticeable ways. "Difference" is what validates the claims and facts of religion if anything does, not the elegance of a grand but gratuitous religious philosophy.

For James, philosophical idealism is merely an interpretation, a redescription, of the facts of naturalism. It has no original facts of its own. Common or conventional religion may spawn its own facts, including the infusion of personal energy and meaning resulting, for some, from faith. These are practical facts, but their spiritual significance cannot be overstated.

If we are afforded the luxury of an occasional transcendent moment, it is only because we have so effectively habituated the rest of our time and attention to the immanent details of when and where we are, whence we have come, and what we propose to do when the spell of absorption lifts. But even more important than a broad and general grasp of our relation to the workaday world is the ability to apply such knowledge in the relatively simple but unceasing transactions (many unforgiving of neglect) that we must manage in a practical way, day after day. Some philosophers and mystics may find quotidian reality relatively uninteresting, from the airy standpoint of pure thought to which they may aspire, but they disregard it only at their peril. Those who lose or abandon their moorings in spatio-temporal particularity when they are fortunate enough to dodge all the gross potential disasters of daily living—street traffic would be one banal but deadly example—may be less nimble in avoiding the subtler kinds of collision with hard reality that result in mental disorientation and disordered lives.

But some point remains in calling attention to a peculiar kind of forgetfulness about the conditions of our life when we are absorbed in the moment, not in plotting the future or in regretting the past but just in reaping the enjoyment of present awareness. Yet, James also reminds us that the "luster of the present" is always backlit by possibilities just offstage, and our appreciation of possibilities is conditioned by what we have made and will continue to make of the past. Past and future thus impinge upon the present moment in ways that not only do not injure or compromise the experience of transcendence, but actually propel it.

We *can* be absorbed in a moment of passive contemplation or active engagement with some memory or past event as the focus of a transcendent experience. And we can be swept into a reverie about the future, whether our own or a far more distant and fantastically removed time and place; witness the phenomenon of fanatical enthusiasm provoked in some by science fiction. But these species of regard for past and future are different from that which obliterates the present moment in a rush of abstracted concern, worry, or disappointment. They represent a sense of time as dynamically continuous but also affording pockets of silent stillness in which we may slow down and contemplate its majestic sweep.

There are good reasons why James, with a personal and professional interest in abnormal psychology (he taught courses in the subject), should have wished to explore fringe experiences. He was vocationally committed to the project of seeking, through the study of mental pathology, greater insight into the normal. Whether abnormality is parasitic on the normal or vice versa is an intriguing question. James was convinced that every kind of experience may be instructive and that madness may be an even better teacher than what we have taught ourselves to call sanity. The line between pathology and exceptionality (which carries with it the possibility of profound insight) can be difficult to trace.

But for the majority of us who have not experienced that sort of exceptional mental state—paranormal or supernatural encounters, spirit or alien contacts, an overwhelming sense (possibly induced by an ingested substance) of the veil being lifted and Reality flashing a teasing glimpse and then receding into evanescence—we may still enjoy our moments of transcendent absorption. James seems to have regretted his own paucity of fringe experiences, as though he were missing something deep or revelatory that he might hook into if only he found the right "medium," listened to different voices, or swallowed or inhaled certain chemicals. The world would surely be a more enchanted place, in supernaturalistic terms, with more such "facts" in it. But it would be no more wondrous; there are wonders aplenty in the natural world, even if dry and prosaic naturalistic descriptions of it have tended to suppress this truth. James, we have noted, speaks of "facts" generated by unconventional beliefs that motivate such actions as he credits to mental "healers," whose cause he championed even as he disavowed any definite confirmation of their beliefs. A fact in this sense is not "scientifically" verified but is, he insists, a datum suggestive of a reality that convention, to its detriment, has missed.

James thinks that the "multiplication of facts" is necessary if our understanding is to grow. The naturalistic viewpoint is that in principle, in theory, and in the long run all of the facts will be accounted for by natural assumptions and standardized processes of inquiry. James says he would choose, if choose he must, to ally himself with the supernaturalists rather than with the naturalists and materialists.[56] But this is because the supernaturalists in question are really *global naturalists* in James's sense: they affirm the reality of their experience, and so they inhabit a wider and more various universe than "mere" or "pure" naturalism can recognize. They do not resist the multiplication of facts, points of view, perspectives, unconventional beliefs, and so on, as potentially instructive or even revelatory.

So, while many of us have not encountered the "fringe," we have had our moments of relatively "joyous and forgetful absorption in present perception" (while walking, reading, talking, engaging in various recreational activities). Every such moment may point the way to transcendence. We are not discussing some ethereal or exotic thing, but the usually small and passing events of daily living. The mystic has his Moments, and the rest of us have ours. I do not know whether we should call the difference one of kind or degree, and really we must suppose that it is only the full-fledged mystic who, presumably having experienced moments of transcendent absorption both large and small, is in a position to make such a determination (putting aside, if he can, any bias on the side of the heaven-rending Big Revelations he claims to know).

"Below, behind, above" ordinary experience is something glittering, transforming, and preeminently real: this is an attitude no longer quite respectable, for those who have read in modern philosophy a certain prohibition of old ways of thinking and speaking about reality.[57] The transcendent has to be located within ordinary experience, or else philosophy should leave it alone (leave it to religion and to the privacy of personal conviction) as beyond the scope of useful generalization.

But has not the foregoing discussion of fringe experiences suggested that, in James's view, there may be transcendent realities unavailable to ordinary consciousness? Yes and no. We need to be careful not to misunderstand "ordinary" here. As a radical empiricist, James disavowed interest in what was unexperienced or unexperiencable. All experience is "ordinary" in contrast to alleged transcendence that exceeds actual and possible experience. Some individuals, however, report "exceptional" experiences that are out of the ordinary in this sense. A radical empiricist is vitally interested in these reports *as* experience. Are they revelatory, hallucinatory, or what? Whatever they are, they are real (even if not compelling or coercive for others). What is real is a candidate for becoming ordinary, however rare or exquisite it is to the outsider, and however unexpected to the percipient.

Ordinariness for James is a recognition of continuity as a fundamental human reality. The common, ordinary, or everyday that James and Dewey exalt, following Emerson, blurs the lines between inner and outer, personal and public. James talks about "extraordinary mental states," for instance, as distinctively "inner" but not on that account irrelevant, unreal, or artificial. How telling it is that some defenders of artificial intelligence call our ordinary occupations and social conventions "artificial" as well. But the ordinariness to which Emerson and the Pragmatists urge our return is as real as can be. The ordinary is good *because* it is real, because it affirms the reality of our most familiar experiences and occupations. What we do, day to day, is real. To deny this is to invalidate the bulk of our experience.

We also need to invoke a distinction between the subjective experience of transcendence versus particular theories that purport to explain how transcendence occurs, whence it comes, and what it means. Theories do not yet matter, at the level of experience. And for the theorizing intellect it may be tempting to treat particular kinds of subjective experience as predictable variables (if theory X is true, then experience Y is likely) and to "explain them away." From either standpoint we face a disturbing disparity between subjective and objective, personal and theoretical issues. James's way of acknowledging the disturbance was to introduce the concept of "pure experience," with uncertain results.

There is another kind of ordinary-yet-exceptional experience that draws back from the fringe but pulls us closer to the transcendent temper undergirding James's global naturalism. It is the experience of "eternity" in a moment, the subject of the next section.

## Naturalism and Eternity

I have seen the sun break through
to illuminate a small field
for a while, and gone my way
and forgotten it. But that was the pearl
of great price, the one field that had
the treasure in it. I realize now
that I must give all that I have
to possess it. Life is not hurrying

on to a receding future, nor hankering after
an imagined past. It is the turning
aside like Moses to the miracle
of the lit bush, to a brightness
that seemed as transitory as your youth
once, but is the eternity that awaits you.

R. S. Thomas, "The Bright Field"

WILLIAM JAMES'S "SPRINGS OF DELIGHT"

> So live, that when thy summons comes to join
> The innumerable caravan which moves
> To that mysterious realm where each shall take
> His chamber in the silent halls of death,
> Thou go not like the quarry-slave at night
> Scourged to his dungeon; but sustained and soothed
> By an unflattering trust, approach thy grave,
> Like one who wraps the drapery of his couch
> About him, and lies down to pleasant dreams.
>
> William Cullen Bryant

Poets have often rhapsodized on the themes of eternity and transience, finding in them a point of convergence perhaps more obscure to most philosophers and traditional religionists (particularly those of a theistic bent). For some, eternity is nowhere *but* in that perception of passing illumination that is indifferent to past and future. These lines by Thomas and Bryant encapsulate a view of "eternity" and how we can best approach it—a view, I want to suggest, that fits very nicely with James's account of transcendence.

So do these by Whitman:

> There is that in me—I do not know what it is—but I know
>   it is in me. . . .
> I do not know it—it is without name—it is a word unsaid,
> It is not in any dictionary, utterance, symbol. . . .
> It is not chaos or death—it is form, union, plan—it is eternal
>   life—it is Happiness.[58]

Mystical William Blake also found "eternity in an hour." These poems lend themselves to a naturalistic interpretation according to which the concept of eternity is brought down to earth, back from the ethereal and the otherworldly. When eternity is thus available for our enjoyment—when we come to realize that it *is* available, that indeed it is all around and within—we then have attained a level of self-possession that surely marks an epoch in our development and a milestone on the path to our full assumption of responsibility for the conditions of our own happiness. This concept of eternity is not uniquely Jamesian, having been articulated by many other philosophers and poets; but his distinctive version of transcendence is illumined by an appreciative understanding of naturalized eternity.

The naturalized concept of eternity as a quality of perception, not a redemptive destination on the other side of life's door, is closely related to what I have called "transcendence as absorption," and it clarifies James's naturalism. In *Varieties*, especially, he is anything but hostile to supernaturalism. But this attitude only complements his persistent commitment to the overall project of furthering our naturalistic comprehension of every dimension of experience, religion included. *Varieties,* after all, grew out of a lecture course in *natural* religion and was consecrated to the advancement of a *science* of religions. The content of any particular religious philosophy or bundle of attitudes might teem with supernaturalism, but James (like Dewey) was dedicated to the task of explicating a natural framework within which the varieties of religious experience and the "logical respectability of the spiritualistic position" can be commonly gathered. "If there be such entities as Souls in the universe," James coyly proposes," they may possibly be affected by occurrences in the nervous centres."[59] This is vastly different from reducing religious experience to a single explanatory principle, which would violate James's sense of the irreducibility of the subjective. Reduction has no place in a science of religions as James intends it. But he nonetheless considers it an undertaking of great promise, in terms of our potential for "expanded consciousness," to discover and analyze something universal in the experience of religious feeling.

Religious feeling may (but need not) coalesce with transcendence. Most transcendent experiences are perhaps not "religious" in any traditional sense. The more prevalent phenomenon, certainly the least subject to unchecked speculation, is the biological-natural. It is not more "fundamental" than the religious or the subjective, but it is more nearly universal. That is, the biological manifestations of transcendent experience *are* universal, even if they are not universally reported or emphasized. Religious feeling is a particular manifestation of a more general, biologically rooted feeling of "zest" or "excitement" which James celebrates in various contexts.

When James refers to "the natural," he usually intends a contrast not with the supernatural but with the *artificial,* the experientially adventitious. Notice that this sense of artificiality is not the same as conventionality, and neither term gains significant meaning from a contrast with the biological. Much is natural that is not biological, and much that is conventional is natural, for James. And as I am using the term, *supernaturalism* for James is not strictly opposed to what I have called global naturalism. If all of this nonstandard terminology is confusing, we can regain our Jamesian balance by remembering that James takes experience seriously. He does not use any of these terms in order to exclude anyone's sincere conviction as to the real meaning of his or her own firsthand experience.

James's naturalism becomes problematic in weighing the distinction between a subjective experience of transcendence versus some particular theory purporting to account for it not in its own terms but in the theory's. Again, theoretical speculation does not arise at the level of "pure experience." If James is a naturalist, we suppose, he must accept the hypothesis that we can in principle "explain" transcendence. But as a radical empiricist, and a defender of experience of all kinds, he'll stubbornly refuse to explain it *away*. He deftly balances the two standpoints in part by recognizing explanation as a relative and instrumental, not absolute, good.

A further factor in the equation is James's belief that "fringe experiences" may reveal realities unavailable to normal or ordinary consciousness. It is not obvious how a naturalist per se actively entertains, and in James's case urgently seeks evidence for, the hypothesis of alternative "realities" and "worlds of consciousness," but the case is somewhat clarified for a global naturalist who is also a radical empiricist with a decisive orientation toward the future: we do not know, in advance, about the limits of "nature." Today's supernatural spookiness may be tomorrow's verified datum. Our evidence is slim. We do not know.

The idea of transcendence seems for many to connote, automatically, the immaterial and the ideal. Perhaps that is because of its traditionally religious associations or because of Western philosophy's long and unconsummated flirtation with dualism. It may seem, for whatever reason, a short and "natural" step from the ideal to the supernatural. Into this mix we must throw the question of naturalism. What kind of a naturalist is James? How does this bear on the "ideal" status of his version of transcendence?

I am going to propose a connection between transcendence and naturalism that the idea of "eternity" helps us to see. If this connection can be made perspicuous, we may then be in a position to reject, confidently, the criticism that radical empiricism is really idealism in sheep's clothing.

"When we try in good faith to believe in materialism, in the exclusive reality of the physical, we are asking our selves to step aside; we are disavowing the very realm where we exist and where all things precious are kept—the realm of emotion and conscience, of memory and intention and sensation."[60] But here we need to distinguish materialism from naturalism and to understand that it is possible both (1) to deny the exclusive reality of the physical, and (2) to assert the in-principle total inclusiveness of the natural. We can say most of what we want to say about our real and "precious" selves without recourse to the supernatural. And I think that James can say most of what he wants to say from a naturalistic perspective, even though he has very sympathetic things to say about supernaturalism in general.

James, despite his own dalliances with the supernatural—mostly, that is, with the reports of others who boasted of their own supernatural *liaisons*, James's attitude being more that of the voyeur—was firmly persuaded that perfectly natural accounts of transcendence were available and might for some natures be enough. Whether or not James thought a naturalistic idiom enough for himself, clearly he denied that others should settle for any form of explanation that seemed to them inadequate to the immediate realities of their own experience. But he usually resisted the popular confusion that mistakes naturalism for narrow materialism. We do not know nature's ultimate extent, its limits, or its largest "possibilities." That is why James was such a champion of ever more experience, more "facts" than materialism or any other theory can deliver. In this light, naturalism, though an invitation to theorize, is not just another theory; it is an attitude expressing our resolve to learn and advance. It is that candle in the darkness of superstition and un-self-critical supernaturalism and of whatever is unnatural in the sense of being alien to experience. For James, as for Dewey, experience and nature are twined. John Edwin Smith thinks Dewey had "an overriding concern to avoid the 'supernatural,'" and "never confronted a sophisticated version of what it might mean to 'transcend nature.'"[61] But he and James, despite differing emphases, regarded transcendence *within nature* as one of our most sophisticated possibilities. I agree with Ray Boisvert: "Philosophically the challenge becomes that of determining whether a radical empiricism can consistently admit the sacred. An open question thus replaces the closed rejection of the supernatural."[62]

With the explicit casting of nature *for us* as inextricably bound up with experience, we cannot allow ourselves to think that "nature" is a terminal concept, a fixed and settled point against which we may measure transitory experience. In this we must sometimes admit an inconclusiveness dictated by the evolving state of our own natural understanding. Whether we consider something "natural" at any given time is a function of the confidence we place in our current ability to account for it in familiar terms, or else in our ability—our "negative capability," Keats called it—to suspend any final accounting. Confidence and familiarity are fluid states, not immune to authority, fashion, or resolve. New paradigms of understanding, James noted, often undergo a predictable reception beginning in derision and ending in the critic's self-servingly forgetful acclaim.[63] And "if Messrs. Helmoltz, Huxley, Pasteur and Edison were simultaneously to announce themselves as converts to clairvoyance, thought transference, and ghosts, who can doubt that there would be a prompt, popular stampede in that direction?"[64]

Neuroscientists and medical physiologists continue learning more about the detailed workings of body and brain. In our nonspecialist attempts to assimilate these findings, we inevitably wander into interpretive territory that exceeds anything the scientists have "verified." Yet, such wandering is essential to our self-understanding. So long as we continue to think of scientific research as a disclosive activity adding to our total understanding of nature and her processes, and so long as we continue to pursue self-knowledge, we will continue to promulgate theories that radiate from basic research as spokes from a wheel. Not all of the spokes contribute to the wheel's structural integrity, nor do they all even add to its worth ornamentally. Some are gratuitous, some are aesthetically objectionable, some are hindrances to the wheel's natural function of rolling. But not to contribute our bit to the wheel's construction—and by the terms of this admittedly strained

metaphor this means to risk a false account of nature and our relation thereto—is just not an attractive alternative, for most of us.

What becomes slippery—to press the wheel metaphor just a little further—is the determination of proximity to the wheel's hub, the attempt to
specify how close a thought, statement, or theory comes to nature. "Nature" is a moving target and we are moving marksmen. The idea of nature
always reflects our current understanding and attitudes, and conditions
them as well, in a perpetual ballet. This is not a circumstance to deplore,
except insofar as it may frustrate our wish to draw ever closer to nature
and to possess confidence at any given moment in our having done so.
In the end, as many have observed, such movement—and the scientific
progress it promises—may be no less an article of faith than any speculative tenet of the religious imagination. But unlike dogmatic supernaturalism, such a faith is at least compatible with fallibilism, pluralism, and
cultural diversity.

The element of arbitrariness or caprice as an insulator of the supernatural is less than obvious, perhaps, when the "host" is not an individual but a
church or a faith-centered culture. Historically, societies in which religious
institutions pervade and shape every aspect of life have tended not to exalt
natural understanding as an ideal distinct from piety. But here we may
pause for a moment to consider some increasingly prominent possible ex-
ceptions to the claim that cultures with a heavily religious orientation, and
a tradition of specific religious values interpenetrating all spheres of life,
tend to denigrate nature and the ordinary. Kabbala is the tradition of Jewish
mysticism that finds occasions of transcendence in daily life. It fosters an
approach to living infused with a spirited and passionate sense of Godliness
in everything. "Jewish mysticism insists on finding God within the world
rather than escaping from the world,"[65] and in this we may observe in
passing an affinity with various spiritual traditions including Emersonian
transcendentalism and several subtraditions that trace some part of their
lineage to it. A crop of recent literature devoted to the "sacredness" of the
ordinary reflects a revival of interest in Jewish as well as New England mysticism, along with the more commonly recognized popular influence of
eastern thinking, especially Zen Buddhism. All of these separate traditions
converge on a shared attitude that is something relatively new in the context of most Western religious life, although the kabbala has a long, long
history (dating at least from the twelfth century A.D.).

Emerson, striding exhilaratedly across his "bare common," would heartily endorse this gloss on kabbala: "there are sparks of God hidden within all
material existence. The spiritual path is to discover these sparks, to raise
them and restore them to God—to become aware of the divine potential
within other people, within life situations."[66] In the Jewish tradition of spirituality, *transcendence* is another name for holiness or sacred practice, the

natural fruit of ritual observance aiming not for salvation beyond the present life but for fulfillment *in* life. And the Christian tradition, as well, marks
out this path: "I came that they may have life, and have it abundantly"
(John 10:10).

In less theological language, James similarly echoes this theme when
he insists on endorsing the identification of religious impulse with love of
life and a will to enhance it. "Not God but life, more life, a larger, richer,
more satisfying life, is . . . the end of religion."[67] There may be a significant
difference, however, between saying that God (or whatever name we wish
to give the focal object of a transcendent experience) is "hidden" in nature
and saying that he or it is latent, manifest, or immanent in nature. In the
former case we may have in mind a picture of nature as the film or screen
behind which reality resides and through which it occasionally peeks (or
through which we peek at it). In the latter, we can intend the full-blown
identity of nature and the object(s) of transcendence, without a metaphysical gap left unplugged. It seems fairly clear that mysticism opts for the language of hiddenness and revelation because this is the picture mystics find
most congenial and attractive. They do typically believe that reality in an
important sense is rooted "elsewhere," although it makes cameo appearances here in the palpable world, perhaps on a fairly constant basis.

A naturalist cannot truly accept the idea of an elsewhere in any ultimate sense, although its possibility may be open to him to map a geography
of nature that includes largely uncharted regions, such as the subconscious. If James is a naturalist, then, we must find a suitable translation of
his references to alternative realities that brings them back to earth, back to
space and time as we know them, and back to the "mapping" of nature; or
else we must give up the claim that he is a naturalist and not, after all, a
mystic.

Still, our earlier point holds: the naturalistic temper is open to correction, thrives on it, and in fact *requires* critical resistance if it is to endure.
When dogma encrusts science it ceases to be a naturalistic endeavor; the
same goes for everything else, certainly for everything claiming scientific
validation. And we can be more charitable to the mystic; we need not attribute to him a dogmatic temper, just a loyalty to what he perceives as the coercive content of his own experience. In any case, such loyalty is not finally
compatible with the spirit of fallibilism that must permeate the naturalist's
inquiries.

Putting these issues as we have, and viewing naturalism as opposed to
idiosyncratic individualism and mysticism, may seem to create trouble for
an interpretation of James as a naturalist. We have noted repeatedly that he
wants to preserve the integrity of individual experience and subjectivity *as
experienced*. Of course, experience in the first instance—which is a bit of a
redundancy, since experience in the full-blooded sense is by definition "in

the first instance"—is always individual and not collective. "Collective experience" is just a name for a lot of individual experiences that happen to have rendered the same results, converged on the same conclusions.

So, what can it mean for James to accept the authority of collective experience? In the first place, it means that no individual's experience as such has authority beyond itself. By the same token, no consensus is granted authority to undermine an individual's experience in this respect. We might suppose that this is indicative of an irreparable, unbridgeable discontinuity—ontological, psychological, or epistemic—between the subjective and the objective, for purposes of naturalistic explanation. If so, this is no more a special problem for James than it is a "fact of life" for us all.

Materialism may, depending on how it is articulated, be a constricted and impoverished reduction of human variety to an ultimately inadequate theory. It may also be the best available framework in which the correct theory must eventually be established. But naturalism is not committed to any of the main defects normally associated with materialism, such as that quoted earlier from John Updike ("disavowing the very realm where we exist").

James's subworlds are all the realms in which individuals live. We do not all live in exactly the same realms, nor do any of us occupy a single realm exclusively; and no good purpose is served by *counting* these worlds with the intent of limiting or reducing their number. Most of the time, the material realm of familiar objects engages us, sometimes the subatomic material realm; usually, the emotional realm of subjective feeling colors whatever other realms or worlds engage our attention at a given moment. We live in one world "at most"—a favorite saying of Donald Davidson's, according to his colleague John Searle—but in the present context such a claim would be ludicrous. We can speak of the *one* world that contains all actual plus all possible experience, but if we all live in *that* world we nonetheless all fail to cognize its total breadth. A being of "widest actual conscious span" would come closer than most of us do, in fact, to achieving that breadth of awareness; and James is tempted to call such a hypothetical being God. He is also inclined to hope that we will all become gradually, progressively more God-like in this sense.

We may believe that there is one ubiquitous substance or "material" upon which all subworlds supervene, or to which they all stand in some other relation of dependency that unifies *the* world; but if we are Jamesians, we will not be tempted to think that the worlds of experience in which we live are more real for whatever such unity they may be thought to gain from that relation. They are real as experienced. We should all be in favor of as much unity as is compatible with an honest rendering of subjective multiplicity, but no more.

Our emotional lives in particular, some materialists ("physicalists") allege, may be accommodated *as they are experienced by us*, in a naturalistic account that "explains" the relation between emotions and the body, mind and brain, and translates the language of feeling into that of physiology or chemistry but does not thereby trivialize or minimize the significance of the emotions and "all that we hold most precious." This is extremely controversial, and unless those who associate mind with the supernatural are willing to form a new association it is unlikely to be persuasive to them.

But though the materialist may fail to persuade, the point is that naturalism need not automatically shoulder the yoke of sterility that has burdened materialism. Naturalism reflects a grander vision holding that whatever may prove to be the correct theoretical explanation of "mind," nature is large and various enough to encompass it. There is a majesty and beauty in the idea that nature includes such wonders as thinking, dreaming, breathing bipeds like ourselves. Materialists, partly to their discredit but also due largely to the imaginative occlusion of those who cannot fathom a nature rich enough to contain all our experience and our hopes, have failed, historically, to convey this vision.

Materialism may be defined as the theory that only the material is real, and that whatever we believe to be real we must somehow relate, in a dependent way, to the material realm. Naturalism just says that whatever is real, experienced, or experienceable is a part of nature. It need not make any more specific claims about the alleged materiality, or otherwise, of nature, so long as its purpose is to avoid prejudicially foreclosing fresh experience and possible revelation. Global naturalism, like Peircean realism, insists above all that we not allow our philosophies to block the road of inquiry.

There are not very many materialists or "physicalists" nowadays comfortable with the characterization of their attitude as one asserting the "exclusive reality of the physical," if this is taken to exclude all of the relations of dependence not themselves straightforwardly physical. The realm of imagination, for instance, in which art is born, would be accounted a dependent of materiality since thought and feeling are, *ex hypothesi*, its sources. Does it compromise their status, their dignity, to assert such dependence? No, it is not clear why that should be thought to be the case, unless we assume that dependence necessarily entails inferiority in any important respect.

What of the "realm of emotion and conscience, of memory and intention and sensation"? Why is it unacceptable, why an affront to our real "selves," to assert a dependent relation to the material realm? Perhaps it strikes Updike and others as an assault on the freedom of the imagination, to locate the personally creative impulse in physical space and time (whatever exactly we mean by "locate"). But *should* it offend our sensibilities to believe that there is room in nature for all our experiences? Not unless we begin with a straitjacketed conception of nature. Yet, we need a nature with enough independence, enough verified facticity about it, to rein in the more fanciful flights of reported but uncorroborated experience. Pragmatism is a social philosophy in many respects, not least in treating knowledge as a product of intersubjectively converging experiences. Neither straitjacket nor floodgate is an appropriate metaphor to capture the normative relation between experience and nature.

## Santayana, Larks, and Barbarians

> I now understand Santayana, the man. I never understood him before. But what a perfection of rottenness in a philosophy! ... It is refreshing to see a representative of moribund Latinity rise up and administer such reproof to us barbarians in the hour of our triumph. [But] how fantastic a philosophy! ... Bah! Give me Walt Whitman....[68]
>
> James to G. H. Palmer, 2 April 1900

In spite of his bluster, James claimed to have "enjoyed" his former student's and colleague's "reproof," as he calls it, but his reproof of *what*, precisely?— radical empiricism? pragmatism? realism? Santayana's philosophy rejects but also embraces elements of each and was finally an outworlder to all philosophies, indeed to all human collectivities; he was a true and solitary original. But who exactly are the "barbarians" with whom James associates himself here?

For Santayana. Americanism—a mix of mercantile capitalism, Protestantism, philistinism, "genteel" Puritanism and callow optimism—was barbarism, and in his eyes James was its darling and champion, the embodiment of a modern sensibility from which the Latin" Santayana was bound to recoil. Of radical empiricism Santayana, in tones not necessarily critical, said that it is a "literary subject." James was being neither disingenuous nor sarcastic in expressing appreciation for Santayana's "style"[69] and deft advocacy of a point of view in philosophy that he, James, nonetheless found repugnant. "Santayana is both a 'gentleman' and a 'scholar' in the real sense of the words, an exquisite writer,"[70] he effused.

It is a tribute to Santayana's originality and elegance as a thinker as well as stylist that he could evoke such appreciation even from those whose views—like James's—he skewered. And "skewered" is just the right word to convey the tone of much of Santayana's polemic against views he found inhospitable. His writing abounds in frequent, withering professions of "abhorrence," "contempt," and wide-eyed astonishment at the credulity of those whose attitudes and opinions he disdains. When he wished it to, his pen could leak venom.

But "skewered" is surely not the right word to express the quality of the relationship, a somewhat complicated one, between these two men. They maintained a mutual respect despite the most pronounced philosophical and temperamental differences. And on at least one occasion Santayana declared himself to James in a way which, he insinuated, was for him uncharacteristically intimate ("I seldom write to anyone so frankly"). Speaking of the "tears" that stain his *Life of Reason,* he unveils in a letter to James a depth of real feeling for the ideal, the "vision of perfection" at the heart of his philosophy:

> It is not the past that seems to me affecting, entrancing, or pitiful to lose. It is the ideal. It is that vision of perfection that we just catch, or for a moment embody in some work of art, or in some idealized reality; it is the concomitant inspiration of life, always various, always beautiful, hardly ever expressible in its fulness. And it is my adoration of this real and familiar good, this love often embraced but always elusive, that makes me detest the Absolutes and the dragooned myths by which people try to cancel the passing ideal, or to denaturalize it. That is an inhumanity, an impiety, that I can't bear. And much of the irritation which I may betray . . . comes of exasperation at seeing the only things that are beautiful or worth having, treated as if they were of no account.[71]

Here are many intimations of eternity and transcendence, as Santayana regards them, and as many blunt and subtle points of difference with James. But the differences share strikingly common roots. The ideal as such excites James as it does Santayana, though for James it is much more a projection and goal than a realized thing caught in charmed moments of transient revelation. The phrase "always various" signifies heavily for James, too, as do the suggestions of inexpressibility, elusiveness, *and* familiarity. But in the end these two philosophers personify very different approaches to perfection and beauty and very different attitudes toward the total meanings of life.

Santayana is an oddly compelling figure and would deserve our attention here even if he had not articulated a position that highlights, by contrast, the Jamesian idea of transcendence. Santayana's philosophy actually echoes and reinforces James's at a number of points, particularly in its sometimes acerbic scorn for the profession of philosophy and the way it has nurtured an attitude of remoteness, on the part of philosophers, from the issues of real life. Like James, Santayana is a naturalist and an individualist. "A spirit with any honor is not willing to live except in its own way."[72] James would certainly endorse the individualistic ethos here, but would as certainly refuse to endorse the rest of the statement: "and a spirit with any wisdom is not over-eager to live at all." This refusal is one clue to the fundamental difference between their two opposed conceptions of transcendence. Unlike James, Santayana eagerly calls himself a materialist and is a classicist casting an image redolent alternately of Plato and Aristotle.

Despite the most profound differences they also share a deep conviction of the integral value of philosophy as the centering focus of a life well lived and of the ultimate worthlessness of philosophies that do not reciprocally guide and learn from life. Both were contemptuous of philosophies and conceptions that did not make a noticeable difference in the daily affairs of those who entertained them, and this is the firm basis upon which Santayana's intellectual heirs and enthusiasts may file a claim on his behalf for inclusion in the mainstream of American philosophy (a membership *he* might have wished to avoid, in any case). But Santayana was not merely being polite when he credited James with planting "seeds . . . which have sprouted into native convictions" and reported "a rather surprising happiness that I can invoke your authority in support of a great deal that I feared might seem rash in my opinions."[73]

Santayana has been the most prominent spokesman for a version of transcendence I want to examine in just enough detail to set it off from James's own version. And again, it is interesting to see how two very different perspectives derive from common ancestry. In this case, the two versions of transcendence—and of course there are many others that do not concern us here—derive in part from the shared incubus of naturalism and a naturalized concept of eternity. And when Santayana asks, rhetorically, "why should we not look on the universe with piety? Is it not our substance?"[74] he owns squarely to a naturalism that James also held, if more guardedly. The official neutrality of "pure experience" forced upon James a greater caution than he probably felt in admitting his own naturalist and even materialist biases. In addition, his libertarianism forbade as tough minded a declaration as Santayana's that "all our possibilities lie from eternity hidden in [nature's] bosom." But he had no difficulty sharing the view that "soul is the last bubble of a long fermentation in the world" and that nature "is the dispenser of all our joys" and "the home of all our happiness." He was less willing to assert—but not, I think, to believe—that nature is the "source of all our energies."[75]

Most of all, on this issue of transcendence, James and Santayana are united in the belief that it is indispensably ingredient to our happiness and that happiness is the crown of life. But perhaps the crown sits more comfortably and as a matter of course for James, whereas for Santayana it must be wrested deliberately and with effort from a reality that in the normal run of events is hostile to our happiness. Jamesian transcendence is a gift and a spontaneous eruption out of ordinary living that reconfigures the landscape of one's self-conception, while Santayanan transcendence is a particular turn of mind suggesting deliberate and calculated forethought and intent. The Santayanan "self" is relatively self-contained and self-assured, less transformed by the experience of transcendence than consoled and reinforced.

"Eternity, taken intrinsically, has nothing to do with time, but is a form of being which time cannot usher in nor destroy; it is always equally real, silent and indestructible, no matter what time may do, or what time it may be."[76] This view anticipates Wittgenstein's famous remark in the *Tractatus* about "eternity" being timeless and, therefore, the possession of those who "live in the present."[77] Santayana goes on to speak in this passage, and elsewhere, of "eternal being" and of our intuitive grasp of such being. This may suggest one point of difference with James on the question of transcendence: while James regards the experience of eternity as a quality of perception rooted in the subjectivity of the experiencer and in every instance of transcendence, Santayana's idea that we survey or "peruse" eternity in a contemplative and detached way—by deliberately regarding things, ideas, and relations in and for themselves as pure being(s)—is something apparently altogether different. And this evident difference echoes James's above observations on Santayana. The "perfection of rottenness" is really, for James, the rottenness of "perfection": he spurns the Platonic valuation of universal Ideas as superior to the particular objects to which they may refer. He is repulsed by the notion that particulars possess full and genuine reality only to the extent that they are bathed in the glow of supernal being, as cast by perfectly formed universals in the mind.

Yet, James clearly reveals more than a trace of admiration for Santayana's masterful presentation of his philosophy of essence, along with the dominant distaste that renders a judgment of "rottenness." His *Bah!* for "harmonious and integral systems" in philosophy mingles with a small smile of appreciation for *this* system. Perhaps he recognizes the irony and good humor with which Santayana would later preface his *Scepticism and Animal Faith:*[78] "Here is one more system of philosophy. If the reader is tempted to smile, I can assure him that I smile with him. . . ." For the philosopher, this comes as close to intellectual self-deprecation as anything ever does. James was sure to appreciate that quality in Santayana, as well as the aesthetic appeal of his "system."

James's letter to G. H. Palmer quoted in the epigraph to this section, and which contains James's *Bah!* and his terse description of Santayana's "perfection of rottenness," shared that letter with Santayana. Santayana's response is telling. On the one hand, it reveals a degree of misreading and misunderstanding on James's part and. on the other hand, a degree of vindication for James's overall assessment of Santayana the man as more of a "spectator," temperamentally, than an "actor."[79] James and Santayana are finally divided by their opposed judgments of the relative value of the active and contemplative virtues, respectively.

James's letter had continued, "those who *do* insist," contrary to James's understanding of Santayana's position, "that the ideal and the real are dynamically continuous are those by whom the world is to be saved." And it included a curious illustrative analogy, of bad eggs for breakfast: "A man whose egg at breakfast turns out always bad says to himself, 'Well, bad and good are not the same, anyhow.' That is just the trouble!" James's point about the eggs may not be transparent. The intended analogy is with Santayana's classical devaluation of fact, or the real and existent, in contrast to the ideal: his eggs are always bad because they have been prejudged by a standard of ideality and goodness that assumes the inferiority of every actual mouthful. At every breakfast he can discover only bad eggs. His pessimism is not an empirical discovery but an a priori decree.

Still, Santayana could reply to James that "I am nearer to you than you now believe":

What you say, for instance, about the value of the good lying in its *existence*, and about the continuity of the world of values with that of fact, is not different from what I should admit. . . . And the point in insisting that all the eggs at breakfast are rotten is . . . the consequent possibility and endeavour to find good eggs for the morrow. The only thing I object to and absolutely abhor is the assertion that all the eggs indiscriminately are good because the hen has laid them.[80]

And here is a hint of a reverse misunderstanding, by Santayana of James. James does not contend that "all the eggs are good." In fact, James convicts others (notably Whitman, and notably not Emerson) of excess in their "indiscriminate hurrahing for the Universe."[81] "Whitman's verse, 'What is called good is perfect and what is called bad is just as perfect,' would have been mere silliness" to the Greek tragedians and was so to James, too.[82]

But if *all* facts are inferior to their ideal counterparts, then the prospect of *eating* better eggs on the morrow rather than just thinking of them seems remote. Some may find sustenance in the contemplative intuition of perfection, but James prefers a more sensual and particular nourishment. Yet, it makes sense for Santayana to say what he says: *his* transcendence does improve the quality of his own experience, *in his own estimation*. This is simply not something that can be fruitfully debated between individuals of opposed taste and temper.

We find the question of realism again broached in an exchange of letters between the two after Santayana's reading of *Does Consciousness Exist?* and *A World of Pure Experience*. Santayana purports to find common ground in "a real efficacious order discovered in the chaos of immediate experience."[83] But, minding his radical empiricist p's and q's, James declines to endorse wholeheartedly Santayana's assertion that "the materials which experience is composed of must be credited with an existence which makes them material elements and gives them a mechanical order." James is reluctant to impute to experience a material composition or any other determinate composition that might prejudge it. But he does believe, with Santayana, in a "real efficacious order" beneath the flux. He never renounces his early belief in "something external really existing" to which we should "conform our wills."[84] He just does not want to characterize that order, whatever it may ultimately be, in terms that replicate Santayana's antiquarian and classical sensibilities. And so he says to Santayana, "I am very glad you find some of my ideas so congruent with yours. Yours are still one of the secrets of the universe which it is one of my chief motives to live for the unveiling of. . . ."[85]

When James first read *Life of Reason*, he was moved to remark on Santayana's "constricted Emersonianism": Emerson "handles life through a funnel," Santayana a "pin-point." Yet, both are in-takers, seeking to infuse experience and not to close it off. The complex triangulation of James, Emerson, and Santayana promises much insight into our tradition's divided philosophic conscience. Those who view Santayana as an aberration, an incongruously European presence in the halls of American philosophy, have yet to sort out this lineage. If Emerson belongs, so does Santayana.

James's radical empiricist scruples and hesitations looked to Santayana like a "conversion" to panpsychism and idealism: "I should think the same empirical reserve or abstention which makes you rebel against my materialistic Platonism would make you rebel against [them]"[86] Meanwhile, Santayana's materialistic Platonism looked to James like a cloistered philosophy of inaction. They may have been importantly mistaken about one another's rhetorical intent but not so much about their respective ultimate commitments. These are sharply divergent approaches to life, and they yield distinctive philosophies of transcendence.

James had his moments, as most of us do, when he could easily have seconded the sentiment of Santayana's poem that begins "I would I might forget that I am I" and concludes, "Wretched the mortal, pondering his mood, / And doomed to know his aching heart alone."[87] But James philosophized in order to conquer such moments, Santayana to beatify them. Jamesian transcendence is steeped in the personal identity and biographical history of the transcender. Santayana's, to the contrary, aspires to the forgetfulness of total (if momentary) immersion in eternity. This is a subtle but profound difference, and it reflects an unsubtle divergence of valuation for mortal life in general. Santayana offers a curious analogy, in a discussion of the English national character,[88] that implies a sharp contrast between his own conception of transcendence and that of James: James is a skylark, a lilting and carefree romantic whose song of joy belies, ignores, or represses its ultimately earthbound materiality—an irrealist, Santayana warns, who may unwittingly invite crushing disappointment.[89] The fundamental contrast between Santayana and James is that of personal and impersonal transcendence.

*Impersonal* transcendence abandons what has been called the "principle of practical interest" and seeks surcease of all pain, struggle, and care in arrested moments of contemplation. Such moments constitute a turn away from the world, from life. Impersonal transcendence is fundamentally a disengagement from life, that is, from life understood as an unfolding *mortal* narrative (with a beginning, middle, and especially an end). It is, we have indicated, a taste of immortality, a figurative dipping of our psychic toes in the seas of eternity. It is in that sense a detached form of experience.

*Personal* transcendence, alternatively, retains the principle of practical interest and involves intimately and directly the personal history of the transcender. Too, it allows a release from pain, struggle, and care, and though this is not its main aim it may still be its primary worth. But from the perspective of the transcender, the intrinsic value of personal transcendence lies in the way it seems to return us to ordinary life with a fresh and invigorated sense of things. In that respect it represents a turn *toward* the world, an *engagement* with life. It may also possess elements or even the structure of contemplation, but its fundamental import is that it does not detach the experiencer, the transcender, from the totality of one's personal history. Rather, it reinforces that history as one's unique personal "take" on life. And one more broad stroke may be useful: impersonal transcendence follows a line of descent from the pessimistic and world-weary tradition of Schopenhauer. Personal transcendence is another chapter in the great book of life, a celebration and expression of something like cosmic joy in living.[90]

"He carries his English weather in his heart wherever he goes, and it becomes a cool spot in the desert, and a steady and sane oracle amongst all the delirium of mankind."[91] This observation of Santayana's on English character indicates a type of measured self-regulation that at first blush reminds one of Santayana's own approach to the internal cultivation and invocation of "Essences." Is he "English" in this respect, or does there lurk behind this apparent appreciation another shoe, about to drop? Certainly there is here the possible implication that those who carry their mental weather with them also cut themselves off from ranges of experience that they might otherwise encounter. And the other shoe in fact fell earlier, in the somewhat patronizing remark that the English inner "weather" is "nothing particularly spiritual or mysterious."[92] But he continues, "it will be a black day for the human race when scientific blackguards, conspirators, churls and fanatics manage to supplant him."[93]

We noted that for Santayana, radical empiricism is a "literary subject." In *Character and Opinion in the United States* he avers that the subject of immediate experience "can be treated only poetically." "Literary psychology" for Santayana is "the art of imagining how [we] feel and think."[94] James did not, however, share the view that such "imagining" is strictly an art if this means to exclude a more systematic or scientific approach to the understanding of experience. As psychologist he studied subjectivity as "scientifically" as then possible, through introspection and phenomenological description; as metaphysician and pragmatist he believed that subjectivity is the keystone human reality, worthy of study from every angle, including those of literature, biography, and religious fervor.

James's view certainly does echo Santayana's in that it admits the imaginative gap that opens between another's experience and subjectivity, on the one hand, and the firsthand experience of our own thinking and feeling, on the other. He might agree that the only way of closing the gap is through a stretch of the imagination and the extension of empathy, and he would still deny the adequacy of such devices for conveying others' experience. We cannot finally fill the gap. The difference between them on this is probably not important, but still it seems misleading to say either that radical empiricism is a literary *subject* or that it is the product of literary *psychology*. It is literary in its appreciation of the importance of imaginative sympathy, but its origins and implications are at least as extraliterary as Santayana's own philosophy.

Santayana "finds little religion in Emerson, and not a great deal of poetry."[95] He finds Emerson religious, although in only a conventional sense, apparently, and in general finds the sage of Concord unoriginal and uninspired! But James surely was on target in saying of Santayana that "he is a paragon of Emersonianism—declare your intuitions, though no other man share them. . . ." Whether we find such declarations venerable or reckless, though, may be beside the present point, and no sharp delineator of James and Santayana in any event. It is more helpful to notice that divergent intuitions are the rule, not the exception, among creative thinkers.

But, to return to the "bright field" (R. S. Thomas's meditation on naturalized eternity), the greater emphasis on James's part is that not just any field will do. Some of us, because of (not despite) who we are, will be left cold by the vision of the field. We may be transported, alternatively, by something else that leaves some of our compatriots unmoved in their turn. If we would understand any particular episode or occasion of transcendence, then, we must acquire a great deal of background understanding pertaining to the specific biography, the inner life, and the enthusiasms of the individual whose experience we are considering. The experience itself may share certain elements with others, in virtue of which we may notice its transcendent dimension; but to appreciate it we must still make the effort to grasp empathically what has brought each of us, individually, to this or that particular "field" of transcendent experience.

Who are the "barbarians," for Santayana? The list is long, and James—whatever the personal affection or respect Santayana may have held for him—is on it, with the likes of Shakespeare, Browning, Whitman, and

Emerson. James qualifies for inclusion on many counts: as an empiricist, a celebrant of particularity, an exponent of multiplicity and variety as *at least* coeval with unity in the total makeup of the world; as an enthusiastic believer in the externality of things and relations to one another, or in the character of mere conjunctive "with-ness" that he finds emblematic of so much human experience; as an opponent of the "harmonious and systematic," the intrinsically unified, and of whatever speaks of ultimate completion, containment, closure. Above all, James is a barbarian because he is a champion of subjectivity.

Shakespeare, as barbarian, comes in for a somewhat puzzling Santayanan analysis. "The silence of Shakespeare [on religion] and his philosophical incoherence have something in them that is still heathen," yet "the absence of religion in Shakespeare was a sign of his good sense." *Heathen* and *pagan* are not in themselves terms of reproof for Santayana, who likes the honest and wholesome naturalness of the instinctively irreligious.[96] But clearly, Santayana disapproves of *Shakespearean* heathenism and finds something unnatural, perhaps even dishonest or degenerate, in its indifference to religion. Why? In part, surely, because in his view Shakespeare is such an inveterate enumerator and collector, not interpreter, of things, incidents, souls in conflict with each other and with themselves. He is too much the taxonomist of human frailty, too little a moralist and philosopher. Shakespeare's great appeal is to those "who think it wise or possible to refrain from searching for general principles, and are satisfied with the successive empirical appearance of things."[97] Depending on what we understand by "satisfied," James certainly fills this bill. His confidence in the capacity of principles and general statements to anticipate novelty, surprise, and the unexpected *particular* content of experience is minimal. Yet he is not satisfied with mere enumeration or collection (in the manner of Shakespeare, as Santayana evidently reads him).

We have noted, for instance, James's refusal in *Varieties* to reduce religious experience to a principle or to a single explanatory approach. But his interest in the particularity of experience is intense and vital and is humanely concerned to grasp something universal in the private and personal yearnings of many for the "more" of religious life (as in other, extrareligious contexts, James honors the varieties of ways in which nonreligious persons experience *their* own hearts' desires). In this James's philosophy is the opposite of heathenism. Barbarism for Santayana involves a refusal to idealize the "facts" at our feet. Whitman is another of his prime examples, as someone who believed so strongly in his own creative originality that he therefore boasted an immoderate and correlative scorn for tradition and classical learning. This claim might equally apply to Emerson, but for his evidently greater grasp and appreciation of the tradition from Plato on. Impressed by his own perception, Whitman overrates the prescience and the uniqueness of his own sensibility and taste. He embodies "perception without intelligence, imagination without taste, image without structure."[98]

Without undertaking an aesthetic analysis of Whitman's poetics, we can see in a broad and thematic way that Santayana objects to a certain formlessness in Whitman, the man as well as the poet; and this helps us to see the germ of his own preferred form of transcendence as a measured, controlled, and formal appreciation of beauty. He is drawn to classical ideals of ordered form and symmetry and to a composed rather than frenetic stance toward experience. He disdains frenzied romantic excess. The Dionysian revel is to him a directionless, ultimately pointless and debased exercise, a surrender to chaos. He objects as well to the "egotism" of the barbarians. Whitman's "song of myself" is finally the warbling of a "single separate person."[99] Santayana knows that Whitman means to sing a representative song, or rather to engage in a representative celebration of experience exhorting us all to sing, separately yet still together. He knows, in short, that Whitman is the self-appointed poet of Democracy, whose own song is only rarely offered in chorus but whose solo is supposed also to involve and include the choir, vicariously and through mutual sympathy, fellow feeling, and respect for human dignity. His song is ours, Whitman proclaims.

But Santayana is not persuaded. He does not think that Whitman succeeds in transcending himself, or crude and unbridled earthiness, at all. It is ironic that the author of *Scepticism and Animal Faith* could not transcend his temperamental differences with the poet who "could turn and live with animals" to discover their deeper affinities.[100] But more importantly to us here, despite the serious reservations James attests concerning Whitman's overripe ebullience and "indiscriminate hurrah-ing," his own preferred type of transcendence is actually quite harmonious with Whitman's "song."

Santayana's interest in the poets, and his critical-philosophical attentions to them—along with the link between James and Whitman we have just mentioned—calls for a moment's reflection on the not-always salubrious composting of philosophy and literature. "Poets are being pursued by the philosophers today out of the poverty of philosophy," William Carlos Williams once complained. "God damn it, you might think a man had no business to be writing, to be a poet unless some philosophic stinker gave him permission."[101] It may indeed be unfair to Whitman, Shakespeare, and to literature generally, to freight the verbal arts with so heavy a philosophical cargo. Good writing has virtues of its own; philosophical problems and texts do not define and exhaust the world of our legitimate attentive interest. Santayana understands this, and his philosophical reading of literature is immeasurably richer, deeper, and more satisfying than the desultory common standard of so much contemporary literary criticism. He does not intend to impugn the ultimate literary excellence, within precise literary bounds, even of the "barbarian" poets he opposes philosophically. Unfortunately, not every philosopher who ventures into the domain of literary evaluation is so circumspect. Philosophers who reject a work of literature because they dislike one or another philosophical implication they detect in one of its aspects—in the case of a novel, for instance, in the character and opinions of a protagonist—may be guilty of murdering to dissect. Those who care deeply for both enterprises must hope that a more agreeable working relationship between literature and philosophy is possible.

The relevance of these meta-literary/philosophical ruminations to transcendence is just this: Santayana would convict a number of poets for barbarism, which, on closer inspection, turns out to be less a literary-critical judgment than a profession of favor for one type of transcendence, and of distaste for another type, which mirrors the difference between Santayana and James on this very question.

And here we may profitably digress to ponder, briefly, the relationship of philosophy and writing generally to the social contexts in which they necessarily occur. As an activity that is voluntary—that is, as response to compellingly felt inner urgencies expressed by writers who insist they "have to" write—writing may of itself occasion a kind of transcendence. Stanley Cavell has claimed that it may also function "therapeutically." Cavell finds in Emerson the message that the purpose of writing is to return us to the everyday and the ordinary, from whatever extraordinariness, marginality, or obscurity we have managed to think, feel, *and write* ourselves into. Writing may thus resist or repair alienation, even that which writing itself has authored. But is alienation central to the generic activity of writing? Does much writing, and philosophizing, not represent the natural fullness of a joyous heart?

Doubtless, many writers have a feeling of being alienated from themselves, of missing a vital "fellowship with the self," of needing to write in order to quell in their own breasts currents of discomfort or disorder that they may be unable to name but cannot escape, or of failing to integrate some inchoate sense of self with the outer persona. But is this emphasis not skewed so far toward the strictly personal dimension that it nearly forgets to address the issue of the writer's fellowship *with his fellows*?

It is not surprising if writers and philosophers sometimes feel alienated not only from themselves but especially from the preponderantly nonwriting, semiliterate world of popular culture. But this, too, may paint a false picture. Emerson regarded writing as a distinctive and important act, and Cavell is right to draw attention to characteristic Emersonian remarks that may well be *about* the act of writing even if they seem to be about something else. Yet Emerson *the unifier* means to write as a "representative man" who happens to be a writer but who presumes to speak for us all. He knows, though, that we must all speak for ourselves. No one else shares the unique perspective each of us is privileged to own. Writers are not especially privileged in this regard. While they may certainly entertain the laudable objective of instantiating the figure of "man or woman thinking," an alienated writer needs to find the way back to ordinary life *personally*, like everyone else. Vicarious salvation is not available here.

Still, there is in Emerson a sense of writerly mission promising to bring us all back to something vital that we have misplaced, to whatever extent we identify with the species act of reflective thinking that *is* reading and writing. It is not just about overcoming self-alienation, but about bridging the distances between persons. Books are so unprepossessing in form to offer such extraordinary possibilities for self-expansion and significant communication not only between contemporaries but across the generations. Billy Collins notices this when he writes of "anonymous men catching a ride into the future / on a vessel more lasting than themselves,"[102] through the medium of the printed word.

The sense of a gulf between oneself and others is a feeling most of us have known at one time or another; it belongs to our condition. But with just a little cultivation so does the sense of connectedness. Emerson, for one, seems to have felt more connected to others generally than many intellectuals of our ironic and specialized age allow themselves to confess. Clear and honest writing can return the writer to ordinary life, to feelings of fellowship and continuity. But not all writing communicates clearly, certainly not all philosophy does. Not all philosophers want to. Heidegger is said to have withheld the manuscript of *Being and Time* from publication until all reviewers pronounced it impenetrable. The anecdote may be apocryphal, but it is at least consistent with the text!

For Emerson the writer/philosopher has a social mission, based on what Cavell calls an "American faith" in hopefulness and cheer: "Emerson seems to take despair not as a recognition of [life] but as a fear of life, an avoidance of it."[103] This is the form of optimism, or meliorism, permeating James and Dewey *and* standing awkwardly beside a suggestion Cavell once made to a gathering of philosophers about the shakiness of the concept of transcendence for James in particular. James's philosophy generates "a mere surmise of transcendence," he told them;[104] in fact, transcendence is for James, as for Dewey, the constant, natural, "ordinary" harvest of the subjective imagination. It supports a vision of the writer/philosopher as a beacon of hope, personal *and* social. Emerson viewed his own writing as the pursuit of unsecured ambition or aspiration, an investment of himself and of his time, energy, and identity in the act of writing. That is a personal act and a hopeful one: after all, if Emerson *knew* that it would succeed (in his own terms), hope would be gratuitous. Can any of us be certain that our personal aspirations will prevail?

Surely we must be hopeful on our own behalf, but not only our own. Emerson is notorious for insisting that he has a greater obligation to cultivate his own talents than to help some of those less fortunate. "Are they my poor?" he asks.[105] But of course he also believed that in cultivating our own talents we perform the greatest social service we (and only we, individually) can. He wants to erase the line between duties to self and to society, and urges that we learn to respect the conscience of every individual in apportioning his days as he sees fit. This is conveniently self-serving. Is it also selfish? This is a big question for Emerson and Cavell, and for each of us.

Why write? There is no more Jamesian a statement of the imperative to symbolize our flowing streams of experience than this from Vita Sackville-West:

> It is necessary to write, if the days are not to slip emptily by. How else, indeed, to clap the net over the butterfly of the moment? for the moment passes, it is forgotten; the mood is gone; life itself is gone. That is where the writer scores over his fellows: he catches the changes of his mind on the hop. Growth is exciting; growth is dynamic and alarming. Growth of the soul, growth of the mind. . . .[106]

That is reason enough to write, but is it reason enough to be read? For that we might heed the message of Faulkner's 1950 Nobel address:

> The basest of all things is to be afraid. . . . It is [the writer's] privilege to help man endure by lifting his heart, by reminding him of the courage and humor and hope and pride and compassion and pity and sacrifice which have been the glory of his past. The poet's voice . . . can help [humanity] endure and prevail.[107]

A word more about Santayana and subjectivity: he is certainly as quirkily "subjective" in his own preferences as James, indeed, as all of us are, though we may be less willing to admit to our own quirks. But Santayana's preferences embody a classical ideal of objectivity that seeks, in an Aristotelian spirit, to plant itself in a "middling zone" of consensual agreement about matters of taste and temper. No such proprieties inhibit James, and in this he is unabashedly "barbaric" and *flighty*.

A skylark is a bird noted for singing in flight, a playfully mobile creature, and a source of endless consternation to spirits more centrifugally anchored in terra firma. Thus was James's avowedly personal philosophy a mystery to Santayana, in its unabashedly intense romanticism. Can it be coincidental that one of James's favorite tropes, used by Shelley in his "To a Skylark," likens our consciousness of reality to the avian "flights and perchings" of a

perceptual life in near-constant motion, resting only to gather the strength
and will for yet another transition?

> Hail to thee, blithe Spirit!
> Bird thou never wert,
>   That from Heaven, or near it,
> Pourest thy full heart
> In profuse strains of unpremeditated art.
> . . . . . . . . . . . . . . . . . . . . . . . . . . . . . .
>   What objects are the fountains
> Of thy happy strain?
>   What fields, or waves, or mountains?
> What shapes of sky or plain?
> What love of thine own kind? what ignorance of pain?

James was not ignorant of pain, but his song was his own even as it reveled
in the songs of others. Its objects included the large exterior forms of the
geographic landscape, but did not exclude the small interior features of the
private imagination.

> We look before and after,
> And pine for what is not:
>   Our sincerest laughter
> With some pain is fraught;
> Our sweetest songs are those that tell of saddest thought.

Here the poet envies the lark's capacity to sink luxuriantly into the moment.
This is an admiration James shares but does not entirely mean to engrave in
the experience of transcendence as we most typically possess it. We are
temporal beings, and our sincerest laughter is tinged with memory, expectation, and the openness of possibility.

> Better than all measures
> Of delightful sound,
>   Better than all treasures
> That in books are found,
> Thy skill to poet were, thou scorner of the ground!

If the "ground" is brute facticity, without the enlivening possibility of alteration at our and others' hands, James does scorn it. Like Emerson's, his
faith in books is great but not unbounded, his appreciation of "delightful
sound" ample but expectant of better.

Teach me half the gladness
That thy brain must know,
Such harmonious madness
From my lips would flow
The world should listen then, as I am listening now![108]

James was learned but preferred to learn. He thought our happiness the antithesis of madness, yet he looked to the "mad" not only for instructive contrast but also for the example they offer of impassioned and singular
purpose.

James mentions Shelley briefly in "A Certain Blindness," in tandem
with Wordsworth, as belonging to the stable of poets and other writers who
have voiced a sense of inner joy as somehow related to the outer phenomena of nature. The nature poets, among whom we can also include Emerson
and Whitman (whom James mentions, along with Stevenson and others)
are flush with the perception of a "limitless significance in natural things,"
things like the hills and fields of Wordsworth's Lake District or the songs of
Shelley's skylark. Their "strange inner joy" may bespeak a "mystic sense of
hidden meaning," but not only a *mystic* sense. We have already touched on
the organic "springs of delight" and the global naturalism which supposes
that whatever is experienceably real has a place in an eventual, full account
of nature.

In "Human Immortality" James quotes from Shelley's "Adonais" in defense of supernaturalism:

Life, like a dome of many-colored glass,
Stains the white radiance of Eternity. . . .[109]

James launches from this image into an extended, speculative meditation on
what possible sorts of incursion, delivered through the mediumship of nature, might just give substance to the poet's dreams: "Suppose, now," he proposes, that Shelley's dome "could at certain times and places grow less
[opaque], and let certain beams pierce through into this sublunary world . . .
so many finite rays, so to speak, of consciousness." James's Shelley-inspired
thought experiment continues: "Only at particular times and places would
it seem that, as a matter of fact, the veil of nature can grow thin and rup-
turable enough for such effects to occur. But in those places gleams, however finite and unsatisfying, of the absolute life of the universe, are from
time to time vouchsafed. Glows of feeling, glimpses of insight, and streams
of knowledge and perception float into our finite world." And here is
James's really pregnant suggestion about how we may wish to take such moments, such apparent "glimpses": "Admit now that our brains are such thin
and half-transparent places in the veil. . . ." He implies the reasonableness

of construing this hypothesis in conventionally supernaturalistic terms; that is, he invites speculation about rendings of the "veil" through which the mystic may claim to glimpse something spectrally remote, extraordinary, and privileged.

But I think the more intriguing implications are not supernatural; they are naturalistic. "The brain would be the independent variable" in the scenario he imagines; "the mind would vary dependently," according to the variable experiences and commitments of individuals. Cryptic though it is, this suggestion nudges us further toward an explicit interpretation of Jamesian transcendence in naturalistic terms and an appreciation of James's basic consanguinity with the assumptions of a naturalized spirituality. In the words of Wallace Stevens:

We live in an old chaos of the sun,
Or old dependency of day and night,
Or island solitude, unsponsored, free. . . .
And, in the isolation of the sky,
At evening, casual flocks of pigeons make
Ambiguous undulations as they sink,
Downward to darkness, on extended wings.[110]

# V

# Futures

Gatsby believed in the green light, the orgiastic future that year by year recedes before us. It eluded us then, but that's no matter; tomorrow we will run
faster, stretch out our arms farther; so we beat on, boats against the current,
borne back ceaselessly into the past.

F. Scott Fitzgerald, *The Great Gatsby*


Real generosity towards the future lies in giving all to the present.

Albert Camus, *The Rebel*

## "The Green Light"

Up to now we have been emphasizing mainly the *timeless* quality of personal transcendence: that aspect of eternity concerned not with temporal
breadth but with focused presence. There is in the more dazzling instances
of transcendent consciousness a clock-stopping sensation of the fullness of
the present moment, a suspension of our usual temporal preoccupations
that excludes consideration of the past and, particularly, scheming for the
future. It is a paradisiacal moment when we look neither ahead nor behind
but repose contentedly where and when we are. It may be that any experience deserving to be called "transcendent" must exhibit this quality as its
dominant note. "The belief in the genuineness of each particular moment
in which we feel the squeeze of this world's life . . . is an Eden from which
rationalists seek in vain to expel us. . . ."[1]

But here we face a challenge, if we suppose personal transcendence capable of capturing and conveying that triadic marriage of inner excitement,
exterior extravagance, and personal transformation that has so gaudily typi-
fied the historical experience of so many of James's countrymen. Gatsby is
the perfect symbol and paradigm of what transcendence has most often
meant, has been "experienced as," in a distinctively Americanized context.
It is decidedly *not* ahistorical, timeless, or an instantiation of some pure

*present,* neither forward nor backward looking. To the contrary, Gatsby represents an almost lascivious displacement of present experience (viewed as existing for its own sake, carrying its own self-certified justification) by the aggressive pursuit of an envisioned future in which the past is neither present nor fully real, and the present becomes a kind of dramatic production, a costumed actor's appearance on a stage of his own devising. Gatsby constructs a persona cut off from his own past, but the flash and mirrors with which he maintains an appearance of dash, energy, and glamour are not wholly contrived: he really aspires to be what he seems, and aspires with such earnest and energetic conviction that he almost is. Paradoxically he is both chasing a dream and living it (or a fantasy simulation of it) in the present.

In the end, of course, the dream dies with Gatsby along with unfortunate innocents who trail in his wake. He does not fulfill his quest, in part because it depends upon his possessing the affections of a woman who does not entirely share his vision. Along the way he manages to achieve a kind of transcendence, degraded, incomplete, and fleeting though it is. But at last we cannot admire his journey, approve his itinerary, or allow that the "romantic egoist's" dream resulted only in self-regarding disappointment and frustration. It brought unforeseen ruin in other lives as well. What went wrong?

Gatsby fails to coordinate his own dreams and visions with those of others, viewing them mostly as players and "extras" who populate his lavish parties and thereby furnish a kind of immediate external validation of his own egocentrism. He does not think of them as individuals in possession of their own dreams and visions. Mostly he does not think of them at all. He does not take their experience, their *subjectivity* seriously. And in failing to appreciate or accept the autonomy of the one person his dream of the future is built upon, his failure becomes tragically destructive.

For those Americans who have internalized the ethos of a materially defined, status-based life (the "bitch-Goddess success,"² in James's startlingly memorable phrase), personal salvation lies exclusively in pecuniarily quantifiable achievement. Only the future promising permanent possession of all those good *things,* the outer trappings of wealth, is fully real; and because there are always more things, more trappings to chase, it is only an idyllic, elusive, possibly chimerical future that shimmers with the prospect of transcendence.

For Gatsby, all desire and possible attainment including personal affection is mistranslated into consumable form. This definition of the good life may work for us up to a point, but not beyond the point at which the desires and dreams of others collide with our own. Gatsby might have learned this lesson had he lived, or he might simply have been embittered and mystified by the intransigence of a world that includes autonomous centers of subjectivity not responsive to his own egoism.

Can personal transcendence avoid the shoals of unenlightened egoism and correct its excesses, or merely confirm them? Despite James's obvious contempt for our "national disease," pragmatism *is* a philosophy of action in time, of plans and consequences and the futures that may realize them. If personal transcendence is similarly oriented to the future, it must find a way to avoid Gatsby's mistakes or else succumb to the disease.

The "green light" is a variable construction of the will and the imagination, made partly of real materials (the beholder's own experience and abilities) but filled out with hope or fantasy, less frequently with practical aspiration. It is an ever vanishing object presenting just enough of a fleeting glimpse, for some, to furnish a lifelong purpose (or obsession, if Melville's Ahab is our prototype and model). It is for each of us different. It marks whatever is uniquely alluring about a possible or at least conceivable, imaginable, or daydreamable future. It conspires with our idealizing tendencies to create a vision that we hold in our hearts if not in our heads and that may be more satisfying as vision than as concrete possibility. It bathes the present in a light of prospective deliverance. It informs our self-descriptions, even if only by contrast with what we soberly imagine as more realistic.

A friend of mine is smitten with Scotland. He never speaks of it except with a distant gleam in his eye and an evident longing to return. He occasionally entertains a fantasy of living there, making a new life, realizing his vision. And I would not be entirely shocked to learn one day that he has indeed set out for that bonny land with that intention. Not entirely. But I would at least be surprised, not because he does not truly dream of that place and the life he might live there, and not because he is a dreamer in any special sense. He is a kind of "romantic," I suppose, in his way of deriving active pleasure from the contemplation of alternative realities and calling them often to mind without any formed intention of enacting his reverie, while in a corner of his imagination still treating the alternative as indistinct from practical possibility; but that surely is true of many more of us than realize or admit it. The surprise would come on reflecting that most of us are dreamers of one kind or another, "live more or less on some inclined plane of credulity,"[3] carry torches for something presently and perhaps permanently out of reach. Yet the torch, the dream, is a valued possession, cradled so intimately that to swap it, even in exchange for its realization in outer form, might be profoundly disorienting. I think my friend would be lost without his Scotland, and if he were *in* Scotland he might very well lose it.

The "green light" may be an illusion, a kind of self-deception. It may create tragedy and pathos, as for Gatsby. But it may also be the "torch" guiding our passage through turbulent waters, the beacon showing us a vision of personal plenitude that the present alone cannot inspire. It may be the glowing center of personal transcendence.

The personal kind of transcendence I am attributing to James frequently owes its transcendent appeal to the dream or vision similar in kind to my friend's Scotland of the imagination. So long as my friend entertains his idealized, indefinitely unrealized vision, he in some sense transcends everyday facticity. Yet he cannot transcend *himself* and still have his vision, too. Self is, after all, the locus of our dreams. His Scotland is not available to me, even though his vision may appeal to me or to anyone. I understand and even share some part of his feeling, perhaps because in my own case I feel a particular fondness for the British countryside, an enthusiasm possibly not so different, after all, from the excitement of a stock-car racing fan for his preferred pleasure, or that of the "creative anachronist" decked out in medieval finery. But because it is always my friend's vision of Scotland, someone else's of the road races or jousting arena, and mine of the Lake District and Cotswolds (and ballpark) that dominate our respective inner lives, we each find a different avenue to transcendence. The imaginative leap from one to the other, however, can be approximated (or at least simulated). In grasping the evident surface resemblance between my pal's Scotland revery and my own attraction to Wordsworth's native grounds, I come a large step closer to an empathic appreciation of his inner landscape. I begin to recognize the eye-twinkle with which he relates his Scottish tales as akin not only to the sunny glow that attends my own thoughts of Britain, but even to my thoughts of spring training! The gap between our respective sensibilities need not hinder our mutual understanding and respect.

Here, by the way, is a Jamesian answer to the charge of "barbarism" from critics like Santayana who complain of an overweening facticity and refusal to idealize experience. If I am right about James and personal transcendence, he defends the idealization of facts to a degree never approached by "idealists" who do not take experience and subjectivity so seriously. What kind of transcendence is it that insists on the presence and the active participation of the person? Or, better, what exactly is it that gets transcended in personal transcendence?

It would, I think, be useful to review here the distinction between personal and impersonal transcendence as we have drawn it thus far.

Impersonal transcendence abandons what has been called the "principle of practical interest" and seeks surcease of all pain, struggle, and care in arrested moments of contemplation. Such moments constitute a turn away from the world, from life. Impersonal transcendence is fundamentally a disengagement from life, that is, from life understood as an unfolding *mortal* narrative (with a beginning, middle, and especially an *end*). It is, as I have indicated, a taste of immortality, a figurative dipping of our psychic toes in the seas of eternity, a detached form of experience.

Personal transcendence, by contrast, retains the principle of practical interest and involves intimately and directly the personal history of the transcender. It, too, allows a release from pain, struggle, and care, but this is not its primary aim, focus, or function, though it may still be its primary worth. From the perspective of the transcender, however, the intrinsic value of personal transcendence lies in the way it seems to return us to ordinary (nontranscendent) life with a fresh and invigorated sense of things. In that respect it is a turn *toward* the world, an engagement with life. It may also possess elements or even the structure of contemplation, but its fundamental import is that it does not detach the experiencer, the transcender, from the totality of his personal history. Rather, it reinforces that history as his unique personal "take" on things, the world, and life's largest meanings. It places the whole person at the center of personal happiness, and finds there—in the experience of happiness—intimations of eternity.

Impersonal transcendence is probably closer in meaning to what philosophers, religionists, mystics, and litterateurs have always meant by transcendence: an experience leaving self behind and uniting finite consciousness with something that seems, either immediately or upon reflection, vast, unlimited, and free of opposition or internal contradiction. The scale and impersonality of the experience is just the source of its traditional appeal, to those who have been drawn to it. It is self-annihilating, subserving what seems an expanded awareness and a unification so total that the net transaction is experienced not as loss but as immeasurable growth.

Personal transcendence is something new on the block. It appeals to those who are not comforted by dissolution of personality and disintegration, however brief and transient, of self. But, recall: in radical empiricism, "self" is not fundamental. We have noted that James even uses the term *incidental* to describe the relation and relative importance of self to the discovery of pure experience. James does not wish to disparage personality; the reverse is true. But he does wish to indicate that our respective individual constitutions, preferences, and "dreams and visions" radiate—uniquely and individually, to be sure—along paths untrod by any other, from a vital center of experience that is not experienced as yours, mine, his or hers, as it transpires. Yet is has to *be* yours, mine, or theirs, in order to have transpired. Its foreground and its reverberant after-ripples must be personal. The seeming paradox is not really so difficult to dismantle here: our personalities make us receptive to transcendence in relation to this or that vision, but in having the experience we surmount facts and realities for its duration.

When my friend is truly enthralled with Scotland, for however long the pitch of excitement lasts—a moment, several consecutive or contiguous moments, rarely longer—he does not think of it as *his*. It is just Scotland, and he treasures it. In personal transcendence we tap into a vital and impersonal center of pure experience. What do we then transcend? Well, there is surely a sense in which we do transcend our fact-ridden individual selves, in the manner suggested. But more importantly, we transcend intellectualism and conceptual confusion; and we may transcend care, worry, sorrow, and personal distress. If so, personal transcendence achieves the same lofty ends sought by impersonal transcendence, but without abandoning the subjective anchorage of selfhood.

Gatsby lives "in" an imagined and hoped-for personal future; but he also surrounds himself in the present with the visible trappings of the life and persona he aspires to. He ritually enacts a personal fantasy to such an extent that it becomes his present reality, and the observer (reader) has difficulty distinguishing Gatsby's reality from illusion. To all appearances he *is* the mysterious, charismatic tycoon he affects to be; with his lavish and extravagant personal style, an apparently spontaneous casualness, an air of cosmopolitan knowingness and a larger-than-life aura of affirmation, he indeed projects an impressive facade. Thus does he define himself, and thus do others readily accept him.

The key to this charade—though of course it cannot be a "charade," strictly speaking, if there is no other "real" Gatsby to perform the pantomime—is Gatsby's and everyone else's complicity in not taking the past, anyone's past, seriously. And that is the myth of America that makes Gatsby's story ours: we are forever creating ourselves, leaving history in the dust of unconsulted memory. Our national life is one of movement toward a shimmering, exciting, vibrant future, as quickly as we can throw off the cumbersome baggage of an unwanted and often-unacknowledged past. But it is also one in which the national psyche constantly courts the "conflict of spirituality caught fast in the web of our commercial life," the "meanness of spirit" and "insensate selfishness" of a culture whose scale of value is weighted by price.[4]

A number of threads weave Gatsby's story. The thread usually attracting critical attention is his tragedy, his sacrifice of a stable personal identity in exchange for a flashy surface that annihilates his own humble but honest origins. There are lessons to learn about Jamesian transcendence in this tragic aspect. Another thread is Gatsby's success, in his own terms. His personal ending is tragic, gratuitous, even absurd; but his life, measured by his own standards, is successful. Here, too, there are useful points to make in connection with James. For one, the value of any life cannot be measured in terms which ignore the subjective evaluation of the individual who lives it.

But most important, for present purposes, is to distinguish Gatsby's form of transcendence from James's, with respect to the progressive and non-self-centered essence of pragmatism. Gatsby is an egoist, James a defender of subjectivity. These are not unrelated but they are very different. Their contrary implications revolve around the central issue (for James) of growth: James's emphasis on subjectivity is a crucial aspect of his overriding interest in the varieties and possibilities of human experience in advancing the growth of individuals in their respective social circumstances and, ultimately, in promoting the growth of humanity. No small interest, this!

We should, therefore, follow our discussion of Gatsby and his form of future-oriented transcendence by considering a very different kind of future-oriented transcendence, one that connects with the historic mission of pragmatism as a progressive and extrapersonal, nonegoistic endeavor. Put another way, the aim is to show that for James the pragmatic moralist there is (meaning, of course, that there *ought to be observed*) a continuity between inner or psychic satisfactions and outer achievement, between transcendent happiness, on one side, and success in meeting the exterior challenges of living, on the other. This implies an engagement in affairs that goes beyond any narrow emphasis on our personal happiness, in a sense of relatedness between our happiness and the welfare of others, in the future of humanity at large.

Here the distinction between two kinds of transcendence, James's and (for instance) Santayana's, is illuminating. Jamesian transcendence is personal, not impersonal, and this connects vitally with subjectivity, contrasts with "pure" experience, and, finally, reflects and reinforces the progressive character of pragmatism. There are fundamental issues surrounding evolution and the experience of what has been called "flow," which I will want to touch on in spelling out some of the main implications of the Jamesian perspective. We will be reminded again of the inescapable Jamesian and pragmatic preoccupation with growth as an organizing principle and a touchstone in the construction of meaning and value in our lives.

The future has been defined ironically, in *The Devil's Dictionary*, as "that period of time in which our affairs prosper, our friends are true and our happiness is assured."[5] Making the future a personal repository of our most pleasant, tranquil, and unrealistic dreams suggests one way of interpreting Gatsby's experience; some would suggest that pragmatism is similarly spellbound by an unreasonably sanguine expectation of future deliverance. But besides projecting a rosy and unfocused orientation toward the future, Gatsby also betrays an element of pretense, a superficial persona rather than an authentic personality taking possession of his own true identity and conducting an honest if less flashy life. The old aphorist was right: "We are never so ridiculous for the qualities we have as for those we pretend to."[6]

I want to suggest that Gatsby's relation to the future is indeed problematic but mostly for reasons other than these. As Americans we are Gatsby's spiritual countrymen, like it or not, and those of us who freely espouse some part of the American pragmatic tradition ought to like it, or at least acknowledge it. He and *we* are right, therefore, to care so much about the future that it invades and alters our present conduct, even informs our present identities. But with this complicity comes a caution: the future about which we care and in which we invest ourselves had better not be too narrow or egocentric, lest by our efforts we reap a solitary tragedy.

For the pragmatist, the future is neither an impersonal abstraction nor a personal fantasy. It is an inspiring, ennobled vision of merging destinies, the fruition of hope and hard work. If the pragmatist's keynote is happiness, its resonance comes from his conception of a future rich with the whole chorus of life, inextinguishable in the trajectory of an individual's life span. When we come to feel ourselves attached in the strongest way to the best of which our kind is capable, we no longer resist the recognition of our own individual limits, for these define the character of our unique contribution to the large tapestry of life. We may feel an especially intimate and proprietary relationship to that personal contribution, the pride of ownership. But the point here is also to own the whole tapestry, not only the small thread at our hands. Self-enlargement requires identification with the whole as well as our small part. The future becomes a part of our "self" and our present, as it does for Gatsby, but shorn of narrow egoism that shrinks self. This is Gatsby's paradox: he is a shrunken self, less than he was and might have been. He has lost more essential humanity than his material successes have been able to put in their place.

How may the future properly impinge on the transcendent consciousness? A Gatsby-like attitude is problematic but not fundamentally wrong: we are right to care so much for the future that it invades and alters our present. Gatsby's error, and maybe humanity's greatest danger, is a shrunken conception of "self." We are elevated by our solitary dreams so long as they do not displace our sense of human solidarity. But when personal aggrandizement becomes our primary goal—and not the happy consequence of a wider, richer identification with others and with past and future—we invite catastrophe. Fitzgerald's narrator supposes that personality may consist of "an unbroken series of successful gestures,"[7] but pure gesture, conspicuous display, in itself is empty. Personality that betokens solidity of self is not just for show, it is the realization of perennial human energies derived in part from one's sense of relatedness to a human community larger than one's own origins and personal aspirations.

Yet in the character of Gatsby we recognize, besides his own blinded sense of personal mission, a more universally admired (or at least, recognized) trait of Americanism: the urge to *do* something (and always to be doing *something*), to capitalize on time, to exploit possibility. When Daisy Buchanan wonders, "What'll we do with ourselves this afternoon? And the day after that, and the next thirty years?"[8] she symbolizes a specter of purposeless, directionless ennui that haunts and threatens the national paradigm of successful industry.

Gatsby is a transcender, though a tragically flawed one. He is doing his limited best to live up to an ideal, to rise to an occasion—substantially of his own devising—which is beyond his native capacities but not beyond his dreams. The peculiarly personal, uniquely stylized shape of Gatsby's ideal ultimately yields to a more expansive mood and a capacity for something approaching real wonder. This is part of his claim on our fascination: we recognize the irrepressible, unfathomable Americanism of his hopefulness:

> For a transitory enchanted moment man must have held his breath in the presence of this continent, compelled into an aesthetic contemplation he neither understood nor desired, face to face for the last time in history with something commensurate to his capacity for wonder.[9]

This passage immediately precedes the ringing pathos of the "boats against the current" image and suggests one historical source of the attitude that Gatsby embodies, the beginning of an explanation of why so many of us find it an arresting image.

But we also may recognize a much larger phenomenon than Americanism: the quest for personal flourishing, the energizing experience of the quest, as a perennial, native plant indigenous to the human heart. We do not quite grasp *his* dream, but we grasp dreaming and we sympathize.

The trouble with Gatsby is not that he allows the future to dominate his life, but that he allows himself to be no more than the imaginative construction of an *exclusively* personal future. Gatsby's future, despite its vision of blissful romantic possession, is really a solitary future because it subordinates others—especially the beloved object of his exertions—to his own subjective demands of life. His is a constricted, self-aggrandizing self, not an enlarged, sympathetic, and humane citizen of the race. And he has an unhealthy relation to the past, as well as to other people. He is selfish (not the same as self-interested), and his "self" is much, much too small. He takes care to appear generous, but this is a plotted identity intended for public consumption. In fact, his identity is severely stunted. A good heart is not enough to save him from his own consuming egoism.

In brief: subjectivity is the constructive basis of personal transcendence, blind egoism its bête noire. James, we recall, finds nothing wrong with honoring our own subjective "needs," building our personal philosophies and religions upon them. But it must be a thoughtful, sympathetic subjectivity that recognizes as a condition of its own fulfillment the parallel fulfillment of others. That kind of subjectivity is a bridge to others and to past and future. Egoism by contrast is isolated in a sea of narcissism, adrift in its own blinkered subjectivity and insensitive to the similar straits of other persons.

The image with which we began these reflections, that of the green light, naturally invites association with James's appreciative remarks on Stevenson's "The Lantern Bearers," in "A Certain Blindness." We have noted that essay's centrality to the theme of Jamesian transcendence; in the present context, the green light of an endlessly promising, ever beckoning future blends with the cautionary yellow hazard warning of immoderate personal aspiration unbalanced by a strong sense of social identity, communal commitment, and a modestly humane sensitivity to natural limitation, the natural human habitat, and the real context of personal dreams.

Jamesian transcenders, heed and beware.

## From Gatsby to Gates: Proceed with Caution

> Be open to your dreams, people. Embrace the distant shore. Our mortal journey is over all too soon.
>
> Chris Stevens (radio philosopher on NBC television series
> *Northern Exposure*)

Bill Gates, the computer legend and world's richest man, hosted a party at his palatial new high-tech "state of the art" mansion on Lake Washington one spring evening in 1997. In attendance were politicians, corporate executives, and other influential eminences. Of course, the party included a tour of this updated San Simeon of the '90s, a home so wired and "interactive" that different rooms alter their own climate control settings and musical offerings when different individuals enter. In addition, masterworks of art spring to life on the walls according to the preprogrammed preferences of visitors.

In the library of the $60 million castle—it is mildly surprising that Gates's home has a library of *actual* books—is an imposing rotunda around which is stenciled an inscription from *The Great Gatsby*. Mrs. Gates joked that the couple were such fans of F. Scott Fitzgerald that they might install a green light on the end of their dock. "Fulfill your wildest dreams," the host urged his guests, declaring that computing power would continue to increase at a pace allowing them to do so.[10]

Bill Gates, more than any other individual of our time, has sought to impress upon the popular imagination the virtues of "virtual reality" and the allure of a future pervasively, unreservedly mediated by computing technology. The "road ahead," in his personal vision, promises to keep us all plugged in, pretty much all of the time. We will go nowhere without our pocket or "palmtop" computers, which will replace money, track our every movement, and insure that we need never suffer a moment of boredom or solitude again. We will never be out of touch, or reach, will choose exactly what we want to experience and when, and will increasingly tend to disregard the distinction between what is real or "natural" and what is a virtual or artificial imposture. We will transcend the limitations of old-fashioned reality and, indeed, may come to regard it—*reality!*—as increasingly, quaintly irrelevant. Albert Borgmann, for one, deplores the creeping obsolescence of reality in our time, along with a hopeful glance at the silver lining of its resuscitative power: "The preternaturally bright and controllable quality of cyberspace makes real things look poor and recalcitrant in comparison. To be sure, reality at bottom remains inescapable and unfathomable. It is the ground on which the ambiguities of technological information can be resolved and its fragilities repaired. Yet on its surface reality appears lighter and often lite."[11]

We found in the figure of Gatsby the germ of an instructional tale of frustrated dreams and how not to sustain a prolonged and healthy relationship with our ideals. His recklessly egoistic rush to embrace a personal vision of the future was seductive, and for awhile it lit up the world revolving around his personal vision. Eventually, though, the superficiality of this little world became unsustainable. It vanished in the vapor of its own unbearable lightness, collapsing like a house of mirrors. But it exacted a real, human toll.

Are there parallels? Just a few, though admittedly Gatsby and Gates are in most respects as incommensurable as they seem. Gatsby's dreams were very private; although he manifested them in the gaudy public splendor of materially extravagant living, they had nothing, really, to do with effecting changes in the public and social spheres of life. Gates wants to transform the way everyone lives. His own most visible material extravagance, that silicon dream house, is (he says) an attempt to blaze trails for us all. Unfathomably wealthy in early middle age, he has begun to philanthropize on a fantastic scale. Donating unprecedented earmarked sums to public libraries and schools, he has been heralded as the Rockefeller and Carnegie of our time.[12] His beneficence has been anything but selfless, since its ulterior goal is to extend the pervasive presence of computing (and his own company's products). But clearly he believes with earnest conviction that he is doing good, in a public-spirited way. "I am proud to be part of an industry that has revolutionized the world in only 25 years. . . . [T]he computer software industry has created more economic opportunity and empowered more people than any other industry at any other time in history."[13] He predicts an unrestricted future of technological, economic, and computer-enhanced personal flourishing (pending, now, the unforeseen impact of the federal government's antitrust initiative to split Microsoft).

Gates, like Gatsby, symbolizes the power of a driving dream and its capacity to elicit the envy and support (if not the admiration) of others. They are swirling fields of force: somehow through dint of personal energy, uncompromising persistence, luck, and, no doubt, strokes of genius, as well as ruthlessness—they create an atmosphere conducive to the realization of their personal dreams while enlisting the enthusiastic complicity of those around them. Yet, in the end, Gatsby failed because he did not coordinate his passion for a personally compelling vision of the future with the separate passions of others. He did not take their subjectivity seriously, probably lacking the sensibility to grasp what it means to do so. Gates may not be myopic in quite the same way, but his peculiar blindness may bear greater potential for harm if current trends continue. In the largest social sense, his success (meaning not his wealth but the spread of his idea) has already been gained: personal and network computing as a way of life is here to stay, and he deserves much of the credit or blame. It is for the rest of us to sort out the consequences, limit the damage, and secure the gains.

Gates proudly crows, "Your connection [to computer networks] will be your passport into a new, 'mediated' way of life." And "firsthand experiences aren't always so rewarding."[14] So there it is from the horse's mouth: the Information Age is mediation unabashed. There are good and bad forms of mediation, of course. A central theme in this work, key to understanding what is distinctive about Jamesian transcendence, is the idea of connectedness ("connectivity," in Gates-speak) to other people and to possibilities, in ways that break down the more inhumane forms of mediation dominating our lives. The computing revolution obviously has great potential for good in this respect, but it also presents us with the great risk that people like Gates—those with power to alter the day-to-day experience of millions of people—have not grasped, and will not. Gates continues to insist that we need not worry, particularly, about the dangers of "individual overindulgence" in recreational networking. But some of the 'net's own creators, as we shall see, are less sanguine about the hazards of virtual unreality.

Gatsby, by comparison, represents a relatively benign figure or type: the damage done by his misguided pursuit of personal fulfillment and a golden future had limited (though tragic) consequences. Still, there are uncanny parallels between Gatsby and Gates, symbols both of their own times and of paradigmatically narrow but "sophisticated" approaches to life. Their examples seduce millions to embrace the cutting edge of an eviscerated reality and a flattening of the possibilities of self and culture.

Here is a bit more grist for the virtual unreality mill: Tim Berners-Lee, one of the pioneering founders of the Internet as we know it, is disappointed in the typically passive "web" experience of most users. He had hoped for a much more truly interactive, socially constructive, and creative medium than it is turning out to be, and he is concerned that it

> will allow cranks and nut cases to find in the world 20 or 30 other cranks and nut cases who are absolutely convinced of the same things, allow them to set up filters around themselves . . . and develop a pothole of culture out of which they can't climb, [resulting finally in] a world which is full of very, very disparate cultures which don't talk to each other.[15]

He is right to worry about that. The web's potential to feed and magnify fragmentation, mistrust, and misanthropy is frightening. Stanford political scientist Norman Nie, director of a study concluding that our sudden immersion in cyberspace threatens our social cohesion, put it bluntly: "When you spend your time on the Internet, you never hear a human voice and you never get a hug."[16] And yet, it is encouraging to find an influential 'net leader such as Berners-Lee making this kind of sense: "At the end of the day, it's up to us: how we actually react, and how we teach our children, and the values we instill." Gates, also, sounds the right note here (if only we can trust that he grasps its full significance): "The Internet will draw us together if that's what we choose, or let us scatter ourselves into a million mediated communities . . . will give us choices that can put us in touch with information . . . and each other."[17]

A "Doonesbury" cartoon strip once presented a character in front of his computer terminal, bored but oblivious to the beautiful mountain backdrop beyond his window, and thinking to himself, "I feel like [I need] a new information stream. . . . I know, television!" Is our vital information lost or just neglected and overlooked? If the latter, we can still pursue its recovery. We can unplug from our devices and reconnect with the natural information at our feet. We can, but will we?

George Trow has written trenchantly about our ironic, hip television culture, epitomized by David Letterman and the *Simpsons*.[18] His critique invokes the idea of lost "manhood" and an absence of seriousness about life, which was once so ingrained in our collective sensibility that no one thought anything about it and without which we now find ourselves leading lesser lives. This is the sort of thing James talks about in connection with the "gravity" of the religious mind and its refusal of "light irony."[19] Such talk of "manhood" falls right into the irony trap nowadays and is easily lampooned: think of Robert Bly's *Iron John* and the "men's liberation movement" of a few years ago, or about the more recent "Promise Keepers" of the Christian right. But if we can get past our own inveterate irony, we may begin to see the relevance, today, of calls for the renewal of a seriousness that can absorb James's simple, "universal message": "All is not vanity in this Universe."

There is no denying the computer's practical utility and ever growing potential as a mind-expanding tool, a spur to creativity, and a bridge between people, connecting one another's ideas. But as we accustom ourselves to the idea of computer-facilitated "networking," we risk reducing the whole digital phenomenon to one more consumer-oriented data stream that may supplant or, at the least, compete with, a more direct relationship with nature and the information of the senses, which alone can secure us to the palpable soil of Mother Earth. As we develop a dependent relation to uninterrupted streams of electronically mediated information, passively ingested, we risk losing our native capacity to think and feel for ourselves. If all experience is secondhand, we ourselves will become secondhand beings, information processors, virtual persons at best.

This is not a uniquely electronic problem. Emerson, for instance, was at war with mediation and derivative experience in the nineteenth century. But in our time the vehicles of mediation are so much more pervasive and invasive of personal consciousness. A trivial example often noted: young people working in retail jobs nowadays are increasingly challenged by the relatively simple task of exchanging currency accurately; rarely do they know how to "count back" one's change. They have been taught to rely on calculators for even the most basic transactions of daily life, and for the most part the reliability of calculating technology supports this reliance. But we have to wonder whether the next generation, or subsequent generations, will develop so strong a reliance on computers that people will experience steady erosion of their ability to think an original thought, to feel an honest emotion. Are we witnessing the ascendancy of a new form of perception, one that limits possibility to the confined bounds of what is renderable in virtual representations of thought and feeling? If so, human reality itself is being squashed and neutered.

The question of James's naturalism must address not only the issue of its relation to supernaturalism but also to a largely uncritical popular eagerness to embrace every new form of virtual experience. When bodily immediacy no longer secures our grip on reality, we are too far from home. James would recoil from the insular subjectivism of our brave new Information Age, which has been aptly described as an age of *missing* information.[20] What is missing is the information of the senses, synthesized by the *actual* central processing unit of the brain and central nervous system but made user friendly in each instance by the uniquely personal contributions of the users themselves. Without this information, we cannot generate for ourselves the sympathetic appreciation of others' experience, which is a prerequisite of panhistorical human solidarity. That, in turn, is necessary for the personal identification with remote futurity that may fuel forms of transcendence unknown to egoists, sensualists, and (their new cousins) virtualists.

George Lakoff and Mark Johnson have suggested that we can retrieve our missing information by attending more carefully to how biological embodiment structures every aspect of our metaphorical hold on the world and on all our relationships. Like James and Dewey, they discern powerfully spiritual implications in the universally carnal human condition. Our organic form is inherently socializing.

A major function of the embodied mind is empathic. From birth we have the capacity to imitate others, to vividly imagine being another person, doing what that person does, experiencing what that person experiences. The capacity for imaginative projection is a vital cognitive faculty. Experientially it is a form of "transcendence."[21]

Such transcendence is as natural as the body, and as intimately personal as our imaginations are rich. Yet, it relates us vitally to others, surmounting the confines of narrow selfhood. Transcendence defies reduction to computational models of mind which suppose that the neural hardware of our bodies can host any compatible program, indifferently. "Real people have embodied minds whose conceptual systems arise from, are shaped by, and are given meaning through living human bodies."[22] This means specific bodies, and persons.

The Jamesian view, again, is that happiness and unhappiness as personal phenomena are vital mysteries, opening onto ranges and depths of experience not wholly available to unpoetic or unspiritual natures, not even minimally so to those who actively or voluntarily withdraw from the vitalizing immediacies of firsthand natural and social relations. Subjectivity is at the core of this mystery, at once the most familiar and the strangest of phenomena. Life in its endless variety is wondrously beyond discursive capture, as (honest) conscious intelligence is intimately aware. Yet the hubris persists among many sensitive and subtle thinkers that belief in human progress must in principle mean the eventual elimination of mystery (Dennett, again, exemplifies this attitude). James believed in progress but in permanent mystery as well, and this is a clue to what is potentially transcendent in a melioristic metaphysic.

In hitching our own personal sense of well-being to the millennial prospects of the race, we expand the region of wonder surrounding our private destiny so that it can embrace, as well, the ideals of the vast human fraternity, past, present, and future. We engage the permanent possibility of meaningful exertion in behalf of common hopes, but not at the expense of individual dreams. And personal imagination retains the prerogative of defining those hopes and dreams, plotting our advance on them, and ranking alternatives. In short, this is a kind of transcendence through which individuals realize a vitalizing attachment to something immeasurably larger and more enduring than themselves, yet are required to renounce none of those personal, individual, "romantic" elements of selfhood which, though transient and unstable, are the animating centers of our lives, our respective founts of happiness. This is transcendence via expanded selfhood, that is, truly expansive, not self-annihilating. It does not exchange the familiar self for a vague abstraction; rather, it convenes all the idiosyncratic selves in a marriage of hope. But with respect to personal enthusiasm, identity, and aspiration, it is an "open" marriage. It defines faithfulness in terms not of renunciation but of mutual consent, forbearance, and tolerance.

Transcendence is a depth experience, and of course there are as many possible approaches to depth as there are ways of being mindfully attentive. Depth resides in traces of historical experience pointing to rich funds of remembered subjectivity, also preserved in the external memory of books, still the only "storage medium" we can rely on not to become obsolete in a generation or less. Depth is present in the hot current of concentrated perception. And it inheres as well in purposive contemplation of a future which, from our vantage, contains many more possibilities than will actually transpire, many opportunities for rich and rewarding relations of all kinds to be affected, and as many risks of the reverse.

We live in a time when depth experiences are increasingly difficult to come by, when experience itself is treated as a "virtual" commodity, and mysterious subjectivity is recycled as prosaic "information" to be skimmed from the theoretically unlimited network database the world is rushing to wire itself into. "Bits are steadily supplanting atoms," writes Sven Birkerts. "Our living has gradually less to do with things, places, and human presence, and more to do with messages, mediated exchanges, ersatz environments, and virtual engagements of all descriptions."[23] There is a bit of the apocalyptic curmudgeon in Birkerts, but his elegant and sober challenge to the unexamined assumption that printed text on paper is inconsequentially interchangeable with phosphorescent text on computer monitors is important and timely. Has our infatuation with the web's promise of infinite information clouded our judgment? Are we releasing our grip on the distinction between the real and the virtual, between what is immediate and what is filtered or fabricated? And are we, in consequence, experiencing an unprecedented "crisis of subjectivity"?

There does seem to be a deliberateness to the pace of reading a book and meditating one's response to it, and to the pace of writing and rewriting until words and thoughts form a unity of intention and meaning, which seems oddly inappropriate online. So, it becomes a cause for some concern when an influential scholar announces that "I find myself increasingly unlikely to consult material that is not online" and replies to reading-list suggestions that "if they put their books online I might read them."[24]

One way of disarming such concern might be to suggest that the virtual/real distinction is not so distinct after all, that "all reality is virtual [and] the only reason for calling a simulation a virtual reality is that its virtuality is more obvious."[25] But this is not persuasive. If we take our own experience at all seriously, we must agree with C. S. Peirce that daily encounters with "limitation, conflict, constraint," in general the "teaching of experience" that he calls "Secondness," furnishes the "main lesson of life."[26] But is this only a "virtual" kind of lesson, and what can *that* mean? This sounds like a professional philosopher's puzzle, maybe even a pleasantly diverting one, but it does not seem much engaged with most people's actual experience of life.

What is "virtual reality?" It has always been with us in one form or another. Literary fiction and poetry often succeed by implanting illusory experiences of virtual reality in a reader's consciousness. Great art and music may do the same, in less straightforward ways. The sophistication of those "virtual" experiences available to us in lieu of inaccessible actual ones is, in some respects, a measure of our progress as a civilization. There is nothing intrinsically or uniformly desiccating about them. But, to spend an inordinate portion of one's conscious existence reading even the best literature, or patronizing the finest museums—never mind sporting a VR suit and headset—surely would be. Serious intellectual or aesthetic activity is, of course, very different from the passive form of virtual entertainment to be ingested from television or computers, if only because it *is* active and engaged with our intelligence and our more humane sympathies. At the opposite extreme, too many of our contemporaries are already plugged in—to television mainly but with the Internet beginning now to capture a growing share of their leisure time—far beyond acceptable hygienic limits. Between the extremes of hyperaestheticism and immersion in an increasingly debased pop culture—daytime TV has become a misanthropic abomination, from Geraldo to Beavis and Butthead; primetime is a nightmare of "reality" programming, often as contrived as professional wrestling, itself inexplicably resurgent in popularity. It is increasingly difficult to imagine sane virtual environments for the masses.

There are many reasons to be disturbed by present trends, none more compelling than the question of the legacy we are preparing for our children: what sort of natural environment will be there for them to enjoy, and what habitual relations to it will we teach them to prefer? Birkerts has confessed a "swarm of angst" about this, imagining (like E. M. Forster in "The Machine Stops") "a future gone virtual in the extreme" in which people "devote themselves almost exclusively to the exchange of information and ideas by means of a peculiar apparatus. . . ."[27] We are not there yet, but this vision is no longer safely consigned to the science fiction racks.

A good way of confronting one's pessimism is by the hopeful act of uncovering its causes and conditions, so far as these are not strictly of one's own peculiar and personal constitution. Not "The sky is falling!" but "Look, the sky seems unstable; what shall we do, now, to steady it?" The sudden emphasis on modes of experience with the world that shut out sensory contact with fresh air and open landscapes seems to some of us one source of instability. Others think that the "limitations and even perversions of communication and learning that are inherent in practices based on the paper-embodied word"[28] can be ameliorated by computer networking. Let us all hope they are right. And let us hope that everyone's focus will eventually regain enough of the combined spirit of Jamesian pluralism and Peircean fallibilism to converge on repairs to salvage what is valuable in every medium of expressive human communication.

Meanwhile, many proclaim a world just around the corner in which we will all be "connected," superficially. And in a world so homogeneously unified, we might be right to worry about the persistence of anything but surfaces. Unless we choose to revive and to revere the mystery of our own and others' subjectivity, the depth of the richest forms of experience could be lost to us. Can we follow the current trend of digitizing most aspects of our lives, plug in to extensive computer networks, indulge the fantasies of virtual reality, *and* still feed and shelter the flame of subjective mystery which, for James and others, contributes so much of the richness and dimensionality of personal experience?

Yes, if we remember how and when and why to pull the plug. There can be no virtual substitute for the real experiences of depth and transcendence, of triumph and joy, of disappointment and sorrow. We will not find reality in bits and simulacra, useful and even transforming though they may be. We must continue to seek it within ourselves and in our reflective relations to others and to nature. And we must continue to express it in our art and in our free actions and dispositions. Then the world will be safe for network mediation.

There is room in the world for a multiplicity of delights and enjoyments; that is part of the meaning of pluralism. So a Jamesian must welcome the "virtual" deliverance of meaningful or pleasant (even if derivative and secondhand) perceptions. But our Jamesian will still hesitate to concede depth, in the honorific sense, to an experience that elides the distinction between what is immediate and real and what is mediated, contrived, and artificial. Recalling James's disdain for subjectivism that treats consciousness as the mise-en-scène of our private amusement, we can be sure that whatever transcendence anyone may be fortunate enough to glean under the auspices of virtual experience, it is not all that it might be: actual, connected fruitfully with nature and the social world.

When I speak of the virtual as shallow, I am thinking not only of the donning of multimedia headsets or the strapping on of body suits with millions of little stimulators to trick the senses. I mean the day-to-day tissue of experience in a culture that views such promised entertainments not only as not inferior but in some cases as clearly superior to the pedestrian pleasures that have always, heretofore, gratified human beings: breathing and moving in fresh air, conversing with real people in real time, delighting in the sensual aesthetic of our own solitary senses. The holographic presentation of a walk in a gentle spring rain, which I hope someday to enjoy for myself on some dreary winter's day, can never replace the real thing. Such an experience may be stunningly satisfying, and taken on its own terms there is no reason to deny that it may have its own kind of depth and resonance. But if we ever find ourselves not bothering to notice whether we are indoors or out, in the holosuite or in the rain, we will have lost an important hold on who and what we are.

Is this an implausible science fiction horror story or a real danger? Perhaps I and others are being needlessly alarmist, but I would rather risk overreacting than allow the virtualists to lure us onto the unreflectively digitized "road ahead," paved though it may be with honorable intentions. I remain steadfastly unwilling to risk the future of experience to those who often describe themselves as "geeks" and "tech-nerds" and who have spent the better part of their waking lifetime glued to screens, never registering a flicker of concern or even recognition that there might be an issue of the social and personal impact of these new media of experience.

This is one motive for insisting on a sense of mystery at the heart of subjective experience. The rush to translate all into data and information may leave us without the will or the wish to prefer what is original and authentic, or even to recognize that category at all. If we acknowledge the untranslatable mystery of our selfhood, we will not be fooled by so much superficially seductive and mesmerizing information. But if transcendence is to be naturalized, so must this mystery. If we find the coupling of mystery and naturalism somehow counterintuitive and untenable, if we believe that naturalized understanding must be prosaic, demystifying, and dull, we have misread the mystery. We need to turn back before we can move ahead.

Our biology lies behind that mystery but does not solve it. We reengineer our world both physically and imaginatively, we interpolate ourselves amidst the countless causal forces having made up the world heretofore, and now we believe it in our power to reconstruct the world to some degree, as causal forces in our own right. How shall we use that power? What kind of world are we in the process of making? What "sub-worlds" will it contain? Can it ever not be boundless in containing more points of view or dimensions of reality than can fit into any conceivable database?

But this last question serves as a reminder that virtual forms of experience may also be meaningful and illuminating, may open partially on those elusive dimensions of reality, if we learn from them even just a little of how others may perceive the world. One clear way in which "the virtual also has its depth and meaning"[29] is in its vestigial capacity to provide experiences we would otherwise miss altogether—"vestigial" because we have always had virtual reality and virtual experiences; the computer-generated version is only the latest and possibly the most atypical example. Anything that stands surrogate for something else and invites us to experience that other thing vicariously, through its mediation, is virtual. Some of those surrogates are contrived and artificial, but that should not automatically discredit them.

The printed word, like all human communication, is a deliberate contrivance. One of its "killer apps" is literary fiction, a virtual universe owing its existence and whatever salutary properties it possesses to that contrivance. Through the medium of fiction we can enter for a time into the subjective space, may gain interior access to the sensibilities, of another. We can virtually experience what it might have been like to be a peasant farmer in medieval England, to be a Hindu mystic, to walk on the moon, or to see the world as our grandparents saw it in their youth—virtually, not actually. That is limiting, of course, but far less than the condition of near-total ignorance, which is our aboriginal state. So, virtual reality can—in principle—deepen our sense of mystery. The important assumption here is that by learning more of another's subjectivity from the inside, virtually, we come to know that person, that self, better and also better appreciate the mystery of selfhood. The mystery does not vanish; it grows in richness and complexity.

But the narrowly scientistic paradigm cannot compass the idea of mystery as a virtue. A popular definition of information, in the computer world, is the reduction of uncertainty. This understanding places a premium on the exponential growth of data, but has no use for the kind of foggy uncertainty embodied in mysterious selfhood. This is not the way to naturalize mystery. If the purpose of naturalizing mystery is not to "solve" or eliminate it but to strengthen our appreciation of how it animates human souls—and in the process to grasp something basic about our condition—then it is fundamentally mistaken to define mystery as the absence of data. The digital rendering of experience is a boon for many purposes, but not for this one.

An affirmative statement of how to naturalize the enduring mystery of selfhood must take account of what we know about our origins. We are back on the terrain of evolutionary biology, not biology sequestered from the rest of life but smack in the middle of it all.

This is why—despite Dennett's un-Jamesian suggestion that evolution tends toward the perfect disposal of mystery—a Jamesian should still prefer Dennett's expansive position on the breadth of "Darwin's Dangerous Idea" to the deceptively humane scientism of Stephen Jay Gould, among others. But Dennett has his own deflationary tendencies, too. His vision is not James's.

Somehow our thinking about evolution must make room for the insight that the perfections we are reaching for as individuals and as a species need not answer, or abandon, all the perplexities of living. We become larger and more interesting, the more questions we are comfortable with leaving open. This suggests a boundary, a point beyond which a certain kind of evolutionary thinking may be unhelpful: nature fosters random variation and mutation and vastly more differentiation of form than is sustainable in finitely integrated ecosystems. Hence, whereas competition for survival among plant and animal species produces an overall healthy genus, family, or order, it may become pernicious and oppressive if applied in human society.

Even after we have absorbed the necessary lessons about what is wrong with social Darwinism, we must welcome a degree of competition in the social world, too: some ideas must compete for favor; not all points of view are sustainable; some ought to perish. Subjectivity, though magnificently various, is not infinitely so. Some forms of subjectivity are self-destructive, some are dangerous to the community at large, but, in general, the social world can afford to be much more hospitable to variety than can the lower realms and is more likely to profit from its tolerance.

This is one of the more inspiring implications of personal transcendence, and it is important that we see it, itself, as an evolutionary result. Indeed, we have grown into whatever respect we evince for the virtue of tolerance and have a great deal more growing and evolving to do. But here is the "grandeur in this view of life" of which Darwin wrote, that from so simple and asocial a beginning we have evolved a civilization that can appreciate and defend its own internal variety and can see the positive worth of it. Out of this broadly biological awareness, I believe, can grow the understanding (not a solution) of mystery we seek.

Calling the appreciation of variety a human-biological imperative, and enlisting the sciences of life into the service of mystery, may itself mystify those who philosophize mainly to answer questions and not equally to profit from their mere asking. Impatient for results and unreceptive to complicating nuance, they will have little use for James's approach, finally a variant of this ancient cosmic conundrum: How comes the world to be here at all instead of the nonentity that might be imagined in its place? Why something rather than nothing? The mystery of subjectivity is not only about the ultimate mystery of all that is—the bare fact of our perspectivally limited recognizance places each of us behind a veil to some extent—but it is about that, too. It is our subjectivity, our questioning, our origins and unfated destiny, our *mystery*, which is at issue.

Old ideas about evolution must give way to fresh thinking about our place in nature. The explosive impact of "augmented" extensions of ourselves—including new information technologies—has resulted in a fundamental redirection of the path we are taking as a species. We are becoming very different from what we would have been otherwise.[30] That is somewhat overstated, since we could undoubtedly point to many such watershed developments in the natural and cultural history of humankind, from the discovery of fire to the printing press to internal combustion. But there is something excitingly and disturbingly different about what is happening now. "Augmentation" may just be another name for mediation, with consequences both good and bad. But it also means, in theory, that we can all be major players now, major influences in the total process of plotting our trajectory into an uncertain future. "In theory" covers much ambiguous ground, but that expression is rich ground, worth digging into.

There is a lot of trendy talk in the air these days about "horizontal" and "vertical" relationships, and clearly the rise of personal computing and networking offers unprecedented opportunities for a much wider and deeper range of contact between individuals and institutions. Contact means influence, but it remains to be seen whether the influence will on balance be salutary or depletive of our capacity to have experiences that strengthen our respective holds on life.

This question of influence, and of our role as responsible sponsors of it, is central to the pragmatic interest in evolution. The next section deals with this: How can we, as individuals and as a race, influence the future? Has purposive goal-seeking behavior a place in the evolutionary account of our destiny, or must we accept a picture of mindlessness and purposelessness as the engine of natural history even after purposive human intelligence has arrived on the scene?

Evolution is a broad concept. Its usefulness as such depends upon our imaginative ability to grasp its significance as more than just a descriptive theory of how certain natural events might be explicated. Pragmatic naturalists see in it as well the exciting spectacle of an intelligent species taking its first hesitant but thrilling steps toward real self-regulation and the direction of its own destiny, toward nothing less than the "conquest of happiness" and a bright future. In this light, those who insist on a narrow construction of what may properly be called "evolutionary," excluding culture and society altogether, seem pedantic and stifling of the spirit.

It seems much better to agree with James and the Pragmatists that we should not to be rigid or ideological about this, but see how fecund the evolution idea may turn out to be when we loosen the grips on its scope as a creative and metaphorical story about the human journey. If it shows us possibilities we had not noticed, for ourselves and our descendants, it will have paid its way. Evolution creates and configures life, including culture, and we need to express the cultural (or human) aspect of this grand process in a way that does not gratuitously diminish us. The concept of natural transcendence is useful in this regard because it preserves human creativity without assimilating it to what Dennett calls mindless, purposeless, mechanical or "algorithmic" methods of creation. Transcendence is creative because it engenders the imaginative worlds we enjoy and from which we reap the meanings of our lives.

But it is creative not only in an interior or private way, unless we live utterly isolated and uncommunicative lives. There may in fact exist a kind of vehicle, as we will discuss in the next section, that can carry personal transcendence beyond the borders of our skin, but—to strain a metaphor—we have to remain in the driver's seat if we do not want the car (and the meanings of our lives) to get away from us. If that were to happen, creativity—which in this context means responsibility for the human future, to our heirs—would be lost. Or as James would say, we would be stuck with the fatalists' Block Universe, and that optimism which turns on our hopefulness about acting deliberately and responsibly would no longer be an option for us. It would be sad irony indeed if that were the final outcome of philosophical reflections on evolution.

## A Pragmatic Perspective on Evolution and Culture

> ...the vigorous, the healthy, and the happy survive and multiply.
>
> Darwin, *Origin of Species*

> Evolution is a change from a no-howish untalkaboutable all-alikeness by continuous sticktogetherations and somethingelsifications.
>
> James's lecture notes[31]

Daniel Dennett has made much[32] of English biologist Richard Dawkins's idea of "memes," source of one of the bigger firestorms to have emerged from recent attempts to philosophize in the key of Darwin.[33] A meme is a unit of influence, a kind of cultural gene alleged to function in the world of ideas, much as genes function in biology, conveying information and influence that spread through speech, writing, and the myriad ways in which human beings enter one another's orbits. Dawkins introduced the term in 1976:

> Examples of memes are tunes, ideas, catch-phrases, clothes fashions, ways of making pots or of building arches. Just as genes propagate themselves in the gene pool by leaping from body to body via sperm or eggs, so memes propagate themselves in the meme pool by leaping from brain to brain via a process which, in the broad sense, can be called imitation. If the idea catches on it can be said to propagate itself, spreading from brain to brain.[34]

The whiff of determinism here bothers most pragmatists. James and Dewey held that subjectivity, mind, and consciousness attach quite naturally to a species in the throes of evolutionary development. Selfishness and magnanimity are for them marks not of the genetic or memetic but of the volitional, personal, and human. We, not memes, are the "meaning-makers" of our own evolutionary epic. Perhaps, then, we can make something of them, too, writes Connie Barlow, "conscientiously using memes for the good of the whole Earth community. Life, evolution, and the universe can then become exuberantly conscious of themselves."[35] The contribution of happiness to survival and flourishing is central to James's and the Pragmatists' compelling interest in evolution. The hope that happiness may "multiply," by evolutionary forces that in time become modestly responsive to our wills, is why modern pragmatists will insist on the possibility of our ultimate independence from memes or anything else that might coerce or exhaust our thinking.

Memeology's philosophical lineage is cloudy but worth pondering, in light of the Hegelian influence that Dewey had to cast off before coming to a more individualistic understanding of how influence itself actually occurs in the perpetual struggle of ideas. "Hegel seems to have done a lot of harm by making people believe that ideas and social forms can reproduce themselves."[36] I do not know whether Dawkins or Dennett would happily confess the influence of the Hegel meme, but their view seems to invite speculation about such sources. It must also be noted that Dennett dismisses "silly" or "greedy" reductionism with un-Hegelian circumspection about the reach of rational understanding: "*Of course* you can't explain all the patterns that interest us at any one level," biology not excepted.[37] Cultural phenomena, then, require explanation in their own terms, not in those of biological evolution univocally construed.

The suggestion that memes propagate themselves—effectively untethering them from individuals and their deliberate acts—is an echo of Dawkins's metaphorical attribution of selfishness to genes. We might find it useful, at the level of metaphor, to think of these units of biological information exchange as using persons for the genes' own ends. But if we wish to retain an older and still more useful self-concept as whole persons acting with foresight and some degree of self-determination and enlightened altruism, we will check this metaphor at the door and reassert the more complex picture of organism-environment interactivity, which retains for us at least partial relevance as "environmental factors" (among others). The point was nicely put this way by Robert Sapolsky:

> By now I hope we have gotten past "genes determine behavior" to "genes modulate how one responds to the environment" . . . to "genes can be convenient tools used by environmental factors to influence behavior" . . . [I]t's less accurate to think "evolution is about natural selection for different assemblages of genes" than it is to think "evolution is about natural selection for different sensitivities and responses to environmental influences."[38]

And as environmental factors we act in reference to the purposes and needs of our own variable natures, under descriptions capable of inspiring purposive acts. Steven Pinker has also commented,

> Resist the temptation to think of the goals of our genes as our deepest, truest, most hidden motives. Genes are a play within a play, not the interior monologue of the players. As far as we are concerned, our goals, conscious or unconscious, are not about genes at all but about health and lovers and children and friends. . . . People don't have the goal of

propagating genes; people have the goal of pursuing satisfying thoughts and feelings.[39]

This is surely right, but it seems gratuitous of Pinker to add that our goals are "subgoals of the ultimate goal of the genes." If we take experience *including our goals* seriously, there is nothing more ultimate than the purposes to which we voluntarily subordinate our acts.

If the metaphorical idea of selfish genes is troublesome, the idea of memes is even more so. This idea threatens to swamp a potentially useful heuristic tool with abstraction and irrelevance. It implies a profoundly false picture of how ideas gain influence and inspire imitation. The pragmatic individualism of James and Dewey may offer a constructive alternative.

The philosophical stakes involved in this debate are immense. Daniel Dennett has come to Dawkins's defense against charges of "sociobiology" and "reductionism," and in the process has sounded some disquieting notes. Dawkins concedes,

> We have the power to defy the selfish genes of our birth and, if necessary, the selfish memes of our indoctrination. . . . We are built as gene machines and cultured as meme machines, but we have the power to turn against our creators. We, alone on earth, can rebel against the tyranny of the selfish replicators.[40]

Dennett, however, thinks that Dawkins concedes too much. Dennett argues that the "we" that stands apart from memes, surveys them, and selects some for favor and targets others for opposition is a myth: memes replicate themselves in hot pursuit of their own "selfish" survivalist agenda. Our minds and purposes are epiphenomenal to the evolutionary process; memes' (and genes') purposes are somehow just the evolutionary process. What we call our ideas turn out to be self-proprietary memetic entities in their own right, and our minds are "artifact[s] created when memes restructure a human brain in order to make it a better habitat for memes."[41] *We* are those memes that have infested our consciousness; *memes are us.*

This leans toward caricature but not far enough to allay reasonable doubt about the benignity of its implications for human autonomy, agency, identity, and critical self-correction. Memes challenge the liberal faith that we may gain independent purchase on ideas and ourselves and direct our social behavior in ways for which we may rightly accept real responsibility. "What makes a person the person he or she is are the coalitions of memes that govern—that play the long-term roles in determining which decisions are made along the way."[42] Such task-force teleology seems flatly incompatible with personal responsibility and autonomy.

How shall we find a handle on these cumbersomely large issues? One handle is the idea of progress. In *Descent of Man,* Darwin does not cavil about the "progress" of civilization: "Progress has been much more general than retrogression. [Humanity] has risen," thanks to bodily adaptation, intelligence, and cooperation.[43] But according to Darwin's own account it seems we deserve little credit, being the spawn of inexorable, impersonal nature. If our first impulse is to feel insulted by an account that sends mind and culture to the sidelines, we should balance that response by recalling the sordid history of those who misappropriated Darwin, those self-serving and malefic social predators who lurk in every culture and era. Better, perhaps, to absorb insult than to court a systematically misanthropic misreading of the great book of nature. Danger lurks at the nexus of science and society, the most egregious of historical examples being the shameless leisure-class apologia of "Social Darwinism" in the Gilded Age and its crude, lingering "survival of the fittest" ethos. Small insult in the form of some cultural irrelevance in the unfolding drama of natural history would, perhaps, be a fair price for social rectitude. If treating one another equably requires the downscaling of our exalted self-estimation as historical agents, so be it. But the total irrelevance of cultural direction in our ascent from Hobbesian primitivism seems a price too steep and deflating. It feels like surrender, as we confront unprecedented challenges seeming to demand more effective thoughtfulness, not less.

Darwin himself, while insisting that "not one living species will transmit its unaltered likeness to a distant futurity," also trumpets an unabashed hopefulness about the future. "Hence we may look with some confidence to a secure future of great length. . . . [A]ll corporeal and mental endowments will tend to progress towards perfection." And it is in this context that *Origin of Species* concludes with its stirring but measured homage to the "grandeur in this view of life . . . [F]rom so simple a beginning, endless forms . . . have been and are being evolved."[44]

The idea of evolutionary development through the "multiplying" not only of genetic but of "memetic" materials is a twist on the theory about which we can only speculate as to Darwin's own response. Some may find it instructive to search for the "founder's intent" in this regard; but whatever he might have said about the evolution of the *idea* of evolution in our own time, and about the astonishing range of new conditions it has been stretched to clothe, we have our hands full scrambling for an appropriately human and humane response to the rapidity of change. Perhaps Darwin's words can help a little, but (to select one of many possible examples) the advent and ascendancy of computing and "information" technologies is new territory for our species. It calls for a resourcefulness of response that cannot allow itself either to repose in archaic attitudes and stale assumptions or to leap unreflectively into an unlit future.

"Progress" is possible but not inevitable, James and the ameliorative pragmatists contend. The most optimistic of us must admit that the world does continue to challenge our belief in cultural evolutionary progress. What, for instance, would an advanced extraterrestrial observer make of the spectacle of millions of people paying to watch, in the name of sport, a onetime violent felon attempt to render his opponent unconscious and who, when unable, became so enraged that he tried to bite off the opponent's ear?[45] Or what would our observer think of our nauseating, predictable penchant for spilling one another's blood for land? Or of our "ethnic cleansing," our "final solutions," our perpetual refusal to coexist peacefully with those who look or think differently from us, our inability to nurture and educate all our children in safety? Not so much, let us hope, as they might think of our undeniably rapid advances in technology and the appurtenances of physical comfort. Those successes, perhaps especially those enhancing our capacity for significant communication, permit us to anticipate more advances ahead, possibly even in the moral sphere. "[H]ere we be," muses Annie Dillard, "I at my laptop computer, you with a book in your hands. We are . . . the [animals] whose neocortexes swelled, who just happen to write encyclopedias and fly to the moon. Can anyone believe this?"[46] It *is* nearly unbelievable but strangely true.

But even if nature works mechanically for the survival of some of our distant descendants, theirs will not automatically be a progressive inheritance. The view of progress as hanging in the balance, awaiting our next and subsequent moves (among other indeterminate variables), is directly implied by a pragmatic understanding of human freedom that stipulates the relevance of choice and act subject to the lessons of subsequent experience. Progress, for the pragmatist, means applied and creative learning that is purposive, mindful, spontaneous, and ever at risk of regress. The public function of critical intelligence, which must be the philosopher's most valuable role in a democracy, seems demeaned by the equation of ideas with self-replicating memes pursuing a cultural agenda not our own. From this angle all bets are off, once minds and purposes take the stage of history. What we and our progeny do matters.

Daniel Dennett presents an "algorithmic" interpretation of human progress, saying bluntly that "all the fruits of evolution can be explained as the products of an algorithmic process."[47] An algorithmic process is mechanical, mindless, purposeless, and automatic, so long as nothing interferes with the initial conditions of its operation. Of course that is just what free will is supposed to do: "interfere." Depending, therefore, upon how literally or to what degree he believes in this quasi-mathematical talk, we must declare him an antipragmatist (in the sense indicated in the previous paragraph).

There are at least two main counts on which an algorithmic account of human progress may run seriously afoul of the pragmatic view. First, such an account—pushed to the limit—would be a version of fatalism. Even short of that limit, it may still leave less latitude for autonomy than a Jamesian will accept. Second, it may validate survival as such, in whatever guise, as "progress." A pragmatist will reserve that validation for a future that has effectively rectified some of the ills besetting us, that exhibits a flexibility or adaptability to unforeseen challenges capable of inspiring renewed and confident hopefulness, and in which our descendants retain a devotion to at least some of those values that by our lights are ingredient to responsible personhood. Foremost among the those values is a willingness to examine reflectively, to revise, and to replace ideas that do not cohere with experience at large. Such willingness would mean nothing, however, uncoupled from belief in our ability to transcend whatever external genesis our ideas may have had and either to make them our own or to effectively renounce them, to internalize or to expel the ideas that shape our humanity for good or ill.

Why should it not be possible to reconstruct memeology so as to accommodate the contingency, risk, and bracing open-endedness that the pragmatic sensibility so ardently requires?[48] Indeed, we might credit Dennett with proposing just such a reconstruction if only he can square the apparent incongruity of entirely algorithmic evolution with such statements as this:

> Whereas animals are rigidly controlled by their biology, human behavior is largely determined by culture, a largely autonomous system of symbols and values, growing from a biological base, but growing indefinitely away from it . . . to overpower or escape biological constraints in most regards. . . .[49]

A pragmatist has no quarrel with memeology thus qualified, and might even welcome it as offering real insight into those insidious inertial prejudices we allow to root and fester, unchallenged, too much of the time. The image of minds as being "infected" or "infested" by invasive memes is not a bad depiction of the unexamined life. It is a powerful reminder to be more self-critical, less complacent about the genesis, merit, and application of our favorite ideas. This is the language and the mission of pragmatism par excellence: to test all our beliefs by acting on them, noting the results, and revising belief and conduct accordingly.

One tenet of pragmatic faith implied by all this is the conviction that after we have reflected, parsed, debated, and, especially, *acted* upon our ideas with open eyes and supple reflexes, the remaining meme complex must be critically stronger than it was; and it must be something we will be prepared to endorse and call our own.[50]

Dennett points out that we do favor a large number of the meme-ideas that do, in fact, get replicated but that we do not favor a great many more we consider relatively benign and not worth the trouble of resisting. The truly pernicious and evil memes are a relative minority, although of course that does not in any way mitigate their potential destructiveness. The Nazi idea, and before that the anti-Semitic idea, has always been vastly outnumbered by others that most persons would have said they preferred. And that is no consolation at all to the Nazi meme's millions of victims. What matters most is not whether it is the memes that stimulated the favor of majorities and that do in fact get replicated and become influential, but whether someone's favoring them is causally decisive for their success. Unless our favoring or resisting certain memes can in principle decide their fate, we are relegated to a spectator's role. The fact of our favor or animus will be epiphenomenal and irrelevant to *their* impersonal agenda.

The Nazi meme was extraordinarily successful for an astonishing length of time, in a culture that had long been esteemed as a pillar of civilized sophistication. In addition, anti-Semitism remains unextinguished, as does racial intolerance generally. Consequently, because we so ineffectually resist so many memes, the suggestion that memes are self-replicating and resistant to our wills has a strong superficial allure. This phenomenon seems to explain their apparent immunity to so many of our exertions.

"Obviously a meme that causes individuals bearing it to kill themselves has a grave disadvantage, but not necessarily a fatal one . . . [A] suicidal meme can spread. . . ."[51] A literally suicidal meme would not spread without its hosts' complicity, and publicity: a solitary and private suicide is unlikely to inspire imitation. But the pathetic example of mass suicide cultism—Heaven's Gate or Jonestown, and the like—reminds us just how quickly a bizarre idea can find hosts willing and eager to proselytize and then heed a message of self-annihilation. On a monstrously larger scale, Nazism is a horrific example of a meme both self-destructive and murderous (if not literally or deliberately suicidal), but not *murderous* in the full sense, if we restrict talk to memes and not to persons. Memes cannot differentiate good from evil, and they cannot take a long view or a widely sympathetic view of human good. They cannot "take views" at all.

But we must take views and think ourselves autonomous, at least to the degree that we can plausibly intend to appraise our stock of ideas and the new ideas constantly coming down the pike, to search for flaw and prejudice in our own and others' thinking and to resist them with all the resources at our disposal. Thoreau said that "it is never too late to give up our prejudices,"[52] Dewey spoke of "subjecting to the test of consequences [our] most cherished prejudices,"[53] and James says the same in countless ways. Glib talk of memes takes none of this to heart. Dennett is not glib—not always—but his algorithmic approach to evolution needs to make elbow room for as much individual autonomy as we need in order not to feel help-less before the invasion of the memes.

Finally, all of this talk of memes replicating themselves, of colonizing human brains to that end, is potentially very misleading. Worst of all, it encourages abandoning the philosopher's most important social role: the exercise of critical intelligence. Dennett makes this mistake when he says things like, "there is no necessary connection between a meme's replicative power, its 'fitness' from its point of view, and its contribution to our fitness. . . ."[54] A meme simply has no point of view; neither has a gene, for that matter. Having a point of view, or subjectivity, to a degree capable of sustaining purposes, intentions, and symbolic achievements of the sort we routinely hatch and execute, is evidently just not in the make-up of anything much less complex than a person.

Some of my best friends, though, are not persons. I am very fond of my Labrador retrievers, for instance, and impressed by their above-average canine smarts and savvy, but they have not pondered any books (good or bad) lately. I do not doubt that they and I share a significant range of thoughts and feelings, perceptions of pleasure and pain, and various kinds of (memetic?) brain events. But they have given me no reason to suppose that they bring to their experience of the world—whatever that is precisely like, for them—a unique, personally ordered point of view that takes subtle account of time, regret and despair and cosmic hopefulness, and a sense of the existential burden and opportunity of metaphysical freedom, all refracted through an unrepeatably, unprogrammably complicated particular combination of experiences, preferences, aversions, and aspirations—in short, a sensibility anywhere near as evolved and supple as that of the common run of humans.

This seems too obvious to say, but it has not been obvious enough to meme researchers who think they can learn something important about the transfer of influence among humans by studying lower animal life—though birds, larks in particular, do have something to teach us! and as Whitman noticed, in some ways the lower animals display a higher dignity. My dogs are more trustworthy and good-natured by far than the common run. I would not say that about our cat, but I do envy her serene, supine contentedness in a shaft of morning sunlight and sometimes her evident indifference to external influence in any form. In general, though, the gene-meme analogy goes awry whenever it ignores the fact that humans, unlike lower forms, constantly formulate conscious and (in respect of survival) gratuitous personal ends and devise complex, impenetrable strategies to achieve them. Our interest in flourishing, beyond surviving, is our special mark. Our complexity of intentions is not always mirrored by moral sophistication, but we can learn.

The pragmatic position on memes is somewhere in the cross fire of those (like Dennett) who favor a computational, demystifying approach to consciousness and others (like Thomas Nagel and John Searle)[55] who are impressed by questions of "what it is like" to possess a subjectivity that is "deep" in a sense possibly applicable to bats and dogs but certainly to humans, defining, and at last beyond words and translations. Neuroanthropologist Terrence Deacon is another who expresses the pragmatic temper in this area. Deacon construes mind, in evolutionary and emergentist terms, as a bio-organic, nonmechanistic, tool-wielding source of creative spontaneity. Unlike computational models, he thinks, this picture of mind "provides a way of understanding that aspect of our experience that is least like clockwork: our experience of being the originators of our own thoughts, perceptions, and actions." Pragmatists take such experience seriously and mostly at face value: "We are what we experience ourselves to be. Our self-experience of intentions and will are not epiphenomenal illusions. They are what we should expect an evolutionlike process to feel like!"[56]

In pragmatic terms, such experiences are the vital pulse of our relatedness to a global process of inexorable transition. Asserting the existence of mind and consciousness not as entities but as functional phenomena, as James put it in his landmark essay *Does Consciousness Exist?* is to insist on our proper place in the total scheme of an evolving nature. We are both product and agent in that grand process: the part of creation that retrospectively witnesses its own genesis and possesses either the genius or the hubris to think itself fit to begin driving a part of the process as evolution proceeds. The "function in experience" that our thinking performs is, as James says, to know it; and for the pragmatist, knowledge is no mere spectator sport. Knowing experience, knowing reality is the enthusiastic acceptance of a contributing role in the unfolding drama of intelligent life, of the self-propagation of human influence and accomplishment. Deacon's view harmonizes nicely with James's neutral monism, and with the general proposal that we not devalue personal experience by pegging reality claims to prior, independent ontological commitments that may be less flexible than the flowing currents of time and change, mutation and selection that are constantly surprising us.

In addition, Deacon's approach contrasts with the predilection of behaviorists for "explaining" consciousness and mind in exterior, third-person terms that usually strike the pragmatist as explaining *away*, unsatisfactorily. Deacon speaks pragmatically when he says that "we do not need to explain away the subjective experience," that we need to accommodate it as a rung on the evolutionary ladder, not a stopping place but a stepping-stone, and as real as we find it at a given moment. This is an important token of something genuinely new under the sun: the early stirrings of self-aware, self-critical, self-assertive, and multiply self-propagating intelligence, which constantly overspills its own biogenetic container. "We are capable of what genetic evolution is not: forethought."[57] "Forethought" is a good name for this capacity of ours to wield influence that might otherwise play out—in the absence of our intelligent and self-possessed intervention—as something like memetic invasion. Dennett himself grudgingly concedes that "unlike natural selection, we are somewhat foresightful choosers of memes."[58]

How foresightful and forethinking can we be? Pragmatists see this as an open question, and they allow themselves to hope that we are getting more visionary and thoughtful as we go. It is an optimism, or meliorism, that they see as echoing Darwin but also as reinforcing him where he is weakest, in the domains of subjective consciousness and social hope. "When should we say that we, masters of our ideas, evaluate and choose the doctrines we will live by?"[59] Dennett is content not to answer his own question but simply to blur its lines with those of the insinuation that memes in some sense chart a course independent of our judgments and choices. This approach a pragmatist cannot endorse. It is always *we* who evaluate and choose (or who, in failing to choose, still have chosen) and we who reap the consequences and either learn to choose more wisely or else repeat our errors.

But perhaps that word *progress* (even more than the idea of it) remains indigestible for some. If so, let us inveigle the support of no less stalwart an opponent of the easy imputation of progress to the evolutionary process than Stephen Jay Gould. Recognizing the life-and-death stakes surrounding our acknowledgment that our natural history is indeed directional, he responds this way when asked what he most "dreads" about the next quarter century: "The possibility that human beings will come up with some invention that will cause us to permanently change our evolutionary direction and destroy ourselves."[60] If "our evolutionary direction" is slowly but steadily drawing us away from the precipice of probable extinction—even if not toward anything more definite that we can yet target or envision—that, like it or not, clearly is a kind of progress. We may as well like it, there being no better alternative.

But however we feel about whatever we call it, we ought not to sneer at movement that may just possibly secure our species' maturity, new possibilities of constructive social engagement and cooperative achievement. We can speak of all this as an "evolutionary direction" without intending any determinate destination or final outcome. We have no reason to refuse the path toward "ideal novelty," as James writes in a passage answering the memeologists' suggestion that we cannot gain an independent critical purchase on our ideas:

> the thing of deepest . . . significance in life does seem to be its character of progress, or that strange union of reality with ideal novelty which

it continues from one moment to another to present. To recognize ideal novelty is the task of what we call intelligence. Not every one's intelligence can tell which novelties are ideal.[61]

But if memes are in charge of our thinking, no one's intelligence can nominate fresh and worthy ideals, which is precisely why pragmatists will not underwrite a view asserting the dominance of memes, the dissipation of responsible choice, and the practical disappearance of persons.

If this seems an overstatement, to say that memeology must (if accurate) imply the end of personhood as we have known it, we must consider how easy it is *not* to grasp the extent to which the real existence of memes should overturn our most familiar ways of thinking and speaking. For example: if memes exist, and if they truly are pervasive and "*selfish* replicators," then it no longer makes sense to credit individuals with originating and promoting ideas. In such terms, memes do not come from persons; it has to be the other way around: persons are assemblages of dominant memes. We should not, then, explain the brilliance of Einstein's theories in terms of Einstein's creative genius; rather, we must explain Einstein's creative genius in terms of the memes that have found a niche in Einstein's brain, *if* memeology is correct. This will bother us and should, if we believe that human beings, their purposes and their unpredictable achievements, are real instigators in life. If we believe this, we will not believe that memes are us. Dennett has attempted to disarm such concerns by labeling them the "bugbear" of agency, but I am not persuaded that he has said anything to frighten the bugbear away. If there are to be agents at all in the universe, better that they should be persons instead of info-bits.

It may seem that the foregoing discussion finally offered less than it first promised in suggesting the possibility of a reconciliation between pragmatism and a suitably pruned memeology. I am not sure they can be reconciled. I do, however, think the concept of memes could be useful metaphorically as a cultural analogue to genes that might allow for the elaboration of an explicitly intelligent and purposive transmission of influence in human affairs—unlike the concept anchored in the mindlessness and purposelessness of genetically driven natural selection. But memes have to be defanged, made "compatible" with our purposes, before any such reconciliation can be entertained. That may be impossible. Intelligence and purpose are the dominant keynotes of human culture, and we need to find a way of recognizing this fact about ourselves in our discussions of transgenerational influence. Memes are worth exploring in this respect, but they may finally fail to fill the bill.

The rejection of meme-centered determinism is one consequence of the Jamesian/pragmatic defense of human purposefulness. The possibility of infusing present experience with transcendent expectation for our future depends upon the plausibility of representing our purposes and goals as partly constitutive of that future, because our choices may contribute to its determination. If so, evolution may be said to have entered a new phase. In order to appreciate and participate in evolution as a creative process, we must be able to lay personal and imaginative claim to the ideas by which we describe to ourselves a desired future.

Dennett has remarked on the special human capacity for "fun" and its failure to receive adequate philosophical attention. "We certainly won't have a complete explanation of consciousness until we have accounted for its role in permitting us (and only us?) to have fun."[62] The next section suggests that a kind of fun, called "flow" and related in interesting ways to James's philosophy, underscores the evolutionary relevance of our goals and purposes, and of our subjectivity.

## "Flow" and the Stream of Thought

> Most animals play. Evolution itself plays with lifeforms. Whole cultures play with customs, ideas, belief systems, and fashions. But it's a special caliber of play—deep—that leads to transcendence, creativity, and a need for the sacred.
> Diane Ackerman, *Deep Play*

> Consciousness does not appear to itself chopped up in bits. . . . It is nothing jointed; it flows.
> *The Principles of Psychology*[63]

James's famous "stream of consciousness," coined in his *Principles of Psychology* (1890), implies that our lives proceed with an ever forward-inclining momentum that sweeps our personal histories smoothly along in its wake. It is an image of inexorable succession that seems little interested in those "bits" of experience that pause to savor the richness of pure presence or of a pres*ent* that partakes of the transcendent. Indeed, James says in the same rhetorical breath in chapter 11 of *The Principles of Psychology* that "it would be difficult to find in the actual concrete consciousness of man a feeling so limited to the present as not to have an inkling of anything that went before"[64] or, we should add, that is to come in the future. But we must remember that James is also a philosopher of transcendence, a celebrant of "the sufficiency of the present moment," on those prized occasions, those electric moments when we are graced with an immediacy of perception in which past and future fall away and our attention is fully riveted on what we see, hear, taste, feel, or apprehend in consciousness now. "This feeling of the sufficiency of the present moment—this absence of all need to explain it, account for it, or justify it—is what I call the Sentiment of Rationality."[65]

This is an unexpected usage of *rationality*, but clearly James is here indicating an element of what we are calling "transcendence" as ingredient to the sense of well-being that puts a stop to our philosophizing. James applauds the sufficiency of the present moment, most of all because it is vitalizing in a way that reverberates and is continuous with the flowing streams of our temporal lives. The present moment is a kind of abstraction, real-as-experienced but distorted badly if left permanently detached from the moving pageant of life.

The insistence on linking transcendent moments with the larger contexts of both our personal and species life suggests a convergence of Jamesian transcendence with what contemporary psychological researchers have dubbed "flow."[66] The coincidence of terminology here may be accidental. Mihaly Csikszentmihalyi does not credit this concept to James, nor does James nominalize the flowing attribute of consciousness in the way that Csikszentmihalyi does. But it is nonetheless fortuitous and striking, and it underscores the continuity of consciousness that is at the heart of the experience of flow as Csikszentmihalyi discusses it, just as continuity is for James the hallmark of any experience attended without preconception. "Consciousness flows," says James; and because it does so—because it flows rather than lurches, in the normally healthy consciousness—we humans can experience that complex state of enjoyment that Csikszentmihalyi calls "flow."

Flow takes many forms, many not embodying overt or specific purposefulness.[67] I have been an ardent walker my entire adult life, and have reaped the predicted cardiovascular and other therapeutic benefits ("I have two doctors, my left leg and my right"[68] But mostly I walk to buoy my spirit, becalm my mind, and ignite that "surge of well-being" and "inner joy" so many walkers report:

> It comes with the welcome surprise of a cairn in a mountain fog and brings the confidence that you are one the right path. Such feelings combine the ecstasy of childhood with the joy of the mountains and the contentment of maturity.[69]

This is something like the "runner's high," perhaps, but in my own experience I can report that it usually feels more leisurely, meditative, composed, and less ecstatic—in a feet-on-the-ground sort of way—than the slightly feverish excitement which can descend on the body after it has passed a hard physical challenge. Yet the walker's high is also energizing and renewing, at once conveying powerful impressions of life's fleeting quality and its fullness. This is one instance of a kind of natural transcendence which may be cultivated but which never feels contrived or artificial. I always expect to feel good during and after a walk. But the specific quality of that good feeling, its intensity, the particular perceptions it gets related to, the actions it inspires, and so on, are almost always surprising. There is no way that I know of to cultivate that element of surprise. The experience itself remains fresh, spontaneous, and real. "Give me the blue sky over my head, and the green turf beneath my feet, a winding road before me, and a three hours' march to dinner—and then to thinking!" wrote English essayist William Hazlitt in 1822. "I begin to feel, think, and be myself again . . . [M]ine is that undisturbed silence of the heart which alone is perfect eloquence."[70] Others achieve this state of mind in countless ways, many more adventurous than mere traveling on shanks' mare. But I am content to share the imaginative company of the country of walkers, which includes (besides Hazlitt) Whitman,[71] Emerson and Thoreau,[72] Wordsworth, Dickens, Stevenson, Frost, Stevens,[73] Kazin, and James.

"Green turf" can spark the state of flow in other ways for me, not always when it is literally under foot. Every baseball fanatic of years who contracted this blessed affliction in childhood understands "the thrill of the grass," the ripple of pleasure and anticipation and the promise of happy absorption that comes with that first glimpse of outfield through the grandstand tunnel. The aesthetic timbre of such moments is not opposed to intense, active, self-forgetful involvement, but it is something subtly different. This is a neglected dimension of flow, involving as it sometimes does a rapt (but undistanced) spectatorship rather than the engaged technical proficiency and expertise of the chess player, climber, or team athlete. But Dewey's antipathy for spectator theories of knowledge did not block his acute perception of "the sources of art in human experience [that] will be learned by him who sees how the tense grace of the ball-player infects the onlooking crowd. . . ."[74] Like James, Dewey meant to naturalize but not desacralize the sources of delight in everyday life. Dewey's critics charge him with an obsessive instrumentalism, but he understood well enough what William Carlos Williams called the "spirit of uselessness" which for some of us can drench an afternoon or evening at the ballpark, or a morning in the garden, in delight.[75] It is the spirit of those perceptive moments, sometimes stretching to hours, when our own personal experiences and valuations seem to forge real ties to the universe. Is this a "secular spirituality, reflect[ing] an attempt to locate optimal human experience within a nonreligious context of existential and cosmic meaning?"[76] Or was Morris Cohen just right in proposing baseball as our "national religion?"[77]

We should not make too much of the fact that transcendence is sometimes a spontaneous, unexpected, unforeseen product of happenstance, and sometimes punctuates a deliberate process of cultivation. Santayana, for instance, favors a methodical deliberateness in his pursuit of intuited essence; indeed, in a very different way James also is a cultivator of delight. There is no one way delight has to come to us, or we to it.[78]

For Csikszentmihalyi, too, flow often is the outcome of quite deliberate preparation and intention. Consider Joe the welder and his rainbows, artfully devised for no other purpose than personal gratification: "Joe is a rare example of what it means to have an "autotelic personality," or the ability to create flow experiences even in the most barren environment."[79]

Controlling consciousness is at the heart of flow, of stoicism, and perhaps of Jamesian transcendence as well. The operative values are complexity, challenge, skills, and growth rather than stasis, arrest, or contemplative repose in momentary, temporally discontinuous perfection.

Flow betokens inner harmony and personal reserves which may be called upon more or less at will: "A person who rarely gets bored, who does not constantly need a favorable external environment to enjoy the moment, has passed the test for having achieved a creative life."[80]

Flow requires letting go of the self long enough, at least, to experience the marvels of the world. But "letting go" does not mean transcendent abandonment, it means being receptive to novelties in experience which may alter and enrich the self. This receptivity involves a temporary self-indifference and fascination in the wider world, the sort of attitude Bertrand Russell talks about in *Conquest of Happiness.*

> Flow can be meditatively self-forgetful, but we need to mark a difference with eastern and quasi-eastern approaches. "Yoga [is] a very thoroughly planned flow activity. Both [flow and meditation] try to achieve a joyous, self-forgetful involvement through concentration, which in turn is made possible by a discipline of the body. . . . [But] whereas flow attempts to fortify the self, the goal of Yoga and many other Eastern techniques is to abolish it."[81]

Yet this difference is more superficial than real, since eastern *practice* requires the self's very active involvement. The ability to surrender and then recover the self *repeatedly,* with every meditative exercise, implies great self-possession.

James was intrigued by techniques of self-administered control of conscious experience, as we have noted in connection with his fascination for exceptional mental states. Here, east and west reach a partial accommodation in James's thinking. The implicit control of consciousness which must be mastered in order to integrate flow experiences into one's life crosses borders. In 1904 James heard a Buddhist monk lecture at Harvard on

. . . the Buddhist conception of personality as an ephemeral heap or conglomeration of conditions; the idea of *anatta*, that in all existence there is no evidence for a permanent, enduring underlying self; and that liberation meant the transformation of consciousness. Consciousness was liberated from its enslavement in the normal everyday waking state of passion and released into the freedom in *nirvana*, a process that takes place through intensive exploration of normally unconscious states using meditation. Afterwards, James rose and proclaimed to the audience, "This is the psychology everybody will be studying 25 years from now."[82]

For James, though not perhaps for many Buddhists, a conception of *nirvana* which restricts it to the interiority of a meditative moment is interesting but insufficient. This Jamesian sense of insufficiency in those forms of inner life which do not prize overt manifestation in more explicitly social and forward-looking continuities of activity is characteristically pragmatic and western; and it harmonizes with the goal-directedness of much that Csikszentmihalyi calls flow.

A great deal can and should be said about the many convergences between the concept and experience of flow and James's philosophy in general, but this is the central convergence to which I want to draw particular attention here: the implicit goal-directedness crucial to most "optimal" experiences is also crucial to James's pragmatic, radically empiricist, future-looking philosophy of transcendence. The telic dimension is part of that fundamental continuity between inner and outer, and personal and social, forms of experience so important to James and the other "classical" American philosophers. And it is importantly related to the pragmatist's special interest in the processes of evolution as large cultural (as well as biological) phenomena related to personal flourishing and the perpetual renewal of novel opportunities for creative, complexly textured, *happy* experiences. Life itself is "optimized" in the conscious regulation of flow, and "conscious regulation" is much of what pragmatists understand by critical intelligence.

The optimistic or melioristic and forward-looking temper that conduces to transcendent moments and more generally to a transcendent bearing in life is founded in a belief that one's own experience may be optimized not only firsthand but, also, through an imaginative identification with the remote experiences of others, which present action may help to engender, in a future that both is and is not ours to enjoy in the present. James's metaphor of *streams* (of thought and experience) is thus nicely complemented by that of a chain of life.

## Hope and the Chain of Life

Hope is itself a species of happiness, and, perhaps, the chief happiness which this world affords.

Samuel Johnson, letter to unnamed woman, 8 June 1762

Nothing that is worth doing can be achieved in our lifetime; therefore we must be saved by hope.

Reinhold Niebuhr, The Irony of American History

William James died in 1910. In that same year John Dewey published *The Influence of Darwin on Philosophy.*[83] What an exquisitely symbolic, soul-satisfying confluence of events: the transfer of pragmatism's baton, punctuated by the philosophic expression in pragmatic terms of a liberating and transforming vision of life they both treasured. And there was an earlier chronological epiphany, the coincidence of Dewey's birth and the publication of *Origin of Species* in 1859.

"A chain is no stronger than its weakest link, and life is after all a chain."[84] We are each links in a chain of influence, inherited *and* chosen, extending from our lowliest origins to humanity's ultimate, unknown destiny. We have begun to think about how we can improve the chain, strengthen its links, and thereby transmit waves of intelligent direction along its open length. In the process we have encountered a new form of transcendence, one bringing remote futurity closer, laying claim to it, making it ours; and we have dared hope that we may earn the reciprocal embrace of remote posterity.

Dewey and James share the sense of hopefulness implicit in the image of life as a chain. Dewey, with a pronounced communal emphasis, is more explicit about the spiritual implications of this sensibility. And Dewey strengthens James's legacy with a more explicit sensitivity to the inherent risk of perversion that can befall personal ideals in the absence of corrective, balancing social influences. He emphasizes the importance of rooting individual flourishing and growth within a communal context large enough to spot and eradicate the worst perversions. He thus complements James in resisting the seductions of hypersubjectivity to which James did not himself succumb but which he also may not have said enough to discourage in others. We have become all too familiar with many varieties of mass delusional behavior and communal insanity that would have disturbed and confounded James no less than it does us and that might have spurred his further reflections on this vexing question of personal ideals and their perversion.

A horrific example of the perversion of personal ideals and the sanctity of the imagination occurred in 1997 and provides a case in point: the members of a stranger-than-average Southern California cult of computer programmers, known to Internet web surfers as Heaven's Gate, took their own lives in an act of mass insanity that they had convinced themselves would be their ticket to intergalactic adventure on the tail of the comet Hale-Bopp. By all accounts they went voluntarily, with bags packed and grins on their faces. Plans, dreams, and happy dispositions alone do not make for the Good Life.

Such lunacy comes as a sobering reminder that there is a real threat of tragic instability inherent in the unchecked imagination: a point not to lose sight of, alongside the laudable aspects of Jamesian transcendence and subjectivity that I have been concentrating on. It is all very well to honor private dreams and visions, but in the last analysis we have to keep our feet anchored in the terra firma of intersubjective reality. Such mass delusion is pointedly instructive of how not to think about dreams and the future, and we need to wonder whether James was recklessly imprecise about the limits of sane imaginative license in the service of personal ideals. He probably underestimated the susceptibility of ideals to perversion or the potential consequences of perverse ideals. That may be more objectionable, less excusable, on our side of the twentieth century than it was on his.

Is there a way to argue, in strictly Jamesian terms, that the mental state of these pathetic, deluded would-be star trippers lies outside a kind of transcendent consciousness the rest of us condemn only in violation of the most basic precepts of pluralism? There may be, but such argumentation is not highly visible in James's own words. Dewey helps here, reminding us that our enthusiasms are most laudable when they do not set us radically apart from the communities and the larger society in which we dwell but instead further our personal growth. To grow is to relate, to renounce isolation, to form connections with all kinds of possibilities and persons, while retaining a strong sense of one's own identity and personal commitments.

But this highlights a perhaps-unavoidable tension between being open to possibilities—including the possibility of correction when an idea becomes a dangerous and irrational obsession—and "following your dreams." James's attitude, to judge on the basis of his sympathetic treatment of religious pathology, especially in *Varieties of Religious Experience,* is that he prefers to resolve any such tension by erring on the side of dreamy excess. Do we pay too high a price for such liberality? But how can we uphold our commitment to individual autonomy if we do not pay it? What sort of autonomy is even possible in the shadow of a controlling insanity? These are difficult questions, and a serious challenge to the pragmatic libertine.

The connective tissue binding most of the themes of this long meditation, in one way or another, is the idea of growth. In social terms it takes the form of cultural progress and amelioration. Individual growth is more variably idiosyncratic: my growth may be your stagnation, my happiness your misery. But again, Dewey reins in the Jamesian temptation to exaggerate variability and acceptable idiosyncracy. Beyond a hypothetical (but real) point established by unstated intersubjective consensus, idiosyncracy becomes lunacy. If it is dangerous lunacy, it must be discouraged; some lunacy frustrates growth for both lunatic and society.

We noted at the outset some of the many and various forms transcendence can take; but Jamesian transcendence, with a supportive assist from Dewey, is tied irrevocably to the experience of growth focusing on ideals, possibilities, and instigating purposes. I do not think Dewey was any more insightful than James about the constructive and positively motivating character of ideals, possibilities, and purposes. Jamesian transcendence seeks not solace and escape but challenge and engagement. A Jamesian who was smitten with the idea that a hunk of wayward celestial matter might signify a conversational overture from distant reaches would likely be more interested in finding a way to discover, amplify, and share the communication in question than in making a quick and permanent exit from this vale of tears *and laughter*.

"Growth" in the pragmatic sense is not always literal or simple. It may well be that our growth as individuals and in our communities, and in the widest imaginable community of human endeavor (the one spanning all of human history), depends upon *not* growing in certain respects (economically, consumptively). This is a determination for each generation and each individual to make anew. In the pragmatic sense growth is mostly a matter of learning to diagnose and remedy the deficiencies and projected requirements of all the "situations" and experiences of living.

James and Dewey both remind us that while we draw energy and inspiration from our ongoing relationship with the future, we must not denigrate or neglect the passing present. Both took a naturalized Emerson to heart. As Dewey notes with approval,

> The reputed transcendental worth of an overweening Beyond and Away, Emerson, jealous for spiritual democracy, finds to be the possession of the unquestionable Present . . . [T]he idealist has too frequently conspired with the sensualist to deprive the pressing and so the passing Now of value which is spiritual.[85]

And James's "specious" present is not (as sometimes misquoted) "spurious." Whatever we make of our delightful moments, whatever subsequent conduct or idealism they inspire, they remain beautiful moments, and we ought not allow ourselves to miss a single one of them.

It is too easy, and wrong, to distinguish James from Dewey on the basis of simple labels and conceptual boxes. "I doubt if we have as yet begun to realize all that is due to William James, observed Dewey, for the introduction and use of [a] biological conception of the psyche."[86] One thing that is due is a recognition that we possess as our birthright a native capacity for transcendence of all kinds, including those we have discussed and many more that we have not, rooted in the mix of our respective natural constitutions and personal dispositions .

A biological conception of the psyche also assigns to the aforementioned idea of memes as units of transmissible influence—not determination—a value in personal and cultural history they would not have otherwise. The transmission of certain ideas and the termination of others takes on real urgency when we notice the devastation wreaked by the worst of them. Understanding more about how our psyches work, and how influence occurs especially in the minds of children and in the interaction of adults with children, will strengthen the chain of life if we do not permit this narrowly biological conception to swamp and invalidate our more intimate, personal, subjective experience. Biological naturalism holds out a real prospect of gaining a practical understanding of it, and of much else. But we still need our more floridly, delightfully imaginative self-constructions, and the transcendent possibilities they create, in order to remain happily ourselves.

Education, meaning influence both deliberate and osmotic, is for Dewey the engine of growth. James, too, was deeply concerned with the practical mechanics of childhood education. We have heard much of late about the early neurological windows of opportunity to influence young children; not much of the "new" research would shock the philosopher and psychologist who wrote, a century ago,

> In children we observe a ripening of impulses and interests in a certain determinate order. . . . Of course, the proper pedagogic moment to work skill in, and to clench the useful habit, is when the native impulse is most acutely present. . . . The hour may not last long; and whilst it continues you may safely let all the child's other occupations take a second place . . . for many an infant prodigy, artistic or mathematical, has a flowering epoch of but a few months.[87]

The issue of reconciling the biology of consciousness with the subjectivity of experience is parallel to debates about nature and culture. Are we natural beings who bury instinct under the artificial impositions of civilization, or have we become civilized beings periodically assaulted by our own uneradicated worst natural instincts and tendencies? Are culture and nature at war?

No. Pragmatists like James and Dewey refuse to countenance a sharp discontinuity here. They applaud our civilizing achievements, they cheer for more of the same, but they remain committed to biological naturalism and to what might be called a more global naturalism that recognizes civilization as the crown of nature and not its denial. They do not say that we can effect an easy reconciliation of biology and culture, of neurophysiology and the subjective imagination. But they say we must try. Not to try is to fail, either in ignorance or despair.

Think about "growth" as the gardener cultivates it, and about what that process of cultivation reveals of our complex relation to nature, our status as natural beings who nonetheless exercise a spontaneous capacity for unpredictability, in virtue of which we sometimes stand out from nature, against nature as previously understood. In short, it is about nature and "culture"—culture in the literal gardener's sense, and in the anthropologist's. Human growth involves this relation and our progressive coming-to-terms with what it means to be the bridge between nature and culture. Michael Pollan exhibits a sharp Deweyan global naturalist sensibility in making this point: "Contingency is an invitation to participate in history . . . [A]ren't we also one of nature's contingencies? And if our cigarette butts and Norway maples and acid rain are going to shape the future of this place, then why not also our hopes and desires . . . [T]o exclude human desire would be unnatural."[88]

Growth is not an unqualified good. The gardener is not just a cultivator of new growth and the sustainer of old; he is an opponent of negative growth in the form of wilderness and unwanted spontaneous plant incursions. What kinds of growth are undesirable is a matter of his, of our, standards, preferences, and attitudes. It is partly a subjective and personal-aesthetic decision but is not arbitrary. As in the garden, so in life: we decide which kinds of growth are acceptable to us, and our decision—if soundly taken—reflects our dual nature as biological and cultural beings. There is (1) growth as we experience it directly in our own persons, and there is also (2) growth that we shepherd, foster, nurture in others, in our worlds (natural and social), in our children. In a sense we do experience (2), vicariously yet genuinely in the impact it makes upon the quality of experience now, in the present. When our experience of growth takes this form it is, for lack of a better or more immediately expressive term, a spiritual experience. This is growth of identity, expanding "self" beyond the border of our own skin. "The kind of self which is formed through action which is faithful to relations with others will be a fuller and broader self than one which is cultivated in isolation from or in opposition to the purposes and needs of others."[89]

It is easy to be glib (and wrong) about this, but humanity is a natural occurrence, notwithstanding all the perversities committed throughout history in the name of "nature." Insofar as we manage not to invest the concept of humanity's naturalness with an honorific specific value it does not possess intrinsically, we are perfectly within bounds to say that whatever we do is "natural." In this very broad, nondiscriminating sense, Hitler and Nazism were no more or less natural than the Marshall Plan, just as weeds are as natural as roses. The point is, we are that part of nature that must decide, insofar as we can, what to prune and what to plant.

But of course all of us appeal to nature all the time to back us up, to give positive sanction to our personal and cultural doings. In order for such appeal to succeed, we must specify an honorific sense in which it is not simply a prejudice to favor nature, but a demand of our nature as human beings. And there is no doubt that we can be more or less faithful to nature in any number of ways. Certainly when the issue is our proper relation to nature, a degree of faithfulness is preferable to anarchy. When intelligence, self-consciousness, and creativity reach an evolutionary plateau where simple survival is no longer deemed by most thoughtful people adequate to the achievement of a good and purposeful existence, the concept of nature-as-wilderness, as the antithesis of culture, does not address our deepest needs. But as Thomas Huxley said so insistently over a century ago, nature is no moral teacher. Of course we may choose to model our values on what we take to be natural phenomena, but the result is likely to be unsatisfactory as well as unnatural in any but the broadest and least edifying sense.

We too frequently embrace an all-or-nothing mentality, in the face of such reflections, and we ought to resist it. Our choice is not simply (and simplistically) between treating nature as either a pure, "untouched by human hands," outdoor museum, a "preserve," or as an opportunity for naked "development." Some environmentalists take the attitude that any change in the landscape wrought by human beings is tantamount to degradation; some developers take the attitude of the proverbial coal-mine owner who said, "God put it there and it's our duty to dig it out." This small-minded either/or, of which passionate environmentalists and rapacious industrialists are mutually guilty is a symptom of our failure to think clearly about the fact that we are the nexus of nature and culture.

The recognition that we as a species have exceeded what nature-as-wilderness can teach us about ourselves, what it can model as an ethical standard, does not mean than we can reasonably or prudently ignore the idea of nature as something more-or-less distinct from anything we might wish to label "culture." The coordination of our needs and desires with nature is for us an appropriate and *natural* task, and one required by life. The environment in which we function as biological and social beings is not a fixed or neutral backdrop. It reflects our predecessors' achievements and follies, and so will ours be transmitted to our successors.

Conforming the rules of thinking to the requirements of life, instead of the other way around, is a definite requisite of the "growth" I aim to elaborate. "The other way around" is an instance of what James derided as intellectualism, and is the very antithesis of growth. Growth is what happens when we consistently, efficiently nourish ourselves in whatever ways are most congenial to us and least taxing of our and others' vitality. It is not about unlimited expansion or unconstrained consumption. It may be self-serving but is not selfish. It is linked to adaptation and survival and to realism about the limits of human autonomy in a natural universe.

But more than adapting and surviving, human growth is about flourishing, which requires taking charge of the conditions of our own (personal and collective) fulfillment, our ultimate telos and our happiness day by day. Practically, "taking charge" means taking account of all the ways in which we are and might be fruitfully related to the worlds of our habitation. Growth, once again, means connection and relatedness.

Relatedness to other persons is the form of growth eliciting altruism, sympathy, and empathy—our most ennobling moral virtues. Relatedness to possibilities is the form of growth that draws most directly on our subjective particularity and fuels personal transcendence. Relatedness yields moments of heightened experience in the present but is most at home in the future; or rather, it typically has one foot resolutely straining toward the future.

Growth occurs most gratifyingly when we nurture an improbable dream into manifest reality and add thereby to the stock of what exists to be experienced and reexperienced by ourselves, our peers, and our heirs. That is when happiness, the happiness of the pragmatist and of the Jamesian transcender, comes most to the fore. Survival may be growth's sole reward in the strictly biological kingdom, but in the many-storied worlds of human consciousness the greatest reward and entitlement is a happy disposition.

Here is another way to think about this: some regard transcendence as a sort of divine dispensation, a gift of the gods or of impersonal nature. James, to the contrary, considers it a cultivated product of individual personality, or subjectivity, mixed with hard labors directed toward the attainment of ideals. What is wanted is some way of holding ideals to the flame of our (actual and plausibly possible) experience, and to "the requirements of living."

James sought to articulate a total view of things that would be hospitable to the heart's most intimate and insistent yearnings. In his own case, these included an irresistible need to establish the reasonableness of hope for the future, both for himself and for others. The sense of spiritual connectedness he felt to the great transtemporal human community, in chorus with Whitman, Emerson, Wordsworth, and others, was probably as much an expression of hope as of felt kinship. Apparently, James also needed to cultivate a sense of possible kinship with the (alleged) incorporeal and supernatural community of departed spirits, whom he spent so much time attempting to contact in his psychical researches. Woody Allen said (in very different circumstances), "The heart wants what it wants." And James philosophized, as he lived, from the heart.

Religious experience was for James "any moment of life that brings the reality of spiritual things more 'home' to one." What are "spiritual things" for James? He is more open to supernaturalism than Dewey, but he does not exclusively define spirituality in supernatural terms. So, taking him at his word, we can assert James's agreement with these remarks from Vita Sackville-West in praise of the introspective experience of mental (or spiritual) growth we enjoy when we attend closely to our momentary inner lives: "Growth is exciting; growth is dynamic and alarming; growth of the soul, growth of the mind." The possibility of growth is spiritual in this sense: it is the process of self-expansion and increasing connectedness with others and with possibilities of all kinds.

With such a view it becomes possible to reclaim the spiritual side of naturalized transcendence from popular prejudice, which uncritically mistreats rare and exquisite moments as exclusively supernatural. I am de-emphasizing the narrowly aesthetic ("sublimity for its own sake") aspects of transcendence. Of course we should neglect neither the spiritual nor the aesthetic dimensions of our most exceptional experiences, which in any case are not neatly separable.

But there is a distinct difference of emphasis between locating the greater importance of transcendence in its providing occasions of contemplative elevation and aesthetic enjoyment, versus saying that such experiences also mediate social relations and future conduct. The latter is James's more characteristic emphasis, making transcendence both an intrinsic and an extrinsic good, an end and a means linking the inner life to social values in an overtly spiritual way. This is not to deny the spirituality of a purer aestheticism—to each his own!—but rather to stipulate and clarify a distinctively pragmatic conception of the term.

Jamesian transcendence is hopeful because it does not abandon the particularity of personal experience or view it as an obstacle, but rather seeks to learn from it, to build on it, to grow out of it (which is not, necessarily, to outgrow it). Dewey says in Art as Experience that "in a growing life, the recovery [of equilibrium between organism and environment, following a disruption] is never mere return to a prior state. . . . Life grows when a temporary falling out is a transition to a more extensive balance. . . ."[90] We tend to think of disruptions as negative, but transcendence is a positive disruption ("falling out") of ordinary experience that cannot be sustained indefinitely, though it can be positively assimilated. Assimilation means a larger, more richly related self, intelligently engaged in actual conditions while yet pursuing ideals. That is growth, and its possibility is a ground for hope. This is transcendence not as escape from the temporal but as its embrace. The poet Edwin Arlington Robinson implied some such view when he said, "The world is not a 'prison-house,' but a kind of spiritual kindergarten where bewildered infants are trying to spell God with the wrong blocks."[91]

The more important general point about temporality in James is that when he talks about the present he usually has the future in mind as well, and vice versa. Alternative beliefs portend alternatively imagined futures, and these impinge directly on the quality of present experience. Hence, "the whole function of philosophy ought to be to find the characteristic influences which you and I would undergo at a determinate moment . . . if one or the other [belief, attitude, philosophy] were true." That is why we can say that Jamesian transcendence does not just fall serendipitously from the sky but is cultivable.

Serendipity can suffuse and expand an instant of life and make it seem an eternity, overleaping nature and process. It can seem to take us out of ourselves, transporting us to another realm and swapping "reality" for Reality. Naturalized transcendence, on the other hand, is not about surmounting quotidian reality, aspiring to a "view from nowhere," or seeking solace in supernatural or metaphysical beliefs . But it is very much concerned with expanding our perspective in a way allowing us to acknowledge and even to honor our subjectivity while rejecting narrow or egotistical conceptions of selfhood. So transcendence comes to mean not standing apart from the world but, in a certain way, loosening our attachment to existing conditions. It means vivifying possibilities, and (paradoxically?) looking to future fulfillments as sources of transcendence in the present. And the only function of the idea of the universe as a "unified totality" is as something to work toward, a goal, an ever receding ideal whose pursuit may fuel our most exceptional moments, our most "transcendent" experiences.

The theologian Paul Tillich, though "liberal," is widely supposed to have been a more religious thinker than the naturalist Dewey. Vocationally and sociologically, this may be unquestionable: Tillich was a professional religionist. But was Tillich an "insider" to religious experience relative to Dewey? It depends on how we are to understand Dewey's claim that universal human experience attests a generic religious or "spiritual" dimension from which pragmatic humanists are not excluded. Dewey not only makes room for this insight but exalts it as the implicit "common faith" of us all. If he seems personally unmoved that is probably his congenital Yankee taciturnity, not indifference to the spiritual life. The ground of "ultimate concern" is too important to us all to be left as the exclusive domain of self-anointed spiritualists, theologians, and divines.

Is it possible to give a natural, nonmetaphysical account of transcendence that affirms the continuity and compatibility of inner life with social reality, the ethical consensus of our peers, and the practical requirements of life? I am convinced that James and Dewey think so. If such an account is not "religious" then maybe we need to rethink the hierarchy that places religious values above all. By whatever name, an approach to living that aims to coordinate personal flourishing with the common good is spiritual in the truest sense. Why should we not say then, with Dewey (and James), that an unsecured faith in humane ideals for which we are prepared to work can also be a religious value?

"This world is sacred," Dennett says in explicit echo of Nietzsche. But Nietzsche was a fatalist, finally. It may be emotionally therapeutic to tell ourselves that the world is a sacred, finished, unified totality, but it is much more constructive to say with James that the world is sacred—worthy of veneration and preservation—*in places* but not in others. Parts are best lost. Even Dewey is reported to have taken comfort once in the thought that "what is, is, and you can just lie back."[92] But he did not just lie back, of course. Though even the most committed meliorist may have moments of brief retirement from the battles of living and though his personal mental hygiene may need them, the Nietzschean battle cry *"Amor fati!"* does not serve the purpose. We must be a great deal more selective of our battles and more custodial of our constructive energies than that implies. If (in Emerson's phrase) the days are gods, our divine relation to them must be an active one.

James and Dewey harmonize on the spiritual and social keynotes of continuity and compatibility between individual and communal values. When James invites us to surrender our ideals to "other hands than ours,"[93] I propose to read him in chorus with Dewey—Whitman and the transcendentalists sing in the same choir—as confidently passing the baton of hopefulness about the future to our (immediate and distant) generational successors, entrusting the progress of the race to them. James is equally friendly to supernaturally religious renderings of "other hands," but the more impressive point is that he does not grope for spectral hands on behalf of the ideals we hold in common. The very naturalness of the fact of our diverse, respective ideal interests, more than their objects (spectral or not), is what he is most eager to notice and impress upon us.

The common core of religious feeling for James, we must remind ourselves, is not about God. Love of life is religion's spring. If we do not bungle our watch, we may aspire to transmit a richer inheritance of life than we have received. In that aspiration resides the possibility of one kind of transcendence in the direction of "something larger than ourselves" but possibly not larger than the collectivity of selves past and future whose tangential link is our present. This is transcendence with an irrepressible forward momentum, probing for the "next step" of our evolutionary epic and the chance to endure. So, as Richard Rorty suggests, "we can, with James, relish the thought that our descendants may face live and forced options which we shall never imagine."[94] And if, as Rorty goes on to say, "James was not always content to identify the 'wider self through which saving experiences come'" with some such feeling of human solidarity through the ages, he was much more at ease with this fundamentally naturalistic orientation to spiritual life than is commonly recognized. And if, as A. N. Wilson suggests, such a conception strikes some believers as not *Godly* enough, that is merely a reflection of their own religious assumptions and not a legitimate objection to James's. "When James had asserted as a matter of empirical fact that people had religious experiences which did not fit into any neat, scientific-materialist package of the universe, his work was done. If we make him stay behind after the lecture and say what God is like, that is our fault, not his."[95]

If what is "common and generic" in religious experience *is* a sense of continuity with "something ideal," that "wider self through which saving experiences come," why may that ideal self not be a naturally conceived aspiration of elevated human attainment, in a progressively realized future that is ours, now, to dream of and to work for? And why can that attainment not include the eventual integration of our own private and personal ideals— realities in the most complete sense of the term—with those of our peers? James and Dewey *both* espouse something very like that as the beginning of what could become our acknowledged common human faith. It seems in any event to be a tacit presupposition of effective social engagement.

The death of a friend in 1904 prompted this from James:

> . . . [her] death was so abrupt and bewildering . . . —where is she now? And what does it all mean? I never had the pathos or the mystery brought so sharply home . . . how much more real are people's lives than all our criticisms of them! It is a lesson to cultivate each other, all of us, while we yet have each other.[96]

Now here, now gone: no life phenomenon is so universal or natural—excepting birth—yet it still awakens in us the shudder of mystery. It may be impossible to spell out exactly what mysterium is implicated in our reactions of loss: wishfulness, emptiness, regret—in some natures tinged with fond memory and hope, in others with unmitigated sorrow and despair. Again, words fail.

We could cash it out in terms of speculative curiosity about a supernatural afterlife, and James was as curious as anyone about possible nether worlds. Or we could bury the mystery under mechanistic, clinical explanations of "how we die." But neither of these approaches really engages the subjective imagination where it lives, amidst natural and impermanent forms. Neither does justice to our affections. Neither recognizes the complex experience of death that is, pace Wittgenstein ("Death is not an event in life"), a reality: the broader our sympathies, the more another's death may seem like an experience of our own. Like the cat, we may each of us expect, if we enjoy even a modest longevity, to experience many deaths. Few will register as straightforward departures. The loss of a person whose life has meant something personal to us is never a simple alteration in the exterior landscape or mere material subtraction. "To any one who has ever looked on the face of a dead child or parent the mere fact that matter *could* have taken for a time that precious form, ought to make matter sacred ever after. . . . That beloved incarnation was among matter's possibilities."[97] *Where is she now?* thus lends itself to natural meditations infinitely more subtle and personal than "heaven," "beyond the veil," or "in a better place" can even begin to hint.

Yet the image of the veil of illusion was important to James. He did not regard our consciousness and our experience as illusory, only the premature stipulation of their boundedness by all that has hitherto been perceived and reported. Our history is in its early chapters. There will be more.

We need not exceed nature's bounds in order to encircle this "more," if only we will accept their elasticity from the start. No experience belongs off the map. For those who do not feel it, so much talk about mystery can itself seem all too mysterious. Even conceding that subjectivity must permanently elude the objectifying intellect, that each of us possesses a unique point of view beyond articulation, that we cannot ever hope to possess another's perspective—though of course (as we have noted) fiction allows us a "virtual" experience of other sensibilities and poetry may provide sharp insights and shared sympathies, too—many will shrug this off as obvious and uncompelling. They are right, at the relatively superficial level of speech. We are struggling to find words for an emotion-laden and richly textured phenomenon. We should not struggle too hard. James's counsel is for introspection instead of endless talk. Take a hike (or a preferred equivalent), reside for a time in silence, and see if you do not detect a mystery at the core of your being.

Or, attend to the details of your own grief at another's passing. Such are the pained occasions when most of us are least able to overlook the wonder of one another, unreplicable marvels of nature that we are. How strange that we have come, how strange when we go, how strange the interim. Again, the mystery of subjectivity is inseparable from the universal mystery: why something, why anything at all? It is our privilege not merely to be of that "something," but to know that we are and to care.

Not long ago the oldest human died in France, at age 122. Her intimates credited her endurance to an epicurean reasonableness of temper and to an attitude not uncommon among the happiest older persons: "If you can't do anything about it, don't worry about it," was her credo;[98] Jamesians do not endorse the sloganeering reductionism of "Don't worry, be happy," but they do acknowledge the wisdom of recognizing that peace and justice in the larger world cannot be gained through the abandonment of our own personal sources of satisfaction. This ought to assuage the guilt of some of those who feel self-indulgent, or worse, for taking pleasure in things small and local while bombs fall and genocide rages abroad. The suffering of fellow humanity is real and tragic, but we should not compound its scourge by denying our own enthusiasms. Let us take thought and measured remedial action on behalf of the Kosovars of the world. And let us celebrate the arrival of spring and its diversions, in our gardens and sporting arenas and wherever else the human heart and imagination may find their freedom. Turning from the discursive dead end of ineffable cosmic mystery and the dead weight of socio-historical guilt, let us rejoice in James's "vital mystery" of happiness.

"Temperament," so frequently considered in these pages, names and locates an enigma but still does not explain how a philosopher can recognize wonder as the well-spring of his own intellectual and professional life, yet fail to take in the idea of permanent, natural mystery. But an unsatisfactory explanation can still shed indirect light. It is helpful to realize, for instance, that the positivist's reductive, world-shrinking dismissal as "nonsense" whatever he cannot translate in specified ways may be the philosophic expression of a prior personal aesthetic. If he prefers the symmetrical tidiness of a well-scrubbed cave to the ramshackle messiness—the (present) unverifiability—of a more open and evolving domicile, so be it.

No one ever confused James's temperament for Santayana's, but the former might also have said,

> Each morning the sunrise excites wonder in the poet, and the order of the solar system excites it in the astronomer. Astronomy explains the sunrise, but what shall explain the solar system? The universe, which would explain everything, is the greatest of wonders, and a perpetual miracle.[99]

For those temperamentally disposed to find such reflections powerful and moving, the failure to be so moved is nearly inconceivable. Those differently constituted must feel oppositely (but still similarly) baffled. James's ubiquitous "blindness" is our mutual opacity to one another, and it seems permanently ineradicable. But we may allow ourselves to hope that it is a premature pessimism, in the long view.

Where cosmic mystery slips our grasp, fortunately, we may retain a hold on the more manageable sources of personal fulfillment. Temperament is still key, as instanced by that of the formidable woman whose life spanned a dozen decades. What an edifying life! Wise people have always known (as she evidently did) that personal happiness cannot wait on universal salvation and that the pursuit of happiness avails only with the sane and stubborn distinction between what we can change and what we cannot.

No life is free of worry, but I doubt that hers was beset by worries about the cosmos's ultimate cosmological fate, aeons from now. Of course, we could drench our consciousness in ominous but not unreasonable portents of the eventual entropic dissipation of all that has been. That is a disquieting thing to contemplate but not yet, surely, a suitable object of real worry. Bertrand Russell, in *A Free Man's Worship*, even found it inspirational. It is beyond our conceivable control and will not in any case be propitiated by the sacrifice of real and present goods, such as our happiness.

These thoughts recall at least two avenues by which James approaches the question of happiness. The first is by addressing the element of chance, risk, or luck involved in our avoidance of the worst pitfalls that may visit us from that region beyond our control, and how that element can be moderated by a natural affinity between our "powers" and the demands of successful living. We have been a lucky species. If cataclysmic theories of prehuman natural history are correct, it was literally a meteoric bolt from the blue that annihilated the dinosaurs and thus hastened our ascent. Individually, too, most of us keep our fingers crossed. But how much of luck and of happiness is, in the words of the old baseball philosopher Branch Rickey, the "residue of design"? Nicholas Rescher makes the Jamesian point succinctly:

> It is not just by having children that we become luck-subjected hostages to fortune, but by having a stake in anything whatsoever. Wherever we invest our hopes and aspirations—whatever may be our expectations and goals and plans—good or bad luck can come into operation.[100]

James's second approach is via the question of pessimism. If personal happiness requires frank acknowledgment of our own limitations, how much control can we cede without inviting deep pessimism and its view that happiness is too momentary, ephemeral, and illusory to matter, and that all striving and goal seeking is a vain delusion? And on the other side, what of all those apparently happy New Thinkers, incited in part by their admittedly partial understanding of James, who have credited their own high spirits to a repudiation of limits? A sane and sober middle view is clearly needed here. An accurate rendition of James's philosophy of transcendence would be instrumental to that end, and no one offers a saner, more sober, or more faithful reformulation of James's largest philosophical intentions than Dewey.

Dewey believed that our happiness is best secured by a vivid, conduct-informing consciousness of our inherent ties to one another and to organic nature, ties imposing very definite limits but opening as well onto a vast prospect capable of firing the imagination with the renewal of hope:

> The community of causes and consequences in which we, together with those not born, are enmeshed is the widest and deepest symbol of

the mysterious totality of being we call the universe . . . the matrix within which our ideal aspirations are born and bred.[101]

Awareness of our vital links to this "continuous human community" may
flower into an unshakable natural "creed" centered on amelioration and the
transmission of our "heritage of values . . . [so] that those who come after
us may receive it more solid and secure, more widely accessible and more
generously shared than we have received it."[102] Those partial to more traditional creeds may find this too thin for their spiritual taste, but the issue
ought not be reduced to a simplistic dichotomy between naturalism and supernaturalism. The issue is better put in terms of whether Dewey's naturalized community strikes one as wider and deeper than alternative objects of
devotion. Some are so struck, others are not. We should all be able to live
and let live with this consequence of our variable humanity. As James said,
we are each "a syllable in human nature's total message."

Dewey's commitment to an aggressive and activist brand of naturalisti-
cally based meliorism is itself so "solid and secure" that it requires no extended documentation. But in an uncharacteristic moment of self-revelation
the stolid Yankee once apparently confided in his old student Max Eastman
about a youthful "mystical experience" from his early stint in Oil City, Penn-
sylvania:

> The essence of the experience was a feeling of oneness with the uni-
> verse, a conviction that worries about existence and one's place in it are
> foolish and futile. "It was not a very dramatic mystic experience,"
> Eastman continued. There was no vision, not even a definable emo-
> tion—just a supremely blissful feeling that his worries were over.
> Eastman quoted Dewey, ". . . to me faith means not worrying. . . . I
> claim I've got religion and that I got it that night in Oil City."[103]

This melds very well with a homiletic, therapeutic, stoic, yet somehow
joyous and de novo expression of James's unique view, dating from *his*
prephilosophic youth but anticipating his most mature thought:

> Remember when old December's darkness is everywhere about you, that
> the world is really in every minutest point as full of life as in the most joy-
> ous morning you ever lived through; that the sun is whanging down, and
> the waves dancing, and the gulls skimming down at the mouth of the
> Amazon, for instance, as freshly as in the first morning of creation; and
> the hour is just as fit as any hour that ever was for a new gospel of cheer
> to be preached. I am sure that one can, by merely thinking of these mat-
> ters of fact, limit the power of one's evil moods over one's way of looking
> at the cosmos.[104]

I find it compelling, and not at all coincidental or incongruous, that the two great pragmatic meliorists of classical American philosophy each achieved in their twenties the same quasi-stoic insight that, as we have noted, carried the world's oldest person happily through her days. The power of imaginative self-transcendence to conquer egoistic distemper, especially when coupled with the wide-open perspective of life as a self-replicating, self-correcting chain, is unrivaled. It has been conclusively "verified." The spirit of acceptance and that of reform belong together. The mature James, for one, is full of admiration for the spirit of acceptance in whatever blissful forms it may assume in the lives of men and women. And he is full of expectancy and hope.

Writer and poet Wendell Berry tautly summarizes the call to hope I find so prominent in James and Dewey: "A part of our obligation to our own being and to our descendants is to study life and our conditions, searching always for the authentic underpinnings of hope."[105] But, he elaborates significantly, the search must center on ourselves, in our own time:

> We can do nothing for the human future that we will not do for the human present. For the amelioration of the future condition of our kind we must look, not to the wealth or the genius of the coming generations, but to the quality of the disciplines and attitudes that we are preparing now for their use . . . [T]he man who works and behaves well today need take no thought for the morrow; he has discharged today's only obligation to the morrow.[106]

Berry goes on to illustrate but also to strain this correct emphasis on the present as preparing (and possibly sabotaging) but not simply waiting on the future. He says that disciplined attention to present needs aligns us "with natural processes, [with] no explicit or deliberate concern for the future. We do not eat, for instance, because we want to live until tomorrow, but because we are hungry today and it satisfies us to eat."[107] In fact, both kinds of reasons—present satisfaction and continued existence—are coordinate in human action.

But maybe the simple satisfaction of present desire is, after all, our most reliably pressing motivator, overshadowing even the survival instinct by sheer statistical incidence. We face many more opportunities to satisfy ourselves in small ways, day to day, than we do tangible threats to our survival. Dramatically contrived television survival spectacles, masquerading as "reality" programming, thus are comically misnamed. Might not "satisfaction" be seen as an elemental achievement of happiness? Happiness, we know, ranges across fields of satisfaction vastly wider than the bare purging of rudimentary desire. Why should it not (for some) also embrace contemplation of a future we covet for the palpable enjoyment not of ourselves but of our descendants?

Despite unduly softening the essential triangulation of our hopefulness with (1) responsible industry in the present and (2) unsecured expectation for the future as well, Berry articulates a sensibility here that James would find eminently sane:

> Goodness, wisdom, happiness, even physical comfort are not institutional conditions. The real sources of hope are personal and spiritual, not public and political. [One] is not happy by the dispensation of his government or by the fortune of his age [but] only in doing what is in his power, and in being reconciled to what is not in his power.[108]

Not even a Jamesian wants to tilt at windmills, if that is what he believes them to be. But hopeful and melioristic Jamesians are probably slower than most in acknowledging windmills, and thus in being resigned or reconciled. Temperament again, as so often in James's diagnoses of intellectual predisposition, provides not a barrier but a springboard, in those so constituted, to happiness. It is in our power to dream and to work. "The more ephemeral that humanity appears *sub specie aeternitatis*," writes Hans Koning, "the more essential it becomes to make this a just world. Right now a lot of people are more bent on making themselves feel better about the world, by looking at it through Prozac eyes, than on improving it."[109] But Jamesians feel better when they are working to improve it.

Mind's fundamental purpose, to paraphrase the French poet Valéry, is to produce futures. The plural emphasis here is suggestive and pragmatic: different minds, different futures. Yet we also create various aggregate minds in the groups we choose to identify with. By identifying with collective humanity, one can speak proprietarily about the future (as opposed to a narrowly personal future linked uniquely to a singular point of view and to one's private aspirations). The genius of American philosophy is, in part, its considerable will and capacity to do justice to both kinds of impulse, the personal and the collective, and to draw constructive energy from both aspects of the future. One of my purposes has been to show how James's approach can do justice to both kinds of impulse and how it draws energy from both senses of the future. A subsidiary purpose has been to clarify the link between James and the pragmatic temper to evolution. The "anti-Essentialist double-play combination, Darwin to James to Dewey" (in Dennett's happy phrase) has helped me to pull off this twin-killing.

What, at last, is the source of James's melioristic/pluralistic/radically empiricistic naturalism? Is it personal religious convictions or attitudes expressed in *Varieties* suggesting the yearning for a "grand discovery"[110] or some other motive we have not even thought of? A friend, sympathetic to James's thought but frustrated by its open-endedness, once complained that somehow it all just does not "fit." Getting things to fit—if this is more than a requirement of bare consistency or at least compatibility—is a rationalist worry that does not much interest James. He is not willing to "contradict" himself like a Whitman, but neither is he worried about constructing an elegant philosophical object. It is no tremendous loss if we cannot subsume meliorism by pluralism or radical empiricism. But there is a wellspring for James, the source of all the *ism's* associated with his far-flung philosophical enterprise. It grows out of his fundamental need for hope, for himself and for humankind. Hope for James comes from a reasonable faith in the possibility of free and responsible human activity in response to life and in exercise of those personal and natural enthusiasms that are ours to enjoy together and singly.

Felt personal need and temperament, then, account for James's pragmatism, pluralism, radical empiricism, and all the rest of it. No one of them entirely accounts for all the others. Hope—the need for it, the possibility of it, the sense of it as the only reputable alternative to inadmissible despair— is the center of his vision as I see it. The prime requisite of hope is confidence that what we do matters and may make all the difference further along the chain of life. Meanwhile, conscience and hope command our respect for the immediately contiguous links who are our contemporaries and sometimes command as well our intervention to secure their hold (which is also ours) on the communal life of our species. A chain really *is* no stronger than its weakest link, and James shared the Emersonian sense of life (expressed in the epigraph to "Nature") as a "subtle chain of countless rings." We are all vulnerable, fragile creatures, our luminous time here is brief, and we owe one another support and sympathy. "The truest vision of life I know," wrote Wallace Stegner, "is that bird in the Venerable Bede that flutters from the dark into a lighted hall, and after a while flutters out again into the dark."[111] But the hall's retention of light after our departure, for the use and enjoyment of later migratory transients whose way we have marked, can be our purpose and their deliverance. Meanwhile our human vulnerabilities will always exceed our personal "fortifications," says Anne Lamott, "so the only choice is whether you are most going to resemble Richard Nixon with his neck jammed down into his shoulders, trying to figure out who to blame, or the sea anemone, tentative and brave, trying to connect. . . ."[112] James is with the anemones, and the larks.

"What I like best about William James after all," Henry James scholar Sheldon Novick once told an online community of Jamesians, "is the relentless effort to express experience in ordinary language, as rigorous and coherent in its way as Emily Dickinson's poetry,"[113] and, in its way, as cheerfully restorative of life:

"Hope" is that thing with feathers—
That perches in the soul—
And sings the tunes without the words—
And never stops—at all— . . .[114]

# Abbreviations

| | |
|---|---|
| ECR | *Essays, Comments, and Reviews.* The Works of William James, ed. Frederick H. Burkhardt, Fredson Bowers, and Ignas K. Skrupskelis (Cambridge: Harvard University Press, 1987). This multivolume series is the basic source for James's texts and is referred to hereafter as "Works." |
| EP | *Essays in Philosophy.* Works, 1978 |
| EPR | *Essays in Psychical Research.* Works, 1986 |
| ERE | *Essays in Radical Empiricism.* Works, 1976 |
| ERM | *Essays in Religion and Morality.* Works, 1982 |
| MT | *The Meaning of Truth.* Works, 1975 |
| P | *Pragmatism.* Works, 1975 |
| PBC | *Psychology: Briefer Course.* Works, 1984 |
| PP | *Principles of Psychology.* Works, 1983 |
| PU | *A Pluralistic Universe.* Works, 1977 |
| SPP | *Some Problems of Philosophy.* Works, 1979 |
| TT | *Talks to Teachers on Psychology and to Students on Some of Life's Ideals.* Works, 1983 |
| VRE | *The Varieties of Religious Experience.* Works, 1985 |
| WB | *The Will to Believe and Other Essays in Popular Philosophy.* Works, 1979 |
| Letters I/II | *The Letters of William James.* 2 vols.. Ed. Henry James. Boston: Atlantic Monthly Press, 1920. |
| Perry I/II | R. B. Perry, *The Thought and Character of William James.* 2 vols. Boston: Little, Brown and Company, 1935 |
| Perry (abr.) | *The Thought and Character of William James.* Briefer Version. New York: George Braziller, 1954. |

Besides the scholarly Harvard series The Works of William James and the other sources indicated, I cite parallel references in [brackets] of the following books that may be more accessible for many readers: either the fine pair of *Library of America* volumes or John McDermott's earlier single-volume anthology.

| | |
|---|---|
| WJ I | *William James: Writings 1878–1899.* New York: Library of America, 1992. |
| WJ II | *William James: Writings 1902–1910.* New York: Library of America, 1987. |
| Writings | *The Writings of William James: A Complete Edition.* Ed. John J. McDermott. Chicago: University of Chicago Press, 1977. |

# Notes

Preface and Acknowledgments

1. P, 31 [WJ II, 509].
2. Harold Bloom, *The American Religion: The Emergence of the Post-Christian Nation* (New York: Touchstone, 1992).
3. P, 49 [WJ II, 526–27].
4. P, 49–50 [WJ II, 527].
5. WB, 241 [WJ I, 700].
6. SPP, 63 [WJ II, 1,042].
7. P, 9 [WJ II, 487].
8. PU, 131 [WJ II, 762].
9. VRE, 119 [WJ II, 132].
10. VRE, 116 [WJ II, 128–29].
11. SPP, 9 [WJ II, 985].
12. Patricia Hampl, Introduction, *The Best Spiritual Writing 1998,* ed. Philip Zaleski (San Francisco: HarperCollins, 1998), xv.
13. VRE, 76 [WJ II, 83].
14. Henry David Thoreau, *Walden* (Boston: Beacon, 1997), 2.
15. WB, 104 [WJ I, 555].
16. Lance Morrow, "Deconstructionist at the Super Bowl," *Time,* 18 January 1999, 98. The prime seducers, for those not attuned to the spiritual side of baseball, were Mark McGwire, Sammy Sosa, and Joe Torre's record-setting Yankees (Torre's fading autograph on a baseball that meant much to me thirty years ago means more today, having been joined by teething marks from my sister Kim's beloved, departed old Doberman Pinscher "Bo"). Their gracious heroics restored continuity with the past of "Willie, Mickey and the Duke" and renewed this particular chain of life.
17. ECR, 73 [WJ II, 1,117].
18. A. N. Wilson, *God's Funeral* (New York: Norton, 1999), 328.
19. Scott Russell Sanders, *The Secrets of the Universe* (Boston: Beacon, 1991), 244. And see his *Hunting for Hope: A Father's Journeys* (Beacon, 1998).
20. James Family Discussion List ("Jamesf-l"): jamesf-l@wvnvm.wvnet.edu. John Dewey Discussion List ("Dewey-l"): dewey-l@ganges.csd.sc.edu. Charles Sanders Peirce Discussion List ("Peirce-l"): peirce-l@ttacs6.ttu.edu. For complete addresses and instructions on how to access these E-mail lists (as well as additional information on relevant Web sites), see the end of the bibliography.

21. A phrase reminiscent of E. M. Forster's uncannily prescient story of the same name, in which civilization is paralyzed by its dependence on technology. At press time, the heralded "Y2K" apocalypse doubtless is already fading from memory as a curio in the pantheon of fin de siecle mass delusional weirdness, even as our computing machines monopolize ever-increasing chunks of our personal and collective consciousness.

22. The hopeful impulse seems much in the air at present. Among many worthy new titles on the subject is Patrick Shade's book *Habits of Hope: A Pragmatic Theory* (Nashville: Vanderbilt University Press, 2001). Dr. Shade and I developed our ideas on hope independently, making their contemporaneous publication fortuitous and, just possibly, itself modest cause for hope.

## Introduction: The Glimmer and Twinkle of Jamesian Transcendence

1. Jostein Gaarder—whose astonishing popular success with a philosophical novel aimed at juveniles and entitled *Sophie's World: A Novel about the History of Philosophy* (New York: Farrar, Straus & Giroux, 1994) bespoke a surprisingly wide audience for accessible mainstream philosophy—has derided New Age metaphysics as "philosophical pornography" promising easy spiritual gratification and "instant wisdom" (*American Way*, 15 August 1995, 62). James would not speak so intemperately, but in contrast to many New Age metaphysicians he respected traditional efforts to think and speak clearly about the relation of thought to reality.

2. Andrew Delbanco, *The Real American Dream: A Meditation on Hope* (Cambridge, Mass.: Harvard University Press, 1999), 5.

3. The grave-site marker is modestly tucked away in the shadow of a classroom building on the Burlington campus of the University of Vermont. Its inscription is from the final paragraph of *A Common Faith*.

4. The career of the Czech writer and statesman Vaclav Havel—who said "a human action becomes genuinely important when it springs from the soil of a clear-sighted awareness of the temporality and the ephemerality of everything human . . . the salvation of this human world lies nowhere else than in the human heart, in the human power to reflect, in human meekness and human responsibility"—is illustrative of the transcendent improbabilities of this remarkable period of recent history. *Disturbing the Peace* (New York: Knopf, 1990), 113.

5. "The game is a repository of age-old American verities . . . and yet at the same time a mirror of the present moment . . ." *Baseball: An Illustrated History* [New York: Knopf, 1994], xviii). Burns is not alone. Baseball has always had an uncanny appeal to intellectuals and poets, from Whitman ("I see great things in baseball") on, including this short roster of all-stars: Morris R. Cohen, Robert Frost, Bartlett Giamatti, Doris Kearns Goodwin, Stephen Jay Gould, David Halberstam, Donald Hall, Christopher Lehmann-Haupt, Bernard Malamud, John Updike, and William Carlos Williams.

6. F. Scott Fizgerald quoted in *A Companion to American Thought*, ed. Richard Wightman Fox and James T. Kloppenberg (Cambridge, Mass.: Blackwell, 1995), 57.

7. But for an interesting recent discussion arguing that James and Kant have more in common than James wanted to admit, see Thomas Carlson, "James and the Kantian Tradition," in *The Cambridge Companion to William James*, ed. Ruth Anna Putnam (New York: Cambridge University Press, 1997), 363–83.

8. Like Proust's madeleine cake in *Remembrance of Things Past*, for example, or Will Barrett's cave epiphany in Walker Percy's *The Second Coming*. Percy's protagonists

are always questing for a message or sign to fuse their own personal experience with something transcendently salvific.

9. Alfred Kazin, *God and the American Writer* (New York: Knopf, 1997), 168. Kazin belonged to that sadly dwindling fraternity of "public intellectuals" that included Edmund Wilson and Lionel Trilling. Like them, and in the spirit of Whitman, Emerson, and James, he read books not as disembodied "texts" but as spontaneous, creative expressions of individuals in their freedom. Michael Kazin says his father "taught me that sensing the world through language was painful, inescapable, and, far too rarely, sublime" (*American Scholar* [Winter 1999]: 23).

10. It seems petty in this context to mention the dental chair or the shopping mall, but transcendence of a sort has its place there, too. Not everyone is pained by the mall but I will bet most readers understand my dental phobia.

11. Raymond D. Boisvert, *John Dewey: Rethinking Our Time* (Albany: State University of New York Press, 1998), 141. Professor Boisvert elaborates his explication of Dewey: "What Dewey had in mind was the fully inclusive, somatically integrated person who is motivated by an intense devotion, not just to individual well-being . . . but to 'the sense of a connection of man, in the way of both dependence and support, with the enveloping world that the imagination feels is a universe.' . . . This ideal, says Dewey, 'is not a goal to be attained. It is a significance to be felt, appreciated.' Such a 'significance to be felt' is what Dewey has in mind when he chooses to admit the irreducibility of the 'religious' as an experiential aspect of life."

12. Wim Kayzer, *'A Glorious Accident': Understanding Our Place in the Cosmic Puzzle* (New York: W. H. Freeman, 1997), 240.

13. See, for instance, Rorty's *Philosophy and the Mirror of Nature* (Princeton, N.J.: Princeton University Press, 1980); *Consequences of Pragmatism* (Minneapolis: University of Minnesota Press, 1982); and *Contingency, Irony, and Solidarity* (New York: Cambridge University Press, 1989).

14. These are some of the causal candidates offered by participants in a 1996 conference on consciousness. Specialists in the field may recognize allusions to the pet ideas of Pat Churchland, Roger Penrose (berated by Churchland for propounding a theory of "pixie dust in the synapses" while himself accusing John Searle (!) of lacking a noncomputational model of mind—a claim to which Searle responded incredulously when I asked him about it—and others. And at least one participant—probably not many more—spoke up for mystical and transcendent consciousness as worth attending to (Sandra Blakeslee, "The Conscious Mind Is Still Baffling to Experts of All Stripes," *New York Times*, 16 April 1996.

15. *Letters* I, 228–29. James cast these aspersions in a letter to Santayana, who, despite extreme philosophic and temperamental differences, would have shared the former's sharp antipathy for the youthfully arrogant epistemologists ("never confounding 'Aesthetik' with 'Erkentnisstheorie'"), whose type we will always, apparently, have with us. Santayana must have chuckled, if ever he did, in sympathetic reaction to James's contemptuous "Faugh!"

16. This tendency is most pronounced in connection with nonphilosophers, though James was capable of enjoying the experience of encountering philosophies he nonetheless believed radically flawed. He "squealed with delight," for instance, over Santayana's "perfection of rottenness." *Letters* II, 122.

17. The motion picture *Contact* (based on the late Carl Sagan's novel of the same name) illustrates "the epistemological foundation of James's worldview," says Thom

Carlson. "[James's] situation was akin to that of the protagonist who was given a scientif-ically irresolvable dilemma of direct contact with the radical Other. Although it would have been unreasonable of her to assert the reality of the anomalies of her experience in the face of the conflicting testimony of her peers, it would have been equally unreason-able for her to deny the given evidence of her experience" (post to *James Family Mail List* ("Jamesf-l"), 9 September 1997. For the complete address and instructions on how to ac-cess this E-mail list (as well as additional information on relevant Web sites), see the end of the bibliography.

18. Quoted in Kayzer, *"A Glorious Accident,"* xi.

19. Kitaro Nishida, *An Inquiry into the Good,* tr. Masao Abe and Christopher Ives (New Haven, Conn.: Yale University Press, 1990), 158. Also see *Intuition and Reflection in Self-Consciousness,* tr. Valdo H. Viglielmo (Albany: State University of New York Press, 1987); *Last Writings: Nothingness and the Religious Worldview,* tr. David A. Dilworth (Honolulu: University of Hawaii Press, 1987); Yoko Arisaka and Andrew Feenberg, "Experiential Ontology: The Origins of the Nishida Philosophy in the Doctrine of Pure Experience," *International Philosophical Quarterly* 30, no. 2 (1990): 173–205.

20. Jacques Barzun, *A Stroll with William James* (Chicago: University of Chicago Press, 1983), 4. More recently the nonagenarian Barzun has added: "The work that churned up and recast all my notions about life and the mind, thought and feeling, sci-ence and the art of writing was William James's *Principles of Psychology.* . . . [I]t read like a novel of adventure—which, in fact, it was: the adventure of discovering what was be-lieved about human consciousness. . . . I gathered from its sallies into all regions of cul-ture, that the mind works natively not like a recording camera, not like a logical machine, but like an artist" (Ronald B. Schwartz, *For the Love of Books: 115 Celebrated Writers on the Books They Love Most* [New York: Grosset/Putnam, 1999], 15).

21. A 1909 letter cited by Ignas Skrupskelis in a review in *Transactions of the Charles S. Peirce Society* 28, no. 4 (Fall 1992): 894.

22. Linda Simon, *Genuine Reality: A Life of William James* (New York: Harcourt Brace & Company, 1998), xxii. Simon offers a vivid and charming thumbnail sketch of James the man: "At just over five feet eight inches tall, James was trim, robust, with lu-minous and engaging blue eyes. . . . James's public image, like his finely-crafted writing style, struck some fastidious observers as 'graphic and racy.' Although he was the same age as many of his Harvard colleagues, he appeared younger, fresher, and more vibrant" (xv).

23. *Letters* II, 346.

24. Besides Christian Science, "New Thought" embraces the Unity School of Christianity, Science of Mind, and other sects, not all formally "Christian." These are still popular in our time and actually are on the conservative end of a quasi-religious spectrum that now includes the more radical "New Age." James understood the hunger for personal "meaning" that propels such movements and took their flourishing as evi-dence of mainstream philosophy's general, deplorable unresponsiveness to it. He credit-ed the "mind curists" of his time with America's "only decidedly original contribution to the systematic philosophy of life" (VRE, 85 [WJ II, 93]).

25. He wrote to his brother Henry in 1870, "I can't bring myself . . . to blink the evil out of sight, and gloss it over. It's as real as the good. It must be accepted and hated, and resisted . . ." (*Letters* I, 158).

26. WB, 5 [WJ I, 447].

27. ERE, 24 [WJ II, 1162]. The passage concludes: "This imperfect intimacy, this bare relation of withness between some parts of the sum total of experience and other parts, is the fact that ordinary empiricism overemphasizes against rationalism, the latter always tending to ignore it unduly. Radical empiricism, on the contrary, is fair to both the unity and the disconnection. It finds no reason for treating either as illusory. It allots to each its definite sphere of description, and agrees that there appear to be actual forces at work which tend, as time goes on, to make the unity greater."

28. *The Recovery of Philosophy in America: Essays in Honor of John Edwin Smith*, ed. Thomas P. Kasulis and Robert Cummings Neville (Albany: State University of New York Press, 1997), 270.

29. VRE, 297 [WJ II, 337].

30. VRE, 113 [WJ II, 125].

31. PBC, 13 [WJ I, 15] .

32. P, 99 [WJ II, 576].

33. P, 31 [WJ II, 508].

34. P, 93 [WJ II, 569].

35. Bertrand Russell, *The Conquest of Happiness* (New York: Liveright, 1971).

36. *Principles of Psychology* (Cambridge, Mass.: Harvard University Press, 1983), 179.

37. "Research from large twin studies . . . shows that the personalities of identical twins, even those reared apart from birth, are about twice as similar as those of fraternal twins . . ." (Winifred Gallagher, *I.D.: How Heredity and Experience Make You Who You Are* [New York: Random House, 1996], 64).

38. Natalie Angier notes the evident incoherence of contending both that (1) "countless studies have now documented the paucity of the effect that ordinary families have on children" *and* (2) "the one thing a good family can do is to make a child happy" (Lawrence Wright, *Twins and What They Tell Us about Who We Are* [New York: John Wiley & Sons, 1997], 129); see *New York Times Book Review*, 8 February 1998.

39. See *The Human Cloning Debate*, ed. Glenn McGee (Berkeley: Berkeley Hills Books, 1998).

40. James Gorman, "Consciousness Studies: From Stream to Flood," *New York Times*, 29 April 1997. A schism has emerged between two prominent wings of neuroscientific debate on consciousness, the "east pole" (represented by Steven Pinker), holding that the brain's hard-wiring allows little play for extragenetic variation, and the "west pole" (including Francis Crick), treating the brain as relatively flexible, adaptive, and culturally educable (Sandra Blakeslee, "Recipe for a Brain: Cup of Genes and Dash of Experience?" *New York Times*, 4 November 1997). James would have preferred the westerners in this dispute but would deplore the simplistically destructive dilemma and the reductionism with which both wings still seem smitten.

41. Rita Carter, *Mapping the Mind* (Berkeley: University of California Press, 1998), 13.

42. *New York Times*, 24 January 1998.

43. *Nashville Tennessean* (and other syndicated newspapers), 14 February 1998. Dilbert: "I didn't realize you were such a philosopher." Dogbert: "That's my point."

44. Charles Darwin, *The Descent of Man* (Amherst, N.Y.: Prometheus Books, 1998), 3.

45. Henry David Thoreau, *Walden* (Boston: Beacon Press, 1997), 297.

46. *Letters* I, 337–38. And James was still impugning his own professorial status fifteen years later: "a professor has two functions: (1) to be learned and distribute bibliographic information; (2) to communicate truth. The first function is the essential one, officially considered. The second is the only one I care for" (*Letters* II, 268).

47. This passage from Ford's 1986 novel *The Sportswriter* (New York: Vintage, 1995), 223–24, concludes: "Some things can't be explained. They just are. . . . It is better not even to look so hard, to leave off explaining. Nothing makes me more queasy than to spend time with people who don't know that . . . for whom such knowledge isn't a cornerstone of life." Such a stance is easier to sustain, of course, if you are a former teacher who has achieved subsequent success in other endeavors (fiction writing, for instance).

48. EPR, 99.

49. EPR, 101. Recalling James's great attraction to Bergson's "creative evolution," we can safely speculate that he would be fascinated by Lee Smolin's "cosmic evolutionism" in *The Life of the Cosmos* (New York: Oxford University Press, 1997) and by some versions of the "Gaia" hypothesis of a living, evolving universe—such as Rupert Sheldrake's "morphic resonance" in *The Rebirth of Nature: The Greening of Science and God* (Rochester, Vt.: Park Street, 1994). James likely would sympathize with the increasingly prominent "ecoreligious" attitude that reveres life as such, but he would still resist treating everything as so integrally alive that unity is presupposed and not to be hard-won. In the last analysis James is an anthropocentric humanist.

50. "Transcendence within 'nature' requires a nature that has movement and free-play within it . . . a natural time that is not a determined process, but one which offers up tendencies and privileged possibilities within which sometimes routine, sometimes novel outcomes are realized. . . . If 'transcendence' does not mean 'upward' to the heavens . . . it has to mean outward and onward, an openness, in space and time" (John J. Compton, personal communication).

51. Sandra Blakeslee, "The Conscious Mind Is Still Baffling to Experts of All Stripes," *New York Times*, 16 April 1996.

52. The attitude that everything is in principle explainable and demystifiable pervades Dennett's writings and is reiterated in his response to critics in *Dennett and his Critics*, ed. Bo Dahlbom (New York: Blackwell, 1995). Dennett's reverence for and application of Darwin in his own thought can gathered from statements such as this: "[Darwinism is] a stable system of explanation that does not go round and round in circles or spiral off in an infinite regress of mysteries . . . [T]he cost [of intrinsic, permanent mystery] is prohibitive: you have to get yourself deceived. . . . [T]here is no intellectually defensible way of rebuilding the mighty barriers to comprehension that Darwin smashed" (*Darwin's Dangerous Idea* [New York: Simon & Schuster/Touchstone, 1996], 25, hereafter abbreviated *"Darwin"*).

53. Edward O. Wilson, *Consilience: The Unity of Knowledge* (New York: Knopf, 1998), 12. A constructive alternative to Wilson's view is John Dupre, *The Disorder of Things: Metaphysical Foundations of the Disunity of Science* (Cambridge, Mass.: Harvard University Press, 1993).

54. Francis Crick, quoted in John Horgan, *The End of Science: Facing the Limits of Knowledge in the Twilight of the Scientific Age* (New York: Broadway Books, 1997), 164. Horgan's comment to Crick: The reductionistic hypothesis is by now so tiresomely familiar that it is less *astonishing* than simply *depressing*.

55. One example is the idea that we all choose our mates mainly on the basis of an instinctive urge to transmit our own DNA. Meredith Small comments: "The idea that the human brain was molded only during one period of history . . . is misguided." And, "Genes are passed along in the real world where attraction, love, mating and marriage are not always linked" (Meredith F. Small, "Are We Losers? Putting a Mating Theory to the Test," *New York Times*, 30 March 1999).

56. Nagel had a precursor on bats: B. A. Farrell wondered about bat experience in *Mind* in 1950 (Dennett, *Elbow Room* [Cambridge, Mass.: MIT Press, 1984], 17).

57. Kayzer, *Glorious Accident*, 245.

58. Dennett, *Darwin*, 427.

59. John Searle, *Minds, Brains and Science* (Cambridge, Mass.: Harvard University Press, 1984), 24. Other statements of Searle's seem Dennett's main "mysterian" target: "[T]he mode of existence of [conscious experiences] is a first-person or subjective mode of existence, whereas [that] of the neural pathways is a third-person or objective mode of existence; the pathways exist independently of being experienced in a way that pain does not" (*The Mystery of Consciousness* [New York: NYREV, Inc., 1997], 98).

60. Searle, *Mystery*, xiii.

61. Andy Clark, *Being There: Putting Brain, Body and World Together Again* (Cambridge, Mass: MIT Press, 1997), 4. Some distinguish this new sensitivity to the biological basis of intelligence as research into the conditions of "AL" (artificial life).

62. Merleau-Ponty is the hero, for instance, in David Abram's *The Spell of the Sensuous—Perception and Language in a More-Than-Human World* (New York: Pantheon, 1996).

63. Steven Pinker, *How the Mind Works* (New York: Norton, 1997), 4.

64. Ibid., 52.

65. Horgan, *End of Science*, 246. A recent reply has come from Sir John Maddox, who sensibly predicts that future discoveries will "change our view of our place in the world as radically as it has been changed since the time of Copernicus" (*What Remains to Be Discovered: Mapping the Secrets of the Universe, the Origins of Life, and the Future of the Human Race* [New York: Free Press, 1998], xiii).

66. At least one prominent futurist thinks so: "The disparity in the capabilities of machines and the more advanced animals, such as the *Homo sapiens sapiens* subspecies, will be short-lived. The unrelenting advance of machine intelligence . . . will bring machines to human levels of intricacy and refinement and beyond within several decades" (Ray Kurzweil, *The Age of Spiritual Machines: When Computers Exceed Human Intelligence* [New York: Viking, 1999], 57).

67. John Searle, "I Married a Computer," *New York Review of Books*, 8 April 1999, 38. This is Searle's review of Kurzweil's *Age of Spiritual Machines*. The cover headline: "Can Computers Make Us Immortal?"

68. John Horgan, *The Undiscovered Mind: How the Human Brain Defies Replication, Medication, and Explanation* (New York: Free Press, 1999), 266.

69. Searle, *Mystery*, xv.

70. Ibid., 193.

71. Ibid., 212.

72. Ibid.

73. EPR, 98–99.

74. Owen Flanagan, "Consciousness as a Pragmatist Views It," in *Cambridge Companion to William James*, 26.

75. Richard M. Gale, "John Dewey's Naturalization of William James," in *Cambridge Companion to William James*, 67.

76. *Letters* I, 152–53.

77. VRE, 119 [WJ II, 132].

78. VRE, 119–20 [WJ II, 133].

79. ERE, 19 [WJ II, 1157].

80. VRE, 399 [WJ II, 453.

81. *Letters* II, 149.

82. PU, 131 [WJ II, 762].

83. SPP, 14 [WJ II, 990].

84. Juith Rich Harris, *The Nurture Assumption* (New York: Touchstone, 1998).

85. Emerson's rhetorical question is posed in *Conduct of Life* ("Power"). *Emerson: Essays and Lectures* (Library of America, 1983), 971. The countervailing caution: "I suffer whenever I see that common sight of a parent or senior imposing his opinion and way of thinking and being on a young soul to which they are totally unfit. Cannot we let people be themselves, and enjoy life in their own way? You are trying to make . . . another you. One's enough" (*Ralph Waldo Emerson: Complete Writings* [New York: Wm. H. Wise, 1929], 988).

86. Delbanco, *Real American Dream*, 98. We can hope our children do not fall for the latest fashion in trendy nihilism, exemplified by French novelist Michel Houellebecq: "We live in a world in which there are no more links. We're just particles." Emily Eakin, "Le Provocateur," New York Times Magazine, 10 September 2000, 38.

87. MT, 72 [WJ II, 891–92].

88. *Letters* II, 251.

89. ERM, 144 [WJ II, 1239].

90. John McDermott, addressing the first annual "Summer Institute for American Philosophy" in Burlington, Vermont, in July 1998, criticized James's quake reactions as "obscene" and, with other observations in *On a Certain Blindness in Human Beings* (see below, chapter 2), suggestive of "value-blindness." Notwithstanding my utmost respect for McDermott's wisdom and my unbounded gratitude for his Herculean contributions to the cause of American philosophy, I must respectfully and emphatically disagree.

91. PP, 6.

92. PP, 148.

93. From *Nature*, chapter 7 ("Spirit") in *Emerson: Essays and Lectures*, 41–42.

94. Richard Dawkins, *Unweaving the Rainbow: Science, Delusion and the Appetite for Wonder* (New York: Houghton Mifflin, 1998), x.

95. *Nature*, chapter 8 ("Prospects"), 43. Andrew Fiala says that if we recognize, with Emerson, that "'nature is still elsewhere,' beyond the poet's words and the philosopher's theories, we may regain some respect for nature as that which continually exceeds our attempts to grasp her"("Nature Is Still Elsewhere: Pragmatic Ecology and the Poetry of Nature," presented to the annual conference of the *Society for the Advancement of American Philosophy* (SAAP) in Eugene, Oregon, 26 February 1999.

96. Robinson Jeffers, "Love the Wild Swan," in *A Comprehensive Anthology of American Poetry* (New York: Modern Library, 1944), 357.

97. In *Samaritan Snare* Wesley tells Picard that "William James won't be on my Starfleet exams." Picard answers, "Nothing really important will be. Open yourself to the past—history, art, philosophy—and all of this might mean something." Robert L. McCullough wrote this episode, originally aired 15 May 1989 (Larry Nemecek, *The Star Trek, the Next Generation Companion* (New York: Pocket Books, 1995), 86.

98. VRE, 38 [WJ II, 41]. But James repudiates Renan's own interpretation of these words—"Give ourselves up, according to the hour, to confidence, to skepticism, to optimism, to irony and we may be sure that at certain moments at least we shall be with the truth"—insofar as it counsels an ironic refusal to risk error or commitment. James would have little use for the "vain chatter and smart wit" that is the *lingua franca* of our day, finding in it an absence of due seriousness—not the same as grimness—about life.

99. Diane Ackerman, *A Natural History of the Senses* (New York: Vintage, 1991), 309. Ackerman's implicit total view is very Jamesian; see *Flow and the Stream of Thought* above.

100. Poirier well understands chains of influence: "James is the point of transmission, linking Emerson to Frost, Stein, and Stevens. . . . It is through James that one can most profitably trace an Emersonian linguistic skepticism . . . they share in a liberating and creative suspicion as to the dependability of words . . ." (Richard Poirier, *Poetry and Pragmatism* [Cambridge, Mass.: Harvard University Press, 1991], 5; Jonathan Levin transmits some of Poirier's sensibility about this and extends it in his own original voice in *The Poetics of Transition: Emerson, Pragmatism, and American Literary Modernism* [Durham: Duke University Press, 1999]).

101. *Walden*, 312.

102. EP, 190 [WJ II, 1313]. This was one of James's last living published utterances, appreciatively quoting an obscure "amateur" philosopher named Benjamin Paul Blood ("A Pluralistic Mystic"). James's capacity to appreciate and share the personal philosophic visions of "characters" and "cranks" testifies to his belief in the transcendent power and mystery of subjectivity.

## Chapter One: Taking Subjectivity Seriously

1. TT, 149 [*Writings*, 645].

2. PU, 131 [WJ II, 762].

3. SPP, 54 [*Writings*, 252; WJ II, 1,031].

4. Edward S. Reed, *The Necessity of Experience* (New Haven: Yale University Press, 1996), 12. I am grateful to the anonymous reader at Vanderbilt University Press who first brought Reed's important and insightful book to my attention, noting its parallels to my own.

5. P, 10 [WJ II, 488].

6. SPP, 53 [*Writings*, 251].

7. PU, 122 [*Writings*, 570–71 fn.].

8. WB, 66 [*Writings*, 325].

9. "We are left, as in the other cases, with a puzzle about the role or sense of 'pure experience.' It is evidently of great importance in James's account, and yet also totally inarticulate. . . . For James's pure experience has to be such that nothing whatever can be said about it, if it is to fulfill the very role for which it is cast. Elsewhere James refers to the 'speechlessness' of sensations. . . . Without some ability to characterise the experiences we have no means of determining their identity, and even have no clear means of assessing James's central claim that we are presented with conjunctive relations in experience as well as atomic sensations" (Graham Bird, *William James* [New York: Routledge & Kegan Paul, 1986], 108–9).

10. ERM, 110–11 [WJ II, 1,119].

11. "Self-Reliance," in *Ralph Waldo Emerson: Essays and Lectures* (New York: Library of America, 1983), 270. My emphasis.

12. VRE, 34 [WJ II, 36].

13. Emerson, *Essays and Lectures,* 271.

14. Ibid.

15. Quoted by James in "On a Certain Blindness in Human Beings," TT, 146 [*Writings,* 642].

16. TT, 141 [*Writings,* 637].

17. TT, 144 [*Writings,* 640].

18. TT, 166 [*Writings,* 659].

19. *Walden* (Boston: Beacon, 1997), 124.

20. VRE, 79–80 [WJ II, 87].

21. *Writings,* 7.

22. WB, 77 [*Writings,* 334].

23. *Writings,* 8

24. ERE, 83 [*Writings,* 281].

25. VRE, 134 [*Writings,* 6].

26. Perry (abr.), 368

27. WB, 61 [*Writings,* 321].

28. Ibid., 365

29. Ibid., 258–59

30. Philip Zaleski and Paul Kaufman, *Gifts of the Spirit: Living the Wisdom of the Great Religious Traditions* (New York: HarperCollins, 1997), 107.

31. Perry, 258–59

32. Ibid.

33. EP, 172–90 [WJ II, 1,294–313].

34. EP, 190 [WJ II, 1,313].

35. Perry, 371

36. TT, 146 [*Writings,* 642].

37. Ibid.

38. Ibid.

39. Ibid.

40. TT, 134–35 [*Writings,* 631].

41. I don't know if John McDermott has a "list," but he, too, appreciates the "Say Hey Kid." He illustrates Dewey's idea of the "consummatory" in experience with a Mays anecdote about an eleventh-inning home run which—to his very great delight—defeated the home team.

42. WB, 55 [WJ I, 502].

43. Natalie Angier, *The Beauty of the Beastly: New Views on the Nature of Life* (Boston: Houghton Mifflin, 1995), 194–95.

44. Ibid.

45. David Flick, "If You're Happy and You Know It," *Nashville Tennessean,* 29 July 1999.

46. PP, 1007

47. TT, 163 [*Writings,* 656].

48. PP, 925.

49. This characterization of subjectivity and objectivity follows Nagel: "A view or form of thought is more objective than another if it relies less on the specifics of the individual's makeup and position in the world, or on the character of the particular type of creature he is. The wider the range of subjective types to which a form of understanding is accessible—the less it depends on specific subjective capacities—the more objective it is . . . [O]bjectivity allows us to transcend our particular viewpoint and develop an expanded consciousness that takes in the world more fully. All this applies to values and attitudes as well as to beliefs and theories" (Thomas Nagel, *The View from Nowhere* [New York: Oxford University Press, 1986], 5).

50. Nelson Goodman, *Ways of Worldmaking* (Indianapolis: Hackett, 1978).

51. PP, 921.

52. Ibid., 923.

53. Nagel, *The View from Nowhere*, 214.

54. PP, 940.

55. ERE, 4 [*Writings*, 170].

56. PP, 924

57. Zaleski, *Gifts of the Spirit*, 118.

58. Ibid., 117.

59. TT, 137 [*Writings*, 634]


## Chapter Two: Blindness and Optimism

1. TT, 132 [*Writings*, 629].

2. TT, 132 [*Writings*, 629].

3. TT, 132 [*Writings*, 629].

4. TT, 134 [*Writings*, 631] John McDermott finds evidence of one of James's own moral blind spots in these and surrounding remarks, as we noted in the Introduction. I do not.

5. TT, 134–35 [*Writings*, 631].

6. TT, 141 [*Writings*, 637–78].

7. Susan Hill and Piers Dudgeon, *The Spirit of Britain* (London: Headline, 1994), 98.

8. TT, 144 [*Writings*, 640].

9. Ibid.

10. P, 18, 20 [WJ II, 496, 498].

11. SPP, 73 [WJ II, 1,054].

12. There is a wonderful photograph that captures the spirit of James's and Royce's amicable life-long opposition: they are perched together on a stone wall in Chocorua, New Hampshire, in 1903, evidently in the middle of a heated but friendly exchange; James is wagging his finger at Royce, barely restraining a grin and (reports Perry) playfully riling Royce with the mock-serious curse "Damn the Absolute!" (*Letters* II, 135).

13. This *bon mot* has been variously attributed, for instance to Mark Twain; but it may have been uttered by James B. Cabell. It is certainly a remark worthy of Twain, and if he did not say it first he probably said it often.

14. At the University of Missouri in the late 1970s, Prof. Alexander von Schoenborn sometimes shared with students his lecture notes on Hegel, Heidegger, and other figures

alien to the midwestern undergraduate sensibility. In the margins next to this astonishing equation he had scribbled a model of eloquent pith: "Yikes!"

15. WB, 130 [WJ I, 583].

16. WB, 132 [WJ I, 585].

17. WB, 136 [WJ I, 590].

18. P, 137 [WJ II, 612].

19. Ibid.

20. *Santayana, Pragmatism, and the Spiritual Life* (Chapel Hill: University of North Carolina Press, 1992), 12. Levinson links James and Santayana as "festive critics" whose project was "to highlight how mean suffering was and to find and display ways to overcome things that impeded human joy" (182). Yet Levinson errantly endorses Santayana's dubious distinction "between a Jamesian pragmatism that always pictures thought as conducive to some particular action, and his own festive view that it is in holidays from work, or in 'high moments, when action [becomes] incandescent in thought, that [people] have been most truly alive, intensively most active, and although *doing* nothing, have found at last that their existence was worthwhile'" (184). The distinction is dubious because it inaccurately implies that James was not interested in "holidays" or, more generally, the kind of transcendence sometimes achieved when we are "doing nothing."

21. James's younger ally in Britain, the Oxford *enfant terrible* F. C. S. Schiller, remarked on the Jamesian tendency to attract and enthrall, *and be enthralled by*, persons we might call "characters" (the less charitable called them cranks and kooks): "It was in virtue of his psychological sympathy that James had such a fascination for all sorts of cranks, not only philosophic . . . [W]hen James received them with an open mind and ear, and listened to them and took an interest in their struggles to express themselves, and soothed them and treated them as though they might really have become, by some divine chance, the vehicles for some unsuspected revelation, they promptly fell in love with him, and became his devoted adherents. James treated them tenderly and spent enormous amounts of time and trouble on them and not a little money. . . . On James's death some of his cranks tried [unsuccessfully] to attach themselves to me" (*William James Remembered*, ed. Linda Simon [Lincoln: University of Nebraska Press, 1996], 143–45).

22. VRE, 240 [WJ II, 274].

23. James—like Bradley, says T. L. S. Sprigge—favored a moderate "new kind of asceticism" embracing the "arduous" (*James and Bradley: American Truth and British Reality* [Chicago: Open Court, 1993], 2). In general, James means by "ascetic" any self-discipline that habituates us to doing what inclination and personal preference initially resist. In *Principles* he explicitly urges small daily acts of denial, to mold our characters and build reserves of discipline to call on when life presents real tests.

24. *Letters* I, 158.

25. Perry (abr.), 379.

26. Ibid., 122.

27. A point made by John Updike in "Elusive Evil: An Idea Whose Time Keeps Coming," *New Yorker* 22 (July 1996): 62–70.

28. VRE, 136 [WJ II, 152].

29. Sprigge, *James and Bradley*, 23.

30. Ibid.

31. Gregory Pappas has a nice discussion of this attitude in Dewey . As in so many other respects, what can be said of his attitude towards openness is applicable to James as well. For instance: "Open-mindedness does not exclude firm belief or commitment. One can be open-minded even with respect to those convictions for which one presently has no doubts. All that is required is that one be ready to entertain doubts if they occur, be ready to give up the belief if necessary. Commitment does not have to be dogmatic or fanatical to be legitimate. Decisiveness and flexibility are not mutually exclusive" (Gregory Fernando Pappas, "Open-mindedness and Courage: Complementary Virtues of Pragmatism," *Transactions of the Charles S. Peirce Society* 32, no. 2 [spring 1996]: 318.

32. *Letters* II, 240

## Chapter Three: Pure Experience

1. A popular novel by Pirsig, *Lila: An Inquiry into Morals* (New York: Bantam, 1991), attempted to assimilate Jamesian pure experience to eastern philosophy much as an earlier novel, *Zen and the Art of Motorcycle Maintenance: An Inquiry into Values,* tried to marry Plato and Buddhism.

2. Jean-Francois Revel and Matthieu Ricard, *The Monk and the Philosopher: A Father and Son Discuss the Meaning of Life,* trans. John Canti (New York: Schocken, 1998), 38.

3. Eugene I. Taylor and Robert Wozniak, eds., *Pure Experience, the Response to William James* (Bristol, England: Thoemmes, 1996). Curiously, the editors of this volume identify Royce as one of the "developers" of pragmatism, and there are subtleties of scholarship that might vindicate the claim in some limited respects. But Royce's absolute idealism was largely antithetical to Jamesian pragmatism. More startling is the editors' claim that "the philosophical tradition to which James actually belongs is [not English empiricism but] to a lineage that is more uniquely American and underived; namely, that of Swedenborgian and transcendentalist thought. . . . James was weaned on an intuitive psychology of personality transformation promulgated by his godfather, Emerson, and a Swedenborgian emphasis on the spiritual evolution of consciousness put forward by his father" (xxi). But early exposure to a tradition is not the same as "belonging."

4. MT, 6–7 [*Writings,* 136].

5. ERE, 71 [*Writings,* 272].

6. ERE, 18 [*Writings,* 182].

7. ERE, 73 [*Writings,* 274].

8. ERE, 75 [*Writings,* 276].

9. Ibid.

10. Ibid.

11. Ibid.

12. ERE, 18–19 [*Writings,* 182].

13. ERE, 83 [*Writings,* 281].

14. This is the fictive television filling station attendant, in *Andy Griffith Show* episode 196 ("Goober Makes History"), reflecting on growing a beard and discovering his inner philosopher. Ken Beck and Jim Clark, *The Andy Griffith Show Book* (New York: St. Martin's, 1995), 166. Goober had to shave—not with Occam's razor but Floyd's—to rediscover "his self": a cautionary tale for all professional thinkers.

15. Annie Dillard, *Pilgrim at Tinker Creek* (New York: Harper & Row, 1974), 79.

16. "Ordinary empiricism, in spite of the fact that conjunctive and disjunctive relations present themselves as being fully coordinate parts of experience, has always shown a tendency to do away with the connections of things, and to insist most on the disjunctions . . . [e.g.] Hume's statement that whatever things we distinguish are as 'loose and separate' as if they had 'no manner of connection'. . . [J. S.] Mill's account of both physical things and selves as composed of discontinuous possibilities . . ." (ERE, 22–23 [WJ II, 1,160]).

17. Such critics were legion in the twenties, especially. One example of an influential misreading of James from the period is Lewis Mumford, *The Golden Day: A Study in American Experience and Culture* (New York: Boni & Liveright, 1926).

18. This famous diary entry includes the twenty-eight-year-old James's acceptance of the French philosopher Renouvier's definition of free will: *"the sustaining of a thought because I choose to,"* and of his "first act of free will . . . to believe in free will." The entry repudiates suicide (which James admits to having contemplated in the past) and concludes: "My belief, to be sure, *can't* be optimistic—but I will posit life (the real, the good) in the self–governing *resistance* of the ego to the world. Life shall be built in doing and suffering and creating" (*Writings*, 7–8).

19. I caution the reader here that my use of a single passage from Dillard's marvelous book may tend to mislead about her own overall attitude and the tone of her book. In general it is an ecstatic celebration of continuities between the natural and human worlds. Ironically, the passage I have chosen to exemplify an un-Jamesian view of self-consciousness may be the least representative of Dillard's own personal view, which is delightfully salient in *For the Time Being* (New York: Knopf, 1999).

20. ERE, 14 [*Writings*, 179].

21. ERE, 43 [WJ II, 1,182].

22. Gerald E. Myers, *William James: His Life and Thought* (New Haven, Conn.: Yale University Press, 1986), 566.

23. ERE, 23 [WJ II, 1,161].

24. ERE, 25 [WJ II, 1,163].

25. "Blindness" is a trait we all possess simply by virtue of being unable to comprehend the entirety of whatever spectacle we cast our gaze on, of not uniting all points of view within the compass of our own. "The spectator's judgment is sure to miss the root of the matter. . . . The subject judged knows a part of the world of reality which the judging spectator fails to see, knows more while the spectator knows less . . . [N]either the whole of truth nor the whole of good is revealed to any single observer, although each observer gains a partial superiority of insight from the peculiar position in which he stands" ("On a Certain Blindness in Human Beings," TT, 132–49 [WJ I, 841–60].

26. SPP, 54 [WJ II, 1,031].

27. ERE, 25 [WJ II, 1,163].

28. *Letters* II, 272

29. Quoted in Zaleski, *Gifts of the Spirit*, 106.

30. Ibid.

31. James's anti-"intellectualism" is not the same phenomenon that historian Richard Hofstadter critiqued in *Anti-intellectualism in American Life* (New York: Knopf, 1970). James cautions that we not abuse the powers of intellect by substituting pure intellection for rounded perception. Still, it is in the broader sense an intellectual act to warn against the dangers of intellectualism. We must not forget that James was one of the first to use the term *intellectual* in a positive way, to describe his own activities and

his professional as well as temperamental allegiance to reason, in the sense that is not unfaithful to the actual experience of individuals.

32. One result of going with the flow of experience in the way suggested here is that we may begin to free ourselves from the wearying habit of subordinating all of our acts to remote futurity, and learn to enjoy and appreciate present experience *now*. There is no inherent conflict or final incompatibility between adopting *both* the purposive and goal-oriented *and* the aesthetic attitudes, although we typically cannot embrace both unreservedly and simultaneously. We must exercise discretion to know when each attitude is appropriate. But "normally it is quite within our power to regard our doings as so many ends. This could render each of our acts self-validating and joyous" (John Lachs, *Intermediate Man* [Indianapolis: Hacket Publishing Company, 1981], 41).

33. ERE, 46 [*Writings*, 215].

34. "Your view strikes one at first sight as being a kind of phenomenalism . . ." (Letter to James, 1905, in Ralph Barton Perry, *The Thought and Character of William James*, vol. 2 [Boston, Little, Brown, 1935], 489–90).

## Chapter Four: Pursuing Happiness

1. VRE, 34 [WJ II, 36].

2. Keillor's shriners affirm, in unison: "We were meant to be here, and we were meant to have a large amount of money" (*Prairie Home Companion* broadcast, Minnesota Public Radio, 14 February 1998).

3. The pope, for instance, surely fulfills his pontifical role correctly by insisting on a certain canonical allegiance among the faithful. "Infallibility" means not inerrancy but formal doctrinal finality: like an umpire he can be wrong (many Roman Catholic philosophers surely thought John Paul II was wrong about Pragmatism in his recent *Fides et Ratio* encyclical, for instance), but he cannot be overruled by those who have agreed by their participation in the Church to be bound by his arbitration.

4. WJ II, 118–35

5. Lawrence to Rev. Robert Reid, 3 December, 1907, *The Selected Letteers of D. H. Lawrence*, ed. James T. Boulton (New York: Cambridge University Press, 1997), 7.

6. Cohen records, "When my revered friend and teacher William James wrote an essay on 'A Moral Equivalent for War' [*sic*], I suggested to him that baseball already embodied all the moral value of war, so far as war had any moral value. He listened sympathetically and was amused, but he did not take me seriously enough. All great men have their limitations . . ."(Morris R. Cohen, *Faith of A Liberal* [New York: Henry Holt, 1946], 57, originally published in the *Dial* 67, 26 July 1919).

7. DiMaggio himself did not understand. Simon, in a touching eulogy, reports the austere Yankee Clipper's consternation: "What I don't understand is why you ask where I've gone. I just did a Mr. Coffee commercial. . . . I haven't gone anywhere" (*New York Times*, 9 March 1999).

8. A. Bartlett Giamatti, *Take Time for Paradise: Americans and Their Games* (New York: Summit, 1989).

9. "Religion is the state of being grasped by an ultimate concern, a concern which qualifies all other concerns as preliminary and which itself contains the answer to the

question of a meaning of our life" (Paul Tillich, *Christianity and the Encounter of the World Religions* [New York: Columbia University Press, 1963], 4).

10. G. K. Chesterton, *G.K.C. as M.C.* (1029; reprint, Freeport, N.Y.: Books for Libraries, 1967), 42.

11. Some Jamesian subworlds: the worlds of physical objects, scientific microphenomena, abstract mathematics, illusion, mysticism, religion, opinion, madness, and on and on. "The complete philosopher is he who seeks not only to assign to every given object of his thought its right place in one or other of these sub-worlds, but he also seeks to determine the relation of each sub-world to the others in the total world which *is*. . . . Each world *whilst it is attended to* is real after its own fashion" (PP, 921, 923).

12. VRE, 69 [WJ II, 76].

13. VRE, 71 [WJ II, 77].

14. C. S. Lewis, *A Grief Observed* (London: Faber & Faber, 1961; New York: Bantam, 1976), 28.

15. I have advisedly emphasized the phrase. "*From the outside*" of someone else's subjectivity, that is, from *our* point of view, we simply cannot know what a devotion to truth or duty (or any other attitude) feels like, subjectively, to that individual. I may know that Truth and Duty are cold abstractions *to me*, but from Lewis's point of view (for example) they may feel warm and intimate.

16. I say this even though the imaginative and fanciful character of much of his work, especially his writing for children, may suggest otherwise. This was a man who felt keenly the heart's yearnings and sought to placate them with religion, perhaps in spite of his punctilious scholar's devotion to truth. Many are familiar with Lewis from childhood, others from his popular writings on religion, and still others from his highly respected works of literary criticism, particularly those focused on the late Middle Ages and the Renaissance. I confess to having deliberately avoided him for many years, falsely supposing that he would have nothing of interest to say to me. I did not seek out his writings until the film *Shadowlands* (Savoy Pictures, 1993) depicted a thoughtful, sensitive, engaging figure who did not rest lightly with his hard-won religious faith. For what it is worth, and with whatever degree of insight the filmmakers may have had into the Lewis psyche, it is difficult to view that film and not come away with a sense of the man as deeply consoled but also deeply challenged by the tenets of his belief.

17. WB, 141 [*Writings*, 617].

18. A pluralistic point well made by John Lachs in his essay "Human Natures," reprinted in *American Philosophic Naturalism in the Twentieth Century*, ed. John Ryder (Amherst, N.Y.: Prometheus, 1994), 524–39.

19. WB, 148 [*Writings*, 617].

20. Ibid.

21. WB, 149 [*Writings*, 618].

22. WB, 150 [*Writings*, 618].

23. WB, 150 [*Writings*, 618–19].

24. WB, 150 [*Writings*, 619].

25. WB, 151 [*Writings*, 620].

26. *Letters* II, 127. Perry has a nice summary of his own understanding of "James's personal faith":

James's religion took the form neither of dogma nor of institutional allegiance. He was essentially a man of faith, though not a man for any one church or creed against the rest. Unlike his father, he was not interested in the elaboration and specific formulation even of his own personal beliefs. He confined himself to the intellectual acceptance of what he regarded as the substance of all religions, and to highly generalized emotional attitudes. He insisted upon retaining not only the ideality but also the actuality of God—as a conscious power beyond, with which one may come into beneficent contact; he believed in the triumph, through this same power, of the cause of righteousness to which his moral will was pledged; and he entertained a hopeful half-belief in personal immortality. These specific doctrinal affirmations, together with his belief in believing, his sympathy with every personal belief which brought to an individual the consolation or the incentive that he needed, and the quality of tenderness and ardent good will which pervaded all of his relations with his fellow men, make up the substance of his personal religion. (Perry [abr.], 270)

27. *Letters* II, 248

28. It is easy to forget that James was a trained M.D. In 1894 James wrote, in opposition to strict and exclusive licensing proposals that would have injured the cause of alternative "healers," "I assuredly hold no brief for any of these healers, and must confess that my intellect has been unable to assimilate their theories. . . . But their *facts* are patent and startling; and anything that interferes with the multiplication of such facts, and with our freest opportunity of observing and studying them, will, I believe, be a public calamity" (ECR, 148 [WJ II, 1,338–39]). He wrote that testifying before the Massachusetts legislature in 1898 on behalf of these "facts" and the "extremely important experiences" that generated them required the greatest "moral effort" of his life (*Letters* II, 66–67). Finally, in *Varieties* he derides conventional opposition to unconventional therapies as "pedantic and over-scrupulous" (VRE, 104 [WJ II, 115]).

29. *Letters* II, 199. James continued in this 1903 letter: "[The desire to formulate truths] has contracted an alien alliance in me lately with a feverish personal ambition. . . . I actually dread to die until I have settled the Universe's hash in one more book! Childish idiot—as if formulas about the Universe could ruffle its majesty, and as if the common-sense world and its duties were not eternally the really real!"

30. *Letters* II, 76.

31. Robert Pinsky, *The Sounds of Poetry: A Brief Guide* (New York: Farrar, Straus & Giroux, 1998), 8. Elaborating his view of poetic expression as natural to our biological form, Pinsky says that it is "an ancient art or technology: older than the computer, older than writing . . . evolved for specific uses: to hold things in memory, both within and beyond the individual lifespan" (9). It helps secure "deep, ancient links that join memory, human intelligence, [and] culture" (116).

32. *Letters of John Keats,* ed. Hyder Edward Rollins (Cambridge, Mass.: Harvard University Press, 1958), no. 65 (27 Feb. 1818), 238.

33. Patricia Hampl, Introduction, *The Best Spiritual Writing 1998,* ed. Philip Zaleski (San Francisco: HarperCollins, 1998), xx. "Sunday Morning" is in *The Collected Poems of Wallace Stevens* (New York: Vintage, 1990), 66–70. If Stevens was America's great secular-spiritual poet, our contemporary Billy Collins is a Stevens for the millennium: more accessible, lighthearted and funny, but still acutely perceptive of everyday life.

See his *Picnic, Lightning* (Pittsburgh: University of Pittsburgh Press, 1998) and the earlier *Art of Drowning* (1995), which includes an amusing paean to Stevens in "Monday Morning," 63.

34. These were never published as such in his lifetime, but have recently been reconstructed: Eugene Taylor, *William James on Exceptional Mental States: The 1896 Lowell Lectures* (Amherst: University of Massachusetts Press, 1984). In the preface to his book, Taylor traces how he reconstructed this material from scattered volumes containing James's own marginalia in Harvard's Widener Library and from newspaper and other eyewitness accounts.

35. See John Lachs, "Transcendence in Philosophy and in Everyday Life," *Journal of Speculative Philosophy*, n.s., 11, no.4 (1997): 247.

36. MT, 6–7 [*Writings*, 136].

37. VRE, 307 [WJ II, 349].

38. For instance: Wendy Kaminer reports the attitude of psychiatrist John Mack that an alien-abduction story was credible if "'what was being reported was felt to be real by the experiencer . . . and communicated sincerely' (as if sincerity in these cases might not be simply a measure of the intensity of delusion). The truth lies in what you feel . . ." ("The Latest Fashion in Irrationality," *Atlantic Monthly*, July 1996, 104. In our time, many people "feel the truth" of alien abduction and conspiracy, guardian angels, and universal spiritual awakening through the agency of vibratile transformational energies and harmonic convergences that render the mark of Enlightenment invisible to the rest of us.

39. VRE, 307 [WJ II, 348–49].

40. Especially in Lectures IV and V of *Varieties*. See VRE, 83 ff. [WJ II, 91ff.].

41. Ken Wilber, *One Taste: The Journals of Ken Wilber* (Boston: Shambhala, 1999).

42. James Redfield, *The Celestine Prophecy: An Adventure* (New York: Warner, 1993).

43. An earnest melioristic impulse is one of the salutary common themes of many of these writers. This particular expression is from James Redfield's *Celestine Prophecy Experiential Guide* (New York: Warner, 1995), a workbook designed for use in the thousands of "study groups" that grew up around the phenomenal success of this surprise bestseller.

44. *Reaching to Heaven: A Spiritual Journey through Life and Death* (New York: Dutton, 1999), 188.

45. Taylor, *James on Exceptional Mental States*, 3.

46. SPP, 27 [WJ II, 1,002].

47. Thomas Carlyle continued, "Silence is deep as Eternity; speech is shallow as Time" (*Critical and Miscellaneous Essays*, vol. 4, in *The Oxford Dictionary of Quotations* (New York: Oxford University Press, 1966), 126.

48. *Tractatus Logico-Philosophicus* [1921], trans. D. F. Pears and B. F. McGuinness (1922; reprint, London: Routledge & Kegan Paul, 1974), 3.

49. Karl R. Popper, *Conjectures and Refutations* (New York: Harper & Row, 1965), 213. Popper credits this remark to Franz Urbach.

50. Walker Percy, "Bourbon," in *Signposts in a Strange Land*, ed. Patrick Samway (New York: Farrar, Straus & Giroux, 1991), 103.

51. VRE, 408 [WJ II, 463].

52. Alfred Kazin quoted in Jonathan Rosen, "Alfred Kazin's Tie," *American Scholar* (Winter 1999): 25.

53. VRE, 407 [WJ II, 461].

54. SPP, 60 [WJ II, 1,038].

55. VRE, 408–9 [WJ II, 463–64].

56. VRE, 409 [WJ II, 464].

57. John Lachs lays this conclusion at Kant's door, in "Transcendence in Philosophy and in Everyday Life." See n. 35 above.

58. Walt Whitman, *Leaves of Grass* (New York: Vintage/Library of America, 1992), 246.

59. PP, 181

60. John Updike, *Self-consciousness* (New York: Knopf, 1989), 250. Updike may appear to yearn for the supernatural, but in fact his books are full of appreciation for the natural, simple satisfactions of everyday life. He would love nothing more, it seems, than to "be a self forever."

61. *The Recovery of Philosophy in America: Essays in Honor of John Edwin Smith,* ed. Thomas P. Kasulis, and Robert Cummings Neville (Albany: State University of New York Press, 1997), 293.

62. Raymond Boisvert, "Repast, Reliance, Religion: Beyond Naturalism and Spirituality," presented to the annual meeting of the *Society for the Advancement of American Philosophy* in Eugene, Oregon, February 25, 1999. Professor Boisvert urges abandoning the terms "naturalism" and "spirituality" as unhelpfully broad. But if nature is whatever gets transformed and selected by the processes of evolution, and spirit is whatever reacts to and participates intelligently in these processes, they cannot be anything but widely inclusive.

63. P, 95 [WJ II, 572].

64. EPR, 99–100

65. Daniel P. Matt, *The Essential Kabbalah: The Heart of Jewish Mysticism* (San Francisco: HarperSanFrancisco, 1995), cited in "The Kabbalah Craze," *Utne Reader* (December 1996): 24–26.

66. Ibid.

67. VRE, 399 [WJ II, 453].

68. With his aforementioned "squeal of delight," James professed "intensely [to] have enjoyed Santayana's attack . . ." (*Letters* II, 122–23). This was James's reaction (together with the aforementioned "squeal of delight") in 1900, upon reading Santayana's *Poetry of Religion.*

69. James supported Santayana's Harvard promotion in these terms, in an 1898 letter to President Eliot: "Whatever shortcomings may go with the type of mind of which he is a representative, I think it must be admitted to be a rare and precious type . . . with his style, his subtlety of perception, and his cool-blooded truthfulness" (Perry [abr.], 270).

70. Perry (abr.), 270.

71. Perry II, 403. Santayana explains his willingness to be so "frank" with James: "I know you are human, and tolerant to anything, however alien, that smells of blood."

72. *Little Essays Drawn from the Writings of George Santayana,* ed. Logan Pearsall Smith (New York: Charles Scribner's Sons, 1920), 164.

73. Perry II, 396

74. George Santayana, "Reason in Religion," in *Life of Reason, or the Phases of Human Progress,* 2 vols. (1905–6; reprint, 2 vols. in 1, New York: Charles Scribner's Sons, 1953), 263.

75. Ibid.

76. *Scepticism and Animal Faith* (1923; reprint, New York: Dover, 1955), 112.

77. "Death is not an event in life: we do not live to experience death. If we take eternity to mean not infinite temporal duration but timelessness, then eternal life belongs to those who live in the present" (*Tractatus*, 72).

78. George Santayana, *Scepticism and Animal Faith*, v. By the way, a word in passing concerning the alternative *skeptic* instead of Santayana's preferred *sceptic*: Santayana was (in James's words) a proud representative of "moribund Latinity" and followed the Latinate form, from the Roman Scepticus, even though Scepticus's Greek mentor Pyrrho was a *skeptic*.

79. Perry II, 252

80. Ibid., 320–21.

81. *Writings*, 586

82. VRE, 78 [WJ II, 85].

83. Perry II, 397

84. *The Selected Letters of William James*, ed. Elizabeth Hardwick (Boston: Godine/ Nonpareil, 1980), 82.

85. Perry II, 398

86. Perry II, 400

87. *The Philosophy of Santayana*, ed. Irwin Edman (New York: Modern Library, 1936), 23.

88. Ibid., 343–50.

89. Santayana makes no explicit claims about James's being a "skylark" and does not in fact mention James at all in this particular discussion. But these are not difficult lines to read between.

90. James declined in 1883 to participate in a public ceremony honoring Schopenhauer, "the burden of whose song . . . was the annihilation of personal selfhood." It is a hypertrophied optimism indeed, he observed, which "takes to hurrahing for pessimism itself" (Perry I, 723). But he appreciated "the immortal Schopenhauer's" praise of sympathy for others' joy (Perry [abr.], 233).

91. George Santayana, *Soliloquies in England, and Later Soliloquies* (New York: Charles Scribner's Sons, 1922), 32.

92. Ibid., 30–31.

93. Ibid., 32.

94. Santayana, *Scepticism and Animal Faith*, 252.

95. John McCormick, *George Santayana: A Biography* (New York: Paragon House, 1988), 138.

96. "Irreligious" following conventional if chauvinistic usage; of course, there are religions outside the Judeo-Christian and Muslim fold, but they too seem to have escaped Shakespeare's interest.

97. McCormick, *Santayana*, 135.

98. Ibid., 136.

99. Ibid., 137.

100. Including many of the sentiments implied here: "They do not sweat and whine about their condition, / They do not lie awake in the dark and weep for their sins, / They do not make me sick discussing their duty to God, / Not one is dissatisfied, not one is demented with the mania of owning things, / Not one kneels to another, nor to his kind that

lived thousands of years ago, / Not one is respectable or unhappy over the whole earth" (Whitman, *Leaves of Grass*, 58).

101. "But, the shabby little stinkers all want to write poetry themselves . . ." (*William Carlos Williams and James Laughlin: Selected Letters* [New York: Norton, 1989]), 97.

102. Collins, "Marginalia," in *Picnic, Lightning*, 15. See also note 32 of this chapter.

103. Stanley Cavell, *Conditions Handsome and Unhandsome: The Constitution of Emersonian Perfectionism: The Carus Lectures, 1988* (Chicago/London: University of Chicago Press, 1990), 130.

104. "Something Out of the Ordinary," Presidential address delivered before the Ninety-Third Annual Eastern Division Meeting of the American Philosophical Association, *Proceedings and Addresses of the APA* 71, no. 2 (November 1997): 27.

105. Cavell, *Conditions*, 134.

106. Vita Sackville-West, *Twelve Days* (1928; reprint, London: Michael Haag, 1987), 9–10. Nicholas Delbanco supplements her admirable answer to the question *Why write?* with the recognition of writing's evolutionary and social utility: " because we will not advance as a species without the advantage of hindsight and foresight: both retrospect and prospect fused in what's composed" (*Harper's*, January 1999).

107. William Faulkner, "Address Upon Receiving the Nobel Prize for Literature," *The Portable Faulkner* (New York: Viking, 1968), 724. Originally published 1946.

108. *The Complete Works of Percy Bysshe Shelley*, ed. Roger Ingpen and Walter E. Peck, 10 vols. (New York: Charles Scribner's Sons, 1927), 2:302–5.

109. ERM, 86 [WJ I, 1,110–11]. All quotations from James in this paragraph come from "Human Immortality" in this source.

110. Wallace Stevens, "Sunday Morning," in *Collected Poems*, 70. Stevens is one of many in his generation of poets (like Eliot and cummings) to have been influenced by the Harvard atmosphere of James and his contemporaries. Richard Wilbur recalls an occasion when Stevens, late in life, reminisced fondly "all about his teachers in philosophy" including Royce and Santayana. Peter Brazeau, *Parts of a World, Wallace Stevens Remembered: An Oral Biography* (San Francisco: North Point, 1985), 169.

## Chapter Five: Futures

1. SPP, 60 [WJ II, 1,039].

2. *Letters* II, 260. James complained to H. G. Wells of our "general fund of optimism and respect for expediency," and "the moral flabbiness born of the exclusive worship of the bitch-goddess SUCCESS. That—with the squalid cash interpretation put on the word success—is our national disease."

3. EPR, 100

4. This was the original *New York Times* reviewer's description of Gatsby's world, 19 April 1925, reprinted in *Books of the Century: A Hundred Years of Authors, Ideas and Literature*, ed. Charles McGrath (New York: Times Books, 1998), 64–66.

5. Ambrose Bierce, *The Devil's Dictionary* (1911; reprint, New York: Dover, 1993), 41.

6. *The Maxims of La Rochefoucauld* [1678], tr. Louis Kronenberger (New York: Random House, 1959), no. 134, p. 57.

7. Fitzgerald, *Gatsby*, 8.

8. Ibid., 106.

9. Ibid., 159.

10. Carrie Goldberg, "Bill Gates Speech Draws CEOs," *New York Times*, 10 May 1997.

11. Albert Borgmann, *Holding On to Reality: The Nature of Information at the Turn of the Millennium* (Chicago: University of Chicago Press, 1999), 216.

12. In June 1999, "in the largest gift ever by a living person to a charitable foundation, [Gates] donated $5 billion to support education and health care causes." Weeks later, "in a few hours of stock market trading, [his] holdings surged by just about that amount . . ." (Amy Harmon, "Gates Hits $100 Billion Mark, More or Less," *New York Times*, 17 July 1999).

13. Steve Lohr, "In Senate Testimony, Gates Champions Microsoft," *New York Times*, 4 March 1998.

14. Bill Gates, *The Road Ahead* (New York: Viking Penguin, 1996), 5.

15. "Robert Wright, "The Man Who Invented the Web," *Time*, 19 May 1997.

16. *New York Times*, "The Lonelier Crowd," 20 February 2000. The study was conducted by the Stanford Institute for the Quantitative Study of Society.

17. Gates, *The Road Ahead*, 314.

18. George W. S. Trow, *Within the Context of No Context* (New York: Atlantic Monthly Press, 1997) and *My Pilgrim's Progress: Media Studies 1950–1998* (New York: Pantheon, 1999). Young Jedediah Purdy has joined the anti-ironic backlash with his *For Common Things: Irony, Trust, and Commitment in America Today* (New York: Knopf, 1999).

19. VRE, 39 [WJ II, 41]. As noted in the Introduction, religion for James "favors gravity, not pertness; it says 'hush' to all vain chatter and smart wit." See note 93 of the Introduction.

20. Bill McKibben, *The Age of Missing Information* (New York: Random House, 1992).

21. George Lakoff and Mark Johnson, *Philosophy in the Flesh: The Embodied Mind and Its Challenge to Western Thought* (New York: Basic Books, 1999), 565. The authors praise John Dewey's understanding of "the full richness, complexity, and philosophical importance of bodily experience" (xi). Dewey himself, as noted, credited James with pioneering the "biological conception of the psyche."

22. Ibid., 6.

23. Sven Birkerts, "The Fate of the Book," in *Tolstoy's Dictaphone: Technology and the Muse* (St. Paul, Minn.: Graywolf Press, 1996), 199.

24. Posts to "Peirce-l" Internet mail list by list manager Dr. Joseph Ransdell, January 1999. For the complete address and instructions on how to access this E-mail list (as well as additional information on relevant Web sites), see the end of the bibliography.

25. Ibid.

26. *The Essential Peirce: Selected Philosophical Writings*, 2 vols., ed. Nathan Houser and Christian Loesel. (Bloomington/Indianapolis: Indiana University Press, 1992), 2:249.

27. Sven Birkerts, "The Millennial Warp," in *Readings* (St. Paul, Minn.: Graywolf, 1999), 20.

28. Joe Ransdell, "Peirce-l," 18 February 1999. For the complete address and instructions on how to access this E-mail list (as well as additional information on relevant Web sites), see the end of the bibliography.

29. John Lachs, personal communication.

30. A point entertainingly argued by Walter Truett Anderson in *Evolution Isn't What It Used to Be: The Augmented Animal and the Whole Wired World* (New York: W. H. Freeman, 1996). Anderson represents a growing cadre of social commentators and "third culturists" whose hasty attempts to pinpoint the central human significance of new technologies have not quite found the mark.

31. This was James's parody of Spencer, recorded in his lecture notes. Dennett relates its uncertain lineage in a footnote in *Darwin's Dangerous Idea* (New York: Simon & Schuster/Touchstone, 1996), 393. It underscores the muddle and silliness surrounding so much philosophizing about evolution, in James's day and in ours.

32. *Consciousness Explained* (Boston: Little, Brown, 1991), 200–210; and *Darwin's Dangerous Idea*, 341–70.

33. See, for example, Stephen Jay Gould, "Darwinian Fundamentalism," *New York Review of Books*, 12 June 1997; and "Evolution: The Pleasures of Pluralism," *NYRB*, 26 June 1997.

34. Richard Dawkins, *The Selfish Gene* (New York: Oxford University Press, 1989), 192.

35. Connie Barlow, *Green Space, Green Time: The Way of Science* (New York: Springer-Verlag, 1997), 56.

36. John Lachs, personal communication.

37. Dennett, *Darwin's Dangerous Idea*, 102.

38. Robert Sapolsky, "A Gene for Nothing," *Discover* (October 1997, Special Issue: "Why We Do What We Do"): 46.

39. Steven Pinker, "Against Nature," *Discover* (October 1997, Special Issue: "Why We Do What We Do"): 94–95.

40. Dawkins, *The Selfish Gene*, 200–201.

41. Dennett, *Consciousness Explained*, 207. Here Dennett takes the hard line that Dawkins ducks by advancing the independent credentials of certain cherished memes: "the selective forces that scrutinize scientific ideas are not arbitrary or capricious" (Dennett, "Viruses of the Mind," in *Dennett and His Critics*, ed. Bo Dahlbom [New York: Blackwell, 1995] 26).

42. *Darwin's Dangerous Idea*, 368.

43. Charles Darwin, *The Descent of Man* (Amherst, N.Y.: Prometheus, 1998), 151

44. Darwin, *Origin of the Species*, 408.

45. This allusion, for those fortunate enough to have missed the sickening news of this "sporting" debacle in the summer of 1997, is to a boxing prize fight in which convicted rapist Mike Tyson bit his opponent. But in our confessional culture all is forgiven, if only the transgressor will humble himself with a public apology—disgraceful, but morbidly fascinating from a socio-anthropological point of view.

46. Annie Dillard answers her own question: "Yes, because cultural evolution happens fast. . . . Once the naked ape starts talking 'the unit of reproduction becomes'—in the words of anthropologist Gary Clevidence—'the mouth'" (*For the Time Being* [New York: Knopf, 1999], 93–94).

47. Dennett, *Darwin's Dangerous Idea*, 60. He also says that "evolution is, in the end, just an algorithmic process" (266). Dennett's views are typically difficult to box, but in *Elbow Room: The Varieties of Free Will Worth Wanting* (New York: Oxford University Press, 1984) he seems to defend a version of determinism.

48. A reconstructed memeology might not appeal to Dennett if it invokes an "open-endedness" that implies ineradicable cosmic mystery and a picture of humans as in any respect falling outside the framework of naturalistic understanding. Cultural "skyhooks" are *verboten* on his account; Darwinian "cranes" are not. But perhaps the framework is more elastic than Dennett assumes.

49. Dennett, *Darwin's Dangerous Idea*, 491.

50. Here it is interesting to notice Dennett's defense of his view in Leibnizian /adaptationist terms: ours must be the best possible world (*Darwin's Dangerous Idea*, 238ff). Although Dennett's is not the rationalists' a prioristic, necessitarian kind of possibility, it is still too confining to suit James and most pragmatists.

51. Richard Dawkins, *The Extended Phenotype* (San Francisco: Freeman, 1982), 110–11.

52. *Walden* (Boston: Beacon, 1997), 6.

53. John Dewey, *Reconstruction in Philosophy* (Boston: Beacon, 1957), 160.

54. Dennett, *Consciousness Explained*, 203.

55. Computationalism is "obviously false about consciousness," Searle confidently insists. "The correct approach, which we are still only groping toward in the cognitive sciences, is to forget about the obsolete Cartesian categories and keep reminding ourselves that the brain is a biological organ, like any other, and consciousness is as much a biological process as digestion or photosynthesis" (John Searle, "Consciousness and the Philosophers," *New York Review of Books*, 6 March 1997). It is unclear whether Dennett disagrees with any part of this statement, but clearly he and Searle (and the others) have very different ideas about the extent of sui generis novelty and uniqueness that bio-organic forms may claim to monopolize.

56. Terrence W. Deacon, *The Symbolic Species: The Coevolution of Language and the Brain* (New York: Norton, 1997), 458.

57. Ibid.

58. ". . . but we should not underestimate the myopia and astigmatism created by the other memes that are our accomplices." And: "Every meme is potentially a Trojan horse. What is 'visible' to us, the (willy-nilly) selectors of memes, is one thing; what we thereby actually end up replicating is another. . . . We don't consciously take on all the logical implications of the ideas we adopt, and we can't assay in advance the practical effects of adopting them" (Daniel Dennett, "Back from the Drawing Board," in *Dennett and His Critics*, 232.

59. Ibid., 231.

60. *Utne Reader* (September–October 1997): 101.

61. TT, 164 [WJ I, 876].

62. Dennett, *Consciousness Explained*, 62.

63. PBC, 145 [WJ I, 159]. "Consciousness, then, does not appear to itself chopped up in bits. Such words as 'chain' or 'train' do not describe it fitly as it presents itself in the first instance. It is nothing jointed; it flows. A 'river' or a 'stream' are the metaphors by which it is most naturally described . . . *the stream of thought, of consciousness, or of subjective life.*"

64. This in the context of examples of full temporal perception like "thunder-breaking-upon silence."

65. WB, 58 [WJ I, 505].

66. Mihaly Csikszentmihalyi, *Flow: The Psychology of Optimal Experience* (New York: Harper & Row, 1990); *The Evolving Self: A Psychology for the Third Millenium*

(New York: HarperCollins, 1993); *Creativity* (New York: HarperCollins, 1996); *Finding Flow* (New York: HarperCollins/Basic, 1997).

67. Indeed, as Diane Ackerman notes in the epigraph beginning this section, flow as often has to do with unpurposive—not to be mistaken for pointless or ineffectual—play. The quote is from *Deep Play* (New York: Random House, 1999), 26.

68. George Macauley Trevelyan, quoted in Philip Zeleski and Paul Kaufman, *Gifts of the Spirit: Living the Wisdom of the Great Religious Traditions* (New York: Harper-Collins, 1997), 77.

69. Ron Strickland, ed., *Shanks Mare: A Compendium of Remarkable Walks* (New York: Paragon House, 1988), xix.

70. "On Going a Journey," in Aaron Sussman and Ruth Goode, *The Magic of Walking* (New York: Simon & Schuster, 1967), 227.

71. "Done with indoor complaints, libraries, querulous criticisms / Strong and content I travel the open road" (Whitman, *Leaves of Grass*, 297).

72. "Yesterday I went to the Cliff with Henry Thoreau. . . . Here is a new scene, a new experience. 'Ponder it, Emerson' . . ." (*The Heart of Emerson's Journals*). In his recent essay "Useful Ignorance: Reflections on Thoreau's Walking" (SAAP Conference, Eugene, Oregon, 2/27/99), Russell Goodman wondered whether it is possible to "saunter," in Thoreau's sense, in an automobile. Not for me: prerequisite to the transcendent delights of walking, in my experience, are locomotion and its attendant physiological manifestations.

73. Annie Dillard has documented the fertile consistency of Wallace Stevens's peripatetic (and other) routines: "He rose at six, read for two hours, and walked another hour—three miles—to work. He dictated poems to his secretary. He ate no lunch; at noon he walked for another hour, often to an art gallery. He walked home from work—another hour. After dinner he retired to his study; he went to bed at nine. On Sundays, he walked in the park. I don't know what he did on Saturdays. Perhaps he exchanged a few words with his wife, who posed for the Liberty dime. (One would rather read these people, or lead their lives, than be their wives)" (*The Writing Life* [New York: Quality Paperback Book Club, 1990], 33).

74. *The Philosophy of John Dewey*, ed. John J. McDermott (Chicago: University of Chicago Press, 1981), 527. The passage, from the first chapter of *Art as Experience* (1934), continues: ". . . who notes the delight of the housewife in tending her plants, and the intent interest of her goodman in tending the patch of green in front of the house; the zest of the spectator in poking the wood burning on the hearth and in watching the darting flames and crumbling coals. . . . He does not remain a cold spectator" (528).

75. "The crowd at the ball game is moved uniformly / by a spirit of uselessness which delights them" ("At the Ball Game," *The Collected Poems of William Carlos Williams*, 2 vols. (New York: New Directions, 1986), 2:233. This is the spirit Whitman knew on Brooklyn Ferry.

76. *Spirituality and the Secular Quest*, ed. Peter H. Van Ness (New York: Crossroad, 1996), 7. See also other contributions in this volume, especially the very insightful essay by Nancy Frankenberry, "The American Experience," 102–26.

77. See above, note 5, chapter 4.

78. Santayana's personal circumstances late in life underscore the very Jamesian insight that we cannot grasp the inner worth of another's ways of living. Santayana spent the war years of the 1940s, apparently quite contentedly, in a Roman convent. Edmund

Wilson visited him there. "A few days later, in my hotel room, the thought of his spending night after night, so far from Harvard and Spain, alone in that little bed . . . appall[ed] me . . . but the intelligence that persisted in him was the intelligence of the human race: he was thinking all their thoughts, taking part in all their points of view—so how could he be lonely? He had made it his business to spread himself through every human consciousness with which he had made any contact. He slept, in his plain single bed, in the consciousness of the whole human mind" (Edmund Wilson, *The Forties* [New York: Farrar, Straus & Giroux, 1983], 67.

79. Csikszentmihalyi, *Flow*, 149.

80. Ibid., 171.

81. Ibid., 105.

82. Eugene Taylor, *William James on Consciousness beyond the Margins* (Princeton, N.J.: Princeton University Press, 1996), 147.

83. *The Influence of Darwin on Philosophy and Other Essays* (New York: Henry Holt, 1910). The title essay first appeared in *Popular Science Monthly* in July 1909. The book's preface was signed just months before James's death.

84. VRE, 116 [WJ II, 128], and: "each of [our activity experiences] is but a portion of a wider world, one link in the vast chain of processes of experience out of which history is made" (ERE, 87 [*Writings*, 285]).

85. Dewey, *Philosophy of John Dewey*, 29.

86. Ibid., 11. Dewey then offers a wedge useful to those who would pry him apart from his predecessor: "I do not think that he fully and consistently realized it himself."

87. TT, 45 [WJ I, 748].

88. Michael Pollan, *Second Nature: A Gardener's Education* (New York: Atlantic Monthly Press, 1991), 184–85. Pollan has written another marvelous book on the general theme of nature and culture called *A Place of My Own: The Education of an Amateur Builder* (New York: Random House, 1997), concerned specifically with architecture and the tangible realization of personal dreams and ideas in outer form. The recurrent education motif is no accident; the author acknowledges Dewey's strong influence (personal communication).

89. John Dewey, *Ethics* [1932], in *The Essential Dewey*, vol. 2: *Ethics, Logic, Psychology*, ed. Larry A. Hickman and Thomas M. Alexander (Bloomington/Indianapolis, Indiana University Press, 1998), 350. "Having a good sense of continuity with life, of belonging intimately, of being able to depend on nature, including human nature, is all part of spirituality," comments Jim Garrison on this summary of responsible Deweyan selfhood. I thank him for recalling the statement to my attention. See his "John Dewey's Philosophy as Education," in *Reading Dewey: Interpretations for a Postmodern Generation*, ed. Larry Hickman (Indiana University Press, 1998), 63–81, and fine contributions by Tom Alexander, Ray Boisvert, John Stuhr, and others.

90. Dewey, *Philosophy of John Dewey*, 535.

91. Robinson, quoted in James D. Hart, *The Oxford Companion to American Literature*, 5th edition (New York: Oxford University Press, 1983), 645.

92. George Dykhuizen, *The Life and Mind of John Dewey* (Carbondale: Southern Illinois University Press, 1973), 22.

93. VRE, 412 [WJ II, 467].

94. Richard Rorty, "Religious faith, Intellectual Responsibility, and Romance," *Cambridge Companion to William James*, 99. "In Whitmanesque moods he could identi-

fy this wider self with an Americanized humanity at the farthest reach of the democratic vistas."

95. A. N. Wilson, *God's Funeral* (New York: Norton, 1999), 331.

96. Perry II, 357

97. P, 50 [WJ II, 527].

98. Her obituary appeared in the *New York Times,* 5 August 1997. We should not overstate the contribution of this credo to her longevity, in view of the fact that this woman's immediate forebears also are reported to have reached ripe old age. But genes may be educable, too.

99. George Santayana, *The Idea of Christ in the Gospels or God in Man: A Critical Essay* (New York: Charles Scribner's Sons, 1946), 80.

100. Nicholas Rescher, *Luck: The Brilliant Randomness of Everyday Life* (New York: Farrar, Straus & Giroux, 1995), 16.

101. John Dewey, *A Common Faith* (1934; reprint, New Haven: Yale University Press, 1980), 85.

102. Ibid., 87.

103. Dykhuizen, *Life and Mind of John Dewey,* 22. Commenting on this unfamiliar episode, Tom Alexander observes that "the origin of the word 'mystic' is Greek *muein,* 'to be silent' (echoed in our word 'mute'). Dewey managed to be pretty mute about this experience most of his life, didn't he?" (Personal communication).

104. *Letters* I, 128

105. Bill McKibben used this Berry quote as the volume epigraph for *Hope, Human and Wild* (New York: Little, Brown, 1995).

106. Wendell Berry, "Discipline and Hope," in *Recollected Essays 1965–1980* (San Francisco: North Point, 1981), 190.

107. Ibid., 195.

108. Ibid.

109. Hans Koning, "Notes on the Twentieth Century," *Atlantic Monthly,* September 1997, 96.

110. John Lachs, personal communication.

111. Wallace Stegner, *The Spectator Bird* (Lincoln: University of Nebraska Press/Bison, 1976, 1979), 213.

112. Anne Lamott, "Why I Don't Meditate," in *The Best Spiritual Writing 1998,* ed. Philip Zaleski (San Francisco: HarperCollins, 1998), 154.

113. Post to "Jamesf-l" mail list, 11 February 1999, replying to another participant's allusion to an Emily Dickinson poem: "This was a Poet—'It is That / Distills amazing sense / From ordinary Meanings.'" For the complete address and instructions on how to access this E-mail list (as well as additional information on relevant Web sites), see the end of the bibliography.

114. *The Complete Poems of Emily Dickinson,* ed. Thomas H. Johnson (Boston: Little, Brown, 1960), 116.

# Bibliography

Abel, Reuben. *Humanistic Pragmatism: The Philosophy of F. C. S. Schiller.* New York: Free Press, 1966.

Ackerman, Diane. *A Natural History of the Senses.* New York: Vintage, 1991.

———. *Deep Play.* New York: Random House, 1999.

Barlow, Connie. *Green Space, Green Time: The Way of Science.* New York: Springer-Verlag, 1997.

Barzun, Jacques. *A Stroll with William James.* Chicago: University of Chicago Press, 1983.

Berners-Lee, Tim, and Mark Fischetti. *Weaving the Web: The Original Design and Ultimate Destiny of the World Wide Web by Its Inventor.* San Francisco: Harper-SanFrancisco, 1999.

Berry, Wendell. *Recollected Essays 1965–1980.* San Francisco: North Point, 1981.

Bird, Graham. *William James.* New York: Routledge & Kegan Paul, 1986.

Birkerts, Sven. *The Gutenberg Elegies: The Fate of Reading in an Electronic Age.* New York: Ballantine/Fawcett Columbine, 1994.

———. *Readings.* St. Paul, Minn.: Graywolf, 1999.

———. *Tolstoy's Dictaphone: Technology and the Muse.* St. Paul, Minn.: Graywolf, 1996.

Blackmore, Susan. *The Meme Machine.* New York: Oxford University Press, 1999.

Block, Ned, Owen Flanagan, and Guven Guzeldere, eds. *The Nature of Consciousness: Philosophical Debates.* Cambridge, Mass.: MIT Press, 1997.

Bloom, Harold. *The American Religion: The Emergence of the Post-Christian Nation.* New York: Touchstone, 1992.

Boisvert, Raymond D. *John Dewey: Rethinking Our Time.* Albany: State University of New York Press, 1998.

Borgmann, Albert. *Holding On to Reality: The Nature of Information at the Turn of the Millennium.* Chicago: University of Chicago Press, 1999.

Borradori, Giovanna. *The American Philosopher.* Chicago: University of Chicago Press, 1994.

Brown, Hunter. *William James on Radical Empiricism and Religion.* Toronto: University of Toronto Press, 2000.

Caspary, William R. *Dewey on Democracy.* Ithaca, N.Y.: Cornell University Press, 2000.

Cavell, Stanley. *Conditions Handsome and Unhandsome: The Constitution of Emersonian Perfectionism—The Carus Lectures, 1988.* Chicago: University of Chicago Press, 1990.

————. *In Quest of the Ordinary: Lines of Skepticism and Romanticism*. Chicago: University of Chicago Press, 1988.

Cohen, Jack, and Ian Stewart. *The Collapse of Chaos: Discovering Simplicity in a Complex World*. New York: Penguin, 1995.

Collins, Billy. *The Art of Drowning*. Pittsburgh: University of Pittsburgh Press, 1995.

————. *Picnic, Lightning*. Pittsburgh: University of Pittsburgh Press, 1998.

Cotkin, George. *William James, Public Philosopher*. Baltimore: Johns Hopkins University Press, 1990.

Crick, Francis. *The Astonishing Hypothesis: The Scientific Search for the Soul*. New York: Simon & Schuster, 1994.

Croce, Paul Jerome. *Science and Religion in the Era of William James. Vol. 1: Eclipse of Certainty, 1820–1880*. Chapel Hill: University of North Carolina Press, 1995.

Csikszentmihalyi, Mihaly. *The Evolving Self: A Psychology for the Third Millennium*. New York: HarperCollins, 1993.

————. *Flow: The Psychology of Optimal Experience*. New York: Harper & Row, 1990.

Dahlbom, Bo, ed. *Dennett and His Critics*. New York: Blackwell, 1995.

Damasio, Antonio. *The Feeling of What Happens: Body and Emotion in the Making of Consciousness*. New York: Harcourt Brace, 1999.

Darwin, Charles. *The Descent of Man*. Amherst, N.Y.: Prometheus, 1998.

————. *The Origin of Species by Means of Natural Selection*. Last (6th) Edition. Amherst, N.Y.: Prometheus, 1991.

Dawkins, Richard. *River Out of Eden: A Darwinian View of Life*. New York: Basic, 1995.

————. *The Selfish Gene*. New York: Oxford University Press, 1989.

————. *Unweaving the Rainbow: Science, Delusion and the Appetite for Wonder*. New York: Houghton Mifflin, 1998.

Deacon, Terrence. *The Symbolic Species: The Coevolution of Language and the Brain*. New York: Norton, 1997.

Dennett, Daniel C. *Consciousness Explained*. Boston: Little, Brown, 1991.

————. *Darwin's Dangerous Idea*. New York: Simon & Schuster/Touchstone, 1996.

————. *Elbow Room: The Varieties of Free Will Worth Wanting*. New York: Oxford University Press, 1984.

Desmond, Adrian. *Huxley: From Devil's Disciple to Evolution's High Priest*. Reading, Mass.: Addison Wesley, 1997.

Dewey, John. *A Common Faith*. [1934]. New Haven, Conn.: Yale University Press, 1980.

————. *The Essential Dewey*. 2 vols. Ed. Larry A. Hickman and Thomas M. Alexander Bloomington: Indiana University Press, 1998.

————. *The Influence of Darwin on Philosophy and Other Essays*. Ed. Amherst, N.Y.: Prometheus, 1997.

Dillard, Annie. *For the Time Being*. New York: Knopf, 1999.

————. *Pilgrim at Tinker Creek*. New York: Harper & Row, 1974.

Dupre, John. *The Disorder of Things: Metaphysical Foundations of the Disunity of Science*. Cambridge, Mass.: Harvard University Press, 1993.

Edelman, Gerald. *Bright Air, Brilliant Fire: On the Matter of the Mind*. New York: Basic Books, 1992.

Eldridge, Michael. *Transforming Experience: John Dewey's Cultural Instrumentalism*. Nashville: Vanderbilt University Press, 1998.

Emerson, Ralph Waldo. *Ralph Waldo Emerson: Essays and Lectures*. New York: Library of America, 1983.

Everdell, William R. *The First Moderns: Profiles in the Origins of Twentieth Century Thought*. Chicago: University of Chicago Press, 1997.

Feyerabend, Paul. *Conquest of Abundance: A Tale of Abstraction Versus the Richness of Being*, edited by Bert Terpstra. Chicago: University of Chicago Press, 1999.

Fontinell, Eugene. *Self, God, and Immortality: A Jamesian Investigation*. Philadelphia: Temple University Press, 1986.

Flower, Elizabeth, and Murray G. Murphey. *A History of Philosophy in America*. New York: G. P. Putnam's Sons, 1977.

Fox, Richard Wightman, and James T. Kloppenberg, eds. *A Companion to American Thought*. Cambridge, Mass.: Blackwell, 1995.

Fraser, Caroline. *God's Perfect Child: Living and Dying in the Christian Science Church*. New York: Henry Holt, 1999.

Gale, Richard M. *The Divided Self of William James*. New York: Cambridge University Press, 1999.

Gavin, William Joseph. *William James and the Reinstatement of the Vague*. Temple University Press, 1992.

Goodenough, Ursula. *The Sacred Depths of Nature*. New York: Oxford University Press, 1998.

Goodman, Nelson. *Ways of Worldmaking*. Indianapolis: Hackett, 1978.

Gould, Stephen Jay. *Rocks of Ages: Science and Religion in the Fullness of Life*. New York: Ballantine, 1999.

Hall, Donald. *Life Work*. Boston: Beacon Press, 1993.

Harris, Judith Rich. *The Nurture Assumption: Why Children Turn Out the Way They Do*. New York: Free Press, 1998.

Haught, John F. *God after Darwin: A Theology of Evolution*. Boulder, Colo.: Westview Press, 2000.

Heim, Michael. *The Metaphysics of Virtual Reality*. New York: Oxford University Press, 1993.

Hickman, Larry A., ed. *Reading Dewey: Interpretations for a Postmodern Generation*. Bloomington/Indianapolis: Indiana University Press, 1998.

Hodges, Michael P. *Transcendence and Wittgenstein's Tractatus*. Philadelphia: Temple University Press, 1990.

Hofstadter, Richard. *Anti-intellectualism in American Life*. New York: Knopf, 1970.

Hook, Sidney. *John Dewey: An Intellectual Portrait*. Amherst, N.Y.: Prometheus, 1995.

Horgan, John. *The End of Science: Facing the Limits of Science in the Twilight of the Scientific Age.* New York: Broadway Books, 1996.

———. *The Undiscovered Mind: How the Human Brain Defies Replication, Medication, and Explanation.* New York: Free Press, 1999.

Horn, Jason Gary. *Mark Twain and William James: Crafting a Free Self.* Columbia: University of Missouri Press, 1996.

James, Henry, ed. *The Letters of William James.* 2 vols. Boston: Atlantic Monthly Press, 1920.

James, William. *William James: Writings 1878–1899.* New York: Library of America, 1992.

———. *William James: Writings 1902–1910.* New York: Library of America, 1987.

Johnson, George. *Fire in the Mind: Science, Faith, and the Search for Order.* New York: Vintage Books, 1996.

Kasulis, Thomas P., and Robert Cummings Neville, eds. *The Recovery of Philosophy in America: Essays in Honor of John Edwin Smith.* Albany: State University of New York Press, 1997.

Kayzer, Wim. *"A Glorious Accident": Understanding Our Place in the Cosmic Puzzle.* New York: W. H. Freeman, 1997.

Kazin, Alfred. *God and the American Writer.* New York: Knopf, 1997.

———. *A Walker in the City.* New York: Harcourt Brace Jovanovich, 1951.

Kuklick, Bruce. *The Rise of American Philosophy: Cambridge, Massachusetts, 1860–1930.* New Haven, Conn.: Yale University Press, 1977.

Kurzweil, Ray. *The Age of Spiritual Machines: When Computers Exceed Human Intelligence.* New York: Viking, 1999.

Lachs, John. *George Santayana.* Boston: Twayne Publishers, 1988.

———. "Human Natures." Fourth Annual Patrick Romanell Lecture, delivered at Eastern Division Meeting, December 29, 1989. *American Philosophical Association Proceedings* 63, no. 7 (1990):30–39.

———. *In Love with Life: Reflections on the Joy of Living and Why We Hate to Die.* Nashville: Vanderbilt University Press, 1998.

———. *Intermediate Man.* Indianapolis: Hackett, 1981.

Lakoff, George, and Mark Johnson. *Philosophy in the Flesh: The Embodied Mind and Its Challenge to Western Thought.* New York: Basic Books, 1999.

Lamberth, David C. *William James and the Metaphysics of Experience.* New York: Cambridge University Press, 1999.

Larson, Edward J. *Summer for the Gods: The Scopes Trial and America's Continuing Debate over Science and Religion.* Cambridge, Mass.: Harvard University Press, 1997.

Levin, Jonathan. *The Poetics of Transition: Emerson, Pragmatism, and American Literary Modernism.* Durham: Duke University Press, 1999.

Levinson, Henry Samuel. *The Religious Investigations of William James.* Chapel Hill: University of North Carolina Press, 1981.

————. *Santayana, Pragmatism, and the Spiritual Life.* Chapel Hill: University of North Carolina Press, 1992.

Lewis, C. S. *A Grief Observed.* London: Faber & Faber, 1961; New York: Bantam, 1976.

Lewis, R. W. B. *The Jameses: A Family Narrative.* New York: Farrar, Straus and Giroux, 1991.

Lupica, Mike. *Summer of '98: When Homers Flew, Records Fell, and Baseball Reclaimed America.* New York: G. P. Putnam's Sons, 1999.

McCarver, Tim (with Danny Peary). *The Perfect Season: Why 1998 Was Baseball's Greatest Year.* New York: Villard, 1999.

McCormick, John. *George Santayana: A Biography.* New York: Paragon House, 1988.

McDermott, John J., ed. *The Philosophy of John Dewey.* Chicago: University of Chicago Press, 1981.

————. *The Writings of William James: A Complete Edition.* Chicago: University of Chicago Press, 1977.

McGinn, Colin. *The Mysterious Flame: Conscious Minds in a Material World.* New York: Basic Books, 1999.

McKibben Bill. *Hope, Human and Wild.* New York: Little, Brown, 1995.

Maddox, (Sir) John L. *What Remains to Be Discovered: Mapping the Secrets of the Universe, the Origins of Life, and the Future of the Human Race.* New York: Free Press, 1998.

Mumford, Lewis. *The Golden Day: A Study in American Experience and Culture.* New York: Boni & Liveright, 1926.

Myers, Gerald E. *William James: His Life and Thought.* New Haven, Conn.: Yale University Press, 1986.

Nagel, Thomas. *The View from Nowhere.* New York: Oxford University Press, 1986.

Nishida, Kitaro. *An Inquiry into the Good.* Tr. Masao Abe and Christopher Ives. New Haven, Conn.: Yale University Press, 1990.

Peirce. Charles Sanders. *The Essential Peirce: Selected Philosophical Writings.* 2 vols. Edited by. Nathan Houser and Christian Loesel. Bloomington / Indianapolis: Indiana University Press, 1992.

Percy, Walker. *Signposts in a Strange Land.* Ed. Patrick Samway. New York: Farrar, Straus & Giroux, 1991.

Perry, Ralph Barton. *The Thought and Character of William James.* 2 vols. Boston: Little, Brown, 1935.

————. *The Thought and Character of William James,* Briefer Version. New York: George Braziller, 1954.

Pinker, Steven. *How the Mind Works.* New York: Norton, 1997.

Poirier, Richard. *Poetry and Pragmatism.* Cambridge, Mass.: Harvard University Press, 1992.

Pollan, Michael. *A Place of My Own: The Education of an Amateur Builder.* New York: Random House, 1997.

————. *Second Nature: A Gardener's Education*. New York: Atlantic Monthly Press, 1991.

Purdy, Jedediah. *For Common Things: Irony, Trust, and Commitment in America Today*. New York: Alfred A. Knopf, 1999.

Putnam, Hilary. *Pragmatism: An Open Question*. Oxford: Basil Blackwell, 1995.

————. *Renewing Philosophy*. Cambridge, Mass.: Harvard University Press, 1992.

Putnam, Ruth Anna, ed. *The Cambridge Companion to William James*. Cambridge: Cambridge University Press, 1997.

Reed, Edward S. *The Necessity of Experience*. New Haven, Conn.: Yale University Press, 1996.

Rescher, Nicholas. *Luck: The Brilliant Randomness of Everyday Life*. New York: Farrar, Straus & Giroux, 1995.

————. *Pluralism: Against the Demand for Consensus*. New York: Oxford University Press, 1993.

Richardson, Robert D., Jr. *Emerson: The Mind on Fire*. Berkeley: University of California Press, 1995.

Ridley, Mark, ed. *Evolution*. New York: Oxford University Press, 1997.

Ridley, Matt. *The Origins of Virtue: Human Instincts and the Evolution of Cooperation*. New York: Penguin, 1998.

Rolston, Holmes, III. *Genes, Genesis and God: Values and Their Origins in Natural and Human History*. New York: Cambridge University Press, 1999.

Rorty, Richard. *Consequences of Pragmatism*. Minneapolis: University of Minnesota Press, 1982.

————. *Contingency, Irony, and Solidarity*. New York: Cambridge University Press, 1989.

————. *Philosophy and Social Hope*. New York. Penguin, 1999.

Rose, Michael R. *Darwin's Spectre: Evolutionary Biology in the Modern World*. Princeton, N.J.: Princeton University Press, 1998.

Rue, Loyal D. *Everybody's Story: Wising up to the Epic of Evolution*. Albany: State University of New York Press, 2000.

Ruse, Michael. *Mystery of Mysteries: Is Evolution a Social Construction?* Cambridge, Mass.: Harvard University Press, 1999.

————. *Taking Darwin Seriously*. Amherst, N.Y.: Prometheus, 1998.

Ryan, Alan. *John Dewey and the High Tide of American Liberalism*. New York: Norton, 1997.

Ryder, John, ed. *American Philosophic Naturalism in the Twentieth Century*. Amherst, N.Y.: Prometheus, 1994.

Sagan, Carl. *Billions & Billions: Thoughts on Life and Death at the Brink of the Millennium*. New York: Random House, 1997.

Sagan, Carl, and Ann Druyan. *Shadows of Forgotten Ancestors: A Search for Who We Are*. New York: Random House, 1992.

Sanders, Scott Russell. *Hunting for Hope: A Father's Journeys*. Boston: Beacon, 1998.

——. *Writing from the Center*. Bloomington/Indianapolis: Indiana University Press, 1997.

Santayana, George. *The Life of Reason, or the Phases of Human Progress*. 2 vols. 1905–1906. Reprint (2 vols. in 1), New York: Charles Scribner's Sons, 1953.

——. *Scepticism and Animal Faith*. 1923. Reprint, New York: Dover, 1955.

Searle, John. *Mind, Language and Society: Philosophy in the Real World*. New York: Basic Books, 1998.

——. *Minds, Brains and Science*. Cambridge, Mass.: Harvard University Press, 1984.

——. *The Mystery of Consciousness*. New York: NYREV, Inc., 1997.

Seigfried, Charlene H. *William James's Radical Reconstruction of Philosophy*. Albany: State University of New York Press, 1990.

Simon, Linda, ed. *Genuine Reality: A Life of William James*. New York: Harcourt Brace & Company, 1998.

——. *William James Remembered*. Lincoln: University of Nebraska Press, 1996.

Smith, David C. *The Transcendental Saunterer: Thoreau and the Search for Self*. Savannah, Ga.: Frederic C. Beil, 1997.

Smith, John E. *America's Philosophical Vision*. Chicago: University of Chicago Press, 1992.

Solnit, Rebecca. *Wanderlust: A History of Walking*. New York: Viking, 2000.

Sprigge, T. L. S. *James and Bradley: American Truth and British Reality*. Chicago: Open Court, 1993.

Suckiel, Ellen Kappy. *Heaven's Champion: William James's Philosophy of Religion*. Notre Dame, Ind.: University of Notre Dame Press, 1997.

Taylor, Eugene. *William James on Consciousness beyond the Margins*. Princeton, N.J.: Princeton University Press, 1996.

——. *William James on Exceptional Mental States: The 1896 Lowell Lectures*. Amherst: University of Massachusetts Press, 1984.

Taylor, Eugene, and Robert Wozniak, eds. *Pure Experience: The Response to William James*. Bristol, England: Thoemmes, 1996.

Thoreau, Henry David. *Walden*. Boston: Beacon Press, 1997.

Thwaite, Anthony, ed. *R. S. Thomas*. London: J. M. Dent, 1996.

Townsend, Kim. *Manhood at Harvard: William James and Others*. New York: Norton, 1996.

Trow, George W. S. *My Pilgrim's Progress: Media Studies 1950–1998*. New York: Pantheon, 1999.

——. *Within the Context of No Context*. New York: Atlantic Monthly Press, 1997.

Van Ness, Peter H. *Spirituality and the Secular Quest*. New York: Crossroad, 1996.

Whitman, Walt. *Leaves of Grass*. New York: Vintage/Library of America, 1992.

Wilson, A. N. *God's Funeral*. New York: Norton, 1999.

Wilson, Edward O. *Consilience: The Unity of Knowledge*. New York: Knopf, 1998.

————. *Naturalist.* Washington, D.C.: Island, 1994.

Wright, Robert. *The Moral Animal: Evolutionary Psychology and Everyday Life.* New York: Vintage, 1995.

————. *Nonzero: The Logic of Human Destiny.* New York: Pantheon, 1999.

Zaleski, Philip. *Best Spiritual Writing 1998.* San Francisco: HarperCollins, 1998.

Zaleski, Philip, and Paul Kaufman. *Gifts of the Spirit: Living the Wisdom of the Great Religious Traditions.* New York: HarperCollins, 1997.

### E-Mail Lists

DEWEY-L (John Dewey List). To subscribe, send the message (in message area) <subscribe dewey-l (your first and last name)> to <listserv@ganges.csd.sc.edu>.

DEWEY-L list archives. To access the list archives using E-mail, first send the message (in message area) <index dewey-l> to <listserv@ganges.csd.sc.edu>. The server will respond with an E-mail message listing all the archive files, in chronological order, e.g., <LOG9802B> (second archive file in February 1998, roughly a week's worth of dewey-l posts).

EMERSON-L (Ralph Waldo Emerson List). To subscribe, send the message (in message area) <subscribe (your first and last name) to <emerson@field.uor.edu>.

JAMESF-L (James Family List). To subscribe, send the message (in message area) <subscribe JAMESF-L (your first and last name)> to <listserv@wvnvm.wvnet.edu>. According to its current manager, this list no longer sponsers discussion of William James, although discussion of his father and siblings continues.

WILLIAMJAMES-L (William James List). To subscribe, send the message (in message area) "subscribe williamjames-l (your first and last name) to <listserv@austin.cc.tx.us>.

PEIRCE-L (Charles Sanders Peirce List, <peirce-l@lyris.acs.ttu.edu>). To subscribe, send the message (in message area) <subscribe (your first and last name)> to <lyris@lyris.acs.ttu.edu>.

## William James Sites on the World Wide Web

The most complete is Frank Pajares's site at Emory University: <http://www.emory.edu/EDUCATION/mfp/james.html>.

LeRoy Miller has a site on "New Age, New Thought: William James and the Varieties of Religious Experience": <http://www.tekdok.com/james/index.htm>.

Randall Albright's James website offers links to those above and serves as a "virtual" bookstore for books in print by and about James: <http://world.std.com/~albright/james.html>.

The official Website for the William James Society is maintained by John Shook: <http://www.pragmatism.org/societies/william_james.htm>.

# Index

life; future); "glimmer and twinkle," 1, 48; "gulls skimming down at the mouth of the Amazon," 206; habit, 50, 95, 126, 195, 222n. 23; "hands off," 6, 29, 36; happiness, 12, 49, 94–95, 122, 130, 140, 152, 158, 160–61, 175–76, 198, 207–208 (*see also* joy); happiness and mystery, 17–27, 96, 168, 204–5; healthy-mindedness, 12, 70–71, 74–75, 87; human community, 10, 109, 198 (*see also* James: "wider self"); humanism, 31, 106–7, 200, 216n. 49; "ideal novelty," 185–86; "ideal and real dynamically continuous," 141; ideals, 8, 43, 55, 110, 139, 193–94, 198–99, 201–2; ideals, surrendered to "other hands," 201; immediacy, 57, 80, 82–83, 86, 96–98, 114, 121, 167, 187; immortality, 152–53 (*see also* eternity); importance, 42, 50, 52–53, 58–60, 63, 85; individualism, 37, 90, 99, 135, 178; intellectualism, xiii, 18, 23–24, 38–39, 47, 79, 94, 121, 159, 197, 224n. 31; "interest, no truth without some," 78; "'interesting' aspects of things," 85; "joy, peculiar sources of," 51 (*see also* James: happiness, "springs of delight"); Keene Valley, 34; language, limits of, xiii, 20, 39–40, 48, 51, 86, 93–94, 96–97, 120–22, 128, 168, 204 (*see also* talk); "life always worth living," 51; "lustre of the present hour," 28; materialism, 58, 128, 132–33, 136–37, 140, 202; meaning of life, 43; metaphysics, 1, 5, 32, 62, 67, 95, 97; metaphysics, defined, 33; metaphysics, New Age, 212n. 1; "mind cure" movement, 70–71, 115, 214n. 24; "Moral Equivalent of War, The," 71; "Moral Philosopher and the Moral Life, The," 106–7; "more life," 29, 135; Mt. Marcy ("Walpurgisnacht"), 31, 113, 117; "my creative power," 46, 88; "my religious act," 110; mystery, 101, 116, 120, 168, 171–74, 202–4, 219n. 102; mysticism, 112, 115; naturalism, xi, xiii, 28, 30, 129, 131–32, 137, 152, 195; neutral monism, 91, 184; nitrous oxide, 110, 123; "On a Certain Blindness in Human Beings,"

17, 59–60, 218n. 90, 224n. 25; "One and the Many, the," problem of, 80; "our national disease," 231n. 2; panexperientialism, 99; personal faith, 102, 226n. 26; personality, xii, 9, 15, 53, 79–80, 87, 158, 198; pessimism, on Schopenhauer's, 64, 230n. 90 (*see also* meliorism); "Ph.D. Octopus," xv; on philosophy, 7–8, 11, 16, 39–40, 43, 47–49, 71, 88, 110, 112, 227n. 29 (*see also* James: explanation, intellectualism); "philosophy must pass from words to life," 49; "pining, puling, mumping" moods, disdain for, 45, 87; pluralism, 5–6, 8, 10, 13, 22, 27–29, 33–34, 37, 50, 65, 80, 89, 91, 119, 134, 170–71, 193, 208–209; *Pluralistic Universe, A,* 29, 34; prayer, 103, 110; *Principles of Psychology,* 33, 56, 60, 187, 214n. 20, 222n. 23; "professional philosophers, inveterate habits dear to," 16; on progress, 185; pure experience, 79–100, 214n. 19; pure experience as "a primitive stage of perception," 84; questionnaire on religion, 102–3; radical empiricism and dogmatism, 75; —and Exceptional Mental States, 128; —and goal-seeking, 191; —and meliorism, 66–67; —and naturalism, 132; —, postulate of, 82, 116; —and relations, 88, 91–99; 219n. 9, 223n. 16; —and the sacred, 133, 201, 203; —and Santayana, 138, 142–45; —and the self, 93, 158; —and subjectivity, 100, 125; —and value, 82–84; reality, "deeper features of," 38; reality, defined, 58; reality, *fons et origo* of, 55; religion, 1, 29, 102–3, 110, 135, 142; religion, defined, 101; religious experience, defined, 199; resistance, feeling of, 46, 86; "return to life," xi, xiii, 38; rock, parable of the, 109; Russell and concreteness, 47; salvation, 29–30, 35, 65, 68–69, 102–3, 105, 149, 155; "salvation, incapable of believing the Christian scheme of," 29 (*see also* salvation); seances, James's, 111; sensualism, 68; "Sentiment of Rationality," 187; "Seth," 119; Shelley, 150–53;